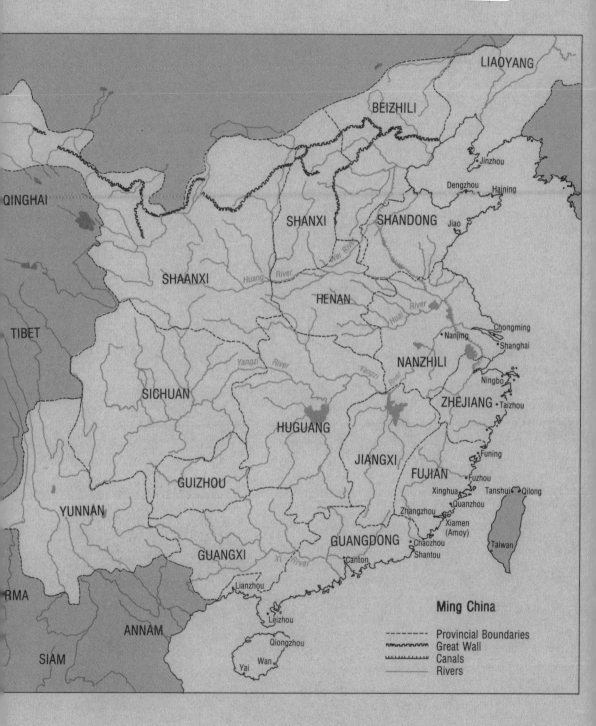

LIAOYANG

BEIZHILI

Jinzhou

Dengzhou   Haining

QINGHAI

SHANXI   SHANDONG

Jiao

SHAANXI   Huang   River   Wei River

HENAN

Huai   River

TIBET   Chongming

Nanjing   Shanghai

Yangzi   River   NANZHILI

Ningbo

SICHUAN   Yangzi   River   ZHEJIANG   Taizhou

HUGUANG

Funing

JIANGXI   Fuzhou

GUIZHOU   FUJIAN

Xinghua   Tanshui   Qilong

YUNNAN   Quanzhou

Zhangzhou

Xiamen   Taiwan

GUANGDONG   (Amoy)

GUANGXI   Xi   River   Chaozhou

Canton   Shantou

Lianzhou

RMA

Leizhou   **Ming China**

ANNAM   - - - - - -   Provincial Boundaries

Qiongzhou   ꞈꞈꞈꞈꞈ   Great Wall

SIAM   Yai   Wan   ꞈꞈꞈꞈꞈ   Canals

Rivers

EIGHTH VOYAGE
OF THE DRAGON

EIGHTH VOYAGE OF THE DRAGON

A HISTORY OF CHINA'S QUEST FOR SEAPOWER

By Bruce Swanson

NAVAL INSTITUTE PRESS
Annapolis, Maryland

Copyright © 1982
by the United States Naval Institute
Annapolis, Maryland

Library of Congress Cataloging in Publication Data
Swanson, Bruce, 1937–
  Eighth voyage of the dragon.

  Bibliography: p.
  Includes index.
  1. Sea-power—China—History.   2. China—
History, Naval. I.Title.
VA633.S93   359′.03′0951   81-85443
ISBN 0-87021-177-3   AACR2

To my wife RoseAnn
and our children
Erin, Meghan, Shannon, and Bruce

I think the greatest difference between
China and the West, which can never be made up,
is that the Chinese are fond of antiquity but
neglect the present.

Yan Fu, chancellor of the Tianjin Naval Academy
from "Lun Shibian Xhiji" (1895)

CONTENTS

FOREWORD

A lot has been written about navies and naval warfare, but the story of the efforts of the world's oldest civilization to develop seapower is little known. The case of China is an enigma: she is a country with a vast coastline and more than three thousand offshore islands, and yet she rates only a lengthy footnote in the histories of seapower.

Bruce Swanson's meticulously researched and carefully documented narrative details China's historical struggle to determine the nature and size of her navy. Today's bureaucratic battles have less to do with Communist ideology than with the age-old conflict in China about the type and direction of naval power. The author's efforts have created an invaluable framework for seeing the forces behind this struggle.

If we in the West can know and better interpret China's long history, it will help us sift out the transitory from the lasting elements of her institutions. This work makes a sizeable contribution to that knowledge, particularly in developing an understanding of China's attitude, as it is embodied in her navy, toward the sea.

GENERAL VERNON WALTERS
U.S. Ambassador-at-Large

PREFACE

This book is primarily intended for those interested in naval history. It resulted from many conversations with naval historians and students who wanted to know about China's maritime affairs, past and present. No single work measuring that history from early times to the present exists, and only China's imperial period has been addressed in any detail. Thus, it was necessary to devote the early portion of this work to a survey, which relies heavily on the research of a number of Asian scholars. For a fuller appreciation of specific events, the reader is urged to consult their works. The author takes full responsibility for errors of fact and interpretation.

I am greatly indebted to Professor J.P. Lo, who did a lot of original research on the Song, Yuan, and Ming navies. Dr. William Braisted deserves thanks for his work on the U.S. Navy in China. Professor John Rawlinson's painstaking analysis of China's nineteenth-century efforts to acquire a navy was immensely helpful, as was Knight Biggerstaff's work on China's first modern schools. Joseph Needham's wondrously detailed volume on Chinese nautical accomplishments provided rich bibliographic background. Equally valuable were Richard Smith's in-depth study of Qing military institutions and Immanuel C.Y. Hsu's study of the 1874 debate about maritime and frontier defense. Joseph Fletcher's chapter in the *Chinese World Order* gave crucial information about the Ming voyages. And without the aid of J.V.G. Mills' important translation of the Ma Huan diary, this book would lack significant details of those voyages.

I owe a special debt to John King Fairbank. His many books and articles made research on the imperial period a joy, and his encouragement made it possible for me to continue working on the history.

The early idea for this book was suggested by the late Dr. Ralph L. Powell. Without his backing and that of his wife, Helena, the initial research could not have been undertaken.

I am indebted to Dr. Richard D. Mathieu, associate dean and director of research, U.S. Naval Academy, for supporting my early research at the Naval Academy. Appreciation is extended to the successive chairmen of the U.S. Naval Academy history department, Professors John W. Huston, Larry V. Thompson, and Philip W. Warken, who provided research space and assistance when it was sorely needed. I also thank Father John Witek at Georgetown University for the valuable advice he gave after carefully reading through the galleys.

Heartfelt thanks go to Eric Yuan, whose fine Chinese characters appear on the jacket cover and in the appendices. I also appreciate the work of Ms. Alice Creighton, Special Collections Department, Nimitz Library, U.S. Naval Academy. She located and made available the valuable photographs from the Ltjg Moses Lindley Wood album.

Without the cooperation of Mr. David Kassing and Mr. Brad Dismukes at the Center for Naval Analyses, the final stages of this book could not have been finished. I most gratefully acknowledge the help of General Vernon Walters at a critical period in the preparation of this book.

I wish to thank Ms. Constance Buchanan, who edited the manuscript to the reader's benefit, Ms. Beverly Baum and Ms. Cynthia Taylor, who worked tirelessly on the art and layout, and Ms. Kay Berman, who typed the manuscript.

Lastly, I thank my wife, to whom this volume is dedicated. Without her love and support the work could not have been accomplished.

Annapolis
2 February 1982

EIGHTH VOYAGE
OF THE DRAGON

CHAPTER 1

CONTINENTAL CHINA

 Chinese naval history over the past millennium has been characterized by the clash between two great cultural entities: continental, Confucianist China and maritime China. The former sprang from the unification in north central China of several distinct warring kingdoms in 221 B.C. During the ensuing thousand years, two major dynasties, the Han (202 B.C.–220 A.D.) and the Tang (618–907 A.D.), transformed China into a magnificent land-based cultural empire. The seat of power remained in the economically self-sufficient riverine region formerly occupied by members of the old warring kingdoms. A high degree of consonance and independence marked the development of Confucianist China.

The fall of the Tang in 907 A.D. coincided with the evolution of maritime China. By then the old riverine culture had spread down the rivers to the sea and encompassed many disparate "tribes" that populated the southeastern coasts. If continental China represented the steadiness of an elder, maritime China was characterized by the unruliness of an adolescent given to disobedience. Over the second thousand years, four dynasties—the Song (960–1279 A.D.), the Yuan or Mongol (1279–1368 A.D.), the Ming (1368–1644 A.D.), and the Qing (1644–1912 A.D.)—attempted to handle the challenges posed by sea travel, ocean trade, and the introduction of foreign ideas.

Some emperors and officials saw the advantages of maritime expansion, but their policies were often thwarted by land-oriented bureaucracies. In the early Ming period seven magnificent voyages (1405–33 A.D.) were authorized that extended Chinese seapower southward into the Indian Ocean and on to Africa. However, pressure was exerted by the continentalists, and almost as suddenly as they began, the voyages were terminated. In the ensuing centuries laws were frequently enacted that retarded naval and maritime development to the extent that navies and merchant fleets were ineffective and unable—even sometimes forbidden—to sail on the open sea.

What follows is an account of the historical forces and issues underlying the conflict between Chinese continentalism and the maritime spirit. In many respects the conflict represents China's eighth voyage—a journey to restore Chinese seapower, one beset by troubled seas and a strong tide of continental tradition. It is a struggle that has survived to this very day; the present Chinese "dynasty" remains as divided as its predecessors over how to deal with matters of the sea.

GEOGRAPHY, MARKETING, AND TRANSPORT

During the first millennium, the north was the center of Chinese civilization. Fertile areas dotted the lowlands of northern China, the Yellow River, and the 3,400-mile-long Yangzi River. Most of the population and economic activity was concentrated in these valleys and plains. The region was agriculturally labor intensive, with wheat and millet crops grown in the northernmost zone and rice in the southern area of the Yangzi River Valley.[1]

A self-sustaining marketing system, which was to have important implications for all spheres of Chinese society and government administration, arose in the agrarian countryside early on and ruled out dependence on the sea for commercial needs. According to one authoritative study, the system resulted from the evolution of four basic market units: the core village, the standard market town, the intermediate market town, and the central market city. Traced vertically through the market hierarchy from village to city, the population increased and the number of farmers decreased. Magistrates, merchants, landowners, and people who provided specialized services were concentrated in the city.[2]

The north China coast, except for the slightly mountainous Shandong Peninsula, was flat and artificially banked. North of the Yangzi lay great expanses of coastal marshes and reeds, together with large tracts of salt pans. The harbors were subject to heavy silting and icing during the harsh winters. Even in this early period the areas's soil was too poor to support forests. As a result, shipbuilding was limited to small riverine vessels. The barrenness and relative inaccessibility of the northern coasts resulted in the commonly held notion that the sea was nothing more than an uncommanded natural defense barrier. Thus, ancient imperial courts ignored matters of naval and maritime speculation.

Two other factors encouraged north China's independence of the sea: a highly developed pisciculture and a river-canal transport system. Regarding the former, most core villages had a pond of several acres that the peasant was able to use in the raising of "domesticated fish." In the large towns and cities near rivers or lakes, it was also the custom for private individuals to claim ownership of part of the river or lake area for the raising and harvest of aquatic plants and fish.[3]

The river and canal system was the most important transport link in continental China. From the sixth to the twelfth century A.D., Chinese emperors kept architects and engineers at work perfecting a canal system that was to connect most of the principal rivers in north China. The

The traditional fish pond (1884). For hundreds of years, the Chinese have success-fully raised domesticated fish in such ponds. As a result, ocean fishing did not prevail. (From the Ltjg Moses Lindley Wood album dated 1884–85, courtesy of the Special Collections Department, Nimitz Library, U.S. Naval Academy.)

longest, the Grand Canal, stretched nearly 600 miles from Hangzhou, in modern Zhejiang Province, across Jiangsu Province to the city of Jining in Shandong Province. Later, during the Yuan (Mongol) dynasty, the Grand Canal was extended another 150 miles to the city of Linqing on the Wei River, which served as an important northern link to modern Tianjin (Tientsin), which was in turn connected by river and canal with the Mongol capital at Dadu (Beijing).[4] Although these water links were often severed by floods, silting, or warfare, they were usually repaired and re-mained an important lifeline for food transport. The canals were also useful for flood control, drainage, and irrigation.

The importance of the canal system is evidenced by a government record of the eleventh century, when Song dynasty engineers built ice-breakers to keep the canals open in the winter. The account states the following:

> The Bianqu [a main artery of the Grand Canal] was always closed by the 10th month of each year, so that no traffic could use it. But when Wang Jinggong [Wang Anshi] was prime minister he used to have transportation carried on in the winter as well, and kept it open. Apart from the low water levels, which hindered movement, much damage was caused to the vessels by floating ice. So he had several dozen "foot boats" [probably paddle-wheelers] equipped with trip-hammers at the bases to break up the ice.[5]

Grand Canal (1793). (Courtesy of the Cambridge University Press, Cambridge, England.)

The Yangzi River, its tributaries, and canals accounted for nearly 6,000 miles of navigable waterways and linked six major provinces of central China with the north. The system promoted political unification and served as an important route for economic and cultural exchange. Even as early as the Han dynasty, this vast water-transport system had become ingrained in imperial strategic thought. Emperors and their advisors knew that whoever controlled the Yangzi controlled China.

THE CONFUCIAN IDEOLOGY

Confucius was a teacher who lived around 551–479 B.C. His philosophy was molded during a period of warfare between competitive Chinese states. He yearned for the restoration of an ancient cultural system that united China as a single state under one master. Confucius envisioned the state to have been a golden society over which a benevolent and virtuous emperor presided. Rule was carried out by moral suasion and ritual rather than by law, and a loyal, competent government bureaucracy managed daily affairs. Within Confucius's idealized society, virtue, education, cultural unity, and stability were stressed.[6]

Confucianism did not prevail for another two and a half centuries, however. The first dynasty to unify all existing Chinese states, the Qin (221–206 B.C.), was legalist, being characterized by authoritarian rule that used severe laws and harsh punishments to secure obedience.[7] China's first dynasty created a totalitarian state where right was what the ruler decreed. It was also noted for its development of a strong military and the advocation of materialism, although merchants and intellectuals were only grudgingly tolerated.

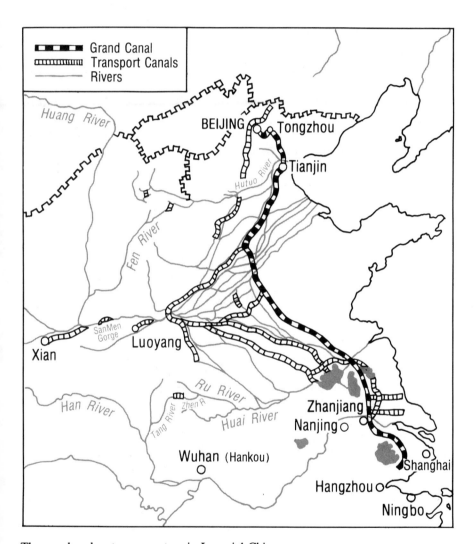

Grand Canal
Transport Canals
Rivers

Huang River

BEIJING Tongzhou

Tianjin

Hutuo River

Fen River

SanMen
Gorge

Xian   Luoyang

Ru River

Han River   Tang River Zhen R

Huai River

Zhanjiang

Nanjing

Wuhan (Hankou)   Shanghai

Hangzhou

Ningbo

The canal and waterway system in Imperial China

When the Qin was succeeded by the Han dynasty, the legalists were swept away and replaced by Confucians, who viewed man as basically good.* Theirs was a government run by idealistic officials who were both cultured and learned in ritual. To qualify for the position of government magistrate, a prospective official administrator had to possess personal integrity, recognize the value of scholarship, be devoted to high ideals, and believe in established socio-political principles that demanded subservience and respect for authority. No emphasis was placed on developing specialized skills, and the best administration was the one that governed least.[8]

Confucianism stressed harmony with nature. Science was not considered a means of conquering nature. In his lifetime a Confucian sought to achieve a virtuous relationship with people and things. He viewed natural calamities as the result of improper conduct by the ruler. Thus, the most important fuction of the Confucian official was to advise the ruler on conduct that would avoid calamities. The emperor ruled with the "mandate of heaven," which held that so long as the emperor ruled well he enjoyed the sanction of heaven. If his rule was unwise, he forfeited heaven's approval, under which circumstances the people were allowed to overthrow and replace him.

THE EXAMINATION SYSTEM AND LANGUAGE

Integral to the Confucian government apparatus was the examination system that, theoretically at least, made it possible for all persons to compete for coveted government offices. The examination system assured a supply of dedicated Confucian bureaucrats who had achieved literacy in the difficult Chinese language.

The written language was complicated by its dependence upon ideographs, and those who were fortunate enough to have schooling first had to memorize several thousand basic characters in order to read.[9] Once he had mastered the preliminaries, the literate Chinese man had to keep reading and writing or he would soon forget his fund of knowledge. Finally, he was required to read the classics, which stressed morality in government and proper behavior.

By the fifteenth century, civil examinations required the aspirant to write highly stylized essays restricted to eight topics and not exceeding seven hundred characters. Such linguistic rigidity kept the writing system unchanged and cumbersome. Moreover, emphasis on the written language sorely inhibited progress in science and scientific logic.[10]

For the overwhelming majority of the population who were functionally illiterate, the spoken language posed great difficulties as well. Each dynasty had a court or capital language that was not understood nationwide. Broadly speaking, the Mandarin or Han dialect was spoken north of

---

*Legalism was never entirely destroyed. Its latest reincarnation was in the practices of the so-called Gang of Four, who tried to restore many legalist ideas in the People's Republic of China in the 1970s.

the Yangzi, but south of the river, near the coast, there were six other dialects: Wu, Min, Cantonese, Hakka, She, and Tai.Dialectal diversity generated local chauvinism and greatly complicated cultural intercourse and commercial exchange.

THE SOCIAL STRATA

THE PEASANT

The basic strength of continental China's society lay in the peasant-farmer's realization that whatever he derived from life would be limited. Because of this, the peasant developed an extraordinary attachment to his land, which represented the "limited good" of his existence.[11] His world thus was held together by a motivation to cultivate, harvest, and sell crops within the rural marketing system. In theory the peasant could rise to official scholar status by passing the examinations, but such a happening was rare.

Land provided the peasant with an economic, emotional, political, and religious base. It gave him a sense of pride and status, and provided a place for the maintenance of ancestral plots. These factors, together with landowner pressure, tended to keep the peasant tied to his land. To be mobile was risky; it was considered better to emulate one's forefathers by farming the land and accepting whatever fate provided.[12]

THE GENTRY

From ancient times, the fates of the peasant and the government were determined by the gentry.[13] There were two requirements for gentry membership: one was to own land and the other was to be a government officeholder. Hence, gentry status was accompanied by the acquisition of financial and political power. With this came privilege and prestige, as well as a responsibility to look after the peasant and remain politically loyal to the government.

Such power resulted in an enduring conservatism that had preservation of gentry order and security as ultimate goals. One finds no examples of the gentry, as a class, attempting to overthrow the imperial Chinese government and establish a regime of its own. Instead, whoever successfully seized the reins of power and assumed the mandate of heaven could count on the gentry to actively support the new government. Conversely, the new government would maintain the old order and provide security for the gentry structure.

The gentry was able to provide most of its own security through several traditional devices. First, it was essential that at least one family member pass the examinations and gain entry into the degree-holding official class, since gentry membership was not hereditary but rather was dependent upon family influence.

Secondly, it was important for the gentry to own land from which income in the form of rent was collected. Hence, gentry pressure was constantly exerted on the peasant to farm the land.[14]

Thirdly, the family structure of the local gentry was highly organized. Unlike the small peasant family, which was an independent, laboring household, the gentry family unit was made up of an extended clan. It was a patriarchal system with several generations living together in a big house. The head of the house enforced clan laws, administered discipline, and exercised full financial and social power.[15]

The gentry usually lived in the standard market town, the intermediate market town, and the central market city. They managed day-to-day commercial affairs from offices located in teahouses and guilds. The teahouses and guilds represented privilege and status, for in them the leisured gentry could sip tea, gamble, gossip, conduct business, and settle disputes. The latter activity was an important one, requiring adroit arbitration in order for the gentry to command and maintain peasant respect. Significantly, too, it meant that Chinese law depended more on personal confrontation than on a legal system. It was much better to resolve disputes face-to-face than to go to court and risk embarrassment.[16]

The local gentry also managed a complex system of land rights involving peasant loans, mortgages, tenant titles, and taxes. Consequently, the gentry served as middlemen between peasants and government. In this role they were required to carry out natural disaster projects, manage charities, oversee public works projects, and organize and command local defenses, including navies, against internal and external threats.

Shanghai tea house as it appeared in 1884–85. Note members of the gentry in hats and jackets at left organizing stevedores and dockworkers for the day's work. Other smaller groups exchange gossip and information on port activities. (From the Ltjg Moses Lindley Wood album dated 1884–85, courtesy of the Special Collections Department, Nimitz Library, U.S. Naval Academy.)

GOVERNMENT ORGANIZATION

The imperial Chinese bureaucratic administration was an intricate and sophisticated system. While it is beyond the scope of this work to examine in detail the workings and organization of the system, some description is in order to illuminate later discussions of Chinese maritime development.

By the late Qing, the reins of power were held by the following organizations: the Grand Council, the Imperial Household, the Grand Secretariat or Inner Cabinet, and the Six Boards.[17]

The Grand Council was essentially a cabinet composed of so-called ministers who held other important offices. The number of ministers varied, but by the late Qing there were five. They conducted the business of the empire, usually in the presence of the emperor.

The Imperial Household, as the name implies, was a palace organization that managed such things as the court's finances, imperial worship, palace halls and pavilions, and control of eunuchs. Other departments were charged with overseeing imperial flocks and herds, the palace stud, the imperial armory, parks and grounds, and the imperial bodyguard. The Imperial Household wielded great power and was often the focus of intrigue and corruption.

The Grand Secretariat was made up of powerful advisors to the emperor. Although their power was superseded by the Grand Council in the late Qing, their advice and influence ranged across the entire spectrum of state affairs, including military matters.

The Six Boards represented the functional side of the central government. Their titles and general functions were as follows:

1. Board of Rites—two important functions of this board were its administration of the examination system and the management of imperial seals.

2. Board of Revenue—this board carried out population registration, oversaw tax collection, and assessed and registered land ownership. It also controlled mints and banks, and approved state loans. Additionally, it managed the important grain storage system.

3. Board of Personnel—this board directed personnel of the civil service of the empire. Its broad responsibilities included actions pertaining to selection, rank, gradation, rules defining degradation and promotion, and all ordinances related to the granting of investitures and rewards.

4. Board of Punishments—among the many legal functions managed by this board were those related to justice and the promulgation of law codes. It also examined provincial judges' decisions.

5. Board of Works—this was an especially large bureaucracy. Its responsibilities included the overseeing of construction and maintenance of roads, canals, bridges, temples, mausolea, city walls, government buildings, and shipbuilding.

6. Board of War—this board was charged with directing all military affairs. There were sub-departments involved in the selection of officers, discipline, horse or cavalry upkeep, and a commissariat.

At the provincial level the Chinese bureaucracy was even more pervasive. From the Tang dynasty onward, provinces existed that were divided into prefectures and districts.[18] Officials administering these three divisions were representatives of the central government, and most of their activities were managed by the Six Boards. This direct central government role, however, was more for overseeing the actions of provincial administration than for directing daily affairs. Hence, the provinces enjoyed a great deal of autonomy in meeting the responsibilities levied by the central authorities.

During the Qing period, some of the most powerful officials in the empire were the provincial governors-general who had authority over both civil and military officials in the provinces under their jurisdiction (the number of provinces so governed could vary from one to three). Additionally, within most provinces a governor acted as a check to his colleague, the governor-general.

These posts formed the key echelons through which the central government exercised control over the empire. A system of memorials was used so that the emperor could seek advice or communicate regulations to be implemented. Also, the provincial governors-general and governors could convey their views to the emperor via memorial on any issue they considered important, including foreign relations and military strategy.

Special mention should be made of the grain-conveyance bureaucracy, which ensured the passage of grain tribute to the capital. As early as 735 A.D., 165,000 tons of grain were being transported over the canal system. There developed a class of grain magistrates, each of whom directed a staff responsible for such things as grain receipt, transfer, and transshipment.[19] Activities included the operation and maintenance of great fleets of grain barges. In 1831 the system still operated some six thousand grain junks, which employed approximately seventy thousand junkmen. The imperial court at that time assigned more than seventy-five hundred naval officers and sailors to patrol the various grain waterways.[20]

POLITICAL AND SOCIAL EFFECTS OF THE BUREAUCRACY

The Chinese bureaucracy maintained a delicate balance among the three most important strata: the emperor and his court, the gentry, and the peasant-farmer. Such balance demanded a government of historical hierarchies where relationships were perpetuated from generation to generation. No sense of loyal opposition developed in China and political conflicts were frequently fought at a personal level.

CLIQUES

The formation of cliques in Chinese political life was commonplace. Several traditional relationships and affiliations reinforced the existence of factions: the teacher-student association; the patron-client relationship; kinship; the sworn-brotherhood relationship; and regional identification.[21]

The first two relationships were important to Chinese officialdom, for they were founded upon authority and obedience, which allowed proteges and sponsors to support one another's interests. Kinship was slightly less binding, since Chinese leaders usually chose the best qualified people for

Gentry members (1884). Obviously men of rank, these gentlemen and others like them kept the Confucian system in tact for nearly two thousand years. The embroidered jackets and gowns were for the exclusive use of the gentry. Commoners were not permitted to wear such luxury items. (From the Ltjg Moses Lindley Wood album dated 1884–85, courtesy of the Special Collections Department, Nimitz Library, U.S. Naval Academy.)

sensitive positions, regardless of their relation. The sworn-brotherhood relationship usually fostered connections between members of a society or party.[22]

Regional identification was significant. Strong pride in his native province was bred in the Fujian man or the Shandong man. As a result, it was customary for senior officials serving outside their native regions to surround themselves with trusted subordinates who were fellow provincials.

Underscoring the regional identification factor was the ethnocentrism that pervaded Chinese life. Northerners or Han Chinese (Hanren) viewed themselves as the true Chinese. They believed themselves to be ethnically superior to all others, including the southern Chinese (Yueren). The Han Chinese wrote of southerners as follows: "The Yue people by nature are indolent and undisciplined. They travel to remote places by water and use boats as we use carts and oars as we use horses. When they come [north] they float along and when they leave they are hard to follow. They enjoy fighting and are not afraid to die."[23]

When the Mongols conquered China in the thirteenth century, they revived the system of racial hierarchy, placing themselves at the top, westerners (Semu) second, northern Chinese next, and southern Chinese at the bottom.[24] Obviously, such racist views often led to jealousy and disagreement in the conduct of even the most routine bureaucratic affairs.

REFORM

Although there has been a great deal written about Chinese reform during various dynasties, rarely did any of the attempts to readjust the Chinese politico-social system culminate in substantive changes to the status quo. For the most part reforms, no matter how well intentioned, were cosmetic, resulting in greater centralization, conformity, and corruption in the bureaucracy.[25]

The root cause of reform failure can be attributed to the gentry. As ambitious landowners and officeholders strove to attain this exalted status, they expended a great deal of energy. By the time membership was achieved, very often an individual's motivation was depleted, and he led a life dedicated to leisure and scholarship. Social change and political reform thus became obscured by conservatism and backwardness. Stability and perpetuation of the Confucian system were what mattered most.

For those who managed to overcome such backwardness and correct economic, fiscal, and administrative mismanagement, there still remained the near-impossible task of convincing the bureaucracy, which had to be shown that reform was in accordance with the Confucian concept of government.

REBELLION

What then was the recourse of the dissatisfied, the disenfranchised, and the downtrodden? When government became too oppressive and power too absolute, the Chinese exercised their right of rebellion by bringing down the ruling family and passing the mandate of heaven to another. And in imperial China acts of rebellion were ever present. Significantly, these acts were never revolutionary. Thomas T. Meadows, an Englishman and a consular official in nineteenth-century China, made the following perceptive distinction:

> Revolution is a change of the form of government and of the principles on which it rests: it does not necessarily imply a change of rulers. Rebellion is a rising against the rulers which, far from necessarily aiming at a change of government principles and forms, often originates in a desire of preserving them intact. Revolutionary movements are against principles; rebellions against men. . . . Bearing the above distinction in mind, great light may be thrown by one sentence over 4,000 years of Chinese history: Of all nations that have attained a certain degree of civilization, the Chinese are the least

revolutionary and most rebellious. Speaking generally, there has been but one great political revolution in China, when the centralized form of government was substituted for the feudal, about 2,000 years ago.[26]

Because of mobility and concealment possibilities, many peasant rebellions involved riverine and canal warfare. For example, during the northern Song dynasty (960–1126 A.D.), a succession of rebel groups held the government forces at bay in the upper Yangzi reaches. (One of these rebellions later served as the model for the famous fourteenth-century novel *Shui hu zhuan* [*The Water Margin*], from which Mao Zedong developed some of his basic principles of guerrilla warfare.)[27] It is interesting to note that in order to defeat the water rebels, one of the most famous Song generals, Yue Fei, had to drain the lake region that surrounded their stronghold.[28]

Another celebrated rebellion was the so-called Taiping Rebellion, which occurred in the mid-nineteenth century and lasted some fifteen years. Much of the action in this rebellion also took place on the Yangzi River and its tributaries, and the initial Taiping victories were marked by their proficiency in riverine warfare. For instance, throughout 1852 and 1853, the Taiping riverine navy captured thousands of river craft from the inept government forces. They then formed a marine amphibious assault force that fought the government armies in a series of guerrilla-style hit-and-run actions. The effectiveness of these tactics was described at that time by one pro-government writer as follows: "The rebels, depending on their superiority in number of ships, advanced without difficulty. Taking advantage of favorable winds to sail rapidly at a speed several tens of li [mile] within one day, their whereabouts are so unpredictable that it is impossible for us to defend ourselves."[29]

A more specific example regarding the skill of the Taiping rebels occurred in late 1852. At that time, the rebel leadership had decided to attack the heavily defended city of Changsha, the capital of Hunan Province. Initially, the fighting did not go well for the Taipings, and they were soon forced into defensive positions along the Xiang River. Surrounded on three sides, the rebels set about building two floating bridges across the Xiang. Within several weeks, the bridges were completed and the rebels made good their escape. During the next month, while government troops pondered the Taipings' whereabouts, the rebels covered more than 300 miles of river routes, capturing one city after another.[30]

FOREIGN RELATIONS AND THE TRIBUTE SYSTEM

As the great Asian cultural empire, continental China conducted its foreign relations within the framework of the tributary system, a Confucian practice based upon elaborate ritual and rigid imperial controls.[31] Originating in the Han dynasty as a defensive system to protect China's sovereignty, it subsequently evolved into a diplomatic and political system, and finally in the nineteenth century it became a means of conducting trade.

The tributaries were the "barbarian tribes" that inhabited the areas on the fringes of the Chinese cultural state. In the early period they were loosely governed ethnic groups, but later they came to include remote, highly advanced states. The feature that distinguished them from the Chinese empire was their ignorance of and rejection of Confucianism.

The emperor, with the mandate of heaven, was honored by the tributaries through the ritualistic bearing of gifts, which gained prestige for the dynasty. Some tributary embassies went to the Chinese capital, but the majority remained at the borders where the tribute gifts were exchanged. When the gifts were presented, the Chinese emperor, through his intermediaries, was expected to return gifts of greater value. During such exchanges, the principal ritual of *ketou* (kowtow), or three kneelings and nine prostrations, was performed by the visiting embassy as a demonstration of respect for the Chinese emperor's position as the "ruler of all mankind."

At its zenith during the Ming dynasty, the number of Chinese tributaries exceeded one hundred. During the Qing period, the number had been drastically reduced to fourteen.[32] The Qing also utilized several offices that had been established by earlier dynasties to handle foreign relations. One was known as the Lifanyuan or Mongolian Superintendency, which dealt with northern border tribes such as the Russians and Mongols. A second office, the Reception Office, took care of relations with such tributaries as Korea, Japan, and Annam (Vietnam). A third superintendency, which will be addressed later in more detail, was established on the coast to manage relations with tribes that could only be reached by water. These included "tribes" that inhabited such disparate places as the Liuqiu (modern Okinawa) Islands, Sulu, Holland, Portugal, and England.

Imperial governments exercised especially close supervision over the conduct of tribute with northern tribes. Chinese relations with these "barbarians" required skillful statesmanship. Although they were pastoral and nomadic, the northern tribes remained a threat because they sporadically massed together and attacked Han China. The pacifist peasant-farmer was no match for the marauding cavalry of warlike soldiers.

The northern barbarian threat had a great impact on Chinese history. Of the six dynasties that ruled China from the Song period on (from 960 A.D.), four were dominated by foreign conquerors for a total of 676 years.[33] The Chinese dynasties that ruled the remainder of the period could conquer no more than several hundred miles of nomad territory beyond the Great Wall (the 2,000-mile brick and mortar edifice designed to keep northerners out of China).

Conquests by the northerners never endangered China's culture, however. The nomads' lack of a strong cultural heritage prevented them from displacing Confucianism. Moreover, they did not possess the organizational skill required to manage the Chinese bureaucratic system that so effectively kept the populace in check. As a consequence, the conquerors allowed themselves to be sinicized and accepted the idea of Chinese cultural and administrative superiority.

Tributary membership did have an implied military advantage, for a tribe in good standing was eligible to receive assistance from China if attacked. At the same time, if China were attacked, tributaries could render military aid to the Chinese.* This mutual-defense mechanism paved the way for Chinese emperors' later acceptance of advice and military aid from Europeans. For example, in the sixteenth and seventeenth centuries, Jesuit priests were pressured by the emperor to help China in the manufacture of guns.

TRADE AND THE TRIBUTE SYSTEM

Although the tributary system promoted defense and aided political maneuvering, its most important function was to serve as the channel through which trade was conducted. At border meetings, in particular, there was brisk commercial exchange between outside merchants and the Chinese. Such trade usually included goods and livestock such as horses, rugs, jades, and silks. The superintendencies monitored these transactions closely by predesignating the time and place of the tribute meetings. Any other trade was strictly forbidden.[34]

The anti-commercial attitude of the Confucian Chinese state was related to a traditional suspicion of merchants. The merchant, in fact, held a very low position on the Chinese social scale—fourth after the gentry, peasants, and artisans—and he was scorned for being parasitic.[35] Subjected to such social and political pressure, the typical Chinese merchant used his commercial talent as a stepping-stone toward achieving gentry respectability. If he had the money, a merchant could buy a degree, albeit a lesser one, which made him a member of the higher social strata. Once he was able to buy his degree, he usually devoted himself to a life of leisure or scholarship.[36] Thus, a Chinese merchant class never materialized.

The introverted and self-sufficient nature of the Confucian state produced traits which created considerable difficulty for China in the nineteenth century. While the country could tolerate and absorb foreign ideologies and ideas, its ability to do so can be likened to grafting, where the grafted cells soon become indistinguishable from the entire organism. Seeking only short-term results was the age-old Chinese malady. Practicality was often obscured and progress was measured by sudden transition or costly acquisition. Foreign techniques were introduced but, always regarded as inferior, they disappeared when interest waned.

Additionally, Chinese superiority over time produced a dormancy that manifested itself in disdain for the very things that led to the development of Western seapower prior to the twentieth century: commercial pursuits and the establishment of colonies.

---

* Very possibly this idea originated with an anti-Confucianist, Mo Zi, who died around 390 B.C. He was a proponent of defensive wars who worked out a mutual-defense theory similar to that of the League of Nations. The idea was that if a weak state were invaded, other states would come to its aid.

When viewed from another perspective, Confucian China exerted positive influence in east Asia by serving as a model of political, social, and spiritual stability in the region. By the end of the tenth century, however, Confucian China began to experience tremors of instability. This was due, in part, to large population shifts to the coast and the concurrent opening of maritime routes between China and the Middle East by Greeks, Arabs, and Persians.[37] A dynamic maritime spirit was born, which gradually forced reluctant and conservative imperial courts to focus attention on the sea. This development set loose a fierce clash of interests as subsequent dynasties struggled, often painfully, with the question of the most appropriate form and role of Chinese maritime power. Indeed, it is a question which still has not been resolved.

CHAPTER 2

MARITIME CHINA

China's maritime epoch actually began between the eighth and eleventh centuries, when northern China's population tripled and climatic changes shrank the amount of arable land. These pressures caused an extensive migration of people away from the north, particularly down the Yangzi River to the sea and thence southward along the coast. Meanwhile, nomad encroachment in the north led to warfare with the Han Chinese. The fighting resulted in the bifurcation of China in 1127, when the ruling dynasty, the Song, was forced to flee the inland capital at Kaifeng and reestablish its rule south of the Yangzi River Valley. Importantly, the new capital was relocated to Hangzhou, then a minor port city facing the East China Sea. From this vantage point the southern Song set about controlling the coast and the Yangzi as an economic and military defense against the nomads. A dynamic maritime spirit emerged, and the sea became a new frontier for those who dared to conquer it.

GEOGRAPHY

As Han emigrants settled among various southern coastal tribes, they found the littoral from the Yangzi Delta southward to be much different from that of the north. Maritime China included the modern coastal provinces of Jiangsu, Zhejiang, Fujian, and Guangdong. Except for Jiangsu, their coasts were rocky, indented with many sheltered bays, and possessed numerous natural harbors with excellent anchorages. Additionally, there were quite a few large rivers that emptied into the sea and an enormous number of offshore islands—approximately thirty-five hundred. Both the islands and ragged coastal mountains contained some of China's finest forests. Large seagoing vessels could be built from the firs and pines that grew there. Also, the emigrants discovered what the coastal tribes already knew—that the narrow coastal plains had neither the area nor the fertility to support farming. Furthermore, the mountains, which severely inhibited east-west movement, isolated the coastal population from the interior.

COASTAL URBANIZATION AND CULTURAL DIVERSITY

The character of China's central and southeastern coastal cities contrasted sharply with the older and more conservative cities of the north. Maritime China, geographically and linguistically differentiated, developed a more heterogeneous culture than the north did. Cultural diversity flourished for a number of other reasons as well.

First of all, maritime China was directly exposed to foreign influences. As early as the ninth century, in fact, enclaves were permitted to exist in certain selected coastal cities.[1] Hence, extraterritoriality was a feature that distinguished maritime China from continental China.

Secondly, the coastal merchant dominated the population through his pervasive promotion of commercial trade, and the Confucian preachment of the moral value of tribute was only a secondary consideration. Thus, maritime China was more worldly and felt more comfortable carrying out trade with foreigners.

Thirdly, food production on the coast, primarily fishing, did not suffer monopolization by the government like the grain system did in continental China. The variety and exoticism that colored seafood gastronomic displays became the rule rather than the exception in coastal city homes and restaurants.

THE PORT MARKETING SYSTEM

Despite their differences, continental and coastal China followed a similar pattern of commercial development. Ashore, the coastal peoples lived

Fuzhou City (1884). Long a major port, Fuzhou was also the site of the first modern naval academy in China. Note the rugged mountain terrain in the background that hampered communications with the interior and made the Fujianese more reliant upon the sea. (From the Ltjg Moses Lindley Wood album dated 1884–85, courtesy of the Special Collections Department, Nimitz Library, U.S. Naval Academy.)

with an interdependent maritime market and trade-distribution system that resembled the inland agrarian system. Four products of development could be distinguished: the core coastal village, the minor-market harbor, the intermediate-market and trade port, and the major port.

COASTAL VILLAGES

The coastal core village was usually located in a small protected harbor or cove where a river emptied into the sea. It served as home for fishermen or pearl divers rather than for itinerant coastal merchants and haulers. Because of this, the village was located close to the coastal fishing grounds. (For centuries China has benefitted from rich, shallow fishing grounds located just offshore.) The population of a typical coastal village was approximately two hundred fifty households.[2] Family members who remained ashore repaired nets, made hooks and lines, farmed small garden plots, and engaged in pisciculture. Commercial or marine-production exchange was carried out at the village level and was facilitated by a common dialect. Defense against an enemy was carried out by a loosely organized village militia.

At sea the village fishermen usually operated a "coupled-boat" system, in which two boats fished together, with one, known as the "male boat," doing the actual fishing, and the other, the "female boat," handling the catch and performing supply and preparation functions.[3] Alternatively, the village fisherman could fit out his own junk and fish alone, but this practice, because it failed to reap commercial benefits, was an uncommon one. When fishing was poor or the season's run was finished, fishermen could find temporary employment in larger ports as waterborne carters.

Every village had two major structures: the store and the temple.[4] Usually the store was owned and operated by a landsman whose business was conducted largely on credit and mutual trust. It was a meeting place for the village and functioned in much the same way as the trading post of early America. The temple served as the site for festivals and the worship of various deities. One of the favorites was the Queen of Heaven (Tianfei) who protected boatmen.

THE MINOR MARKETING HARBOR

Another home for the fisherman was the minor marketing harbor. Larger in population, this town provided specialized services ashore. For example, artisans made fishing line, sail matting, nets, and rudimentary tools required by the sailing population. Also, a government-controlled salt monopoly occupied offices where the precious commodity could be purchased for preserving fish catches. Some water-transport services were also available, and these towns were the initial marketing points for exchange of aquatic commodities. As a result, the towns housed fishing guilds, fish markets, and teahouses where business transactions were conducted.

Usually, such towns did not have large pier facilities, so the catch was brought ashore by sampan.[5] A shrine allowed for specialized worship. For defense, there were some walls to protect areas such as government administrative buildings. Some of the towns had small coastal defense units, which sometimes included several naval defense vessels stationed in the harbor.[6]

Because of its more varied functions, the minor marketing harbor attracted the more affluent peasant-fisherman. He usually owned a fishing couple and paid for the food and expenses of his crewmen, who worked on a profit-sharing basis.[7] About 30 percent of the profits went to the owner, although he could retain up to 75 percent if he financed the entire expedition.

The minor marketing harbor served as the focus of activities for a unique group of hardy peasant-sailors known as "fish guests" (*yuke*).[8] They were an itinerant class of water people who sailed up and down the Chinese coast purchasing catches and transporting them to the marketing harbor. The fish-guest system evolved early on because fishermen, before the nineteenth-century development of iceboats, had a problem disposing of their catch, which had to be brought to market fresh or salted.[9]

The fish guest had to be well informed about the supply and demand of fish at marketing harbors, for if catches were good, the price might drop, and he would have to sail quickly to another harbor to obtain a better price. Although uneducated, the fish guest had to have expert sailing skills and be able to speak several different dialects.[10]

THE INTERMEDIATE MARKET AND TRADE PORT

The more specialized intermediate market and trade port was usually located in a good harbor. Although fish markets still prevailed, water-transport services and trade were its most important functions. This port differed from the previous two coastal cities in the number of walls and forts that defended it. The fort usually housed a major coastal-defense garrison that had control of naval vessels.[11]

Fishing fleet (1920s). This Shanghai fleet is in port drying nets. (Courtesy of the U.S. Naval Institute Photographic Library.)

The trade port also served as home for most of the local coastal gentry and government magistrates. It was a manufacturing and retailing center that emphasized commerce rather than politics. Shipbuilding yards, bunds, or piers allowed traders, transports, and fishermen to tie up and go ashore to transact business.[12] Onshore the gentry, merchants, and boatmen gathered in teahouses and guilds to work out jobs and wages. The guilds were an important feature of the trade port. Some provided sailing crews and navigation information while others sponsored local water-transport services.[13]

THE MAJOR PORT

In pre-nineteenth-century China, seven ports served as major entrepôts for overseas and coastal trade. These ports, all located from Shanghai south, were: Shanghai, Ningbo, and Hangzhou in Zhejiang Province; Fuzhou, Quanzhou, Zhangzhou, and Xiamen (Amoy) in Fujian Province; Guangzhou (Canton) in Guangdong Province. It is important to keep in mind that China usually operated a closed-port system, and it was not uncommon for the government to periodically close major ports to trade. Even when these ports were open to foreign shipping or when Chinese traders were authorized to sail abroad, strict government rules and regulations governed such trade.

When trade was authorized, the Chinese relied upon the aforementioned system of maritime superintendencies to keep maritime trade under the rules of the tribute system.[14] These superintendencies, together with local guilds and government customs houses, were important agencies in the major ports and were highly specialized in dealing with trade. For example, by the eighteenth century, a foreign merchantman in Canton could expect to obtain a trade permit and then have a Chinese pilot come aboard for the trip up the Pearl River (Zhu Jiang). Upon arrival at Huangpu (Whampoa) Island, a Chinese security merchant, a comprador, and a linguist were assigned to the vessel to take care of contraband inspection,

Pagoda anchorage, Fuzhou City (1884). This landmark was used by many generations of Chinese sailors to safely navigate up the Min River from the Taiwan Strait. It was also the traditional customs checkpoint for foreign vessels. (From the Ltjg Moses Lindley Wood album dated 1884–85, courtesy of the Special Collections Department, Nimitz Library, U.S. Naval Academy.)

loading and provisioning, and unloading and duty payments, respectively.[15] A similar customs procedure was required of Chinese merchantmen.

One seventeenth-century account illustrates such accountability and the types of cargo.

> Commercial vessels coming to Taiwan from Xiamen receive from the Quanzhou defense headquarters an official manifest in which are listed the ages and personal descriptions of the navigator and the seamen, and the cargo carried. At the Dadengmen, a small island between Jinmen and the mainland joint military post, they are inspected for conformity with the manifest and are cleared. When they are to return to Xiamen from Taiwan, they are examined by the Taiwan defense headquarters as to the ages and personal descriptions of the navigator and seamen, and the amount of their cargo, and given an official manifest. At Luermen in Taiwan, they are inspected by the joint military post, [and may then] leave port.
>
> The headquarters at Taiwan and Xiamen each inspect ships entering their harbors. On entering port, if there are discovered any smuggled goods or such illegalities, they conduct an investigation. The manifest must be turned over to the respective [headquarters] and cancelled. If there are [ships] that have not arrived, and those official manifests are for a long time not handed in and cancelled, the [higher authorities] are informed, and an investigation is carried out.[16]

The major ports featured large urban populations and bustling transport and marketing activity. By the nineteenth century these cities were relatively industrialized and served as wholesale centers. Large schools and universities established their reputations as intellectual centers. Politically oriented as well, the ports attracted clusters of magistrates and officials who handled various government agencies.

The cities were heavily defended by troops, forts, and walled sections. Often both local- and central-government defense units were present. Numerous piers, good anchorages, and the best shipbuilding facilities in the empire qualified these ports to house large naval and marine headquarters.

THE BOAT PEOPLE

Early in Chinese history some of the people who lived on the coast and in the estuary areas began living aboard their vessels. They became known as the boat, or Dan, people.[17] The Dan people evolved into a distinct group whose members were regarded as belonging to the "polluted" professions: fishing, water transport, pearl diving, and the like.

The Dan people spoke the language of the shore population nearest their "fleet." Despite linguistic proximity, however, the Dan were viewed with suspicion and prejudice by shore dwellers, who described their marine neighbor as a "dragon on the water but a miserable worm on land."[18]

Since historical documentation is scarce, the reasons for the Dan's social standing can only be speculated on. Mobility must have contributed to their lowly status. By living aboard their vessels, the Dan could move quickly and evade government requirements such as taxes and corvee

Peasant-fishermen, Canton (1884). Many in this group were rough and tough junkmen who worked desperately hard for low pay. They passed on their sailing knowledge from father to son. (From the Ltjg Moses Lindley Wood album dated 1884–85, courtesy of the Special Collections Department, Nimitz Library, U.S. Naval Academy.)

(labor service). They also remained free of the high rents often imposed on their shore-dwelling counterparts by gentry landowners. Uneducated and cut off from the mainstream of culture on the coast, they were incapable of taking civil-service examinations. Hence, for generations they remained the object of abuse by the landed population and government administrators.[19]

Lineage atrophy also distinguished the Dan from the land dweller. On a small boat it was difficult to maintain continuity of generations beyond the immediate family, and over the centuries this hampered the government's efforts to keep the Dan people in check.

COASTAL CONTROL AND POPULATION REGISTRATION

One of the methods used to keep track of coastal peoples was the *baojia*, or mutual-guarantee system.[20] This system originated in the Wei dynasty (386–534 A.D.) as a means of making the peasant-farmer accountable for the actions of his neighbors. It functioned like a vast police network, organizing land districts into units of ten, one hundred, and one thousand

Nineteenth-century boat people. Living in the most austere conditions, these people were hearty, resourceful, and hard-working. They were excellent sailors and fishermen. (From the Ltjg Moses Lindley Wood album dated 1884–85, courtesy of the Special Collections Department, Nimitz Library, U.S. Naval Academy.)

households and maintaining written records on each household.[21] The *baojia* system allowed the government to extend its control down to the individual level and keep track of both crime and good conduct.

Beginning in the Ming dynasty, the *baojia* system covered the coastal ports and villages, the offshore islands, and the afloat population.[22] For example, coastal and island population centers were organized into individual units of *jia*. Ten *jia* formed a *zongjia* (one hundred households) and ten *zongjia* became a *zongbao* (one thousand households). Each household had to provide a list containing the names, ages, and relationships of the individual household members. The afloat population was similarly organized. All vessels were assigned a license number and port, which had to be carved on the hull. Ten vessels formed a *jia*, and each *jia* had an elected chief.

Interestingly, when the Chinese Communists came to power in 1949, this system was adopted with only minor revisions. Junks, for example, were divided into units of ten, but political cadres replaced the elected chief. As will be seen later, the *baojia* system, as imitated and streamlined by the Communists, became the means of control for the modern Communist maritime militia.[23]

THE MONGOLIAN INVASION

In the thirteenth century the pressures of the Mongol cavalry in the north steadily weakened Chinese rule over the southern Song empire. By 1206 the Mongols had consolidated their control over Mongolia and twenty-five years later succeeded in overrunning China's tributary, Korea. In 1227 they swept over northeastern China and established Dadu, or Beijing, as their capital. In the decade that followed they crossed the Yangzi River and pushed to the coast. There they constructed warships and learned naval warfare in order to defeat the Song, who controlled the offshore islands and major ports. Finally, in 1279, using Yue tribesmen as crewmen and Mongols as officers, the Mongol navy defeated the Song in a decisive battle at Yaishan near Canton.

During this same period, the Mongols employed seapower throughout eastern and southeastern Asia. In 1274 their leader, Kublai Khan, sent an amphibious expedition of forty thousand troops against Japan that was foiled by a typhoon. Seven years later the Mongol emperor sent another force of one hundred fifty thousand men against the Japanese. It, too, was struck by a typhoon; some four thousand ships were sunk and about one hundred thirty thousand men were drowned or killed on the beaches of Japan's southern island of Kyushu.[24] Despite these naval disasters, Kublai Khan retained strong faith in seapower. From 1283 to 1288 he oversaw a series of sea assaults against Annam (Vietnam). In 1292 he sent a force of one thousand ships to strike Java (Indonesia).[25]

Around this time the capital at Dadu became a mighty military center where strategies were developed to subjugate all of Asia. The city hosted large armies and a civilian population that sprang up in support of the military units. An important priority became the matter of grain shipments to the region that would sustain the swollen population. The problem of food was compounded by severely reduced agricultural production in the north, brought on by worsening climatic conditions and the incessant warfare.[26]

GRAIN TRANSPORT: THE COASTAL ROUTE
VERSUS THE CANAL SYSTEM

The need to transport grain northward led to a dispute over the way to most efficiently haul food to the capital.[27] One group favored improvement of the canal system, while another believed that a coastal merchant marine was needed. An important consideration, which helped the case of the merchant-fleet promoters, was that the canal system had been decaying for many decades. The cost of fixing the canals, when balanced against the cheaper cost of supporting a merchant grain fleet, resulted in the emperor's authorization to build coastal transport ships.[28]

Two former privateers, Zhu Qing and Zhang Xuan, were chosen to build the ships and recruit the crews. Earlier these two had delivered their fleet of five hundred pirate vessels to the Mongol cause, and they subsequently served with distinction in helping the Mongols defeat the Song. The success of their grain-transport effort could be seen in the forty-seven years of operation from 1282 to 1329. In the first year, for example, they successfully sailed a convoy of 146 vessels carrying 6 million pounds of grain from Shanghai to the site of modern-day Tianjin. Thereafter, despite much opposition from the canal faction, the sea-transport service increased its annual deliveries, reaching 16.8 million pounds of grain in 1292. By 1309 the amount exceeded 300 million pounds, and in 1329 it reached a high of 420 million pounds.

Significant problems arose, however. Zhu and Zhang were so successful that they soon gained a private monopoly over the grain-transport business. (This was unusual, since the canal system was a government monopoly.) They began to charge high rates for the transport of grain. For example, they purchased rice in the Yangzi Valley for 3 taels a picul (approximately one cent per pound) and charged the government 8.5 taels a picul to transport it north. A history of the period tells how these revenues were developed and subsequently used.

> At this time the currency was stable and prices low. Rice in Jiangnan [Lower Yangtze Valley] cost only 3 taels a picul in Zhongtong currency. To pay 8 taels and 5 candareens to transport one picul of rice was to pay almost three times the cost of rice. The freight charges were paid each year in the ninth and tenth months in sound currency. The shipping people then bought materials for building ships. The construction cost of a ship of 1000 units [capacity of 6 tons] was only a 100 ting [5,000 taels, which by modern standards would have been approximately 3,000 dollars], but by merely shipping 1000 piculs of rice they make 170 ting [8,500 taels]. With such large profits everyone was eager to build ships and to engage in the transportation business.[29]

The Grand Canal grain transport service. This Qing scroll shows how grain was transported up the Grand Canal at the expense of the coastal route. (Courtesy of Cambridge University Press, Cambridge, England.)

It was inevitable that Zhu and Zhang would enter into conflict with the imperial court, for they had created a regional economic power base that potentially threatened the traditional balance between interest groups in the capital and provinces. Such regionalism had always been part of the Chinese political scene, and in order that it be neutralized, intrigue and drastic action were usually required.

Zhu and Zhang were no exceptions. Jealous rivals in the Mongol court kept up a steady barrage of rumors about their corruption, and many of the complaints were not unfounded. Their Shanghai-based maritime empire had become so lucrative that they had even undertaken extensive trade with southeast Asian tributaries. A Yuan history recorded their activities as follows:

> Grain transports and merchant ships gathered like clouds. More than a hundred members of the households of [Zhu] Qing and [Zhang] Xuan wore gold and silver badges. Merchants from foreign lands brought gifts of rare objects, rhinoceros horns and peacock feathers to fill the warehouses. Their pomp was imposing and their wealth the greatest in the southeast.[30]

Having overstepped their authority by receiving tribute, Zhu and Zhang had to bear the consequences. In 1302 they stood accused of treason. Zhu committed suicide. Zhang, his son, and grandson were executed in Beijing.

Their deaths resulted in the grain-transport service being reassigned to the government as a centrally managed operation, and it continued efficiently for the next twenty-five years. However, a number of factors worked against it: corrupt and untrained officials were assigned to administer the fleets; inflation was rampant; storms resulted in losses at sea; and piracy increased. Soon the Mongol emperor gave up on the sea route and ordered grain transport to be carried out by the safer and more easily defended system of canals and rivers.

The experience of Zhu and Zhang is interesting because it embodied what were to become common patterns in relations between the government and merchants. (The relations became known as *guandu shangban*, or "government supervision and merchant operation.") The usual government policy of close supervision and interference made trade a high-risk venture. Merchants like Zhu and Zhang tended to be profit motivated rather than inclined to reinvest in an enterprise subject to social criticism and imminent government takeover. Additionally, the government execution of Zhang's son and grandson showed how dangerous it was to make merchant enterprises a family affair. Last of all, the shutdown of the sea route was an imperial solution repeated again and again in succeeding dynasties. Despite the commercial advantages of trade and the efficiency of the coastal transport service, the Confucian view of merchants usually prevailed and government support of the sea route was temporary at best.

CHAPTER 3

CONTINENTAL AND MARITIME IDEOLOGIES IN CONFLICT: THE MING DYNASTY

 In 1405, China's progressive attitude toward exploitation of the sea culminated in a series of naval expeditions into the South China Sea and the Indian Ocean. The latter expeditions included visits to Ceylon, India, the Persian Gulf, and Africa.* These spectacular voyages, in fact, proved that China was the supreme world seapower whose shipbuilding techniques and navigational abilities were unmatched by any other nation.

But China's prominence as the world's greatest naval and maritime power was short-lived. The last of seven expeditions ended in 1433; never again were naval expeditions attempted by emperors.[1] As a result, it is tempting to dismiss these voyages as a temporary aberration of the Chinese emperor who sponsored them. To do so, however, would be to ignore the ineluctable influence of the maritime spirit on China, particularly the growing awareness of the potential of seapower to expand and control the tribute system. At the same time, the subsequent cessation of the voyages clearly highlights the equally strong force of continentalism among members of the imperial court as they attempted to steer China away from maritime pursuits.

EARLY MING STRATEGIC CONSIDERATIONS

Before discussing the voyages and their itineraries, it is important to examine certain factors that reflected China's continuing struggle between supporters of continentalism on the one hand and the maritime ideology on the other.

THE FIRST MING EMPEROR

The first Ming emperor, Zhu Yuanzhang, was an orphaned peasant from the riverine area near Nanjing. As a child, he had been taken in by Buddhist

---

*Historically, at least, China was the first country to have an "Indian Ocean naval squadron"—today a point of strong contention in Beijing, since the Communist leadership there loudly criticizes the United States and USSR for having naval vessels in the Indian Ocean.

monks and educated in a monastery. Upon leaving the monastery, he was unable to gain employment and was soon begging for a living. At the age of twenty-five, the vagrant joined a rebel band that fought government soldiers for over a decade in the central China river valleys.

Warfare finally wore down the Mongol-backed local forces and the entire Yangzi Valley came under rebel control. In due course, Zhu assumed leadership of the rebels and defeated the government forces. He then established his capital at Nanjing in 1356. Twelve years later, after taking his rebel army north and capturing Beijing from the Mongols, Zhu founded the Chinese Ming dynasty.[2]

Although Zhu, being from a riverine area, had presumably come into contact with many men who had knowledge of the sea, his initial concerns lay in consolidating Chinese rule and making China's borders and strategic cities safe from Mongol invasion. Accordingly, he took several actions that temporarily stifled maritime activities.

WALLS, CANALS, AND COASTAL DEFENSE

With the Mongols only recently defeated, Zhu set about improving city defenses. For example, he directed the construction of a protective wall some 20 miles in length around Nanjing. The barrier was 60 feet high and nearly impenetrable by a force armed with the weapons of the time.[3]

On the coast, Zhu faced the problem of piracy by Japanese and Chinese freebooters, which had increased alarmingly. He ordered that Chinese not be permitted to go overseas—those who violated his edict would be executed as traitors. In 1374 Zhu backed up his decree by abolishing the superintendencies of merchant ships at the ports of Ningbo, Quanzhou, and Guangzhou. Next, he strengthened coastal defenses by constructing forts; in the four-year period from 1383 to 1387, more than one hundred thirty forts were built in the Zhejiang-Fujian coastal zones. In Zhejiang alone, more than fifty-eight thousand troops were conscripted to man the provincial coastal forts.[4]

Zhu also directed the Board of Works to undertake extensive reconstruction of the canal system, which had been damaged by flood and warfare. One of the long-term projects called for enlarging the Grand Canal, which upon completion was to replace the pirate-plagued sea route. The latter route had been reopened earlier when civil strife closed down the canal.[5]

THE TRIBUTE SYSTEM

The first Ming emperor wasted little time before trying to reestablish the tributary system. He ordered missions to proceed to peripheral states such as Japan, Annam, Champa, and Korea, where it was proclaimed that all who wished to enter into relations with China must acknowledge the suzerainty of the new emperor.[6] Very soon some of these states sent reciprocal missions to Peking where Zhu received their kowtows acknowledging him as the Son of Heaven. These missions also served other purposes, such as providing the new Chinese dynasty with information on the current situations in border areas.

紅搶河引

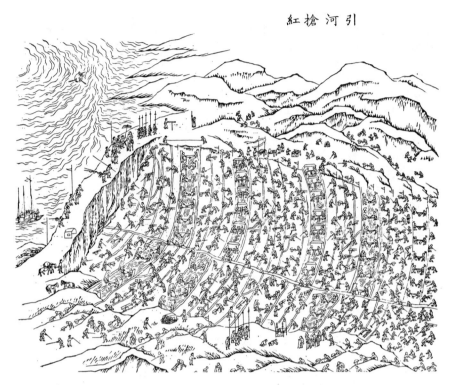

Excavating a canal (1833). A nineteenth-century Chinese engineer has provided a fascinating picture of the vast numbers of people used to dig a new canal. (Courtesy of Cambridge University Press, Cambridge, England.)

JAPAN

There can be little doubt that the new Chinese emperor desired to reestablish Ming China's suzerainty over the Japanese, for in the period from 1369 to 1372, Zhu sent three missions to Japan to persuade the ruling shogun to recognize the first Ming ruler's "mandate of heaven."[7] He also had another reason for pressing the shogun—the Ming government needed to free the coastal population from the growing threat of Japanese piracy. Zhu's efforts were futile, however, and in an acrimonious exchange he severed relations with Japan in 1387. Zhu wrote to the shogun: "You stupid eastern barbarians! Living so far across the sea . . . you are haughty and disloyal; you permit your subjects to do evil." The Japanese reply did little to salve Zhu's anger. "Heaven and Earth are vast; they are not monopolized by one ruler."[8]

ANNAM AND CHAMPA

Zhu Yuanzhang was also concerned about events in the area we call Vietnam today. In that region, there existed the two tributary states of Annam and Champa, which had been at war for some time. Annam, the northern state on the Chinese border, had been fighting from the beginning of the fourteenth century in an effort to fend off the Mongols, who tried on three occasions to incorporate it as a Chinese protectorate (as it had been in the Tang period).[9] Despite the capture of Hanoi, the capital, the Annamese had been able to withstand the Mongol invasions. Now, however, they faced war with their southern neighbor, Champa. Champa occupied the modern-day Vietnamese coast from about Hue in the north to the vicinity of Saigon in the south. The Cham people were seafarers who carried out extensive trade with China and other southeast Asian ocean states. They also supported piracy, and merchant ships were not safe in the South China Sea.

THE MONGOL-MUSLIM ALLIANCE

The first Ming emperor also had to deal with the continuing threat posed by the retreating Mongols. It took Zhu's armies until 1382 to drive remaining Mongol military units from Yunnan in southwest China. Moreover, during the next twenty years, periodic "mopping-up" operations continued beyond the Great Wall in northeast China and in Korea as well.[10]

For the Ming government, the biggest threat lay westward. A Turkic nomad and Muslim named Timur, or Tamerlane, was conquering the entire central Asian region from Siberia to the Mediterranean and southward to the Indian Ocean. Included in the ranks of his fierce Muslim cavalry were remnants of the retreating Mongol armies.

According to an official Ming history, Zhu was anxious to bring Timur into the tribute system. He sent several small missions on the overland caravan route to seek out the Muslim leader. The Chinese apparently were unaware of just how paltry their offer of suzerainty appeared to the ferocious Timur. The Muslims, in fact, scorned the Chinese. "Because they believe [that] our people [are] wild and boorish, they do not hope for politeness, nor respect, nor honor, nor law from us; and apart from their own realms they do not know of a city [anywhere] in the world."[11]

In 1394, after only a quarter century of Ming rule, an incident occurred that would seriously jeopardize the Chinese dynasty. At that time, Zhu received what he thought was a tribute mission from Timur that delivered a letter acknowledging the Chinese emperor as the ruler of all mankind. The letter, forged by an ambitious merchant or court official, led Zhu to send a return mission to central Asia in appreciation of Timur's vassalage. In 1395, when the Chinese embassy reached Timur and delivered Zhu's note, the Muslim leader became so enraged that he advised his staff to prepare for an invasion of China to bring down the Chinese "infidels."[12] He took the Chinese mission hostage. By 1404 his plans were nearly complete, and he had massed two-hundred thousand Muslim and Mongol cavalrymen in the Pamirs, near modern-day Afghanistan.[13]

Fortunately for the Chinese, Timur died in 1405, following an all-night drinking bout. On his deathbed he reportedly "expressed his regret in having neglected the conquest of such infidel countries as China and drawn his sword against Muslim armies."[14] Two more years passed before the Chinese heard from the freed hostages that Timur had died.

FOREIGN POLICY UNDER THE SECOND MING EMPEROR

While Timur was preparing to invade China, the death of Zhu Yuanzhang in 1398 produced another period of civil war lasting until 1403. Succeeding Zhu was his grandson, a young boy whose court remained in Nanjing. In the north, however, Zhu's fourth son, Chengzu, decided to overthrow his nephew from the southern capital. As the military commander responsible for anti-Mongol operations in the Peking area, he controlled some of the best troops in China.[15] His ultimate success came in 1403, when he defeated the Nanjing forces loyal to his father and assumed the throne with the name Yongle, meaning "perpetual happiness."

Clearly, Yongle's ambition and leadership ability forecast a dynamic reign. As with his father before him, one of Yongle's primary objectives was to establish his sovereignty throughout the tribute system by reinstilling the belief among all foreign states that China was supreme.[16] In order to persuade the tributaries, however, Yongle had to work out a strategy that would both gain respect for Chinese power and enrich the imperial treasuries.

He dealt with Japan first. In 1403 the superintendencies of merchant shipping were reopened and new hostels were built to house Japanese tributary missions coming by sea. A system was devised whereby legitimate Japanese merchants were given trading passports that could be checked by Chinese authorities on each visit.[17] In this way pirates could be identified, while honest Japanese and Chinese businessmen were free to carry on lucrative trade.

In Annam Yongle faced a critical problem. In 1400, while he was fighting to usurp the throne from his nephew, events there were coming to a head. Hanoi had fallen to Champa and the Annamese Tran dynasty was destroyed. The South China Sea was now in the hands of Cham and rebel Annamese pirates, and Chinese merchant shipping, both official and unofficial, was seriously disrupted. In 1406 Yongle decided to attack across the land border in order to pacify the two warring states and then reestablish Annam as a Chinese province. Hanoi was captured in 1406, but the Chinese armies soon bogged down in Annamese cities awaiting reinforcements and supplies. Before long nearly ninety thousand Chinese troops were in Annam attempting to control the countryside through a costly sinicization program.[18]

Problems in inner Asia were developing concurrently with the Annam invasion. Word of the Muslim conquests in central Asia had reached Yongle, but the distance and harsh nature of that western area precluded the dispatch of a large army to confront Timur. Caution got the better of Yongle. He elected to send a small fact-finding mission to Timur in 1402 to inquire why the Muslim leader, since 1395, had failed to pay tribute. In a move that suggested that Yongle would settle for political equality with remote central Asia, he approved the construction of a Muslim mosque in Peking. This may have been done to induce the warring Muslims to keep open the silk route connecting western China with the cities of the Timurid empire (these included Gilgit and Herat, located in modern-day Pakistan and Afghanistan, respectively).[19]

With the silk route used only sporadically, the wealthy classes, the court, and the treasury had become heavily dependent upon southern maritime trade for the import of precious stones, fragrant woods, spices, and rare objects. To ensure the safety of Chinese traders on the sea and the uninterrupted flow of luxury items, it was essential that Yongle build a navy that would convince the ocean states of China's "world supremacy." He devised a forceful plan calling for the aggressive use of seapower to underline Chinese suzerainty over the peripheral southern ocean states. Since the first expedition was to sail all the way to the Muslim states of Aden, Mecca, Djofar, and Hormuz, Yongle likely concluded that the voyages would also be useful in countering Timur's influence in that area.[20]

THE MING SHIPS AND EXPEDITIONS

In 1403, a year of momentous decisions, Yongle directed Chinese shipyards in Fujian to undertake an aggressive shipbuilding effort that would result in the construction of more than two thousand large seagoing vessels over the next sixteen years.[21]

The *baochuan*, or treasure ships, were the largest vessels constructed by the Chinese. Their size has been the subject of many arguments among scholars. Ming histories record that the treasure-ships were 440 feet long and 180 feet wide (an unlikely construction ratio of 5:2).[22] At best, this configuration is an exaggeration, for such broad-beamed vessels would be unresponsive even under moderate sea conditions. In fact, acceptance of these figures degrades the reputation of Chinese shipbuilders of the period, who would have recognized that such vessels were impractical to build. Until research proves otherwise, it is this writer's opinion that the largest vessels were shaped much like the three largest junks, of which records are available. These, the Jiangsu trader, the Beizhili trader, and the Fuzhou pole junk, were built on a proportion of about 6.4:1—much closer to the modern naval architecture ratio of 9:1. The former was about 170 feet long and had five masts, while the latter two had lengths of 180 feet with a beam of 28 feet.[23] It may be significant that Fujian shipyards were given the first-order calling for the construction of 137 ships, since these were the yards that probably developed the technique for building the Fuzhou pole junk.[24]

Another factor often used by scholars to support the larger dimensions is the records that list the number of ships versus the number of people embarked. The best estimates for each expedition are as follows:[25]

	No. of Ships	No. of People	Vessel Types Identified
1st expedition (1405–07)	317	27,870	62 baochuan
2nd expedition (1407–09)	249	?	?
3rd expedition (1409–11)	48	30,000	?
4th expedition (1413–15)	63	28,560	?
5th expedition ?	?	?	?
6th expedition (1421–22)	41	?	?
7th expedition (1431–33)	100	27,550	?

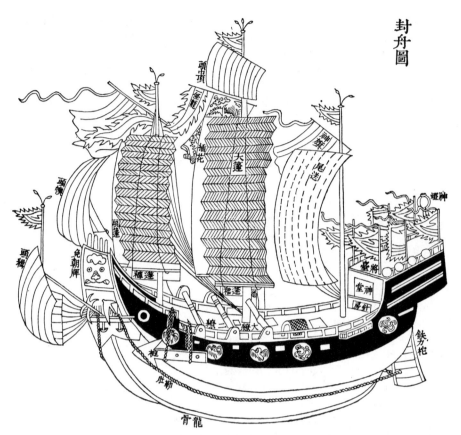

Qing drawing of an oceangoing junk (1757). The translation of the parts depicted are in Appendix K. (Courtesy of Cambridge University Press, Cambridge, England.)

From these estimates, only the first expedition totals seem plausible, for if the total number of people embarked is accepted, the average of persons per vessel is reasonable. Based upon the capacity of large modern junks, it is not unreasonable to assume that a fifteenth-century 180-foot *baochuan* could have comfortably carried at least two hundred persons. Hence, about half of the expeditionary force could have been embarked on sixty-two 180-foot *baochuan(s)*, while the others could have been easily accommodated on the remaining 255 vessels, whose average length was about 100 feet.[26]

NAVIGATION AND SHIPBOARD ROUTINE

There is little doubt that the Chinese possessed the necessary technology to undertake these voyages. Shipbuilders had been constructing ships with watertight compartments for several centuries, and the compass had been used since the Song period. The latter discovery was recorded in an eleventh-century account that describes Chinese geomancy as follows:

> Daoist geomancers rub the point of a needle with loadstone so that it acquires the property of pointing south. But it always declines slightly to the

The 160-foot Chinese junk *Keying* (1884). This vessel was built in the 1840s. It was 160 feet long and is probably the closest approximation to the 180-to-200-foot ships used by Zheng He in the fifteenth century. This vessel displaced 720 tons and sailed to New York from Canton in 1847. Made of teak, it was still in reasonable shape in 1884. (From the Ltjg Moses Lindley Wood album dated 1884–85, courtesy of the Special Collections Department, Nimitz Library, U.S. Naval Academy.)

east and is not due south. Floating it on the water causes too much oscillation, but a fingernail or the edge of a cup may be used to let it spin round very rapidly; being, however, hard and smooth it is liable to fall. The best scheme is to suspend it by a silk fibre, as follows: one should take a single thread from a new skein of silk and attach it with wax of the size of about a mustard seed to the middle of the needle and suspend it on a place where there is no wind. Then the needle will always point south. Some of them are so magnetized as to point north. In my family we have both south- and north-pointing needles. The property of the loadstone to point south like that of the cypress tree to point west, can be explained by nobody.[27]

The typical number of permanent ships' company was about fifty persons, including thirty marines. They stood ten watches daily, with each watch being 2 hours and 40 minutes long. Time was kept by using incense sticks, which burned at the same rate as a single watch. The navigator knew how to ascertain latitude and maintain a course to a predetermined destination. Navigational charts were used and maintained by the chief navigator and his assistants. These charts were guarded jealously and passed down from generation to generation. Known as "water mirrors," some of the Ming charts were still in use in the eighteenth century.[28]

Sailors determined ship speed by tossing a small wood chip overboard and walking to the stern while keeping abreast of the chip. Generally, if the wood chip passed the length of a 150-foot vessel in 51 seconds, the ship speed was estimated at two knots. Regarding sailing speed, one of the fastest trips recorded during the expeditions was a run made from Calicut in India to the northern coast of Sumatra—a distance of about 1,500 miles. The Chinese made the trip in two weeks at a sustained speed of about 4.4 knots. Such sailing abilities were largely the result of the Chinese development of a science for predicting the wind. By the Ming period Chinese navigators had gathered a considerable amount of knowledge about seasons and weather signs, from which they were able to deduce quite accurate estimates on wind direction. Equipped with this knowledge, navigators became skilled in the setting of sails and were thus able to take advantage of various wind directions. Chinese navigators also took frequent soundings and bottom samples, and stayed clear of unfamiliar coasts.[29]

ZHENG HE

In addition to overseeing the construction of the Ming fleet, Yongle selected the senior officers who were to lead the expeditions. For overall commander the emperor picked a Muslim eunuch named Zheng He, who had been in his service since 1382. As a small boy, Zheng He had been taken prisoner in Yunnan during the final rout of the Mongols.

Following his capture, Zheng He, by custom, was castrated and subsequently made an officer in Yongle's army, where he distinguished himself during the successful usurpation campaign of 1403. For his loyal service, Zheng He, at age thirty-three, was made a grand eunuch and appointed superintendent of the Office of Eunuchs. His military prowess, along with his knowledge of Turku languages and Islam, made Zheng He the ideal choice for senior admiral of the Ming fleet.[30] He was given the name Sanbao Taijian, meaning "three-jewelled eunuch."[31]

During his voyages, Zheng He was accompanied by other Chinese Muslims, including one named Ma Huan, who came from the Hangzhou Bay area. Ma was knowledgeable in matters of the sea and in the Arabic and Persian languages. His chief distinction, however, was the account of three voyages he made with Zheng He.[32]

From Ma Huan we learn that Zheng He's general procedure was to bring the fleet together in late spring near modern-day Shanghai, where a series of briefings and religious ceremonies was conducted. Once prayers had been offered, and the fleet had been organized and briefed, it sailed leisurely on a four- to eight-week "shakedown cruise" to an anchorage at the mouth of the Min River in Fujian Province. There the ships would carry out futher intensive training throughout the late summer and early fall. Finally, in December or January, they would set sail during the favorable monsoon.[33]

THE SEA ROUTES

The sea routes followed by Ming naval captains had been known and used for several centuries. Since the Song dynasty, in fact, the routes had been

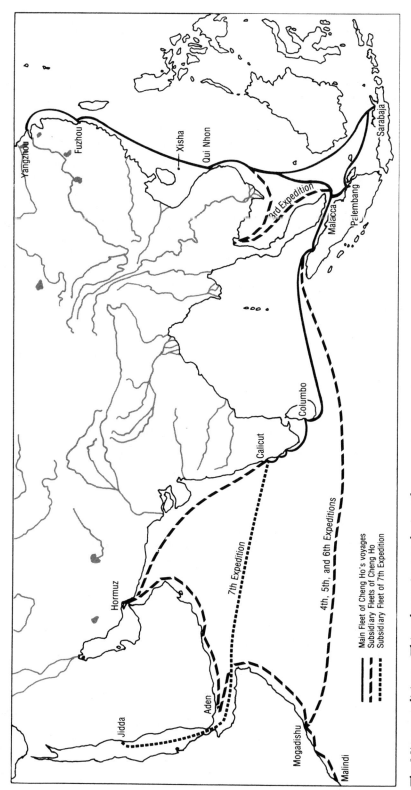

The Ming expeditions. This schematic map depicts the approximate routes navigated by Zheng He's fleets.

Labels on map:

Yangzhou
Fuzhou
Xisha
Qui Nhon
Sarabaja
Palembang
Malacca
3rd Expedition
Columbo
Calicut
7th Expedition
4th, 5th, and 6th Expeditions
Hormuz
Jidda
Aden
Mogadishu
Malindi

Legend:
Main Fleet of Cheng Ho's voyages
Subsidiary Fleets of Cheng Ho
Subsidiary Fleet of 7th Expedition

systematized into two major sea lanes: the East Sea Route and the West Sea Route.[34] Each was subdivided into a major and minor route. For example, the major East Sea Route included Java and southern Borneo, while the minor East Sea Route extended to northern Borneo and the Philippines. The minor West Sea Route encompassed ports in Sumatra and the Malay Peninsula. The major West Sea Route was that route taken to the Indian Ocean via the Malacca Strait.[35]

Following the period of intensive training, the fleet wound its way through the Taiwan Strait and sailed directly into the South China Sea, where land falls were made on Hainan Island and the Xisha Islands (Paracel Islands). From the Xishas the fleet turned westward and made for an anchorage at modern-day Qui Nhon on the Champa (southern Vietnam) coast. The total time of the Fujian-Champa transit was about ten days. Once there, provisions were taken aboard and the crews had "liberty" and "swim call." From Qui Nhon the fleet sailed southward toward the west coast of Borneo, making land falls on the various islands in the southern portion of the South China Sea.

After rounding Borneo, the ships entered the Java Sea and sailed to Sarabaja in Java. At this port Chinese crews were again rested for several months, until about July, when the period of favorable winds occurred. They then sailed through the Malacca Strait via Palembang and thence westward to Sri Lanka. From Sri Lanka the ships made their way to Calicut on the Indian coast, where the fleet was divided into smaller "task forces." Some went to Chittagong in modern-day Bangladesh; others went to Hormuz, Aden, and Jidda; and some visited the African coast near the mouth of the Red Sea. Hormuz usually was reached in January of the first year, and the Chinese returned to Malacca by March. They remained in Malacca only briefly, sailing northward to the Yangzi River by July of the second year.[36]

EXPEDITIONARY HIGHLIGHTS

The first naval expedition got under way in 1405 with more than twenty-seven thousand men aboard an estimated 317 ships.[37] Research of Zheng He's family records indicates the magnitude of the undertaking.

> The men of the expedition included 7 imperial eunuchs as ambassadors, 10 eunuchs as assistant ambassadors, 10 junior eunuchs, 53 eunuch chamberlains, 2 chief military directors, 93 military directors, one senior secretary of the Revenue Ministry, 2 masters of ceremony or protocol from the Honglusi [Department of State Ceremonials] for the audience of foreign ambassadors, one master and 4 assistant geomancer "meteorologists," 128 medical officers and assistants, 26,803 military, braves, "regular" officers, soldiers, reservists, cooks, purveyors, clerks—in all 27,000 men.[38]

The large military contingent played an important role during the return voyage from the Indian Ocean in 1407. When the Chinese ships anchored in the Bangka Strait and went ashore at Palembang (Sumatra), they found many rich and prosperous overseas Chinese living there. One of the Chinese emigrants, a Cantonese named Chen Zuyi, had set himself up as a pirate chieftain and robbed foreign merchant ships. When Zheng He arrived, he was informed of Chen's treachery by another Cantonese resident of Palembang. In a series of sea and land battles, the pirate forces lost five thousand men and Zheng managed to capture Chen. The eunuch admiral transported the pirate back to China, where he was executed. Subsequently, the emperor named the informer, Zhi Jinqing, the governor-general of the Palembang territory.[39]

During the fourth expedition, Zheng He again had occasion to use force, this time in northern Sumatra. Tribal leaders there were fighting among themselves over whose king was the rightful ruler. Zheng He interceded on behalf of the king who had rendered tribute in previous years. His troops defeated forces of several thousand men and then publicly executed their leader. Ma Huan tells us that "the king's son was grateful for the imperial kindness, and [thereafter] constantly presented tribute of local products to the court."[40]

On the Malay Peninsula, Zheng He played a principal role in establishing Chinese suzerainty over the port of Malacca (about 150 miles northwest of modern-day Singapore). In 1409 Zheng He conferred tributary status upon the local Muslim chieftain, who theretofore had been a vassal of Thailand. The chieftain and his family sailed to Nanjing to present tribute.[41]

Zheng He spent a lot of time making the Malacca Strait secure, for even at that time its importance as a trade entrepot linking Asia and the Indian Ocean was recognized. In fact, at Malacca City he set up a Chinese cantonment, whose activities were recorded by Ma Huan.

> Whenever the treasure-ships of the Middle Kingdom arrived there, they at once erected a line of stockading, like a city wall, and set up towers for the watch drums at four gates; at night they had patrols of police carrying bells; inside, again, they erected a second stockade, like a small city wall, [within which] they constructed warehouses and granaries; [and] all the money and provisions were stored in them. The ships which had gone to various countries returned to this place and assembled; they marshalled the foreign goods and loaded them in the ships; [then] waited till the south wind was perfectly favorable.[42]

In 1411, during the third expedition, Zheng He's "marines" fought a series of violent battles with the de facto ruler of a local kingdom near Colombo, Ceylon. The Chinese subdued the insurgents and Zheng He took the captive king and his family to the Chinese court in Nanjing in July 1411. The Yongle emperor subsequently allowed them to return to Ceylon.[43]

On the fifth expedition, Zheng He's sailors encountered unfriendly receptions at Lasa on the Arabian coast and in Africa at Mogadishu (Mogadiscio). In each instance, however, the appearance of Chinese marines was enough to avoid a fight.[44]

Interestingly, with the exception of Ceylon, the Chinese never used force in dealing with the various coastal states west of Sumatra. In some cases the Chinese were awed by the wealth and power of many of the Muslim potentates. Although the Chinese went through the ritual of reading out imperial orders and conferring tributary status on these rulers, there was a feeling of equality similar to that earlier displayed between the Chinese emperor and Timur. For example, during the visit to Aden in 1432, only three Chinese ships journeyed to that strongly defended kingdom. Other areas in the Arabian Peninsula were visited by equally small squadrons. In this regard, Ma Huan's account suggests that the Chinese accepted the presents of certain nations as gifts rather than as tribute.[45]

GIFTS AND CUSTOMS

One of Zheng He's most important duties was to bring back exotic articles to the imperial court. Throughout his account Ma Huan describes rare gems, animals, foods, and customs. For example, in Hormuz, the Chinese were able to purchase sapphires, rubies, diamonds, topazes, coral tree beads, jade, pearls, crystal, and silks. They also acquired lions, horses, and a giraffe (identified as a unicorn), which they transported back to China. Zheng He's sailors were treated to exotic foods like dates, pomegranates, almonds, raisins, watermelons, and apples. In Bengal they ate bananas and bought fine cloths. On the Maldive Islands they noticed that the natives lived in caves and wore no clothes. At Calicut they observed strange religious rituals and traded gold for pepper.

In Thailand Ma Huan noted that if a married woman had sexual relations with a Chinese sailor, the husband remained quite calm, saying only that "my wife is beautiful and the Chinese is delighted with her." He also gives an account of another unusual Thai custom.

> When a man has attained his twentieth year, they take the skin which surrounds the membrum virile, and with a fine knife shaped like [the leaf of] an onion they open it up and insert a dozen tin beads inside the skin; [then] they close it up and protect it with medicinal herbs. The man waits till the opening of the wound is healed; then he goes out and walks about. The [beads] look like a cluster of grapes. There is indeed a class of men who arrange this operation; they specialize in inserting and soldering these beads for people; [and] they do it as a profession.[46]

THE DECLINE OF MARITIME SPIRIT IN THE MING

During the Ming expeditions, a number of political, military, social, and economic factors acted to slow and then finally halt the policies that had promoted maritime experimentation and growth.

THE GRAND CANAL

One of the first indications of China's impending maritime collapse occurred when the Grand Canal was reopened in 1411, making it again possible to ship grain via the inland route. This event marked another closing of the coastal maritime route, and many personnel of the coastal fleets were reassigned to work on the canal. In 1415 the government officially banned grain transport by sea and authorized the construction of three thousand shallow-draft canal barges.[47] This diversion of manpower and shipbuilding expertise was soon felt in the maritime industries.

Oceangoing ship construction lagged and was halted altogether by Yong-le's successor in 1436.[48] At the same time, regulations were issued that reassigned the men of the Indian Ocean expeditionary force to canal duties as stevedores.[49]

POPULATION SHIFTS

Significantly, the conclusion of Ming voyages caused a shift of population away from the sea coast that, from 1437 to 1491, resulted in a loss of eight million people in the three principal coastal provinces of Zhejiang, Fujian, and Guangdong. Meanwhile, inland areas such as Yunnan and Hebei gained four million in population. Many coastal inhabitants also emigrated to southeast Asia.[50]

WARFARE AND BORDER PRESSURE

During the fifteenth century China suffered several serious military set-backs along its land borders that deflected interest in maritime expeditions. In 1418 Annam, tiring of the Chinese presence, launched a war of independence. In a way similar to recent United States efforts, the Chinese tried to carry the fight for some nine years, but Annamese guerrilla tactics eventually prevailed. In 1420 the Ming navy lost a battle on the Red River; in 1427 the Chinese emperor finally grew weary of increased war costs and evacuated nearly one hundred thousand Chinese soldiers from Annam.[51] Chinese suzerainty was maintained, however.

In the north, China faced a graver threat in the form of continued Mongol raids along the entire length of the Great Wall. In 1421, in an effort to counter the resurgent Mongols, Yongle moved the capital from Nanjing to Beijing. Troops were shifted from the seacoast to shore up the northern capital's defenses, which lay less than 100 miles from one of the strategic northern passes that intersected the Great Wall.[52] Despite these precautions, the Chinese emperor was captured in 1449, and the Ming court was forced to resurrect its continental defense strategy completely. These policies did little to diminish the northern nomad threat, however; the critical northern frontier remained under nomad pressure for the next three hundred years. Martial law was periodically imposed, and senior military officials spent their careers defending the north rather than performing naval and coastal defense duties.

CORRUPTION IN GOVERNMENT

Politics within the Ming court also began to turn attention away from the sea, as eunuchs and Chinese bureaucrats vied for power. The praise and favors lavished on palace eunuchs in the early Ming period eventually led to their complete domination of governmental affairs. By the middle of the fifteenth century, the first in a series of eunuch strongmen ascended to power. Very quickly they set about sealing their hold over the most important government agencies, taking control of the army, the police, and finance ministries. When opposed, the eunuchs often resorted to terrorist tactics, arresting and executing those that dared question their authority. Many became quite corrupt, employing ships and crews to transport ill-gotten goods and transferring soldiers to palace construction work.[53]

By 1480 the political intrigues had increased to such an extent that when a powerful eunuch initiated a request to prepare another series of maritime expeditions in emulation of Zheng He, he was greeted by fierce opposition within the ranks of government bureaucrats. Jealous officials within the Board of War conspired to have records of the Indian Ocean voyages destroyed, so as to frustrate any attempt to imitate the early Ming expeditions.[54]

PIRACY

As officials became more absorbed in intrigues at court, they too tended toward corruption, which carried over to coastal trade. Unscrupulous merchants regained control as the government's monopoly on foreign trade was relinquished, and smuggling and piracy flourished. The Ming histories record that "the powerful families of Fujian and Zhejiang traded with the Japanese pirates. Their associates at court protected them and carried out their bidding. . . . Palace attendants outfitted merchant ships and the criminal elements of the coast abetted them in making profit."[55] In fact, while Zheng He and his companions were conducting their voyages, Japanese pirates successfully carried out five major incursions against the Chinese mainland. In 1419 the northern coastguard fleets were helpless in preventing a sizeable force of several thousand pirates from landing on the Liaodong Peninsula. It required a well-trained force of Chinese army troops to subdue the pirates. As an example of the magnitude of this action, the Chinese army commander captured 857 pirates alive and beheaded another 742.[56]

Although Japanese piracy continued to plague the Chinese, it ceased in 1466 when Japan fell into civil war. By 1523, however, Japanese and Chinese raiders were again launching attacks along the coast. Ningbo was burned in that year, and in 1552 a flotilla sailed up the Yangzi, sacking cities without opposition. Natives of the coast fled further inland to escape the ravages of these attacks. In 1555 Nanjing came under seige and the port of Quanzhou in Fujian was plundered. In an attempt to stop these raids, Ming provincial administrators resorted to the Tang dynasty's practice of constructing beacon stations to give advance warnings of pirates. By 1562, 711 beacon stations lined the coast from Jiangsu to Guangdong. By 1563 the army had to be used to combat the sea rovers, who controlled nearly all of the Fujian coast.[57]

SCHOLARSHIP AND NEO-CONFUCIANISM

Finally, a version of neo-Confucianism developed that was markedly idealistic and influenced by Buddhism, resulting in a loss of interest in geomancy and maritime expansion. As early as 1426, a minister memorialized the court, stating the following:

Arms are the instruments of evil which the sage does not use unless he must. The noble rulers and wise ministers of old did not dissipate the strength of the people by deeds of arm. This was a farsighted policy. . . . Your minister hopes that your majesty. . . would not indulge in military pursuits nor glorify the sending of expeditions to distant countries. Abandon the barren lands abroad and give the people of China a respite so that they could devote themselves to husbandry and to the schools. Thus, there would be no wars and suffering on the frontier and no murmuring in the villages, the commanders would not seek fame and the soldiers would not sacrifice their lives abroad, the people from afar would voluntarily submit and distant lands would come into our fold, and our dynasty would last for ten thousand generations.[58]

Such statements helped check Chinese maritime pursuits and force China to restore continentalist policies. Scholars who devoted their lives to the classics were again revered, while the military class was looked upon with great suspicion by the gentry and officials.

By the early fifteenth century, regulations were again in force that made it a capital offense to build a seagoing junk with more than two masts. By 1525 an imperial edict authorized coastal officials to destroy all ships of this kind and place the crews under arrest.[59]

The timing of Chinese maritime decline could not have been worse, for it coincided with European maritime expansion into Asia. The Portuguese arrived in 1516, and although they were expelled in 1521, their exodus was short-lived. They returned and established settlements in Xiamen in 1544 and Macao in 1535. The Spanish occupied the Philippines in 1564 and established trade relations with China shortly thereafter. Then, in the seventeenth century, the Dutch arrived in Asia just as the Ming dynasty was being conquered by the Manchu cavalry that overran Beijing in 1644. Thus was the stage set for the last foreign imperial rulers in China—the Qing.

CHAPTER 4

EMIGRATION, SMUGGLING, AND PIRACY

The rise and subsequent decline of officially sanctioned ocean activity in the Ming period exemplified the recurring clash between the maritime spirit and continentalism. On the one hand, the burgeoning coastal population attempted to use the ocean to support its needs, while on the other hand, the government tried to discourage such practices. Local histories of the late Ming period abound with government dismay over the socioeconomic changes wrought by maritime commerce.

> Almost 90 percent of the common people earn their livelihood by selling their skills or peddling in other prefectures. . . . The people from the middle group or class on down all have no land to till. That there are many merchants or traders among the Huizhou people is a matter of circumstances . . . .
> The land of Min [Fujian] is barren and unfit for crops. The paddy fields do not provide enough; people live off the sea. Those who make their homes on ships number 90 percent.[1]
> The custom of Luzhou has changed radically when compared with the past. Formerly, people wanted to engage themselves in farming; now they want to go into commerce.[2]

The above quotes represent the outcry of a decaying procontinentalist empire. The collapse of the Ming dynasty in 1644 was brought about by the Manchus, a northern tribe that had little interest in naval or maritime matters. Despite brief periods of enlightened trade policies, both the late Ming and early Qing favored the policy of *haijin*, or maritime interdiction.[3] When that policy failed, both dynasties reimplemented the *jianbi qingye* scheme (i.e., the practice of fortifying the walls and moving the population).

More often than not, the government did not possess efficient naval fleets to enforce such policies. Hence, coastal peoples tended to circumvent the government's anti-trade policies, which usually resulted in three things: emigration, smuggling, and/or piracy.

EMIGRATION

When the government implemented trade bans together with the harsher *jianbi qingye* policy, many Chinese coastal peoples were forced to forsake the mainland and migrate southward to seek a better life. These emigrants, 90 percent of whom came from Fujian and Guangdong provinces, primarily represented three classes: officials from vanquished dynasties, merchants, and coastal peasants.[4] The first two groups, well versed in the Confucian system, carried with them extended-family and guild traditions. The merchants were familiar with money lending and possessed substantial experience as middlemen who handled local marketing. As a result, these groups tended to remain loyal to Chinese culture, many to the point of demanding that their families and descendents speak and write their original Chinese dialect.

The poorer emigrants, the coastal peasants, included semi-skilled artisans and sailors who worked as shipwrights, transport workers, and fishermen. These people were less clannish and more willing to adopt foreign ways. Some lost their Chinese identities and most learned the native language of the areas they settled in. This, however, made their lives more difficult, for it meant that they were minority citizens constrained by local conventions; they had less opportunity to succeed than the merchant classes, who tended to ignore local customs and remain Chinese.

CHINESE COMMERCIAL DOMINATION IN SOUTHEAST ASIA

Examples of successful Chinese in southeast Asia are numerous, and only a few will be addressed. For instance, by the nineteenth century, the vast majority of junk fleets used for fishing and transport were owned and operated by ethnic Chinese. As a result, Chinese immigrants in Vietnam controlled all river and coastal transportation, and they had a substantial interest in the fishing industry. The ethnic Chinese, in fact, performed nearly all of Vietnam's deep-sea fishing in the South China Sea, while the Vietnamese fished only the immediate coastal areas. Ashore the story was much the same. By the early twentieth century, for example, Chinese rice merchants in Vietnam owned all but three rice mills in Saigon.[5]

Chinese immigrants were equally successful in other southeast Asian states. In the eighteenth century, in Brunei, they controlled the shipbuilding industry; in Thailand, they became exporters and financiers; in Malaysia they dominated the fishing industry and later controlled tin mines. In the Philippines and Indonesia, the Chinese immigrants monopolized rice distribution systems and banking, and in Sumatra they ran the lumber businesses.

An early commentary on Chinese ingenuity and entrepreneurship is preserved in a sixteenth-century letter from the Spanish bishop in the Philippines to Philip II of Spain.

> What has pleased us all has been the arrival of a bookbinder from Mexico. He brought books with him, set up a bindery, and hired a Sangley [i.e., Chinese] who offered his services to him. The Sangley secretly, and without

his master noticing it, watched the latter bind the books, and lo, in less than [—?] he left the house, saying that he wished to serve him no longer, and set up a similar shop. I assure Your Majesty that he had become so excellent a workman that his master has been forced to give up the business, because the Sangley has drawn all the trade. His work is so good that there is no need of the Spanish tradesman. At the time of writing, I have in my hand a Latin version of Nabarro, bound by him, and it could not be better bound, even in Seville.[6]

Chinese immigrants in Borneo included a number of shipwrights. By the eighteenth century, when mainland China's shipbuilding had deteriorated, it became necessary to purchase junks built in Borneo by overseas Chinese.

In the contemporary period, Chinese commercial domination has continued. For example, in Malaysia, where ethnic Chinese make up 34 percent of the population, they own 20 percent of the coconut and tea acreage and 26 percent of the rubber and oil-palm acreage. In Indonesia, Chinese control more than 70 percent of the local and retail trade. Thailand shows a similar Chinese domination, and there ethnic Chinese control sixty-three of one hundred of the largest Thai manufacturing companies, and are the chief directors of two large Bangkok banks.[7] Chinese dominance in modern Singapore is so complete that the government recently decreed that all children were to be taught Chinese Mandarin.

ANTI-CHINESE SENTIMENT

It is obvious from the foregoing that the Chinese clan immigrant in southeast Asia steadily gained in importance as an entrepreneur and middleman. The overseas Chinese were not always permitted to hold government positions, and so they remained dependent upon business as a means for making a living. With the advent of Western commercial expansionism, the Chinese handled business transactions between the Westerner and the native sector. This meant that the Chinese, through their traditional guild system, conducted most of the money lending, which in turn led them to control housing and land ownership. Resentment occasionally grew among the native population as they became dislocated in the economic system. This led to outbreaks of violence against the Chinese, who became frequent targets of revolutionaries.

Part of the cause for discrimination against Chinese clan immigrants was their long-standing claim of mainland citizenship. The overseas Chinese, or Huaqiao, lived by the unofficial principle of *jus sanguinis*—that is, every child who had either a Chinese father or mother, no matter what his place of birth or residence, was considered a Chinese citizen. Huaqiao adherence to this principle caused considerable problems for southeast Asian states, and despite frequent attempts to ignore it or pass legislation against it, the principle persisted.

SMUGGLING

By the sixteenth century Chinese smuggling had become a widespread and not dishonorable calling; it was practiced not merely by outlaws, but by coastal merchants, government officials, and local gentry as well. Smuggling was so deeply ingrained in the character of the seacoast population that even Chinese of considerable stature would willingly smuggle as the opportunity arose.

The itemization by a seventeenth-century Portuguese merchant of illicit goods transported from China to Japan indicates how lucrative smuggling could be.[8]

Item	China Selling Price	Japanese Purchase Price
Raw silk	80 tpp (taels per picul)	140–50 tpp
Fine silk	140 tpp	370–400 tpp
Gold	5.4 tt (taels per tael)	7.8 tt
Cotton thread	7 tpp	16–18 tpp
Quicksilver	53 tpp	90 tpp
Liquorice	3 tpp	9–10 tpp

Even official foreign missions carried out a brisk smuggling trade. When discovered, their punishment was invariably light. Early Ming histories record that one envoy and his 240-member mission were caught smuggling ivory and spices, but the emperor subsequently pardoned them.[9]

According to other local histories published in the sixteenth century, Cantonese, Fujianese, and Zhejiangese were all engaged in an extensive smuggling network with Japan via the Liuqiu Islands. Many of the smugglers, peasant fishermen or pirates, lacked high-level protection. When caught, they were punished in the severest fashion by beheading.

In southeast Asia, smuggling was promoted by Chinese immigrant enclaves. In many cases, a mainland smuggler contacted the resident

Smugglers being punished. These captured smugglers are being forced to wear the cangue, a traditional form of punishment. (From the Ltjg Moses Lindley Wood album dated 1884–85, courtesy of the Special Collections Department, Nimitz Library, U.S. Naval Academy.)

Chinese headman, who acted as an interpreter and set up trade procedures with local tribes. Some even went so far as to erect warehouses and sleeping quarters for smugglers and their crews.[10]

OPIUM

In the early eighteenth century, smugglers began to transport opium in large amounts.* In 1729 a decree was issued that punished opium dealers, who were relegated to the cangue for one month and subsequently forced to perform military service. Those caught operating opium dens were strangled.[11]

Two principal factors countered the Chinese government's efforts to halt the spread of opium. The British East India Company controlled both the poppy fields in India and the vessels that transported the drug to China's coast. On the coast, Chinese smugglers and unscrupulous officials worked together to bring the opium ashore. Chinese drug smugglers and the British became responsible for an astounding addiction rate. According to Chinese officials of the period, by 1838 fully 90 percent of the population in Fujian and Guangdong provinces were addicts, and cities on key waterways such as the Yangzi River had hundreds of thousands of addicts. On the eve of the Opium War, addiction was infiltrating the military, and the emperor was even informed that addicts were to be found in the ranks of the imperial bodyguard.[12]

Motivated by the large profits in opium trade, Chinese smugglers made improvements in coastal craft. Their work required small, fast vessels capable of carrying substantial opium loads in riverine areas. In the nineteenth century, fast crabs (kuaixie) were built that could outrun any vessel used by the government.† Later the government made use of these boats to interdict smuggling traffic.

Despite constant government attempts to stamp out smuggling, it continued unabatedly into the twentieth century. Even the People's Republic of China (PRC) has been unable to completely halt coastal smuggling. Fishing boats regularly exchange contraband gold, silver, and other valued items between Taiwan and the PRC. There appears to be little honor among the smugglers. Recently (April 1980), while exchanging counterfeit Parker pens and Rolex watches, Taiwanese fishermen received gilded lead bars from their mainland counterparts.[13]

PIRACY

Having provided the Chinese with a model for a fighting tradition, piracy may have been the greatest of all influences on contemporary Chinese naval tactics. In 1938 Mao Zedong located the importance of the piratical tradition for Chinese warfare capabilities.

*Until the arrival of opium, salt was the principal article smuggled in boats. For centuries, salt had been a government monopoly. It was regulated by official agencies, which issued licenses. Because salt was obtained by evaporating sea water, coastal saltpans were maintained by the government.
†These boats were "of great length and beam, the latter increasing rather disproportionately abaft to give quarters to brokers' agents who always went with them."[14]

Objectively speaking, the possibilities of developing guerrilla warfare and establishing base areas are greater in the river-lake-estuary regions than in the plains, though less than in the mountains. The dramatic battles fought by "pirates" and "water-bandits," of which our history is full, and the guerrilla warfare round the Hunghu Lake kept up for several years in the Red Army period, both testify to the possibility of developing guerrilla warfare and of establishing base areas in the river-lake-estuary regions.[15]

INSURGENTS

Generally speaking, Chinese pirates could be grouped into three classes. The first class, to which Mao probably referred, was composed of insurgents who used piracy to oppose repressive dynastic regimes. Interestingly, pirate leaders in this category seldom came from the ranks of the peasant-fishermen. Instead they usually belonged to fairly affluent landowner or merchant families.[16] They took to piracy for a variety of politico-economic reasons, such as overpopulation, high government taxes, concentration of land in the hands of a few, monopolies, and official corruption.

There were two types of insurgent, the river insurgent and the coastal or ocean insurgent. The former were the most numerous and the most successful at inciting rebellion. An example discussed in the preceding chapter is the first Ming emperor, Zhu Yuanzhang, whose prowess in riverine warfare led to the defeat of the Mongols. Throughout China's history, insurgents used riverine areas to advantage and tied down large numbers of government forces. Imperial officials, ever mindful of the need to control the Yangzi and its tributaries, were usually prompt in taking action against such insurgents. If they were negligent, river insurgency could quickly develop into general rebellion.

Coastal or ocean insurgents, although numerous, were never successful at rebellion. Their targets of opportunity were limited, and they could not easily meld with the population ashore. Moreover, government coastal defenses frequently managed to keep the coastal insurgents dispersed or confined to island strongholds. Thus, it was rare that this type of insurgent was able to seriously challenge dynastic rule. In fact, none ever ascended to the throne.

Interestingly, in the one instance where a coastal insurgent did threaten imperial rule, the government chose to avoid direct naval confrontation. This occurred in the late seventeenth century, shortly after the Manchus had established continental domination but still faced Ming opposition in the form of a rebel navy operating from Taiwan, Jinmen (Quemoy), and the Pescadores. For some forty years these ocean insurgents, led by two generations of a Fujian gentry clan, dominated the Taiwan Strait and assaulted the mainland. However, the Manchus, never seriously challenged, continued to strengthen coastal defenses. Finally, riddled by internal rivalries and stymied by Manchu population-control procedures along the mainland coast, the rebels surrendered.

The insurgent pirate, dependent upon the support of river and coastal peasants, enforced rules that promoted good relations among the local populace. For example, food and other goods received from peasants were to be paid for, and anything taken by force was punishable by death. A seventeenth-century statement from a Qing maritime pacification plan tells of the coastal population's loyalty to the principal coastal insurgent Zheng Chenggong.

> The reason why Cheng Chen Jung [Zheng Chenggong] has not been crushed is that he has Foochow [Fuzhou], Hinghua [Xinghua], and other prefectures for his bases of supply. As he gets in the south rice from Huichow [Huizhou], and Chouchow [Chaozhou?], his soldiers lack no food; as he gets wealth in the middle from Hinghua [Xinghua] and Chuanchow [Quanzhou], his soldiers are in no need of pay; as he gets lumber in the north from Foochow [Fuzhou] and Wenchow [Wenzhou], his ships can always be replenished. Although supplies to him from the maritime regions have been prohibited, since the method is defective, the prohibition remains a dead letter.[17]

Rules were intended to allow the pirates to mingle freely with the villagers ashore and thus maintain their inventories of food and gunpowder. Order and discipline were also emphasized at sea. For example, if a vessel left the line of battle during combat and the captain was found guilty in a trial by his peers, he would be beheaded.

In the early nineteenth century (1805) the largest organized band of insurgent pirates in China recorded three rules that were strictly enforced.

> 1. If any man goes privately on shore, or what is called transgressing the bars, he shall be taken and his ears be perforated in the presence of the whole fleet; repeating the same act, he shall suffer death.
> 2. Not the least thing shall be taken privately from the stolen and plundered goods. All shall be registered, and the pirate receive for himself, out of ten parts, only two; eight parts belong to the storehouse, called the general fund; taking anything out of this general fund, without permission, shall be death.
> 3. No person shall debauch at his pleasure captive women taken in the villages and open places, and brought on board a ship; he must first request the ship's purser for permission, and then go aside in the ship's hold. To use violence against any woman, or to wed her without permission, shall be punished by death.[18]

PRIVATEERS

The second class of pirates resembled the European type of privateer. Leaders were usually prosperous merchants or members of the gentry who disguised their private trading fleets when pirating. Crews, often chosen from among servants, were loyal and skilled fighters. The profit motive prompted this group to engage in piracy. Targets of attack included both government and foreign shipping. A sixteenth-century official in Fujian described these pirates as follows:

> In such places as Longqi and Songyu, the land is dangerous and the people are fierce. In general the people lead a seafaring life. Among them, the influential families have often sheltered rascals and privately built big ships and provided them [the rascals] with implements and food so that both parties depend on each other to make a profit. It is respectfully requested that an order be issued to the authorities concerned to prohibit all this.[19]

As in the case of coastal insurgents, pleas by officials for government action against coastal privateers usually fell on deaf ears, because there was little threat to central authority, and coastal defense fleets were often inadequate to deal with the problem anyway. Officials also knew that privateering decreased when conditions were good, and increased when the government was not benevolent or crops failed.

OUTLAWS

The third category of pirates, the outlaws, were primarily of two types, the first comprising coastal farmers or fishermen whose poverty forced them into piracy. The second type were bandits who took up piracy.

The anti-bandit policy of *jianbi qingye*, which was finally abandoned in the late eighteenth century, was sometimes ineffectual in routing the pirates. For example, in 1805 a combined Guangdong-Fujian pirate force totaled nearly seventy thousand men and two thousand ships. It was divided into six fleets identified by colored banners. Within each fleet, a commander was appointed by the pirate chief, assigned a specific raiding area, and forbidden to encroach on others' raiding zones.

Outlaw piracy worsened in the nineteenth century as economic and social problems increased. Between 1661 and 1841 the population controlled by the Qing had grown more than twenty times over, from about 19 million to about 413 million persons, and the amount of arable land had increased only three times over.[20] With his family growing in size, the average peasant was forced to go into debt, and often he had to sell his land

No bound feet in pirate societies (ca. 1931). Pirates, male and female, were the enemies China's navies have most often had to deal with. Note the eighteenth-century cannon, nineteenth-century rifle, and twentieth-century automatic pistol. (Photograph by Aleko E. Lilius, courtesy of D. Appleton and Company, New York.)

to wealthy merchants. Thus, the land came to be concentrated in the hands of a small group of wealthy landowners. Faced with land taxes levied by these landowners, the peasant was soon stripped of his cash. Money itself underwent frequent devaluation due to the continued importation of opium, which drained the provincial treasuries. To make matters worse, the Yellow River and the Yangzi River flooded their banks almost annually, causing the dislocation of population centers.

For these reasons , along with the fact that commercial seaborne traffic had increased significantly, Chinese outlaw piracy was rampant by the mid-nineteenth century. In 1847–48, several pirate groups established a system of strongholds on the offshore islands stretching from the Zhoushan Islands off Shanghai to Xiamen.[21] The local fishing populace in these regions had become so threatened that they were unable to carry out their seasonal expeditions to the rich fishing grounds. Appeals to local Chinese officials went unanswered, as neither the Jiangnan nor Zhejiang fleets dared to venture into the area. As a result, the British navy assumed increasing water-police responsibilities for protection against the pirates. During the period from 1850 to 1866, Chinese governor-generals of the coastal provinces were authorized by the emperor to cooperate with the British in combatting piracy along the coast and in the rivers. Such cooperation took the form of sending several junks along with the British warships to assist in identifying captured pirates. This practice continued even during the period from 1856 to 1860, when China was at war with Britain and France.

The Chinese government's solution usually consisted of offering the pirate leaders a commission in the navy and a civil rank. But piracy continued unchecked, even though British naval assistance accounted for

Pirate fleet under attack. This painting depicts a Royal British Navy ship, HMS *Columbine*, attacking a Chinese pirate fleet in 1849. (Lithograph in colors by Dickinson and Company, after E.H. Cree, courtesy of Beverly R. Robinson Collection, U.S. Naval Academy Museum.)

the capturing or killing of 7,325 pirates in one three-year period.[22] By the late nineteenth century (1898), the problem still remained unsolved, as evidenced in the following letter by the British consul in Canton to his superior:

> Probably never since Canton was open to foreign trade has piracy been so rife as in the year under review. The boldness of the pirates is, however, surpassed by the apathy of the provincial government. I have found no less than forty-one cases of piracy since last December and matters have now reached such a pass that trade on the inland waters of the province is being very seriously interfered with.[23]

Less than thirty-five years later, official Japanese government reports detailed the existence of a huge band of pirates in Bias Bay, some 65 miles east of Hong Kong. This pirate organization consisted of more than fifty thousand persons equipped with modern carbines and machine guns. The Bias Bay pirates had headquarters in Shanghai and Hong Kong, as well as special intelligence centers in Fuzhou, Xiamen, Shantou, and Canton.[24]

Frequent suppression of the maritime spirit by imperial governments stifled Chinese acquisitiveness and seafaring ingenuity. Instead of developing more scientifically, China's ocean commerce and naval spirit were perpetuated through illegal and primitive systems. Emigration, smuggling, and piracy caused China's naval and maritime potential to stagnate at a time when advances in Western naval techniques permitted penetration of China via the sea. The words of the American seapower advocate, Admiral Alfred T. Mahan, in regard to the seventeenth-century French navy, serve equally well to describe the prevailing Chinese attitude. "Yet all this wonderful growth, forced by the action of the government, withered away like Jonah's gourd when the government's favor was withdrawn."[25]

CHAPTER 5

IMPERIAL NAVIES UP TO THE OPIUM WAR

 Despite the ascendency of the maritime spirit, Chinese naval development was uneven and largely influenced by traditional thought. As already seen in the Yuan and early Ming periods, the Chinese were quite capable of dispatching navies to oceans beyond east Asia. Despite such ambitions, influential Chinese managed to deemphasize naval development to the point that seagoing fleets virtually disappeared.

OVERVIEW OF CHINESE STRATEGY

The well-known dynastic cycles had a direct influence on Chinese naval strategy. In general, the cycles can be divided into three phases: consolidation, peace and pacification, and disintegration. In the first phase, dynasties were characterized by a strong military organization that consolidated all warring factions following a period of internal disorder. During this phase, the idea of "grand unification" (*da yitong*) prevailed, and lands or regions recognized to be Chinese territories were occupied in the name of the emperor. Navies were most useful in controlling island holdings as well as demonstrating Chinese suzerainty among oceanic tributaries.

The second phase saw the dynasty flourish, but its very success often produced indifference to maritime and naval affairs. China lapsed into a stage termed "minor unification" (*xiao yitong*) where the coast could not be adequately defended against even pirates and smugglers.

In the third phase, at the end of a dynasty, internecine rivalries and rebellions became more frequent. Open warfare resulted. The capital often shifted and foreign encroachment or conquest resulted. This cycle was termed *pianan* ("partial peace"). China usually lost control over some of its coastal and island territories as well as other continental border regions.

NEILUAN WAIHUAN

At the risk of oversimplification, it might be said that China's disesteem of seapower likely had its origins in the strategic concept of *neiluan waihuan* ("inside disorder and outside calamity"). *Neiluan waihuan* considered the two things that threatened ruling dynasties to be internal rebellion and foreign aggression across northern borders.

In addition to the literal meaning of *neiluan waihuan*, the Chinese had an interpretation concerned with the strategy of defending against these twin threats. It translates simply as "internal weakness invites invasion from without."[1] In this context, the ancient Chinese concept of *neiluan waihuan* closely resembles the modern idea of defensive strategic deterrence; potential enemies had to be convinced that Chinese military forces would respond to aggression with unacceptable counteraction.

This concept forged strong attitudes about military forces. For example, imperial rulers and their advisors sometimes followed the Han dynasty recipe for armies.

> 1. Forces used to settle chaos and to punish the tyrannous are righteous forces, which will dominate all under heaven.
> 2. Forces used reluctantly for self-defense are responsive forces, which will win.*
> 3. Forces used to answer minor grudges are resentful forces, which will suffer defeat.
> 4. Forces used to seize territory and wealth are greedy forces, which will meet destruction.
> 5. Forces used to display great power and numerical strength to awe the enemy are arrogant forces, which will meet extinction.[2]

NAVAL APPLICATION

Applying these ideas to the sea, imperial naval strategists principally pursued a policy of maritime defense, or *haifang*. The Chinese believed that the best way to deal with foes who came by sea was to place naval defense forces in the following key areas, mentioned in order of importance: river approaches, major harbors, and large offshore islands.

Practitioners of *haifang* spoke of "enticing the enemy to enter the inland rivers . . . as if making a pit to wait for tigers or setting a net to wait for fish."[3] The usual method used in springing the trap was to lure enemy vessels into shallow or narrow waters, where they could be immobilized by iron chains, sunken boats, or fire rafts. Then they would be systematically destroyed by soldiers firing weapons from the safety of forts ashore. These tactics were usually effective against poorly organized and sorely equipped rebels, and even foreign pirates such as the Japanese.

Naval strategy, then, was one of defense rather than aggression. Indeed, research of Chinese naval terminology consistently reveals terms like *haifang* and *haian* ("coastal defense"); *haitan fangyu* ("beach defense"); *haijiang fangyu* ("harbor defense"); *yanhai yaosai* ("coastal fortress"); *hechuanzhan*("river warfare"); and so forth. On the other hand, terms like "seapower," "high-seas fleet," and "navalism" have appeared only lately.

---

*The People's Republic of China insists that its border clash with Vietnam in early 1979 was a "victorious" action undertaken in self-defense.

†The Chinese Communist leadership often applies such a description to the contemporary Soviet navy.

The brick-and-mortar system. This massive fortification was representative of China's coastal defense or *haifang* strategy. Forts like these could be found at all principal ports and major islands. Note, on the lower right, the European duck hunter, his dogs, and his day's kill. (From the Ltjg Moses Lindley Wood album dated 1884–85, courtesy of the Special Collections Department, Nimitz Library, U.S. Naval Academy.)

The lack of an aggressive strategy is understandable, for until the nineteenth century China was preserved from serious invasion from the sea, and unlike Europeans in the seventeenth, eighteenth, and nineteenth centuries, the Chinese had little experience with naval warfare on a grand scale. When a threat from the sea proved difficult to handle, the official imperial response often included one or more of the following strategems:

1. Implementation of trade bans
2. Removal of the coastal population inland
3. Enhancement of the coastal and river defense system
4. Inducement of Chinese maritime troublemakers to defect by offering bribes or official rank
5. Use of diplomacy if the troublemakers were foreign and not easily overcome[4]

In the event that these actions failed, the Chinese usually pursued a policy of conciliation. In the case of foreign seapowers, this entailed the granting of trading rights or, as a last resort, the negotiation of a peace treaty.

NAVAL ORGANIZATION

In order to better understand Chinese naval thought, an analysis of the imperial navy as an institution is helpful. Unfortunately, such an analysis must be kept brief, and address only those general themes applicable to the modern naval-building story.

LACK OF A NAVAL MINISTRY

One of the most significant weaknesses of imperial Chinese navies was the lack of a central agency charged with managing or advising on naval matters. In only one dynasty, the southern Song, was a formal headquarters established that had total authority over naval affairs. It was called the Yanhai Zhizhi Shisi (Imperial Commissioner's Office for the Control and Organization of the Coastal Areas), and was located at Dinghai, a port on one of the Zhoushan Islands southeast of modern-day Shanghai. Even this headquarters, however, was limited in its sphere of responsibility, since it defended only the Zhejiang coastal area and major rivers against encroaching Mongol armies.[5]

Two other central agencies having some naval responsibilities were the Board of War and the Board of Works. In time of war, the former could receive reports from all land- and naval-force commands. The latter decided where dockyards were to be established and set regulations for periodic ship overhauls. (In the eighteenth and early nineteenth centuries, naval vessels underwent minor repairs at the end of three years and a major overhaul after six years. At the end of nine years, unless found seaworthy, naval vessels were condemned.)[6]

Without a naval minister, members of the nobility or high civil officials were often appointed to act on the emperor's behalf when maritime crises arose. Their titles varied from dynasty to dynasty, but usually the officials were provided with an imperial seal that gave them plenipotentiary powers. When the matter at hand was cleared up, the seal was returned to the emperor and jurisdiction for naval affairs reverted to the provincial authorities.[7]

In dynasties where overseas trade was approved, maritime superintendents shared certain naval-defense responsibilities. For instance, in the seventeenth century, the superintendent at Xiamen supervised local naval officials, who checked merchant-ship manifests and cleared them for sailing or reentry.[8] In periods when naval fleets were ineffective, the superintendents directed the arming of merchantmen and assigned them to naval duties. Additionally, in wartime they often acquired responsibility for harbor defense and, in cooperation with local gentry and other government officials, oversaw the placement of log booms and chains.[9]

The most common method for exercising naval control rested at the provincial or regional level, since river and seaport defense was considered the responsibility of local armies and navies. Key river cities and coastal ports were supposed to possess sufficient forces to repel invaders who might come by sea. The dispatch of extraprovincial troops and the transfer of fleets between coastal provinces were tactics only sparingly employed.[10]

Normally, a regional military commissioner was responsible for the administration of military forces in his region, which was usually provincial in size. Along the coast, his naval duties involved registration of seamen and the training and preparation of provincial fleets for war. He was responsible for putting down disturbances in his area and transferring vessels or naval manpower to other regions when directed.[11]

The following quote from a nineteenth-century Western report provides an interesting overview of the duties of the provincial officers and fleets of that period:

> The [Chinese] navy has charge to prevent the islands from becoming the resort of pirates and bad characters, the people from emigrating thither or

from the main [land] in any large number. Special annual reports are made to the emperor, upon those of the cruising squadrons, regarding the increase of the island population. From the prevention of smuggling, piracy, and other crimes, there are strict regulations regarding the complement and armament of merchant vessels of different classes, as well as their painting, rigging, etc., the nature of all which particulars should appear in their registration-tickets or sailing-letters. At Macao . . . there are to be no more than 25 vessels of the western men, and these are to be registered by the local officers. The navy or military of the several stations have strict orders to assist distressed merchantmen; and the Inquiry (1825) retains an old Decree of the reign Kiaking [sic] by which officers are held responsible at the same time, for the mischief pirates may inflict, in the Chinese waters upon the vessels of foreigners.[12]

While the above suggests that the emperor had direct management of naval matters, nothing was further from the truth. In practice, the court usually engaged in a time-consuming process of canvassing those who had naval responsibilities for recommended courses of action. The emperor, through his court advisors, then chose from the alternatives offered. However, in times of weak government, the emperor frequently gave approval to individual suggestions without seeking further counsel.[13]

From the foregoing it can be seen that imperial navies were of two types, being either commanded by specially appointed "admirals" to perform special missions or subordinated to civil officials at the provincial level.

INSTITUTIONAL EVOLUTION

During China's first millennium, navies were river and canal defense forces. Sailors in these navies were conscripts, who had to serve annually aboard riverine defense vessels for periods that generally coincided with times of harvest and grain transport. Like the soldiers ashore, the riverine sailors were expected to provide their own support, and in return they received certain privileges such as land allotments, tax exemptions, and exemptions from corvee.[14] Navies in this period were temporary and usually could not cope with the military demands of large-scale warfare.

In the Song period, riverine warfare was extended to the coastal region as the Mongol cavalry pressed down from the north. The old riverine-defense system was applied to the sea as new types of ships were built for operating in the offshore ocean areas. However, the government found it increasingly difficult to guarantee privileges better suited to the farming belts. As a result, the Song found it necessary to create a navy of mercenaries made up of itinerant fishermen, pirates, and salt smugglers from the southeastern coast.[15] Although this navy was an efficient fighting force, it was regarded with great suspicion by Song officials, who were mostly northerners. Nevertheless, due to the Mongol threat, the Song navy grew quickly to twenty squadrons and fifty-three thousand men by 1262. As stated earlier, its primary function was confined to keeping the grain-transport lines of commerce open and patrolling the Yangzi River and its major tributaries.[16]

Following the Mongol conquest of China, the trend towards a mercenary navy was reversed: both armies and navies were conscripted under a traditional tribal military system in which membership was both obligatory and hereditary. On the coast, navies were subordinated to Mongol myriarchies or guard garrisons of one hundred, one thousand, and ten thousand troops. The commanders of these myriarchies were either Mongols, Semu, or Hanren, and like the officers in the pre-Song navies, they were given land and tax privileges.[17] The "enlisted men" aboard ship and ashore were southerners who were appointed by heredity, but they were not landed and possessed few real privileges. Interestingly, the Mongols' high-seas fleets, which participated in naval expeditions against various east Asian and southeast Asian states, were largely made up of the remnants of the Song mercenary navy.[18]

The Ming emperors retained much of the Mongol military organization, dividing the military into two general systems. One, known as the Military Administration System, had hereditary officer ranks, and the other, the Military Command System, had non-hereditary ranks. In the former system, fathers passed their hereditary rank and offices onto sons, but even though a father might advance beyond his hereditary office and rank, the son had to start at the original hereditary level.

In the Qing period, navies were hereditary or non-hereditary and divided along both racial and provincial lines. For example, there were two great armies in the Qing dynasty: the Banner Army and the Army of the Green Standard. The Banner Army was the army of conquest made up of trusted Manchus, Mongols, Semu, or Han Chinese. It was stationed throughout China at strategic areas and guarded important cities, canals, and roads.[19] The Army of the Green Standard, entirely Chinese, acted as a vast police force in the provinces. Both armies had naval forces assigned, most of which were wholly Chinese fleets and therefore subordinated to the Army of the Green Standard. Naval ranks were identical to those of the Ming Military Command System, and each coastal province had its own naval guard fleet. Officers in these fleets, primarily southerners, were conscripted. The Manchus, like the Mongols before them, distrusted the southern Chinese and refrained from granting them hereditary status; the Manchus retained loyalty by keeping southerners dependent upon government pay.[20]

Manchu naval forces subordinated to the Banner Army were located in six regions: the three Manchurian provinces of Heilongjiang, Jilin (Kirin), and Fengtian, and the coastal provinces of Zhejiang, Fujian, and Guangdong. Only in the latter three provinces could Chinese hold hereditary rank (Chinese were not allowed into the three Manchurian provinces until about 1903); however, the Banner naval commands were largely ceremonial and had few men assigned.[21]

NAVAL FORCE CATEGORIES

The process of Chinese naval development gave rise to various forces that had distinct missions and officer classes. The most common were the *shuishou jun*, the *zhenshu jun*, the *yongying*, the *tuanlian*, and the *yong*.

SHUISHOU JUN

The term *shuishou jun* ("naval force") usually connoted military or naval units under a single commander who had the power to act on his own or on behalf of the emperor.[22] The best maritime example can be found in Zheng He and his fleet, which was assigned the task of sailing to the Indian Ocean and reinforcing the tributary system among states located en route. During the Yuan and early Qing dynasties, emperors also designated naval *zhuli jun* ("main forces"), to carry out overseas missions.

There were special instances, too, where *shuishou jun* commanders were civilian officials with imperial authority to direct naval operations. For example, in the dark days prior to the Opium War, the emperor appointed a skilled administrator-scholar from Fujian, Lin Zexu, to take charge of naval forces in Guangdong Province and put an end to opium smuggling.

The most important *shuishou jun*, however, were the river defense navies, particularly the ones that guarded the Yangzi River. There was rarely a period in Chinese history during which a Yangzi River naval force did not exist, a fact that reflected imperial concern over the importance of controlling that vital artery.

ZHENSHU JUN

Main naval forces were augmented by regional navies, or *zhenshu jun*. The precedent for regional coastal-defense navies began with the southern Song and continued under the Mongols. The latter, in fact, had a coastal-defense system built around shore-based garrison forces that were located at strategic sites. Each garrison had both coastal-defense vessels and sea-going ships assigned.[23]

The Ming dynasty improved upon Mongol coastal defense, but at the same time it created a bureaucratic maze. The main element of the Ming system was the so-called *wei*, or regional military guards. *Wei* garrisons consisted of 5,600 men and were located in proximity to major and intermediate coastal ports.[24] The *wei* garrison was further divided into smaller units called *suo*, which in turn were subdivided into minor garrisons of 1,500 (*qianhu suo*) and 120 (*baihu suo*) men, respectively. Each of these minor garrisons occupied a coastal fort or small naval base. Theoretically, each *wei* garrison had 50 ships that could be used for major offensive action against pirates. The minor *suo* garrisons had two ships, each of which were used for reconnaissance and surveillance. In the early Ming period, the six coastal provinces listed an approximate total strength of 54 *wei*, 127 *qianhu suo*, and 1,270 *baihu suo*. Together these units would have had more than 5,000 coastal defense vessels when at full strength.[25] In one province, Zhejiang, there were approximately 90,000 personnel concerned with coastal defense.[26]

By the mid-Qing period, coastal defense forces were subordinate to the Banner Army and the Army of the Green Standard. The former were manned principally by Manchus or Mongols (the forces of the usurping family), and the ranks of the latter were filled by Chinese. Each army possessed naval forces that theoretically could have been used for high-seas operations; however, due to the emphasis on coastal defense, these fleets were decentralized and assigned a specific coastal area to defend. The chain of command was not clear in the least. For example, some admirals commanding squadrons near provincial boundaries could receive orders from each province's Banner Army governor-general. Complicating the picture further, they were also subordinate to senior Chinese officers of the local Green Standard coastal forces.[27]

Personnel of the coastal *zhenshu jun* could also perform non-military tasks. For example, in the Ming period, 70 percent of the defenders were posted on farmlands and employed primarily as farmers.[28] Meanwhile, others were used to build or maintain coastal defense vessels, and in the early nineteenth century, there were units that repaired or built stone-and-earth works used to counter flooding and tidal erosion.[29]

YONGYING

Whenever both central and regional forces proved ineffective, emperors might appoint a proven military or civilian official to recruit and organize temporary forces, or *yongying* (lit.,"encampment of warriors").[30] The official usually given full charge of the military situation was required to return his commission and deactivate his troops when the crisis passed.[31]

Yongying had several advantages. Since they were neither registered with nor funded by the central government, they were less concerned with elaborate command systems. Thus, they were given to better planning, and stressed intelligence collection and mobility in the conduct of operations. *Yongying* commanders also emphasized training and discipline. Officers were expected to be honest and to encourage togetherness within their respective units.

There were also disadvantages. Financing of *yongying* forces was a problem, and the gathering of funds was dependent upon the rank and prestige of the commander. One of the common methods used by *yongying* commanders was to utilize provincial-level taxes, such as transit and sales taxes levied on goods transported and sold by merchants and traders.

Another important drawback to *yongying* forces was that recruitment and close personal relationships between officers and men led to regionalism. Family ties were important. As a result, local vested interests often developed among the *yongying*, which made officer rotation difficult and created rivalries between units.

An example of *yongying* forces that had a naval mission were those created by the sixteenth-century Ming leader, Qi Jiguang. Qi was a member of a Shandong hereditary military family who was sent to Zhejiang Province in 1555 to fight against pirates. His success in Zhejiang soon led to an appointment by the emperor to undertake anti-pirate operations in Fujian, where routine coastal activities were all but paralyzed.

Qi subsequently established *yongying* coastal defense forces, whose organization and modus operandi were to be emulated by others in subsequent centuries. The first step taken by Qi was to divide the Fujian coast into three sectors, the northern, central, and southern. Each sector had two stationary forces consisting of a naval fleet of thirty-two war junks and a shore-based army of an estimated three thousand soldiers. Next, Qi organized two mobile fleets of thirty-two vessels, which were located near the junctions of the north-central and south-central borders, respectively. These fleets were to be used to reinforce any stationary fleet requiring assistance. Ashore, Qi also formed a mobile land force of three thousand soldiers, which could also come to the aid of any land units. Qi also had one remaining land unit permanently assigned to protect the Fujian capital at Lianjiang.[32]

TUANLIAN AND YONG

The fourth category of Chinese military organization involved militia forces of which there were two types, the *tuanlian* (lit.,"grouping and drilling") and the *yong* (lit., "braves"). The former, which dates back to the Tang dynasty, was organized and led by local gentry. Not being a central government organization, its size and scope of operations corresponded with the magnitude of the local threat. Importantly, the civil district magistrate, a representative of the government, was empowered to examine, appoint, or dismiss *tuanlian* leaders. Funding, however, was gotten by donations from the gentry or local guild organizations. Members of the *tuanlian* were conscripts. The usual method was to solicit one out of every three taxable males to serve in the militia.

The *yong* differed from the *tuanlian* in that its recruitment extended beyond local villages, and its troops were paid, fed, and drilled on a regular basis. Like the *tuanlian*, the *yong* was dependent upon the local gentry for support. It made use of *tuanlian* bureaus to register and recruit troops. The most important difference between *yong* and *tuanlian* was that the former could, if required, undertake limited extraprovincial actions.

On the coast, both militia groups usually functioned as auxiliary land forces, but there are historical references to a seagoing maritime militia. In both the Ming and Qing periods, for instance, fishing fleets were used to perform reconnaissance or surveillance duties when pirates were active.[33] These militia fleets, however, had neither weapons nor professional training.

NAVAL PERSONNEL

IDEALISTIC SENIOR COMMANDERS

In imperial China, naval officers were of two distinct types: idealistic senior commanders and career officers. The former were usually appointed by the emperor during periods of crisis to organize and command navies, which could involve either main forces, regional defensive forces, or militia. Invariably, idealistic commanders were chosen from among eunuchs, noblemen, gentry, scholars, or government officials. Their military experience was usually related to the army rather than to the navy. What distinguished them was their devotion to high ideals and an unshakable belief in the established Confucian sociopolitical system. Additionally, most were educated in the Chinese classics. Generally, these men were not inclined to pursue military careers; they returned to civilian life when their services as naval leaders were no longer required.

Unlike most Western maritime nations, imperial China attached little importance to a naval career. A tradition of sorts did evolve, but it closely paralleled the civil system. Hence, naval officers tended to acquire the characteristics that prevailed among the leaders of Chinese society. Sometimes idealistic senior commanders were rewarded with a title of hereditary rank. For example, Admiral Shi Lang, the Fujianese who defeated Zhen Chenggong in the seventeenth century, was made a member of the Chinese Bordered Yellow Banner Army and given the title *shuisi tidu* ("admiral in chief of naval forces"). In 1712, Shi's eldest son inherited the position.[34] In 1659 another admiral, Tian Xiong, was made a marquis and member of the Chinese Plain Yellow Banner Army. His title and rank continued to be inherited until the establishment of the Republic in 1911.

CAREER OFFICERS

The second type of imperial naval officer was the career officer. This type could be further divided into two categories, the conformist and the opportunist. Neither type had extensive classical education but both sought rank and prestige.

The conformist, as the name implies, was opposed to drastic organizational or operational innovations. Usually, the conformist was mildly corrupt and subordinated good leadership principles to authoritative expediency.

A graphic description of a conformist career officer is provided by a Royal Navy observer. He was Lieutenant Henry N. Shore, RN, the first lieutenant aboard HMS *Lapwing*, which visited Fujian in 1875. Lieutenant Shore described the Chinese admiral who commanded the local training ship as "rarely appearing on board, and when he did, shut himself up in a small highly scented den somewhere in the middle of the ship, from which he seldom or ever emerged." Lieutenant Shore observed that the admiral, who spent most of his leisure hours burning incense sticks, did take an active part in the meting out of discipline to the crew. "The old admiral was not all backward . . . for he had a keen sense of the importance of keeping up discipline with the aid of a bamboo, and his liberality of mind occasionally displayed itself in an anxiety to serve out more sticks than was required." Shore went on to say that "whenever one of the jolly tars on board forgot himself, this high functionary was applied to, and came to see the proper measure meted out; and when the punishment had been inflicted the unfortunate delinquent was, with charming irony, obliged to kneel before the admiral and thank him for favours conferred."[35]

The opportunist, or manipulative naval officer, was the opposite of the conformist. Energetic and ambitious, he was an excellent administrator, although he used his naval position to enrich himself. Unlike the conformist, the opportunist supported innovative changes if he believed that they would provide him with more power. This type of naval officer included many ex-pirates and criminals who were bribed by the government to give up their lives of crime in return for a naval commission.

NAVAL PATRONS

In addition to the professional naval officer, the Chinese had naval patrons or advisors. Such advisors could be either native Chinese or foreigners. These patrons often were men of wealth involved in maritime commerce who had purchased official rank. In currying imperial favor, they often offered advice on such things as maritime defense, shipbuilding, navigation, and gunnery.

An example of a prominent Chinese naval patron was Pan Shicheng, who attracted imperial attention during the Opium War (1840–42). Pan's family established a foreign trade firm in Canton in the late eighteenth century and eventually became quite wealthy. Pan Shicheng used his share of the family fortune to build up a lucrative salt- and tea-trading business. He also purchased a degree and set about using his money in the style of the gentry. For example, in the early 1830s, Pan Shicheng was honored by the emperor for his magnanimous contributions to famine sufferers in north China.

In 1840 Pan used his wealth and influence to construct four ships built along Western lines. The ships had copper bottoms, were 133 feet long, and carried 300 men.[36] Pan also purchased foreign guns and subsidized gunnery projects undertaken by a Fujianese engineer, Ding Gongchen.

Pan's efforts were partially successful. In October 1842, the emperor decreed that all warship construction was to be approved and built by Pan at Canton, and that any official who interfered with his work would be severely punished. Unfortunately, the emperor's edict coincided with the signing of a peace treaty with the British at Nanjing (August 1842), and interest in warship construction faded.

In 1842 Pan hired an American naval officer, J.D. Reynolds, to assist the Chinese in developing mines (*shuilei*, or "water thunder") for use against the British. Reynolds was guaranteed a salary of five thousand dollars a month and a bonus of twenty thousand dollars once the experiments were completed. The experiments were successful, but conservatism in the provinces effectively ended the project. When the Cantonese engineers went to Beijing in 1843 to demonstrate the devastating effect of the mine, the Zhili Province governor-general opposed the idea because no one in China had been trained to "put the water-thunder under warships and blow them up."[37] The emperor sent the workmen back to Canton and never made use of the mines.

FOREIGN ADVISORS

The brief episode with Reynolds reflected the Chinese tendency to experiment with technology and make use of foreign advisors. As early as the fifteenth century, in fact, the armament of Europeans had impressed the Chinese. As one official wrote: "The Folangji [Portuguese] are extremely dangerous because of their artillery and their ships. . . . No weapon ever made since memorable antiquity is superior to their cannons." And another Chinese frankly stated: "The Folangji use fire-arms with great skill. The Chinese on the contrary blow off their fingers or their hands or even their arms."[38]

Soon China set about acquiring these weapons through purchase or trade and were able to cast imperfect imitations by 1522. One of the most interesting developments occurred with the arrival of the Jesuits in China in the sixteenth century. They not only established themselves as intermediaries between the Chinese imperial court and the Portuguese, but became trusted technical and scholarly advisors as well. One became a grand secretary and others met daily with the emperor. Another, Father Johann Adam Schall von Bell, organized a gun foundry in Beijing to manufacture cannons to fight the Manchus.[39] Such activities later prompted at least one Chinese scholar to comment, "While Buddha came to China on white elephants, Christ was borne on cannon balls."[40]

The Jesuits also became interpreters for the Chinese. As such they were sometimes employed to help obtain weapons from the West. They also introduced modern cartographic techniques, which later aided the Chinese in mapping some maritime suzerainties, such as the Liuqiu Islands.

In the early nineteenth century, the Chinese were still inclined to obtain help from the Portuguese. At that time, pirate fleets along the southern coasts were causing serious problems. The Portuguese provided six armed corsairs and several battalions of marines to help the Manchus clean up the coastal areas.

China also accepted aid from other European nations, including Holland and England. The former cooperated with the Chinese in the seventeenth century to help defeat Zheng Chenggong on Taiwan, and in the early nineteenth century, the British navy took an active role in putting down piracy.[41]

China's acceptance of foreign aid had important stipulations, however. For example, employment required that the advisor accept an official appointment making him solely responsible to the Chinese government. Regarding the transfer of weaponry or troops, Chinese officials, so as not to risk undue political involvement with foreigners, invariably insisted that such aid be temporary and subordinated to Chinese control. In addressing the problem of how to accept Western aid or advice, a nineteenth-century Chinese statesman aptly summarized China's attitude. "From time immemorial barbarian assistance to China which is followed by success has always involved unexpected demands."[42]

LOCALISM

As noted in previous chapters, defensive systems used by the Chinese depended on decentralization, which had the undesirable side effect of promoting local vested interests. These interests were sustained by networks based upon personal loyalty, and in many cases military leaders selected their staffs from among fellow provincials. This regional factor was further refined by the appointment of trusted clan members or clan adherents to key positions in non-combat offices such as disbursing and logistics. Another method used to preserve regional interests was the time-honored hierarchical relationship. For example, within its unwritten code, a ship's commanding officer and his division officers were bound together by a personal loyalty that demanded each to serve the interests of the other.

An example of localism was that practiced by Qi Jiguang in the sixteenth century. Qi assigned only long-time associates from Zhejiang to key positions in the shore-based armies, but for less desirable shipboard commands, he assigned Fujianese.

Fujian became the most prominent province in naval matters during the Qing period. Zhen Chenggong's insurgent navy was made up of Fujianese, and the Manchus used Fujian loyalists as well to fight Zhen in the late seventeenth century.

It is interesting to note that following Zhen's defeat, the Manchu emperor selected the best Fujian marines to form a temporary riverine combat garrison to fight against czarist Russia on the Amur River. The Amur unit was selected from a "cane-shield" brigade that had fought under Zhen and Shi Lang. They were trained to use cane shields and long knives while fighting in the water. The shields, specially made of impenetrable cotton and rattan, were held over the head for protection while the combatant slashed at his opponent with the long knives. Five hundred Fujianese were used in this brigade, which was sent to the Amur in 1685. Their fierceness and ability to fight in the water helped rout the Russians.

The domination of Fujianese in the naval service is equally evident from a 1685 report on disposition of forces in the Chinese Green Standard Army. It records the naval admiral in Fujian as commanding twenty thousand navy men and marines—a considerably larger force than those in any of the other maritime provinces.[43] Fujian navy men were often assigned by the central government to accompany tribute missions overseas. For example, two hundred Fujianese sailors acted as a protective escort for a convoy bound for the Liuqiu Islands in 1800.[44]

SHIPS AND NAVAL WARFARE

Despite certain successes, the story of Chinese warship development and fighting tactics is generally a sad one. Beginning in the period of Warring Kingdoms and continuing into the Ming period, Chinese naval architecture and tactics advanced at a respectable rate, putting China ahead of European states. But what began in antiquity as an imaginative naval system and progressed through several dynasties to the fifteenth century, ended in the early nineteenth century with anachronistic and hopelessly overmatched provincial navies. While it is beyond the scope of this study to describe in detail Chinese naval development, some examples are in order.

CONSTRUCTION AND NAVIGATION TECHNIQUES

As early as the Tang dynasty, Arab sailors, who regularly visited Annam, Champa, and Canton, had noticed the advantages of Chinese junks. When Arabs returned to the Middle East, they introduced to the European world Chinese innovations such as the leeboard, the centerboard, the balance and slotted rudder, the windlass, and the watertight compartment. The Arabs also borrowed the Chinese idea of painting ships with lime and wood oil to preserve the bottom from corrosion and worm rot.[45]

As noted earlier, the Chinese possessed knowledge of a magnetic needle compass, which was probably borrowed by the Arabs and subsequently passed on to the Mediterranean world.[46] It was divided into 24 points of 15 degrees each. This was much easier to use than the European compass, which still had 32 points divided into 11.25 degrees.[47]

In the Song period, as government backing for maritime affairs expanded, Chinese shipwrights even developed a dry dock—an innovation that did not appear in Europe for several more centuries. An account of this device is contained in the following passage:

> At the beginning of the dynasty [Song] the two Zhe provinces [Zhejiang and southern Jiangsu] presented [to the throne] two dragon ships each more than 200 feet in length. The upper works included several decks with palatial cabins and saloons, containing thrones and couches all ready for imperial tours of inspection. After many years, their hulls decayed and needed repairs, but the work was impossible as long as they were afloat. So in the Xining reign-period [1068–77 A.D.] a palace official Huang Huaixin suggested a plan. A large basin was excavated at the north end of the Jinming Lake capable of containing the dragon ships, and in it heavy crosswise beams were laid down upon a foundation of pillars. Then [a breach was made] so that the basin quickly filled with water, after which the ships were towed in above the beams. [The breach now being closed] the water was pumped out by wheels so that the ships rested quite in the air. When the repairs were complete, the water was let in again, so that the ships were afloat once more [and could leave the dock]. Finally the beams and pillars were taken away, and the whole basin covered over with a great roof so as to form a hangar in which the ships could be protected from the elements and avoid the damage caused by undue exposure.[48]

In the period of Warring Kingdoms, the Chinese built a class of warship known as the *louchuan*, or castled ship. This ship, resembling a seagoing assault tower, had as many as three decks, which were protected by wooden ramparts. The ramparts were built above the decks and housed soldiers, including cavalry, who were equipped with various weapons. The ship had openings for bowmen and spearmen, and was supposedly capable of accommodating several hundred persons. The sides of the superstructure were covered with hide or leather to protect against projectiles. On the upper deck, trebuchets were added that could hurl stones considerable distances. During the same period, the Chinese developed a "covered swooper," a smaller version of the *louchuan* whose upper deck was covered with dried animal hides. The sides of the swooper were enclosed, and had oar ports in addition to the standard openings for crossbows and spears.

Inventions and Skills

In the early seventeenth century the Chinese created a type of minelayer that was suited only for nighttime riverine warfare. The vessel was constructed in two sections connected by large hinges. The forward section

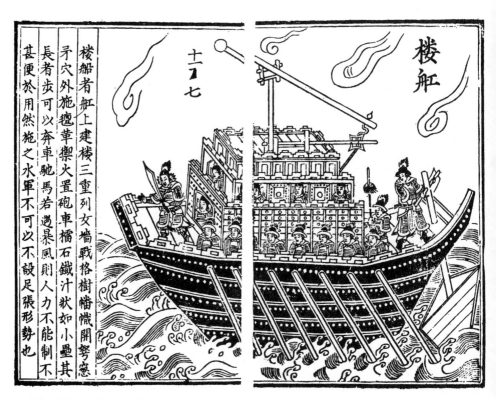

The Chinese battleship *Louchuan* (ca. 600 A.D.). (Reprinted from Joseph Needham, *Science and Civilisation in China*, vol. 4, p. 685, courtesy of the Cambridge University Press, Cambridge, England.)

was loaded with explosives activated by a timed fuse, and in combat the crew of this vessel would carefully row the ship alongside the target and detach the forward section. Then they would quietly withdraw to a safe area to await the devastating effect of their work.

Concerning other types of weapons, the southern Song saw the advent of trebuchets capable of hurling gunpowder bombs. The following passage from a Song history illustrates the high level of naval technology and organization in the early twelfth century:

> In the 3rd year of the Jianyan reign-period [1129 A.D.] the Supervising Censor Lin Zhiping was appointed to take charge of the defenses of the [Yangzi] River and the sea, with authorization to appoint his staff in the region under his command, i.e. from Hangzhou to Taiping. . . . [Lin] Zhiping spoke of the need for sea-going ships and requested that they be chartered from the coastal ports of Fujian and Guangdong [and re-fitted]. . . . These ships should each be equipped with a "Dipper-observer," bulwarks for protection against arrows, iron [-shod] striking arms, stores for projectiles, trebuchets, gunpowder bombs, incendiary arrows, and also other weapons, together with fire-fighting equipment.* [49]

*The Dipper-observer, or *wangdou*, appears to have been a primitive version of the sextant used for determining the position and altitude of stars in the Great Bear constellation. [50]

Minelayer (sixteenth century). Note the hinges amidships. The crew would detach the forward section and rapidly withdraw from the target. (Courtesy of the Cambridge University Press, Cambridge, England.)

During the Song period, Chinese warship construction also included treadmill-operated paddle-wheel ships that mounted as many as eleven paddle wheels per vessel.

The Chinese developed meteorological skills, including a method for predicting the wind. According to the modern Chinese maritime historian, Dr. Bao Zenpeng, the ancient Chinese mariner could predict the direction of the wind based upon season and weather signs. Dr. Bao also notes that during the late Song period, when the Mongols were driving the Chinese southward, ocean charts were used. They included coastal shipping routes, ports, and anchorages. During this time navigational procedures were highly advanced, as Dr. Bao indicates: "The captains knew geography. At night they watched the stars, in the daytime they watched the sun, and when it was overcast they watched the compass."[51]

TACTICS

As Chinese warships and navigational techniques became more sophisticated, so did naval tactics. As early as the period of Warring Kingdoms, the main combatant was the *dayi*, or great wing warship. It was over 120 feet long, had a 16-foot beam, and was propelled by 50 oarsmen. There was also a detachment of 26 marines and up to 10 archers assigned to these vessels. The marines were armed with grappling hooks, spears, and long-handled axes.[52] From this it can be assumed that these early navies used ram-and-grapple tactics during combat.

In subsequent dynasties, as has been mentioned, the Chinese advanced from the ram and grapple to amphibious assault and projectile tactics. However, by the sixteenth century, tactics had declined in sophistication. In 1524 a Spaniard in Macao scornfully described Chinese naval tactics as follows:

> [The Junks] have small iron guns, but none of bronze; their powder is bad. . . . Their arquebuses are so badly made that the ball would not pierce an ordinary cuirass, especially as they do not know how to aim. Their arms are bamboo pikes, some pointed with iron, others hardened by fire, short and heavy scimitars, and cuirasses of iron and tin. Sometimes a hundred vessels are seen to surround a single corsair, those which are to windward throw out powdered lime to blind the enemy, and, as they are very numerous, it produces some effect. This is one of their principal warlike strategems.[53]

Slightly more than a century later, in the early Qing dynasty, Chinese naval tactics experienced a brief renaissance. This was largely due to innovations made by Zheng Chenggong during his maritime rebellion in the late seventeenth century. His admirals, for example, used advanced formations that resembled a diamond formation then being experimented with by the British, French, and Dutch navies. Zheng's battle formation was also imitative of Korean formations used by Yi Sunsin against the Japanese in the sixteenth century.

A typical Zheng battle fleet was organized into five squadrons that duplicated the "quinary system" founded by the ancient Chinese military genius, Sun Tzu. Zheng's fleets were composed of five divisions corresponding to Sun's five military directions: north (forward), south (rear), west (left), east (right), and center. In this arrangement the flagship was usually stationed in the center where it could direct the battle. Until then, the characteristic Chinese system had been for flagships to remain well back from the fighting. Orderliness gave way to melee once contact was made. All pretense to precision ceased, and enemy ships were surrounded and attacked at close quarters.

Despite Zheng's tactical innovations, lack of effective control typified naval tactics, as the most prominent Chinese military journal of the time pointed out: "Fire arms can be used on large boats but the waves make aiming very hard. The chance of hitting the enemy is very slender. Even if one enemy boat should be hit, the enemy should not thus incur severe losses. The purpose of having fire arms aboard [a ship] is purely psychological, namely that of disheartening the enemy."[54]

BRICK AND MORTAR TACTICS

The above statement applied to the principal tactics resorted to by the Chinese, which involved the construction of forts and the blockading of rivers with log booms, fire rafts, and junks lashed together. Such tactics, imitative of what one scholar dubbed the British Brick and Mortar School, were employed in an effort to stop the British navy during the Opium War.[55] Lin Zexu, the Chinese official charged with the defense of Canton, naively reported the following to the emperor in 1839:

Should any unauthorized foreign ships attempt to enter, even if the wind and the time are in their favor, and the ships are sailing as if flying, they will find it impossible to go further than the chained timbers. Granted that the strong foreign boats can break the first line of iron chains, they will be stopped by the second line. Supposing all the chains and lines of timber can be broken, it will take a long time for them to accomplish the task. Meanwhile guns from all the forts will fire on them, and the foreign ships may easily become ashes.[56]

Such thinking, of course, was responsible for the devolution of the war junk. By the nineteenth century, the standard Chinese naval junk was 120 feet long, 25 feet in beam, and had a draught of 12 feet. It displaced from 250 to 300 tons, had a flush deck, and carried guns of poor quality. The crews were armed with spears, swords, and occasionally matchlocks. The old rattan shields were still used but offered little protection against musket shot. The Chinese war junk and its crews put one British observer in mind of a Roman galley, "only less efficiently constructed for venturing away from land."[57]

China's navy was no match for the British. In 1840 England had augmented its Asian fleet with the *Nemesis*, an iron-hulled steamer that carried two 32-pound guns and was flat bottomed. On 7 January 1841, following China's refusal to accept British demands that Hong Kong be ceded to England, the *Nemesis* attacked a Chinese naval squadron of fifteen junks with Congreve rockets. The captain of the *Nemesis* vividly described what happened as follows:

The first rocket fired from the *Nemesis* was seen to enter the large junk against which it was directed, near that of the [Chinese] Admiral, and almost

HMS *Nemesis* in the Opium War. The *Nemesis* was well named. Although she was an iron side wheeler of only 630 tons, with ninety men in her crew and armed with two guns, she easily overcame the Chinese naval junks sent against her. (Courtesy of the U.S. Naval Institute Press, Annapolis.)

instantly it blew up with a terrific explosion, launching into eternity every soul on board, and pouring forth its blaze like the mighty rush from a volcano. The instantaneous destruction of the huge body seemed appalling to both sides engaged. The smoke, and flame, and thunder of the explosion, with the fragments falling round, and even portions of dissevered bodies scattering as they fell, were enough to strike with awe, if not with fear, the stoutest heart that looked upon it.[58]

THE TREATY OF NANJING

On 29 August 1842, a Chinese peace group went aboard the British ship *Cornwallis* and signed the Treaty of Nanjing. The treaty was significant because it represented the first in a series of unequal treaties China would sign under the threat of Western seapower. The essential elements of the treaty were as follows:

1. The Chinese government agreed to pay the English government 21 million dollars of which 12 million dollars was for indemnity, 3 million dollars for the settlement of debts due to British merchants from Hong merchants (the Hong monopoly had been permanently abolished), and 6 million dollars as reparations for destroyed opium.

2. The Chinese government permanently ceded the whole island of Hong Kong to England.

3. The Chinese government established Canton, Fuzhou, Xiamen, Ningbo, and Shanghai as the five trade ports where England could establish factories and where British merchants and their families could come and go freely.

4. A uniform and moderate tariff on imports and exports was to be imposed. The custom duties for British commodities were to be established according to a fixed rate, after the payment of which a commodity could be transported to any spot in the interior without further tax.

5. Official correspondence between the two nations was to be in the form used among equals.[59]

Owing in large part to its naval weakness, China lost the Opium War and was forced to acquiesce to Western demands to open trade ports. Thus, it became alarmingly evident that China's naval stagnation had resulted in barbarian penetration from the sea. The ocean no longer served as an extension of the Great Wall, and the Manchu emperor was moved to comment that "the navy is a nihility. . . . Barbarian ships anchor in our inner seas, without the least notice being taken of them! I look back on the past, and harbour dismal forebodings for the future!"[60]

CHAPTER 6

THE TOTTERING IMPERIAL FRAMEWORK AND NAVAL SELF-STRENGTHENING

 Britain's defeat of China in 1842 led to an important shift of attitude on the part of the emperor toward naval reform. Instead of exhorting his provincial officials to build warships along the lines of Western design, he told them that "if ships cannot be constructed at once and if they can be purchased, by all means purchase them."[1] Meanwhile, a respected scholar from Hunan, Wei Yuan, published a treatise on Qing military operations in which he counselled that "to make guns is not as good as to purchase them." Significantly, Wei also recommended the building of a shipyard and arsenal near Canton, where foreign advisors would teach the Chinese how to build and handle ships and guns.[2]

Before any of these suggestions could be acted upon, other events conspired to delay naval reform for more than twenty years. Two internal rebellions broke out that placed renewed emphasis on riverine warfare and the security of the Yangzi River. Known as the Taiping and Nianfei rebellions, both drew their strength from rebel water forces that controlled key river areas. The Taipings, for example, using insurgent pirates and smugglers, seized control of the Yangzi River Valley and most of the important tributaries. The Nianfei, who were mostly bandits, captured and held parts of canals north of the Yangzi. After nearly sixteen years of civil war the Manchu government found much of its river and canal commerce paralyzed.

During this riverine interregnum (1850–66), several events took place that would influence naval reform in the latter half of the nineteenth century.

NEO-REGIONALISM

By 1851–52, *shuishou jun* and *zhenshu jun* naval forces were badly outmatched by the rebels. Training had become ceremonial and ships were in bad repair. Officers pocketed pay intended for enlisted men. Additionally, long periods of duty at various ports had made the naval forces indifferent. Discipline, highly polarized, was either severe or non-existent.[3]

The emperor responded to such problems in traditional style by selecting several idealistic scholar-generals to organize *yongying* forces and fight against the rebels.[4] While there was never any doubt about the loyalty of these leaders, the subsequent increase in size and efficiency of their armies and riverine navies represented potential threats to the central government. Hence, the traditional balance of power between Beijing and regional interest groups became a matter to be carefully watched.

CHINESE MARITIME CUSTOMS

The initial success of the rebels in river fighting and the desertion by Chinese officials of many traditional trade superintendencies caused serious interruption in the management of foreign trade. Nanjing, in fact, fell to the Taipings in 1853 and was not recaptured until 1864. During this confusion, foreign ships began calling at some ports without paying duties, alarming many responsible Western businessmen.[5] It was determined that new procedures were necessary, and on 29 June 1854 the United States, England, and France concluded an agreement with China that called for the establishment of the Foreign Inspectorate of Customs. This institution was to have a board of foreign customs inspectors and be headed by an English inspector general. Consistent with Chinese tradition, however, the inspectorate was to be under ultimate Chinese jurisdiction and staffs at the various treaty ports were to include substantial numbers of Chinese. This led to the division of China's old maritime superintendencies into two key Chinese offices: the Beiyang Dachen (Superintendent of Trade for the Northern Ports) and the Nanyang Dachen (Superintendent of Trade for the Southern Ports).

However, the establishment of customs did alter Chinese tradition, for it injected Europeans into key maritime advisory roles that had always been allotted to Chinese government officials and local gentry. This quickly led to pressure on China to grant management autonomy to Europeans in matters over which the latter believed the Chinese were slow to take action.

An early example occurred in 1861, when a British customs official convinced a prominent Manchu prince to purchase eight steam-driven warships from Britain. The ships were to be used to put down coastal piracy and smuggling. As the scenario was played out, it soon became evident to all concerned that there were serious flaws in this plan. The British negotiator, Mr. Horatio Nelson Lay, had convinced London that British naval personnel should be assigned to China on half-pay to serve aboard these vessels. Lay also stipulated to the Chinese that the squadron and its commander in chief be controlled and commanded by a European.[6] This announcement caused the Chinese to back off quickly from the negotiations and cancel the warship purchases. The proposed British commander in chief, Captain Sherard Osborn, former commanding officer of HMS *Furious*, wrote his views of the situation as follows:

The Emperor wishes to place the entire control and disposition of the squad-ron under the irresponsible authority of the provincial mandarins, and to supersede me as Commander-in-Chief, leaving it to the local mandarins to form as many squadrons of European vessels as they might see fit under different officers, and under different systems of pay and discipline. . . . To surrender ourselves to the irresponsible orders of local mandarins would certainly make us participators in acts of plunder and cruelty which would bring discrace upon us as British officers and seamen.[7]

FURTHER FOREIGN PRESSURES

The steady influx of foreigners into China created new pressures for fur-ther commercial concessions. This led to the so-called Second China War, which pitted an Anglo-French force against the Chinese. When the war ended in 1859, China was compelled once again to open more ports to trade. Between them, the British and French forced the Chinese to open up eleven more ports. Additionally, England gained control of Kowloon, the peninsula opposite Hong Kong.

The Chinese were also taken advantage of by Russia, who used the war as a pretext to annex Chinese territory north of the Amur River and east of its tributary, the Wusuli (Ussuri) River. In this area a Russian military expedition founded Vladivostok (then a minor Chinese port called Haishengwei) and thereby sealed China off from the Sea of Japan.

NAVAL SELF-STRENGTHENING

By the mid-1860s, *yongying* forces finally defeated the Taiping rebels and imperial attention once again became focused on maritime affairs. One of the first leaders to advocate naval reform was Zuo Zongtang, a scholar-general and commander of one of the anti-Taiping *yongying* armies. Zuo had fought well against the Taipings and in 1863 was appointed governor-general of Fujian and Zhejiang. Within several years, he established him-self as a trusted and efficient administrator by carrying out extensive reform, particularly in education and agriculture. Zuo's reform movement also included a program for Chinese naval development which he had supported since at least 1853.

Zuo was cautious in his approach to naval reform, however. Un-doubtedly he had the aborted British-warship sale on his mind when he wrote: "The method of self-strengthening should be to seek from among ourselves, not seek from others. He who seeks the help of others will be controlled by others, and he who relies upon himself will have the situa-tion under his own control."[8]

Zuo's idealism notwithstanding, he soon realized that some foreign assistance was necessary. This stemmed in part from his purchase of a steamship in 1864 that had foreigners in the crew and was successfully used to reduce piracy along the Fujian and Zhejiang coasts.[9] From this experience, Zuo began to resurrect elements of Wei Yuan's concept from the period of the Opium War that called for China to construct a shipyard and develop the skills necessary to build its own ships. Importantly, however, Zuo did not want to make extensive purchases of warships abroad. Rather, he proposed the hiring of foreign naval technicians to assist China's own small force of progressive, but as yet unqualified, naval experts.[10] The foreign technicians were to be under strict Chinese control and paid in accordance with an agreed contract.

By 1866 Zuo had successfully memorialized the court for the establishment of an arsenal, a shipyard, and a naval academy to be located at Fuzhou in Fujian Province. From its inception, however, Zuo's Fujian naval experiment encountered significant opposition from conservatives and progressives alike. For example, some conservative officials opposed the Fujian naval program because it was too expensive, employed foreigners, and required learning foreign languages and modern mathematics.[11] Others were jealous of the fact that Fujian had been favored as the site. Progressives opposed the plan because they believed that China could only modernize the navy by making substantial foreign purchases rather than by undertaking a purely Chinese shipbuilding venture.

Despite this opposition, in the summer of 1866 Zuo, with the help of several Frenchmen who had been officers aboard his anti-piracy steamer in 1864, concluded a five-year contract with France that called for the building of a dockyard and a naval academy.[12] Sixteen ships were to be constructed and a European staff was to be engaged to train Chinese workmen, foremen, and midshipmen. Although several months later, Zuo was suddenly reassigned to the interior to lead an army against a serious Muslim rebellion, by 1867 the Fuzhou Dockyard, located at the base of Mawei Mountain on the Min River, began to take shape when machinery arrived from France. After nearly two years, the engine shop was completed, and the five-year contract officially began.

THE FUZHOU DOCKYARD AND NAVAL ACADEMY

The Fuzhou naval complex was soon divided into the French school and the English school, which remained distinct from one another. The French school had three departments: the naval construction school, the department of design, and the apprentice school. The English school also was divided into three departments: theoretical navigation, practical navigation, and engine-room operations. To manage and supervise the complex, seventy-five Europeans and twenty-six hundred Chinese were employed initially.

The French school was managed entirely by Frenchmen, and instruction was given in the French language so that students could converse with their teachers and comprehend French technical manuals. Besides language, the five-year curriculum called for learning arithmetic, basic calculus, physics, and mechanics. During the last several years of the curriculum, students were required to put their classroom training to practical use by working in the dockyard plants as both laborers and supervisors. They were not expected to become proficient in new techniques, but rather to reach a state of competency where they could effectively manage construction of vessels. New construction designs were to be mastered by sending promising students to Europe for advanced training.[13]

Steamship "scholars" (1884). These young students were assigned to Li Hong-zhang's China Merchant's Steam Navigation School. Young teenagers were tested and selected for naval training at Chinese naval academies in the late nineteenth century. (From the Ltjg Moses Lindley Wood album dated 1884–85, courtesy of the Special Collections Department, Nimitz Library, U.S. Naval Academy.)

The design department had a three-year curriculum that specialized in engine design. Its purpose was to create a staff of Chinese designers capable of drafting construction plans. At the end of the three-year period, student graduates went on to the department of naval construction for more advanced schooling. The course of instruction called for French, arithmetic, plane and descriptive geometry, and detailed study of the 150-hp marine engine. Students also were required to spend time in the shipyard learning the practical aspects of workshop management.[14]

The apprentice department operated on a three-year program of night classes and was organized to develop foremen from among the more promising workmen assigned to the shipyard. The French supervisor, Prosper Giguel, described the training goals as providing the students with "the ability to read a plan, [and] to design it."[15] Classes were conducted in French and dealt with arithmetic, plane and descriptive geometry, algebra, drawing, and engine descriptions.[16]

During the five-year contract period, as more equipment was acquired and additional buildings were constructed, the physical plant at the Fuzhou Dockyard changed dramatically. By 1874 five permanent shops were created, housing the forges, mills, a boiler construction ship, the engine shop, foundry, and miscellaneous support facilities. Included in the latter was a compass shop capable of turning out compasses, barometers, steam gauges, cannon sights, and chronometers. The ship construction yard also possessed a molding loft, a launching slip for ships up to 2,500 tons, and kilns that produced boiler bricks.[17]

On 10 June 1869, the Fuzhou Dockyard launched its first ship, the *Wannianqing*, a wooden sloop 68 meters long and mounting 14-cm guns. Six months later three ships were launched: two gunboats, each 52 meters long and mounting three guns, and the *Fupo*, a 1,258-ton transport.[18] The following summer, the dockyard succeeded in launching a 100-ton sloop driven by a 150-hp engine built at Fuzhou. Over the next four years, the dockyard constructed eleven more ships of various sizes, and considering the Opium War record of Chinese attempts at naval modernization, this construction was a significant achievement.

Meanwhile, the English school was making similar progress in the training of officers and crews to man the new ships. It was managed entirely by Englishmen. All courses were conducted in English and all technical training materials were read in that language. The department of theoretical navigation was headed by James Carroll, who, in keeping with the idea of a joint-European staff, was hired by Zuo's French director to teach students coastal piloting and celestial navigation. Carroll was assisted by another Englishman and an English-speaking Chinese. Carroll's course of instruction entailed three and one-half years of study covering subjects in English, arithmetic, geometry, algebra, plane and spherical trigonometry, nautical astronomy, theoretical navigation, and geography.[19]

By 1873, thirty-two students had graduated from Carroll's theoretical navigation course and were sent on to the English school's second department for two-year training in practical navigation. This department, set up early in 1870, was initially directed by a Lieutenant Swainson of the Royal Navy. Classes were conducted aboard the training ship *Jianwei*, a Prussian sailing vessel purchased by the dockyard in 1869. Swainson was soon relieved by Captain R.E. Tracey, RN, who had two British navy men as assistants in gunnery and seamanship. Under Tracey's training program, students were expected to learn the fundamentals necessary for command. Exhausting training cruises were conducted, with the outstanding students commanding the training ship and others standing watches in various capacities. Through this process, students were singled out for captaincies; by 1874 fourteen students had been certified under this system.[20]

OVERSEAS TRAINING

Of perhaps more importance than the early naval training at Fuzhou was the subsequent approval by the Manchu court to send selected graduates of the school to Europe for further advanced training. A precedent for this had been set in 1872, when two other powerful regional leaders, Zeng Guofan and Li Hongzhang, had convinced the court to send 120 Chinese to the United States under the auspices of the Chinese Education Mission.[21]

The mission was managed by Yong Wing, a native of Guangdong who had begun studying English while a young boy and was sent to Yale, where he graduated in 1857. In 1864 Yong Wing had been chosen by Zeng Guofan to go to America to purchase machinery for Shanghai's Jiangnan Arsenal. Upon his return he discussed the idea of a mission with Zeng and Li.[22] Eight years later Yong Wing's idea reached fruition when students, mostly from poor Cantonese families, were sent to Hartford, Connecticut, to begin a fifteen-year educational program.

One year after the approval for the educational mission had been granted, Shen Baozhen, the new Chinese director of the Fuzhou Dockyard, memorialized the government to send selected graduates of the French school to France for a three-year course of study in shipbuilding. Additionally, Shen recommended that certain graduates of the English school be sent to England for three years of advanced training in navigation and naval operations. On 6 January 1874, the newly established Zongli Yamen (Chinese Foreign Affairs Office) approved the proposal, citing the American educational mission as the example.[23]

Immediately, Giguel and Shen drew up plans for the selection of thirty students together with supervisors. Importantly, the financing of the venture was to be accomplished entirely by Fujian Province, with two hundred thousand taels (one hundred twenty thousand dollars) estimated as the amount required to pay for the project.[24]

Significantly, the first overseas naval mission was nearly aborted owing to problems with Yong Wing's group in the United States. In 1877, feeling that his young Cantonese students were ready to be sent to West Point and Annapolis, Yong Wing petitioned the U.S. State Department to accept certain students into the American military academies. He received a brusque reply that stated "there is no room provided for Chinese students."[25] Incensed by the anti-Chinese prejudice being championed by Senator James G. Blaine, Yong Wing notified Beijing of his rebuff. At once Chinese conservatives seized upon the incident as proof of failure and urged that the mission be recalled. One official, Chen Lanbin, finally succeeded in halting the mission on the grounds that the students were pursuing courses of study that included Latin and Greek and other "unnecessary subjects."[26] Moreover, Chen complained that the students were disrespectful, lacking in patriotism, and forgetting their mother tongue. Within four years, all of the students had returned to China.

Despite the failure of the U.S. mission, the European naval contingent managed to escape the full wrath of the conservatives. The twelve "line officer" graduates of the English school went to England for various advanced training assignments. Six were ordered to report aboard British ships for sea-duty; four were sent to the Royal Naval College at Greenwich to study shipboard organization prior to their sea-duty assignments; and a fifth student went to Greenwich to study science. The twelfth member was assigned to Portsmouth's naval school.[27]

During their sea-duty tours, the students visited the Mediterranean and several went to the Indian Ocean. Others went to the United States aboard British ships, where they visited various ports. Once the sea-duty assignments were completed, the students returned to England to receive further schooling in electricity, gunnery, and torpedo operations. Additionally, they were assigned to naval shipyards for temporary study in order to observe British shipbuilding and maintenance techniques.[28]

In France the engineering and construction students followed a similar training program. Five of the fourteen, however, studied mining and metallurgy at the Ecole nationale superieure des mines. The other nine students did pursue naval construction studies, with four being sent to the Ecole de construction navale at Cherbourg, and five studied at the Toulon Navy Yard. Their course of instruction lasted two years, followed by tours of inspection at various European shipyards.[29]

In September 1880 all of the students had returned to Fuzhou, ending China's first successful attempt to train Chinese in modern naval techniques. Flushed with the success of the first overseas naval mission, progressive leaders memorialized for a second mission to Europe. Approval was quickly granted, and a second group of nine students departed China in 1882. In 1886 a third group was sent to Britain and France.[30]

All of the returning students were immediately assigned to important positions in the emerging Chinese steam navy. Of the line-officer contingent, several were given commands, while the others were ordered to key billets aboard new ships then being ordered abroad. Those from the French school were assigned to high positions at the Fuzhou Dockyard, where training of students continued at a rapid pace. Although still operating under an outmoded promotion system, the ascendency of the Fuzhou students at the expense of the old Banner and Green Standard officers permanently reversed the balance of power within the developing Chinese naval establishment.

CONFRONTATION WITH THE FRENCH

But disaster for the Fuzhou naval experiment lay ahead as France, the original patroness of the dockyard, threatened to go to war with China. For over ten years the French had been exploring northern Vietnam (Annam) to find a river route into southern China for trade. With the discovery of the Red River, the French had forced a treaty upon the Vietnamese emperor that essentially abrogated Chinese suzerainty over that region.[31] By 1884 French and Chinese armies were engaged in combat in the Yunnan border area, and in July a French fleet sailed into the Fuzhou harbor. One month later, without war being declared, the French admiral, A. A. P. Courbet, attacked the Fujian navy at anchor in the Min River. In less than thirty minutes the firing ended and twenty-two Chinese warships were at the bottom of the river. Thirty-nine Chinese naval officers and two thousand Fujianese sailors and soldiers were dead.[32]

Even more serious than the loss of the Fujian fleet was the destruction that followed when Courbet reduced the dockyard complex to ruin. The foundry, fitting shop, and pattern shop were nearly leveled, as were various workshops and storehouses. By 29 August 1884, the Fujian naval complex was a burned-out hulk—mute testimony to China's continuing naval weakness.

Chinese navy men (ca. 1884). These sailors are conducting drills at Fuzhou aboard the *Yang Wu*. Their uniforms carry the insignia of the ship's name. (From the Ltjg Moses Lindley Wood album dated 1884–85, courtesy of the Special Collections Department, Nimitz Library, U.S. Naval Academy.)

CONTINUING THREATS

The Sino-French War of 1884 has placed us a little ahead of the story of China's nineteenth-century naval reform movement. It is important to put the second half of that story in perspective.

In 1874 China once again faced serious threats to its sovereignty, one from the sea and one from the remote western interior. Japan sent a naval expedition to Taiwan to punish aborigines who, three years earlier, had slaughtered fifty-three shipwrecked Liuqiu sailors. Japan, which had re-

The *Yang Wu* before and after the Sino-French Naval Battle (July 1884). (From the Ltjg Moses Lindley Wood album dated 1884–85, courtesy of the Special Collections Department, Nimitz Library, U.S. Naval Academy.)

cently purchased several small ironclads from Europe, used the incident as a pretext for claiming suzerainty over the Liuqiu Islands. China responded by transporting ten thousand troops to Taiwan, but the sealift took six months to complete and highlighted China's naval weakness. When Japan threatened further action, the Manchu government agreed to pay an indemnity of five hundred thousand taels (approximately three hundred thousand dollars) and drop its claims to the Liuqiu Islands.[33]

Chinese humiliation over Liuqiu was exacerbated as the Muslim rebellion in the northwest, now being supported by Russia, grew progressively worse. By the early 1870s a substantial portion of modern-day Xinjiang and Gansu were under Muslim control, and Russian troops were in the rich Ili Valley. The czar had condescendingly promised Beijing that the troops would be evacuated when Chinese rule was restored.[34]

THE STRATEGY DEBATE, 1874–75

The twin crises set the stage for an intense debate in the capital as to whether a great army should be raised and sent westward or whether modern steam warships should be acquired to defend against Japan on the seacoast.

The leading protagonist in this debate was Zuo Zongtang, who was still in the northwest as commander of the anti-Muslim army. His rival in Beijing, Li Hongzhang, simultaneously held three key posts: grand secretary, governor-general of Zhili, and superintendent of Northern Ports. Li's power, like Zuo's, had been accumulated during the Taiping Rebellion, when he led a *yongying* force from his native province of Anhui against the Taipings. As the fighting subsided, Li, who did not demobilize his army, became a powerful military and political force in the rich Yangzi Valley. In 1870 the emperor brought Li north, along with about twenty-five thousand troops of Li's semi-private Anhui army. Within several years the Anhui mandarin began pressing the court to improve China's maritime posture.

Li Hongzhang made the first move in the debate when he stated the following in a memorial to the court on 12 December 1874:

> Western nations, no matter how powerful, are more than 70,000 li away, but Japan is right on our threshold, capable of spying out our weakness or readiness. She is China's most important permanent problem. Although she has been momentarily restrained to some extent, she still has artfully designed stratagems and plots and is intensely covetous of the riches of our products and people. She hopes to find pretext for further action at opportune moments before we complete our [program of] ships and guns. For this reason, things like ironclads, naval fortresses, etc., must be begun at once. But substantial funds are not available, and besides, purchasing orders take time to fill.[35]

Li's sentiments were supported by most high officials in various coastal provinces, and together they made the following five points:

1. Considering Beijing's proximity to the coast, maritime defense was more important than frontier defense in the far west.

2. The poor state of the national treasury and the possibility of defeat in Xinjiang were two factors that the court had to consider in reevaluating the Western military campaign of Zuo Zongtang.

3. Xinjiang was a wasteland of no value to China, and financial support for the region should cease.

4. With Russia and British India bordering Xinjiang, it could not be adequately defended in the event of a conflict.

5. The withdrawal from Xinjiang would not dishonor the memory of the first Manchu emperor who conquered the territory, but would rather be necessary to the future strengthening of China.

In April 1875 Zuo Zongtang's memorial arrived in Beijing. In his opening remarks he reminded the court that his duties as governor-general of Min-Zhe (Fujian and Zhejiang), where he founded the Fuzhou naval center, had left him with a keen appreciation for maritime defense; it was that experience, together with his nearly eight years in the northwest, that placed him in the best position to judge what policy should be emphasized.[36]

In the course of his rebuttal, Zuo advanced the line that when Mongolia and Xinjiang had been conquered in the past, emperors had spared no expense in efforts to retake the area, for they clearly saw that such regions were China's first line of defense. All previous dynasties, including the Manchus, had fought numerous battles in these regions to preserve the empire, and responsible officials could not simply ignore the lessons of history and cast off the frontier defense tradition. To cease military operations in the northwest would only result in loss of territories that could not be replaced. He predicted that if his campaign were allowed to run its course, China would not have anything to fear from Russia or England, since they would not be able to come to the aid of rebel forces.[37]

Like Li Hongzhang, Zuo Zongtang made five points in his argument as follows:

1. The loss of Xinjiang would weaken defenses in Mongolia—a situation that would threaten Zhili and Beijing.

2. Western nations now operating from the treaty ports were interested in trade and not territorial aggrandizement.

3. Funds for frontier defense should not be diverted to the coast.

4. Territories conquered by past emperors could not be forfeited.

5. Key cities such as Urumqi and Aksu should be recovered immediately.[38]

With the issues now drawn, other officials came forward and presented their respective arguments, and it soon became apparent that Chinese concerns lay first in the unification of the western interior. As one official put it: "The trouble of the various maritime nations is like the sickness of the limbs which is distant and light, whereas the trouble of Russia is like the sickness of the heart and stomach, which is near and serious."[39] The most telling argument, however, was one offered by Zuo Zongtang, who reminded the emperor that if China failed to control the west it would be an admission of dynastic weakness.[40]

On 23 April 1875 the emperor approved Zuo's recommendations and the Xinjiang campaign began in earnest. Over the next six years 51 million taels were spent in the successful recovery of the western frontier regions. At the same time, naval programs were cut back significantly. For example, no new contract was negotiated with France to keep the Fuzhou naval experiment going. Other naval funds were also reduced significantly in order to pay for the western military campaign.

Zuo Zongtang's recovery of Xinjiang and the ouster of Russia from Ili were the results of what in retrospect appears to have been a wise choice. However, that decision and the subsequent disaster in the Min River only strengthened the hand of some maritime supporters. Li Hongzhang, for example, continued to believe that only substantial warship purchases from the West and a greater infusion of advisors could quickly move China into the age of steam. Undaunted by Zuo Zongtang's success, Li set about convincing the emperor to find the funds to "buy" a navy.

CHAPTER 7

THE RUSH TO MODERNIZE, 1874–94

Until the Sino-French War of 1884, China had survived as a sovereign state partly because the European powers had refrained from formally occupying Chinese territory. The treaty-port system was a most satisfactory arrangement for extending economic interests within the Celestial Empire, and there was great hesitation on the part of all the commercial nations to disturb the tottering Manchu bureaucracy through the creation of political divisions.

French ambitions in southeast Asia changed the situation. England became alarmed over the threat posed to its considerable commercial investments in China (Britain controlled slightly more than 60 percent of Chinese foreign trade at that time). The uneasy Anglo-French imperial federation that had lasted for some twenty years was close to disintegration as the French carried out their explorations of the Red River Valley.

Britain had other causes for concern too. Germany was emerging as a leading industrial power, and there was much talk in Parliament about German perseverance and enterprise resulting in gains on trading fronts, including those in China. In 1880, for example, China and Germany concluded the Supplementary Convention, which granted considerable shipping facilities and rights to Berlin and conferred most-favored-nation status upon Germany.

BRITAIN'S ATTEMPT TO GAIN INFLUENCE

Since the mid-1870s, the customs inspector general, Mr. Robert Hart, had been actively pursuing a course intended to strengthen British influence in China, primarily through naval aid. Hart had observed the French conquest of Annam (hereafter referred to as Vietnam), and when the Sino-Japanese crisis appeared ready to erupt into war in 1874, he saw in the situation a new opportunity to enhance Britain's position by cultivating powerful officials such as Li Hongzhang.

Hart's idea entailed establishing the Maritime Customs as an agency responsible to the Chinese government for the "purchase of machinery, tools, arms, munitions, and war vessels necessary for the country's defense."[1] He was acutely aware of the decentralized navy system that permitted coastal provincial officials to sometimes purchase or build warships to be used exclusively within their regional domains. However, when the Japan crisis caused a sudden mobilization, several regional viceroys were compelled to look for funds to buy munitions. When they thought of using customs revenue, it gave Hart an excuse to employ the Customs Service as a central munitions acquisition agency.

Hart was idealistic. He believed that any transactions with officials such as Li Hongzhang should first be cleared with the Chinese foreign office, the Zongli Yamen. In so doing, he undoubtedly ruffled Li's feelings, for Li, who was engaged in the struggle for funds with Zuo Zongtang and others, preferred to carry out his own naval modernization program without Zongli Yamen interference. Accordingly, Li countered Hart's maneuverings by playing off some of Hart's customs subordinates against him. Li was abetted by the protocol system, which permitted only the customs inspector general to communicate with the Yamen, but allowed customs subordinates in the provinces to deal directly with their respective viceroys. Although Hart's commissioners were expected to keep him fully informed on all matters, the international makeup of his staff made this unlikely, especially when warship contracts were at stake. Thus, early on, customs became an easy prey for the old Chinese strategem of using foreigners to control foreigners.

LI'S PURCHASES

In 1874, when Li Hongzhang was engaged in the great strategy debate with Zuo Zongtang, the former wrote that "if we want to put our coastal defense in good order, there is no other way to begin than to change our [old] methods and employ [new] talents."[2] Li believed that Japan represented the main threat to China, and that if the Chinese were to catch up to the rapidly modernizing Japanese, an extensive program of foreign naval purchases would have to be undertaken immediately.

The key word in Li's statement was coastal defense, for despite his emphasis on change, his strategic views were traditional ones. In fact, just a few years before he had urged the building of a wall at Tianjin to bolster China's coastal defenses. Early in his naval reform program, Li showed great interest in acquiring small experimental coastal gunboats then under construction in England. The purchase of ships, which were well suited for defending rivers and seaports, received imperial approval in 1875. Over the next four years, eleven were ordered through Robert Hart and received by Li.[3]

Between 1875 and 1879, China received the first four of these gunboats of the *Staunch* class, which were built by Sir William Armstrong's firm in Britain. These iron ships, named by the British as the *Alpha, Beta, Gamma,* and *Delta,* were schooner rigged, shallow draught, and driven by twin screws. The ships, which ranged in size from 118 to 120 feet in length and 27 to 30 feet at the beam, could steam at 9 knots. However, the unique

Pictured here is Li Hongzhang, the father of the modern Chinese navy. It was through Li's power and influence that the Chinese created the Beiyang steam fleet in the 1880s. At the left is Lord Salisbury and Lord Curzon is on the right.

feature of the ships was the armament, considered to be a daring innovation at the time. Two of the vessels carried 26.5-ton guns, while the two later models mounted 38-ton guns—an unheard-of size considering the vessels' 400-ton displacement.

The guns were worked by hydraulic power, and the powerful recoil was absorbed by rams or pistons cushioned by water beneath a weighted valve. In England, tests with the *Gamma* were conducted in which the 38-ton gun was fired with 130-pound powder charges that delivered an 800-pound projectile. The initial muzzle velocity was 1,500 feet per second and penetrated 19.5 inches of iron in 3 thicknesses padded by 10 inches of teak. In addition to these guns, the ships also carried two 12-pounders and a Gatling machine gun.

In 1879 the superintendent of the Southern Ports, Li Zongxi, also placed an order through Li Hongzhang and Hart for four more of these ships.

Named the *Epsilon*, *Zeta*, *Eta*, and *Theta*, these follow-on vessels differed from the first four in that they were double-ended, with the stern and bow being constructed from the same pattern. The bow was fitted with a rudder, making the ship capable of steaming backward at 9 knots or forward at 10 knots.

As with the prototypes, these ships were small—125 feet long, 29 feet in beam, displacing 440 tons, and entirely dominated by the huge gun. They carried an Elswick 11-inch 35-ton muzzle loader. Although slightly smaller than the 30-ton version carried on two of the original ships, the guns possessed much more power, range, and penetrating power. Fired by 235-pound charges, the projectile weighed 536 pounds and had a range of 7,500 yards.

Interestingly, these guns represented heavier charges than those being carried on any British war vessel. In fact, in 1881 a U.S. naval expert hailed the new Chinese gunboats as having "more powerful guns than [has] any other nation on the globe; for the English *Inflexible* and the Italian *Duilio*, carrying 80-ton and 100-ton guns respectively are not ready for service; while the heaviest guns now mounted afloat by the French, Germans, and Russians burn smaller charges and have less power than the guns on board these gunboats."[4]

Soon after the gunboats arrived in Chinese waters, two other provincial mandarins placed an order with Hart for three such ships: two for the governor of Shandong and one for the governor-general of Guangdong. These vessels, known as the *Iota*, *Kappa*, and *Lambda*, were soon delivered to the provincial fleets.

The total cost of these eleven gunboats came to more than one million dollars and highlighted the buying campaign then getting under way. Indeed, the acquisition of these ships also renewed regional rivalries, as Li Hongzhang arranged for the newer *Epsilon*-series ships to be delivered at Tianjin rather than to Li Zongxi at Nanjing. Once in possession of these ships, Li Hongzhang magnanimously sent the four older ships of the *Alpha* group, which were already in need of overhaul, to Nanjing.

Li Hongzhang was also suspicious of Shen Baozhen, the Fujian naval leader, because Li's new Armstrong boats were manned by Fujian navy men, who periodically sailed them south for training. Afraid that his new ships might somehow become part of the Fujian fleet, Li subverted Shen's attempts to deal with Hart for the purchase of two new ram-type cruisers in 1879. Informing Shen that there was a shortage of funds and the Zongli Yamen would never approve such purchases, Li nevertheless contracted with Hart to buy the cruisers for his own fleet. In 1881 these ships arrived in China to become a part of Li's growing Northern, or Beiyang Fleet.

They were 210 feet long and displaced 1,350 tons. Each carried two 10-inch Armstrong breech loaders as well as smaller pieces. The ships, named the *Chaoyong* and *Yangwei*, also carried rams and spar torpedoes. Although designed for 15 knots, they steamed at 16 knots during sea trials in 1881. Their cost remains unknown.

Another reason for Li's sudden interest in acquiring the cruisers was the deterioration of relations with Russia. In 1879 a treaty had been concluded with the Russian government that was subsequently refuted by the Qing government. The Manchus claimed that the Chinese negotiator had violated instructions and the treaty could not be ratified. Instead, the emperor requested that negotiations be reopened. Russia protested, and besides massing troops in areas bordering China, the czar, in August 1880, sent a Russian fleet to the China coast threatening the Qing government with a naval blockade. Li Hongzhang realized that the Armstrong gunboats were too slow and could not operate on the high seas. In view of the Russian naval threat Li now believed that China needed offensive-type ships that could operate at further distances from the coast.

Although the Russian crisis was over by February 1881, Li and others used the emergency to make extensive weapons purchases abroad. China was fast becoming a lucrative playground for foreign munition salesmen, and many viceroys began to borrow heavily, investing in everything from rifles to torpedo boats.[5] Hart, in fact, was pushed aside by British rivals who looked to Halliday Macartney, the English secretary to the Chinese legation in London, for support. To counter this, Armstrong and Company sent out their own representative to China, a Major Bridgeford, Royal Marine Artillery, Retired, to do business through British firms such as the Jardine, Matheson Company.[6]

Meanwhile, Li had become quite friendly with Gustav Detring, a German and Hart's customs commissioner at Tianjin. Li soon began to play Detring off against Hart, promoting the German to be Hart's successor as inspector general. At the same time (1881), Li corresponded with Li Feng-bao, the Chinese minister to Germany, about purchasing two large iron-clad battleships and one steel cruiser from the Germans. Soon the Berlin-based diplomat arranged for the building of these powerful ships at the Stettin Shipyard. Nearly three years elapsed before the three ships, the *Zhenyuan*, *Dingyuan*, and *Jiyuan*, were delivered (shortly after the Sino-French War) at a cost of more than two million dollars.[7]

To the Chinese, and indeed to the rest of the world, these two battleships were formidable vessels. Constructed of steel and protected by a 14-inch armor belt, they displaced 7,400 tons and generated 6,200 horsepower capable of driving the ships at 14.5 knots. For armament, they each mounted four 12-inch Krupp breech loaders, two 5.9-inchers, eight one-pounders, and three torpedo tubes. Additionally, they carried two 19-meter torpedo boats.

The *Jiyuan* was also an effective fighting ship, being classified by Western naval experts as a modern light cruiser. Although unarmored, it displaced 2,355 tons, was 236 feet long, and could steam at 15 knots. It carried two 8.2-inch Krupp breech loaders and one 5.9-inch Krupp. Auxiliary firepower was supplied by four 6-pounders and six one-pounders. It also possessed four torpedo tubes.

For several years after the arrival of these ships, Li Hongzhang continued to use his German connections to build up the Beiyang Fleet, and in 1887 he took delivery of two more unarmored cruisers, the *Jingyuan* and

The Chinese battleship *Zhenyuan*. This formidable warship was later captured by Japan in 1895. (Courtesy of U.S. Naval Historical Center, Washington, DC.)

Laiyuan. These ships, costing more than $500,000 each, displaced 2,300 tons and could steam at 18 knots. Each also carried two smaller 8-inch Krupps and two 5.9-inch Krupps as major armament.

In addition to these major units, Li bought a number of torpedo boats from the Germans during this period. Research shows that at least twelve such boats were acquired by Li between 1882 and 1895. Typical of these craft was the *Fulong*, which was 144 feet long and capable of reaching speeds up to 25 knots.[8]

The last major units purchased by Li were two cruisers built in England and delivered to China in 1887. These two, the *Zhiyuan* and *Jingyuan* (not to be confused with the German-built cruiser of the same name), cost more than one million dollars.[9] They differed from the German cruisers in that each carried 9.5-inch belt armor and were 270 feet long, displacing 2,850 tons. The main batteries consisted of three 8-inch Krupps and two 6-inch Armstrong breech loaders.[10]

In 1889 Li completed his Beiyang Fleet with the purchase of a Fuzhou-built cruiser, the *Pingyuan*. The ship, which was capable of only 10.5 knots, mounted one 10-inch and two 5-inch Krupp guns.[11]

LI'S MERCHANT FLEET

In addition to his naval purchases, Li Hongzhang pursued merchant-fleet development with equal zeal. As the superintendent of Northern Ports, one of his major responsibilities included managing the transport of tribute rice from the south to Beijing, but the system still relied on the damaged and decaying Grand Canal and a fleet of worn-out coastal junks. Thus, in 1872 Li established the China Merchants' Steam Navigation Company, which bought a fleet of steamers from the American firm of Russell and Company. By the early 1880s Li's coastal steam fleet was competing reasonably well with other Western merchant-shipping firms and showing a reasonable profit.[12]

Despite its initially good performance, the company soon encountered serious problems in the way it managed its operations. The biggest defect lay in Li's reliance upon the traditional *guandu shangban* system ("government supervision and merchant operation"). It is to be recalled that this system, which had been in use for centuries in the grain and salt monopolies, employed government officials as overseers and merchants as managers. The major failing of the *guandu shangban* system was its conservatism, for it severely restrained entrepreneurial reinvestment. Instead, profits went into the pockets of the officials and merchants, and no attempt was made to improve the firm's ships and equipment. Corruption and nepotism became widespread, resulting in an imperial investigation.[13] The fleet soon deteriorated, allowing Western ships to reassume the leading position in China's domestic shipping trade.

BEIYANG BASE AND ARSENAL DEVELOPMENTS

When Li Hongzhang began his grand scheme to purchase a navy, he also undertook plans to create bases and arsenals to support his growing fleet. Early on, Li's larger warships had to undergo semiannual upkeep at Shanghai, while the two larger battleships purchased from Germany could be accommodated only at Hong Kong or Yokohama. One of Li's first moves included seeking advice from German coastal defense experts through Li Fengbao in Berlin. In 1884 a German army officer, Lieutenant Colonel Rheinhold Wagner, supplied the Chinese with a detailed plan that included recommendations on harbors, defensive works, and railways required by the Beiyang Fleet.[14]

Wagner recommended against development of Lushun (Port Arthur), which Li had begun in 1881, on the grounds that it was too shallow and its entrance too narrow to allow for easy maneuvering of ships in times of trouble. Wagner also ruled out Weihai in Shandong Province as a major port for the Beiyang Fleet. Citing its exposure to the weather and shallow waters, he said that defense of the place would require extensive and costly fortifications around the whole bay.

In the end Wagner proposed that the Chinese develop Kiaochau Bay, or as it is now commonly called, Qingdao (Tsingtao). He noted that the entrance was quite wide (nearly 1000 yards), the inner harbors were deep and spacious, and ships could anchor completely out of sight of an enemy at sea. Wagner provided a detailed plan for fortifying Qingdao and outlined the commercial advantages that the harbor offered. Significantly, Wagner's proposals would later be adopted by Germany when that harbor was "leased" by the Germans after the Sino-Japanese War in 1894.

Despite Wagner's careful surveys of the northern coastal area, Li was preoccupied at the time with the Russian threat of a naval blockade and went ahead with plans to build up Lushun. It is clear that Li's strategic views remained traditional, since he preferred to keep his fleet near the approaches of the Gulf of Bohai (Zhili). He entirely overlooked the advantages of having the main body of his fleet stationed farther south at Qingdao, where it could render quicker support for the north, the south, and the Yangzi River.

In 1892, when Li finally did recommend to the court that Qingdao be adopted as a naval base, it was too late. Two years after construction began, plans were abruptly stopped by the war with Japan.

Another factor influencing Li's decision to develop Lushun was, of course, his concern with maintaining control over the Beiyang Fleet. Forced as he was to rely on the Fujian officer corps, Li still feared that he would lose control over the fleet if its main units were given a home port too far south. Qingdao was at the extreme end of Li's northern defense area, and although located in Shandong Province, its proximity to the south would have made it susceptible to southern influence.

Even with the help of a German army engineer, Constantin von Hannecken, whom Li designated as chief supervisor, the effort to modernize Lushun took more than ten years to complete and cost several million dollars. The physical plant ashore was valued at 1,393,500 taels, and when completed in 1894, it housed a dockyard, machine shops, warehouses, a railroad, and an electric lighting system. There was also a torpedo testing station whose wharf accommodated Li's small torpedo-boat flotilla. The machine shops, which possessed modern equipment, listed a boiler ship, pump shop, brassworks, an iron foundry, and a forge.[15]

Li also improved the dockyard at Tanggu (Taku), near Tianjin, and had a 340-foot dry dock constructed. By 1888 this small yard was capable of building small tugs and armored gunboats; however, the Tanggu Dockyard remained a support facility and concentrated on building service craft. In addition to the Tanggu facilities, Li created an arsenal at Tianjin and a machine shop at Weihai. At Lushun he also established an ordnance office and a ship supply depot.[16]

BEIYANG NAVAL SCHOOL DEVELOPMENT

Like the Fuzhou schools, Li's Tianjin Naval Academy was divided into the navigation and engineering departments. Yan Zongguang (Yan Fu), a Fuzhou graduate and emerging intellectual, directed the navigation department, while Commander Sa Zhenping, a Fujianese and Greenwich graduate, was the chief instructor. Importantly, several foreign instructors were added to Li's Tianjin staff. Included in the curriculum were courses in Chinese literature, English, geography, mathematics, navigation, astronomy, engineering dynamics, communications, and practical drill.[17]

The selection of Tianjin students was carefully done, since all had to be healthy, between fourteen and seventeen years old, and capable of reading the classics. Most of the students were selected from Tianjin gentry families. Advertisements, in the form of pamphlets, were circulated around the city describing the naval service as one where substantial salaries and promotions could be earned. Between 1882 and 1894, a total of 136 students were graduated from the school. Among the graduates was Li Yuanhong, who would later play a key role in the 1911 revolution and become president of the Chinese Republic.

In 1886 nine Tianjin students went abroad with twenty-four Fuzhou students to study in France and England. They participated in cruises aboard British training ships and studied a variety of subjects, including hydrography, naval artillery, ship command, and navigation. At least one

Tianjin student, Chen Shoupeng, pursued courses in naval law, specializing in piracy control.[18]

During this period, one other major naval academy was established in the north—the Weihai Naval Academy. Set up in 1889 only to be disestablished after Weihai was ceded to Japan following the 1894–95 war, the school did graduate forty-six students in 1894. Admiral Ding Ruchang, Li's naval commander in chief, was the superintendent, and the school specialized in gunnery and mine training. Interestingly, most of the thirty-six students were recruited from Guangdong Province in 1890 when the Beiyang Fleet made a training cruise to southern ports.

An adjunct School of Application was also established at Fort Taku near Tianjin in 1881.[19] It was headed by a U.S. Marine Corps captain, D. Pratt Mannix, who served on detached temporary duty with the approval of the U.S. secretary of the navy. Modeled after the U.S. Artillery School at Fort Monroe, Virginia, the Taku School of Application was dedicated to teaching the latest theories on coastal defense. Mannix's thirty-month course of instruction included the following subjects:

1. Submarine mining, including mines and torpedoes.

2. Military engineering. This course covered trigonometry, surveying, fortifications, and reconnaissance.

3. Military art and science, "the art and science of warfare, strategy, grand tactics, and military history."

4. International law and the laws of war.

5. Artillery science and practice.

6. Study of military and naval forces of foreign countries.[20]

Captain Mannix expected his students (two hundred midshipmen in the first class) to answer some rather difficult examination questions. For example, in his final test in submarine mining, the student was expected to prepare essays ranging from the making of nitroglycerine, dynamite, gun cotton and fuses, to the use of galvanometers, heliographs, and various types of torpedoes.

THE EMPLOYMENT OF FOREIGN ADVISORS

Li Hongzhang realized that in addition to his massive naval purchase program, his Beiyang Fleet would require the assistance of foreign advisors. Accordingly, in the early 1880s he began to recruit Western naval experts to train his navy. These men were to be answerable to Chinese authority and given Chinese rank. Li was encouraged in this recruitment effort by Robert Hart, who pressed him to select an Englishman as his senior foreign naval advisor. In 1883 William M. Lang, Captain, RN, was selected by Li Hongzhang to be a naval instructor. Three years later, Lang was made an admiral in the Chinese navy, an act accomplished by imperial decree. Li also hired an assortment of other foreigners to help with his navy building. An ex-German cavalry officer served as Li's aide-de-camp; an American graduate of the U.S. Naval Academy was chief navigation instructor at Tianjin; a British customs official became a naval advisor; and a Scotsman noted for his heavy drinking and ability with tugboats was made a vice admiral. There were a number of others who served in lesser capacities, particularly as engineers and gunners.

One of the first foreigners to note the potential problems in Li's international naval "cabal" was an American naval officer, Commodore Robert W. Shufeldt. Shufeldt had been invited to Tianjin in 1880 by Li when the American was attempting to negotiate a treaty with Korea. Impressed with Shufeldt's abilities, Li tried to negotiate for the officer's services but failed. Shufeldt saw much trouble in such an appointment and he sent a letter to his friend, Senator Aaron A. Sargent of California, in which he criticized Li's employment of foreigners. His indictment reads, in part, as follows:

> To increase the inherent defects of this organization [the Beiyang Fleet] and, under the semblance of strength, in reality to add to its weakness, are the intrigue and jealousies of foreign officers both in and about the service. The Inspector-General of the Customs [Hart], an Englishman, in addition to his great power in that office, would also like to administer the navy. The ships [the *Staunch*-class gunboats] were built in England under his contracts. Since their arrival in China the Commissioner of Customs at Tianjin [Detring]—a German—has managed to secure their control. Three Englishmen—"quasi" officers of the Royal Navy, but now belonging to the Imperial Customs services afloat—are on board the ships as "advisers" to the Chinese admiral and captains. Two ex-officers of the French Navy employed at high salaries for some purpose never yet specified, make up three nationalities, each jealous of the other, and all despising the Chinese, while aspiring to control its naval service. With such discordant parts it will easily be seen how difficult it is to create a harmonious whole. The Viceroy [Li], astute in all things but in the wisdom of the outside world, is more or less a vicitm to the flatteries or the arts of these ambitious men, who persuade him that he has a navy.[21]

Shufeldt's observations of the Europeans were uncannily accurate, but he failed to notice how equally ambitious the Chinese could be. Lang, in fact, soon encountered strong opposition from the Chinese naval officer corps. As inspector of the Beiyang Fleet from 1886 to 1890, he had quickly taken charge of training, and his early successes led one British observer to comment that "Chinese ships were well navigated; . . . kept station fairly when in company; . . . fired well at a mark, both with guns and torpedoes; . . . [and] exchanged semaphores with each other in English."[22] Despite his successes, Lang stirred up the resentment of many Fujian officers, who were unhappy with his constant demands for discipline. Lang wrote that he was "irked by the obstacles thrown in his path by ignorant and envious men."[23]

The incident that finally led to Lang's resignation occurred in August 1890. At that time, the Beiyang Fleet was conducting one of its annual training cruises in the south. While steaming in the vicinity of Hong Kong, the Chinese admiral departed his flagship to visit that city. Lang immediately had his own pennant hoisted, but a Fujianese captain ordered Lang's pennant hauled down and his own flown. Lang grew angry and confronted the captain, who claimed that he was second in command and Lang's admiral rank was without authority. Back in Tianjin, Lang reported the incident to Li Hongzhang, but Li, after some deliberation, sided with his captain. Lang resigned soon thereafter.[24]

THE NAVY OFFICE

In May 1885, three months before his death, Zuo Zongtang submitted a memorial in which he recommended sweeping changes to the antiquated naval command system. One of his proposals was that China no longer delay establishing a central office to handle naval affairs. Zuo's decree read in part as follows:

> Formerly, on account of the great importance of coastal defense, the high ministers of the southern and northern ports were ordered to deliberate the case [as proposed by Zuo] and report by memorial. Now, according to their memorials concerning an over-all plan for the whole situation, it is requested that a well-trained navy for the northern ports be organized immediately and be used as an example. Henceforward, naval expansion will be undertaken every year. Their plan seems to be proper and practical. Let Prince Chun be the minister of the Navy Yamen to control and command all naval forces; let the Grand Secretary, Prince Qing and the Zhili governor-general, Li Hongzhang, be the associate ministers; and let the Lieutenant General of the Chinese Red Banner, Shanqing, and the Junior Vice-Minister of the Ministry of War, Zeng, be assistant ministers.[25]

Shortly thereafter, the court, in fact, issued an edict calling for the establishment of the Shuishi Yamen, or Navy Office.

Prince Chun, a Manchu, was appointed navy minister. As father of the Guangxu emperor, who would reach maturity in 1886, Prince Chun's appointment was in reality a political decision. The choice boded ill for the newly established Navy Office, for the prince feared the empress dowager, and had acted as her unwitting tool in court intrigues for a number of years.

During the first several months after it was formed, the Navy Office did undertake certain reform measures. One of its first acts was to prevent provincial leaders from making indiscriminate purchases abroad. The Navy Office also attempted to follow up on one of Zuo Zongtang's recommendations that called for holding periodic intrafleet maneuvers. In 1886 the Southern, or Nanyang, Fleet sailed north to take part in joint fleet exercises.

Despite the initial show of unity, there was considerable jealousy among southern leaders, who objected to Li Hongzhang's growing influence with the Navy Office. One southern leader complained that Li's modern Beiyang Fleet was receiving too much attention, and that the frequent shift of Nanyang superintendents prevented the southern fleets from modernizing with the same degree of continuity that Li enjoyed in the north.

THE BEIYANG NAVAL REGULATIONS OF 1888

The criticism of Li's growing authority over the navy was not unfounded, for during the three years following the appointment of Prince Chun, Li Hongzhang carefully cultivated the confidence of the prince and took him on frequent tours of inspection at various Beiyang facilities. Shortly after one such trip, the prince became so enthused that he wrote a series of poems about coastal defense. His admiration for Li became intense, and he dutifully passed on to the throne Li's proposed regulations in September 1888.[26]

ORGANIZATION

Li's Beiyang regulations basically addressed three things: organization, training, and rewards and punishments. The matter of organization was especially important, for it dealt with the delicate matter of command and authority. Li, as noted previously, was forced to rely upon a large number of the more senior Fuzhou officers to operate his modern warships. Although he was wary of their being southerners, he could do little except insure that his choice for admiral was a "Li man." For this important position he chose Ding Ruchang, a native of Li's own province, Anhui, and a former cavalry officer in Li's Huai Army.[27]

To foreign observers and Chinese alike, Admiral Ding was acknowledged as a brave man, but in the matter of running a modern steam fleet he was a poor choice. His only real experience at sea came in 1880, when he was sent to England to bring back two Armstrong cruisers, the *Yangwei* and *Chaoyong*. On the return trip he shoaled his ship, the *Yangwei*, and she ran out of coal and drifted helplessly in the Mediterranean for several days.

An English observer reported Ding's own estimate of his abilities in the following anecdote about the admiral and one of his foreign advisors. It belies the idea that senior Chinese officers, at least, were afraid to question the proficiency of foreigners.

> A foreign officer posed on somewhat meagre grounds as an expert in torpedo work, and was detailed to inspect torpedo boats. Fiddling about with a bow tube, when the boat was underway, he accidentally released the torpedo, which, sliding half-way out, was bent and ruined by the pressure of water. Ding had the officer brought before him and said: "The loss of a torpedo does not matter much, for unfortunately I see no chance of using them; but what I do not like about this affair is your pretense to be an expert. Here am I Admiral of the fleet. Do I pretend? Do I assume to know anything about a ship or navigation? You know I do not; so take an example from me and pretend no more."[28]

Immediately below Ding in the chain of command were the captains Lin Taizeng and Liu Buchan, both of whom had gone to England with the first group of Fuzhou students. Liu and Lin commanded the *Dingyuan* and *Zhenyuan*, respectively, and were given complete authority over the running of their ships. Their home port was Lushun. Ding's staff also included departments of personnel, engineering, fleet weapons, and a commissariat.

Li's regulations also contained a detailed breakdown of the officer corps, which was divided into three distinct branches: "combat officers," "engineers," and "petty officers." The combat officers were further divided into three groups: an "outer-seas" or "blue-water" group, assigned to the major deep-draught combatants; an "outer-seas ordinary-vessel" group, which served in harbor defense, training, or logistics capacities; and an "inner-waters" group, which served on the rivers or ashore. All recommendations for promotion to lieutenant and above had to be approved by Li prior to the submission of names to Beijing.[29]

TRAINING

Joint training between the fleets received considerable emphasis in Li's regulations. Every winter the Beiyang Fleet was to sail south and carry out extensive exercises with the Nanyang ships. Each spring the Nanyang fleets were expected to come north and perform a similar training mission. Significantly, while Beiyang ships were in southern waters, they remained under Ding's direct command, but when Nanyang ships came north, they were generally answerable to Li Hongzhang. In order to offset Li's influence, the Nanyang superintendent promulgated a similar set of regulations in 1891 and took to sending his own admiral north with the fleet during annual fleet reviews.

REWARDS AND PUNISHMENTS

In Li's regulations on rewards and punishments, examinations were stressed and, as was happening in European navies, captains were expected to write articles on navy topics for publication. Based partly upon the results of their articles, rewards and punishments were administered to these officers. Li also set forth an elaborate scheme for rewarding his shore-establishment personnel. Dockyard workers and translators, for example, could receive awards for making beneficial contributions like translating Western technical manuals.

Li also implemented a new pay system, which was divided into two parts: 40 percent for personal pay and 60 percent for command or sea pay. For example, an officer temporarily assigned to shore duty drew personal pay but did not receive sea pay. An admiral's pay was affixed at 8,400 taels (5,460 dollars) per annum—3,360 taels for personal pay and 5,040 taels for command pay. The lowest officer rank drew 96 taels for personal pay and 144 taels for command pay. In 1888 Li's annual pay for the Beiyang Fleet totaled 669,100 taels (about 435,000 dollars).

THE SEEDS OF FAILURE

Despite the establishment of the Navy Office, its role in unifying China's fleets remained severely limited. For one thing, its annual 4-million-dollar budget soon made it an attractive target for corrupt officials. Compounding problems, Prince Chun died in 1892 and the Navy Office passed into the hands of more inexperienced officials. Although the office was not officially disbanded until after the war with Japan, it was completely dominated by the Imperial Household at the time of Prince Chun's death.

Three years before the Sino-Japanese War of 1894–95, Li Hongzhang ordered Admiral Ding to sail the Beiyang Fleet to Japan and "show the flag." While in Yokohama, individual Japanese were allowed to come aboard China's battleships and cruisers, whose size and evident firepower awed most everyone. One visiting Imperial Japanese Navy captain, however, was not impressed. The officer, Captain Togo Heihachiro, noted that the Chinese crews were slow in carrying out orders, that both guns and other topside equipment needed maintenance, and that laundry hung from mast lines, rails, and stays.[30]

Togo's observations were indicative of the general malaise that infected China's emergent navy. In reality, Li Hongzhang's fleet had no fighting spirit and genuine uncertainty existed among the officer corps as to how to employ modern naval weapons. Failure was in the air and it could be traced to several factors, some of which have as much relevance today as they did in the summer of 1891.

CLIQUES AND EMBEZZLED MONEY

During Li Hongzhang's purchase campaign, the matter of corruption among high officials repeatedly stifled the attempt to create a modern navy. At the apex of corruption lurked the empress dowager, whose unscrupulous court henchmen diverted an estimated 12 million dollars from the navy from 1889 to 1894 for the purpose of refurbishing the Summer Palace in honor of the empress's sixtieth birthday.[31] The only concessions

The empress dowager, Cixi (Tz'u-hsi), is shown here being carried by her eunuch bodyguards. She used more than $12 million of Chinese navy funds to refurbish the Summer Palace grounds in the late nineteenth century. (Courtesy of the U.S. Navy.)

to the navy were steam launches that hauled court ladies about the palace lake, and the infamous Marble Boat, still anchored at the bottom of that lake as rigid testimony to the incredible excesses of the late Manchu period.

Aside from the corruption at the highest levels of government, another more insidious influence was at work—the emergence of a Fujian naval clique. As noted earlier, when Zuo Zongtang received approval to set up the Fuzhou naval center, he turned to the local Fujian gentry for help. A committee of one hundred Fujianese leaders was established to administer the center and assist in gaining operating funds. In effect, the Fujian naval experiment was run like the traditional guilds and power rested with the gentry leadership. Very soon the naval center was awash in plots and schemes described by one observer as "intrigues having for their object the complete control of the fleet, the power of keeping out and admitting whom they chose without reference to qualifications, and the general determination to subordinate the naval service to their personal and family advantage."[32] For example, no Cantonese were included in the first overseas training contingent.

An example of how early the Fujian gentry set about controlling the navy was reported by an English naval officer who visited the school in the early 1870s. He noticed that Guangdong and Fujian students lived apart and had separate cooks. He also observed that although the students who showed the most promise were Cantonese, the Fujian school officials

The $12 million marble boat. Money spent for this birthday present to the empress dowager was taken from the Chinese navy's budget. (Courtesy of the U.S. Naval Institute Reference Library, Annapolis.)

treated them with contempt.[33] For example, no Cantonese were included in the first overseas training contingent.

Although suspicious of their ambitions, Li Hongzhang had no other source of experienced naval officers from which to draw. As an indicator of the proliferation of Fujian officers in his Beiyang Fleet, Li's officer corps was 60 percent Fujianese (123 out of 206 officers). At the senior officer level, the percentage was even more significant: 15 of 18 captains and commanders were from Fujian. Additionally, of the 15 major warships in Li's Beiyang Fleet, 13 were commanded by Fujianese.[34]

Fujian dominance soon gave way to the corrupt notion that the most successful captain was the man who could acquire the most money. Funds allocated for the repair and upkeep of vessels were embezzled. Several senior Fujianese naval officers were even suspected of substituting coal dust for black powder in naval ammunition cartridges and selling the powder for profit.[35]

To a great degree, the Fujian naval officers were aided in their quest for personal prestige and power by the very progressive leaders who sought to build a strong navy. Li Hongzhang, for example, attempted to entice officer candidates by putting a naval career on an equal footing with the respected civil service. Ashore, officers were encouraged to wear dress uniform of their civil service peers, and they were not discouraged from leaving the navy to compete for highly prized civil positions. This ingrained affinity for scholar-bureaucrat status often displayed itself among the students in the various Chinese naval academies. Foreign instructors noted that "it was a far harder task to get their pupils to take part in gymnastic or calisthenic exercises than to attain proficiency in scientific knowledge."[36]

LACK OF CONSENSUS AND COHERENT PLANNING

Throughout the naval reform movement, there was a constant clash between those who advocated self-strengthening programs and those who wanted faster results through foreign purchases. As late as 1885, Zuo Zongtang was still urging the court to undertake a massive naval construction program.[37] This proposal was submitted in the face of Li Hongzhang's extensive foreign purchases and ignored the reality of China's technical weaknesses.

No better example of the confusion over authority and decision making can be offered than that exhibited by the Chinese regarding the French in 1884. Ostensibly, the person in charge of the Fujian fleet was the Nanyang superintendent. The Chinese flagships had five command layers: the Min-Zhe governor-general; the Fuzhou Manchu general; the Fujian governor; the governor's deputy for Fujian coastal defense; and the Fuzhou Dockyard superintendent. None of these officials agreed on how to deal with the French fleet, and as a result, the Chinese admiral afloat had no orders and took no evasive action.

DEPENDENCE ON FOREIGN ADVISORS

In order to maintain authority over the advisors that Li Hongzhang so energetically recruited, the Chinese often had to play off one against the other. As a result, there was always some suspicion among the foreign advisory corps that one nationality was being favored at the other's expense. This gave way to constant infighting and jealousy as the foreigners vied for power within the respective institutions to which they were assigned. In the navy the English enjoyed the preeminent position, particularly among the Fujian line-officer corps, many of whom had trained at Greenwich.

The proliferation of foreign advisors on major warships was particularly debilitating to the gunnery and engineering departments. Very often the foreigner performed duties without consulting his Chinese officer counterpart, and he neglected to instruct enlisted men properly in routine tasks such as how to light off a boiler or maintain a gun.

Another result of the dependence on foreign advisors was the Chinese navy's use of English as its communications medium. No effort was made to develop a flag signal or wireless radio system that used Chinese.

LACK OF INTEGRATED TECHNOLOGY

From 1870—when Chinese engineers first began training on simple steam engines—to 1894, foreign naval engineering plants and weapon systems underwent dramatic changes. As a result, Li Hongzhang's indiscriminate purchases forced the Chinese navy to try and keep up with a wide variety of foreign technologies.

For example, Li's first purchases of the twin-screw English *Staunch*-class gunboats were carried out on poor advice, for even at that time, the French had discovered that twin screws in their coastal defense ships were disadvantageous. Very soon the Chinese also found that these vessels were unsuitable for operations in anything but the calmest of seas.

An important failing of Li Hongzhang's Beiyang Fleet was the lack of standardization among various vessels. There was great disparity in speeds as well as turning radii, and yet no one seemed to be aware of these discrepancies.[38] Another apparent failing was that after ten years of practice, the Chinese did not know that firing the 12-inchers of the battleships dead ahead would destroy the flying bridge and all those located on it.

Chinese navy engine rooms and ships contained an assortment of fairly complicated machinery. There were English Thornycraft small-tube boilers and German Schulz-Thornycraft boilers. Some ships had German Krupp breech loaders, others had French Vavasseur guns, while still others had Armstrong, Nordenfeldt, and Hotchkiss guns.

Obviously, the Chinese were unable to train sailors to maintain such a wide range of foreign vessels, technical engines, and guns. One solution to this was to keep officers and men assigned to their ships for most of their careers. In this way the crew was able to be familiar with and efficiently operate machinery, guns, and engine plants. However, such a practice prevented the Chinese sailor from becoming an all-round professional technician.

ADDITIONAL PROBLEMS

Despite the potential of the Beiyang Fleet, on the eve of the war with Japan there remained strong advocates of the traditional *haifang* fortification strategy. The old riverine troops remained active in many areas and prepared harbor-blocking devices such as sunken junks and fire rafts. Liu Kunyi, the viceroy in central China, effectively sealed off Shanghai by filling the Wusong Channel with rocks.

Meanwhile, although many graduates of Western naval schools had ascended to senior positions aboard ship, most did not display a keen knowledge of naval tactics. Neither did they take much interest in seeing that the ship's gunnery personnel was properly trained and had on supply sufficient ammunition. The Chinese seemed to justify the criticism of one naval strategist who wrote, "In skillful hands the torpedo sometimes misses; managed by the Chinese, it is absolutely inoffensive."[39]

In addition to these problems, the Chinese logistics support system was sadly deficient. There were not enough shells for the big guns, and many of those available were faulty.

Finally, because the Navy Office failed to evolve as a strong central agency, no mechanism existed to bring the various fleets together as a single fighting force. On the eve of the war with Japan, China's navy remained decentralized and controlled by rival provincial officials. When the Chinese and Japanese navies clashed in September 1894, only one Chinese fleet, the Beiyang, was used to defend the coast.

CHAPTER 8

DISASTER AT YALU: THE SINO-JAPANESE WAR, 1894–95

The Sino-Japanese War (1894–95) was the stage for a confrontation between two contrasting military ideologies. On the one hand, China pursued a philosophy expressed in the slogan *zhongxue weiti, xixue weiyong* ("Chinese learning for the fundamentals, Western learning for practical application").[1] China's reforms were cosmetic ones, intended to select certain features of Western material civilization and at the same time to preserve the fundamentals of the Chinese cultural and political system.

On the other hand, Japan modernized with the eagerness born of a nascent nationalism. Young, aggressive samurai leaders encouraged the development of military strength. These men, ruling as oligarchs in the name of the Japanese emperor, were willing to do almost anything to make Japan strong. They supported rapid industrialization as a means of gaining equality with the Western powers and forcing them to abrogate unfair treaties. While young Chinese naval cadets went abroad for maximum periods of two to three years, some of their Japanese counterparts were spending up to seven years in Britain learning naval techniques. As Mr. Frederick Thomas Jane, father of the naval encyclopedia, *Jane's Fighting Ships*, observed at the time, "Japan's energies were concentrated on training personnel, China's on acquiring materiel."[2]

THE JAPANESE THREAT

China's weakness was demonstrated by the continuing Western encroachment along its borders. By 1890 many Chinese dependencies had passed to Western control, and the final curtain was about to drop on China's Confucian world order. In 1881 Russia had taken the western portion of Ili; Vietnam fell under France's control in 1885; the British assumed complete control of Burma in 1886; and Sikkim became a British protectorate in 1890.

Korea, however, remained stubborn in the face of imperialist pressures. Throughout the late nineteenth century, as the West and Japan tried to secure a better foothold there, the rulers of the so-called Hermit Kingdom persisted in proclaiming their allegiance to China. As a result, the Chinese continued to maintain a position of strength in Korea, and Li Hongzhang openly proclaimed, "I am King of Korea whenever I think the interests of China require me to assert that prerogative."[3]

But Li's "kingship" could not immunize Korea from the outside world. In 1875, when one of its naval survey vessels was fired upon by Koreans, the Japanese used the incident as a pretext for forcing negotiations with Korea that resulted in the conclusion of a treaty a year later. This was followed by a series of treaties between Korea and the United States, Great Britain, Germany, Italy, Russia, and France.

Six years later (1882) warring political factions in Korea caused China and Japan to send troops to restore order. The Chinese were able to secure a better advantage, which irritated Japan. During the Tianjin Convention, which was concluded in 1885, China and Japan agreed to withdraw their troops and notify each other in the event that military intervention was required in the future. An uneasy peace ensued until 1894, when rebellion again broke out in Korea's southern provinces. China notified Japan that it was sending troops to Korea, but in the letter of notification it referred to Korea as a tributary state. This upset the Japanese, who said they never recognized Korea as a Chinese tributary, and they too sent troops.

By the time both armies arrived in Korea, the rebellion had been suppressed. Japan then pressed China to cooperate in carrying out reforms in Korea. China demurred, saying that reform was a problem for the Koreans, upon which Japan attempted to force the Korean government to denounce its tributary status. When Korea refused, the Japanese army seized the Korean king and held the government hostage. A new pro-Japanese government was convened, which quickly directed the Chinese to leave Korea. This led to military confrontation, and on 11 August 1894, both sides issued a declaration of war. The Chinese emperor's declaration is worth repeating because it clearly shows China's habit of clinging to the anachronistic Confucian system. It also highlights China's disinclination to fight the Japanese navy at any distance from the coast.

> Korea has been our tributary for the past two hundred odd years. She has given us tribute all this time, which is a matter known to the world. For the past dozen years or so Korea has been troubled by repeated insurrections, and we, in sympathy with our small tributary, have as repeatedly sent succour to her aid, eventually placing a Resident in her captial to protect Korea's interests. . . .
>
> Judge of our surprise then when, half-way to Korea, a number of the Woren [Japanese] ships suddenly appeared, and taking advantage of our unpreparedness, opened fire upon our transports at a spot on the seacoast near Yashan, and damaged them, thus causing us to suffer from their treacherous conduct, which could not be foretold by us. As Japan has violated the treaties and not observed international laws, and is now running rampant with her false and treacherous actions, commencing hostilities herself, and laying herself open to condemnation by the various Powers at large, we therefore desire to make it known to the world that we have always followed the paths of philanthropy

and perfect justice throughout the whole complications, while the Woren, on the other hand, have broken all the laws of nations and treaties which it passes our patience to bear with. Hence we commanded Li Hongzhang to give strict orders to our various armies to hasten with all speed to root the Woren out of their lairs. He is to send successive armies of valiant men to Korea in order to save the Koreans from the dust of bondage. We also command the Manchu generals, viceroys, and governors of the maritime provinces, as well as the commanders-in-chief of the various armies to prepare for war and to make every effort to fire on the Woren ships if they come into our ports, and utterly destroy them. We exhort our generals to refrain from the least laxity in obeying our commands in order to avoid severe punishment at our hands. Let all know this edict as if addressed to themselves individually.

Respect this![4]

NAVAL PREPARATIONS

In the several months prior to the declaration of hostilities, Li Hongzhang approved the assignment of several foreigners to various ships of the Beiyang Fleet to assist the Chinese in combat preparations. The senior foreigner was Major Constantin Von Hannecken, the Prussian cavalry officer who had been hired years before to train Li's army and to supervise the construction of Lushun (Port Arthur). William Tyler, an Englishman and Maritime Customs inspector who was aboard the battleship *Dingyuan*, acted as Von Hannecken's personal secretary and assisted in gunnery and general deck operations. Also assigned to the two battleships were several German and British engineers and gunnery instructors. The lone American, Philo N. McGiffin, was aboard the *Zhenyuan* as that cruiser's advisor to the executive officer. McGiffin had a reasonably strong naval background. He was a graduate of the U.S. Naval Academy and had completed the required two-year cruise following his Annapolis training. However, due to a congressional reduction in funds, only twelve midshipmen out of his class of thirty-six had been permitted to remain on active duty. McGiffin had gone to China and been hired by Li in 1884.

As war fast approached, Admiral Ding Ruchang held several meetings with his senior officers and foreign advisors. During these meetings it became clear that, due to wide variance in individual ship capabilities, some modification in tactics was in order.

The evolving doctrine of the time was to have ships fight in line-ahead formation with the flagship in the van. Thus formed, each ship could use all of its batteries broadside to the enemy. One method for achieving the formation was to get under way in a line-abreast order, and then, at the signal, to turn all ships to port or starboard in the line-ahead formation. Theoretically, opposing fleets using these tactics ended up in parallel columns, steaming in the same direction and firing salvos until an advantage was achieved. The best way to gain advantage was to "cross the enemy's T"; that is, one column, by superior speed or maneuvering, crossed perpendicular to the head of the other column. In this instance, the latter's bow guns of the forward-most vessel were the only that could be brought to bear, while the crossing column could use most of its guns.

Admiral Ding and his officers were aware of these tactics, but Von Hannecken found the Chinese ill prepared to execute such maneuvers. In a report to Li Hongzhang, he noted the following:

> On first going on board I endeavored to become acquainted with the conditions under which the squadron was to be maneuvered, and I remarked among other defects that the new code of secret signals was not satisfactory and that it did not respond to all the numerous exigencies of command for a fleet of twelve ships. I saw also that the ships had very different speeds and turning circles, and that in consequence it was difficult for them to execute correctly changes of formation and to keep their places exactly during evolutions. This inconvenience was aggravated by the difficulty of the signals, or the lack of attention that had been paid to understanding them; but as it was necessary always to be ready to go to sea, I resolved not to change them, fearing to embarrass yet more the crews who might not have time to familiarize themselves with my new code.
>
> These reasons decided me not to regard the twelve ships of the squadron as forming a single group, but to consider them as single ships, able to unite in ordinary times under the command of an admiral, but before the enemy during battle to act individually at their own risk and peril.[5]

Probably as a result of Von Hannecken's findings, Admiral Ding agreed that in the event of a sea fight the tactics would be as follows:

1. In action, sister ships, or each pair of ships belonging to a subdivision or section, would remain together if possible and mutually support each other in attack and defense.

2. Because the forward guns were the more potent ones, the fundamental tactics would be to keep bows on to an enemy.

3. All ships were to follow as closely as possible the motions of the admiral.[6]

In contrast, throughout the first eight months of 1894 the Japanese fleet under Admiral Yuko Ito had been exercising daily at sea. Besides emphasizing gunnery practice, Ito had equipped small steam launches with protective matting and divided them into two squadrons. His senior officers were placed in command of the mock vessels and they were drilled continuously in tactics, signaling, and fighting. Afterwards the battles were critiqued and battle discipline was discussed. For example, Ito discovered that his captains were inclined to use ramming tactics. He pointed out to them that none of Japan's warships were ironclads, and were therefore unsuited for such tactics.[7]

More importantly, the Japanese fleet had the advantage of standardization, for, although smaller than the Chinese fleet, the Japanese vessels were nearly equal in speed and turning radii.

THE BATTLE

On Monday, 17 September 1894, the Chinese fleet lay at anchor off the mouth of the Yalu River in the northern Yellow Sea. It had arrived there the day before in the escort of several troop ships. On Sunday the troop carriers proceeded up the river and disembarked relief troops on the Korean side of the Yalu. The morning was clear, there was little wind, and the seas were calm.

At 1100, as the Chinese crews were preparing for lunch, smoke was sighted to the west-southwest. Within a short time, a large Japanese fleet was identified heading in the general direction of the anchored Chinese naval units. By coincidence, the Japanese had been en route to Takushan near the Yalu River entrance. At about 1115, the Japanese identified the Chinese squadron and the signal "the enemy is sighted" was hoisted. As frequently practiced, the Japanese formation quickly changed to a single column in close order.[8]

Meanwhile, the Chinese hurried lunch and made preparations for getting under way. Significantly, the Chinese engine rooms had to operate at force draft in order to work up speed. The problem of raising steam led to confusion, and instead of signaling for the line-ahead-in-sections arrangement as previously agreed, the *Dingyuan* signaled for line abreast, with the leaders, the two battleships, located in the middle.[9] Thus, the Chinese struggled slowly toward the Japanese column in a ragged crescent-shaped formation.

Admiral Kozo Tsuboi, commanding the Japanese flying squadron, instantly saw that his four small cruisers could gain on the Chinese line, pass across it, and inflict heavy punishment on the weak Chinese left wing. Once he had cleared the Chinese formation, he expected to double back and attack the Chinese right wing. However, he decided to avoid the two formidable Chinese battleships for the moment.

When the two fleets had closed to about 10,000 yards, William F. Tyler, a British advisor on the *Dingyuan*, became alarmed over the disarray of the Chinese formation. He hurried to the flying bridge where Von Hannecken and Admiral Ding were standing and suggested to the German that an order to alter course to starboard would at least bring the battleships into a position that would allow them to make first contact with the fast-closing Japanese. Both Ding and Von Hannecken agreed and the signal was promptly run up. At this point, Tyler records that the *Dingyuan*'s Fujianese commodore, Liu Buchan, played a "treacherous trick."

> I stood above the entrance to the conning-tower below which was the Commodore, and waited for the movement of the helm. None came. "Commodore, the signal to alter course has been hauled down. If you do not port at once you will put the fleet in worse confusion." The Commodore then gave the order "Port," but in a lower voice said "Steady, steady," resulting in the movement being stopped. Sick with rage, I flung a curse at him, jumped the conning-tower top and ran to [Admiral] Ding. I hardly realized that he was now alone, and that I could not speak to him—I knew but little Chinese and he knew no English. I reached the Admiral's side, and then a roar of sound and then oblivion; for Liu had given the order for the ten-inch barbette guns to fire, and Ding and I were standing on the flying-bridge immediately above them. That bridge was quite well named: it flew, and so did Ding and I. And that was how the Yalu battle opened.[*][10]

---

*Admiral Ding and Tyler were standing on the wooden fore bridge, which extended over the muzzle of the 10-inch barbette guns. As noted earlier, during firing it was a dangerous position, and injury from muzzle blast was common if one did not take cover. Ding, in fact, was thrown into the air and his right foot and leg were injured by splinters. He also suffered powder burns on his face. Tyler had all of his clothes blown off and was temporarily blinded.[11]

At such an extreme range the Chinese broadside was useless. Her firing had the disastrous effect of causing the rest of the Chinese ships to commence firing. Thus, much valuable ammunition was expended on targets still too far away.

Regarding ammunition, the foreign gunnery advisors had been jolted by the discovery that most of the ammunition aboard the Chinese ships was useless armor-piercing shells rather than the more effective common shells.[12] For example, on the Dingyuan only fifty-five common shells were aboard, and these were fired away in the first hours of battle. McGiffin, aboard the Zhenyuan, was later quoted as saying that when one of the common shells came up from the ammunition room the crew "nursed that shell like a hothouse plant."[13] It was also discovered that some projectiles for the bigger guns were inferior and did not fit. But the biggest shock came when many shells were found to be filled with sand.[14]

The Japanese held fire until they had closed to 3,000 yards, at which time a furious barrage was loosed from their quick-firing guns. It was only a matter of moments before Chinese ships of the left wing suffered extensive damage. On nearly every vessel halliards were shot away, preventing any further transmission of orders by flag signal.[15] Meanwhile, Tsuboi's flying squadron swept by virtually undamaged. He executed a quick left turn and brought the Chinese right wing under a withering fire.

The Dingyuan and Zhenyuan lumbered ahead bows on in an attempt to intersect the Japanese column. The armor on the two battleships held up well and they remained in good shape in the early going.[16] Still, the lack of effective ammunition prevented them from inflicting extensive damage.

There was at least one brave moment for the Chinese. The Zhiyuan on the left wing had been badly hulled in the initial Japanese salvo and took on a heavy list to starboard. All guns were out of action, so the captain, Deng Shichang, tried to ram Tsuboi's flagship, the cruiser Yoshino.[17] As it lurched forward in a valiant attempt to crush the Japanese vessel, the Yoshino literally blew the Chinese ship to pieces. It sank with all hands.

Aboard the Zhenyuan McGiffin did not see much bravery in his Chinese commander, however. He later wrote the following unfavorable description:

> Commodore Lin was our captain, but he was not to be seen at Yalu. Clearing for action was more than he could stomach even—the fright of anticipation nearly killed him. . . . I kept on hearing a curious noise going on below me in the conning tower every time there was a lull in the firing, and going down there after a while to fight the ship, I came an awful header over Commodore Lin, lying flat on his stomach, cursing and groveling, and praying to Buddha for all he was worth. He belonged to the Mandarin class, and they are all an effete race of arrant [sic] cowards.[18]

By 1510, the Dingyuan was on fire forward, the Zhiyuan was about to capsize, the Jingyuan was ablaze, and most of the other Chinese warships were badly damaged and in distress. The Chinese battle formation was in total disarray and each ship that remained afloat was seeking its own route of escape. The Jingyuan and Jiyuan had broken off from the fight and were

Sino-Japanese naval tactics (1894). These models demonstrate the poor tactics employed by China in September 1894 at Yalu. The Chinese main force, at the right, is arrayed in line abreast while the Japanese, in column at left, bring maximum guns to bear. (Models by Bradley Hahn and photographs by David Pickel.)

fleeing westward toward Dalian; the *Pingyuan* and *Guangbing* were struggling northward to shallow water; and the two battleships, the *Dingyuan* and *Zhenyuan*, were isolated and receiving heavy fire from the Japanese.[19]

At 1730, with darkness approaching and the prospect of torpedo-boat counterattacks, the Japanese broke off contact. The *Zhenyuan* had received some 124 direct hits, and her superstructure was almost completely shot away. The *Dingyuan* had fared just as badly: she was burning forward, had sustained 200 hits, and her fighting top had been blasted into the sea. Later reports indicated that nearly every Chinese deck officer had been wounded and more than 600 men had lost their lives.[20] By contrast, the Japanese had lost no ships, although several had sustained damage. Seventy-eight Japanese officers and men had been killed and 160 wounded.

One post-action assessment by a U.S. Navy observer portrayed the battle's lopsidedness as being largely due to Chinese incompetence. He wrote that "the Mikado's sailors kept their lamps trimmed and were ready when the bridegroom came; while the subjects of the Son of Heaven, like foolish virgins, had let their oil run dry, and the crisis found them unprepared."[21]

Other foreigners on the Chinese ships were critical of the Chinese as well. One report had this to say:

> Some brave officers there doubtless were, but when three out of twelve captains show the white feather what can the physical bravery of crews avail? Someone—I think it was Napoleon—has said, "An army of donkeys led by a lion is better than an army of lions led by donkeys." All praise is due to the foreigners in the Chinese fleet, who, working unsupported against great odds, gave their best service to an ungrateful nation and alone deserve the credit for whatever discipline existed.[22]

McGiffin, who was perhaps in the best position to criticize the Chinese, praised them instead. He summed up the courage and fighting spirit of sailors aboard two of the ships as follows:

> About the middle of the fight the *Laiyuan* caught fire aft, and burned fiercely. The broadside guns could not be manned, being surrounded by flames; but the bow guns were worked steadily, while the crew persistently fought the flames on the quarter-deck. Below, in the engine-rooms, with ventilators stopped on account of fire overhead, and, in darkness, receiving orders only by voice-tube transmitted from the deck through the stoke-hole, the engineers stood to their duty, hour after hour, in a temperature bordering on 200°. After several hours the fire was extinguished; but these brave men were in several cases blinded for life, and in every instance horribly burned and disfigured. . . .
>
> When the *Zhenyuan* was desperately on fire in the forecastle, and a call was made for volunteers to accompany an officer to extinguish it, although the gun fire from three Japanese ships was sweeping the place in question, men responded heartily, and went to what seemed to them almost certain death. Not one came back unscathed. No, these men were not cowards. There were cowards present, as there have been on every battlefield; but here, as elsewhere, there were brave men to detest them.[23]

THE AFTERMATH

The Yalu battle was not the final battle between the Chinese and Japanese navies. The showdown came several months later at the northern Shandong port of Weihai. By then Japan's armies had overrun both Korea and the Liaodong Peninsula, as well as captured Lushun and Dalian. In January 1895 the remnants of the Beiyang Fleet had sealed themselves in the Weihai estuary behind booms and sunken junks. In late January the Japanese attacked the port and sent torpedo boats against the traditional harbor-blocking defense works. Finally, in early February they broke through and engaged the Chinese. On the fifth the *Dingyuan* was sunk. The *Jingyuan* was destroyed four days later trying to break out of the blockade.[24]

Philo McGiffin, Chinese navy advisor. McGiffin is shown as a midshipman at the U.S. Naval Academy in 1881 and after the Battle of Yalu in 1894. He later committed suicide due to the severe head injuries received in the battle. His eyewitness account of the battle was widely acclaimed by naval experts of the period, including Admiral Alfred T. Mahan. (Courtesy of the U.S. Naval Historical Center, Washington, DC.)

Shortly thereafter China sued for peace and the surviving Beiyang warships were delivered up to Japan in partial payment of war damages. The Chinese emperor ordered all surviving captains to be executed by beheading. The order was later rescinded, but not before several officers had been executed. In anticipation of the drastic punishment, Admiral Ding and two other captains committed suicide by swallowing lethal doses of opium. By late February 1895 the million-dollar warships of the Chinese navy were scattered above and below the ocean's surface, and a large percentage of the navy's Western-trained officer corps was dead.

After Japan's victory in 1895, Li Hongzhang traveled to Shimonoseki to sign a peace treaty. The general demands that Japan forced Li to accede to were

1. Chinese recognition of the total independence of Korea
2. The ceding of Taiwan, the Pescadores, and the Liaodong Peninsula (including Lushun and Dalian) to Japan
3. The payment of an indemnity of 300 million taels
4. The signing of a trade treaty that granted Japan most-favored-nation status and required the opening of seven new treaty ports[25]

One Chinese concession was not long lasting, however. Less than a week after the treaty signing at Shimonoseki, Russia, Germany, and France, shocked at Japan's aggressive efficiency, presented a note to the Japanese saying that "the possession of the Peninsula of Liaodong, claimed by Japan, would be a constant menace to the capital of China, would at the same time render illusory the independence of Korea, and would henceforth be a perpetual obstacle to the peace of the Far East."[26]

Under such international pressure Japan dropped its claim to Liaodong and returned the territory to China in November 1895. This action, however, unleashed a series of arguments among the Western powers over Asia. Within three years, under the guise of leases, they began to take possession of many Chinese ports. In 1898 Germany grabbed Qingdao; Britain took Weihai; Russia snapped up Port Arthur (Lushun), thus acquiring a Pacific warm-water port; and France took possession of Zhanjiang in the South China Sea.

CHAPTER 9

REFORM AND REVOLUTION: CHINA'S NAVY, 1896–1911

 Defeat by the Japanese coupled with further Western encroachment forced most Chinese to seriously question the whole Confucian system. They now realized that the old traditions could not be reconciled with even moderate reforms. New and radical measures were required.

A NAVAL INTELLECTUAL'S VIEW

A number of Chinese intellectuals believed that China could be saved only by fully adopting Western ideas. One, Yan Zongguang or Yan Fu, was a graduate of Greenwich and the naval academy in Fuzhou. In 1890 he had become the chancellor of Li Hongzhang's Tianjin Naval Academy. During his ten-year chancellorship at Tianjin he displayed a wide range of interests and introduced many new ideas into China. Two of Yan Fu's favorite pursuits were journalism and intellectual publicizing, but he also studied logic, sociology, jurisprudence, and economics.[1] While at Tianjin he founded two newspapers and translated into Chinese such works as Thomas Huxley's *Evolution and Ethics and Other Essays*, Adam Smith's *An Inquiry into the Nature and Causes of the Wealth of Nations*, John Stuart Mill's *On Liberty*, and Herbert Spencer's *Study of Sociology*.*

But Yan Fu was not naive about the obstacles lying in the path of China's Westernization. Like many intellectuals, he was outraged at China's humiliation at the hands of the Japanese and critical of failed reforms. Yan Fu attacked the nineteenth-century dictum endorsing "Chinese cul-

---

*Several other Fuzhou Naval Academy graduates or their protégés became important political figures. For example, in foreign affairs, Chen Lu, Gao Lu, and Lo Fenglu would hold high positions. Chen went on to obtain a law degree from Paris University in 1906 and served in a variety of important political positions after the 1911 revolution. From 1920 to 1927 he was the Chinese minister to France and a delegate to the League of Nations. Gao became secretary to Sun Yat-sen in 1912 and was soon appointed director of the government observatory. Fluent in German and French, he became minister to France in 1928 and authored a book entitled *The Principles of Einstein's Theory of Relativity*. Mr. Lo left the Chinese navy after 1893 and served as Chinese minister to Great Britain, Spain, and Belgium concurrently, from 1896 to 1901.

ture for the foundation and Western culture for practical use." While still chancellor of Tianjin, he published the following criticism:

> Chinese understanding of the necessity of learning Western methods did not begin until after the defeat of China by Japan in 1895. Since the lifting of the ban on Western merchants coming to China by sea, there have been quite a few developments: (1) the Zongli Yamen; (2) the Tongwen Guan; (3) the Fuzhou Shipyard; (4) the educational mission to send students to study abroad; (5) the China Merchants' Steam Navigation Company; (6) manufacturing; (7) the navy; (8) the Ministry of the Navy; (9) foreign military drill; (10) the opening of schools; (11) the dispatch of Chinese envoys abroad; (12) the opening of mines; (13) the establishment of telegraph and post offices; and (14) the building of railways. If we count everything, there are more than ten or twenty items. Most of these things have served as the foundations on which Europe became rich and strong, but when we applied them in China, they were like a good orange tree on the bank of the Huai River which, after it was transplanted, produced thick-skinned oranges. The tree looks as if midway between life and death and we do not get the fruit we sought. What is the reason?
>
> I think the greatest difference between China and the West, which can never be made up, is that the Chinese are fond of antiquity but neglect the present. The Westerners are struggling in the present in order to supersede the past. Chinese consider a period of order and a period of disorder, a period of prosperity and a period of decline, as the natural course of heavenly conduct of human affairs; while Westerners consider that daily progress should be endless, and that what has already been prosperous will not decline, and that when things are well governed, they will not be in disorder again—all of which they take as an absolute law of academic thought and political ideas.[2]

As evidenced by such criticism, China remained a nation uncertain as to how to proceed. There was a sense of urgency as most intellectuals saw China rapidly dropping behind Japan and the West, but those who held power clearly were not up to the task of implementing efficacious reforms. China adopted the method of the "quick fix" in seeking new ways to survive—and the fix was supplied by adversaries. Against this background China's few remaining leaders had little cause for hope. There was a deficiency of ships, facilities, and technical knowledge. Considering China's recent record of naval reform, prospects were dismal at best.

WHETHER OR NOT TO HAVE A NAVY

In August 1895, soon after the signing of the Treaty of Shimonoseki, a prominent Chinese official, Liu Kunyi, memorialized the court that, because of China's naval impotence, the best way to insure seaboard security would be to give that task to Russia through a secret naval treaty. Another prominent official, Zhang Zhidong, agreed. The essence of his proposal, which was denied by the emperor, is worth repeating, because fifty-five years later it would serve as the basis for Sino-Soviet naval cooperation.

> In everything concerning Russian commercial affairs and boundary matters, we should make some compromises. If Russia resorts to warfare in the

The Chinese cruiser *Hairong*. This vessel and three others were the main naval forces of republican China from 1911 to 1937. Built in Germany in 1897, it carried three 6-inch guns and eight 4-inchers. It was scuttled in the Yangzi River in November 1937 to prevent the Imperial Japanese Navy from sailing upriver. (Courtesy of the U.S. Naval Historical Center, Washington, DC.)

East, we should aid her navy with coal and food, permitting her war vessels to enter our dockyards for repairs. . . . But we should have it settled in the contract that in case China is attacked, Russia will have to help us with armed forces, of which the most important is the navy. . . . If we have the Russians to aid us, in the future, regardless of what country may start hostilities with us, after a few weeks several tons of Russian warships could be sent to patrol the Eastern Seas. Thus we can prepare only the strategy of war on land, and our enemy cannot plan to invade the interior deeply. This is the crucial point in our international relations and the most important policy for saving the situation.[3]

The desperate tone of the memorial prompted the aging Li Hongzhang to exert his influence and revive the navy. Characteristically, he urged the purchase of ships from the West and the emperor approved the recommendation. During the next three years, China acquired five cruisers, four destroyers, and four torpedo boats. Two of the cruisers, the *Haitian* and *Haiqi*, were built by Armstrong and carried two 8-inch guns. They were 4,300 tons each and had a top speed of 24 knots.[4] The other cruisers were German built (Vulcan), displaced 2,950 tons, mounted three 6-inch guns, and had a speed of 19 knots.[5] The destroyers and torpedo boats were also built in Germany. The former were 280 tons, carried two torpedo tubes, and had a speed of 32 knots.* The torpedo boats were of two types typical of the period: one 62 tons and carrying three torpedo tubes, and the other 90

---

*In 1900 China's navy played almost no role in the Boxer Rebellion. Ironically, however, part of the indemnity China had to pay after the rebellion included the transfer of these four destroyers—one each to France, Great Britain, Germany, and Russia.

tons and carrying two torpedo tubes. Their top speed was approximately 18 knots.*[6]

The arrival of the new ships in China did not change the opinions of many foreign naval experts about efforts to buy a fleet. In late 1898 Rear Admiral Lord Charles Beresford visited China, and at the request of the Nanyang viceroy he inspected ships of that squadron, after which he advised the viceroy as follows:

> I recommended [to] them to put what ships they had left in order for police purposes, pointing out that such vessels should be able to stop the piracies at and about Canton. I strongly recommend them not to expend any more money for naval armaments, since the work of protection which devolved upon them demanded rather a military than a naval development. In my opinion, the first thing they ought to do is to provide that security for trade and commerce which only military and police can give. I called their attention to many cases of wasteful expenditure and, in particular, to the fact that they had about the coast and in the river hundreds of men-of-war junks, entailing an absolutely useless outlay of money.[7]

ORGANIZATION AND LEADERS

Lord Beresford's opinion was not without ground, for China's naval organization was little changed. It remained highly decentralized—the Navy Office had not been instituted again. On the Yangzi there were twenty-two navy-subordinated flotillas of junks that required the employment of ten thousand sailors and officers.[8] The remnants of the Beiyang Fleet had been combined with the Nanyang Fleet and given a home port near Shanghai at Wusong. It was no accident that the bulk of the navy was again positioned on the Yangzi, for demonstrations of political unrest were becoming ever more frequent along the river as the Manchu dynasty entered its final years.†[9]

Leadership of the navy was vested in Admiral Ye Zugui, a Fuzhou graduate and student at Greenwich in 1878. Ye was in poor health, probably because of the trauma he had suffered at Weihai in 1895. Although commanding officer of the cruiser *Jingyuan*, he had been ashore when she was sunk in the harbor on 7 February. He had been granted promotion only after his "rehabilitation" in 1899. Ye died in 1906 and command of the navy passed to his deputy, Admiral Sa Zhenping.[10]

SA ZHENPING

The ascendency of Sa Zhenping to naval commander in chief was significant because of his remarkable longevity and the principal naval and

---

*The pro-German nature of the ship purchases paralleled the creation of a new-style army at Nanjing, which was organized like the German army and employed German advisors. The most striking feature about this army, formed by the same official who proposed the Sino-Russian naval alliance, Zhang Zhidong, was that Germans held command positions.

†Shanghai was the center of political agitation, as it would be during the Cultural Revolution in the 1960s.

political roles he would play in subsequent years. Indeed, from the time he entered the navy in 1873 to his death in 1951, Sa had the distinction of having served in the imperial, republican, and Communist navies.

Sa's background was typical of the Chinese navy officer whose career spanned the transition from junk fleets to steam navies.[11] He came from a moderately wealthy gentry family in Fujian. As a youth he received the traditional classical education, and in later life wrote poetry in the old eight-character style. At the age of fifteen in 1873, Sa entered the Fuzhou Naval Academy, where he soon achieved high academic honors. As a result, he was chosen to go to the Royal Navy Academy in Greenwich in 1877 (Yan Fu was a fellow student at Greenwich). In England he studied navigation, natural science, and English language translation. Returning to China in 1879, Sa was ordered to the Tianjin Naval Academy as a navigation instructor. Six years later he was made commanding officer of the Fuzhou-built transport *Tongji*. During the Sino-Japanese War, he was at the Tianjin academy as the head of Yan Fu's navigation department. In 1895, like most naval officers present at the Battle of Yalu, he handed in his resignation. Sa returned to active duty in 1897 as commanding officer of the newly purchased cruiser *Haiqi*.

During his tour as commander of the *Haiqi*, Sa earned a reputation as a stickler for discipline. One of Sa's acquaintances, U.S. Admiral Robley "Fighting Bob" Evans, commander in chief of the U.S. Asiatic Fleet at the time, recorded that Sa's cruiser was "the cleanest thing in the shape of a warship I ever saw."[12] Sa was also quoted by the U.S. naval attaché to China, Commander Irvin V. Gillis, as saying that "China would never have a navy until the officers wore boiled shirts."[13]

Sa differed from his Chinese contemporaries because he practiced Islam. The Sa clan was of the western China Muslim (Semu) minority. Sa's ancestors, in fact, had come to Fujian in the fourteenth century as trusted officials representing the Mongol conquerors. In the ensuing centuries, the Sa family was absorbed into Chinese culture and became an important Fujian gentry clan whose members distinguished themselves as effective administrators and naval leaders.

Because of his Semu heritage, Sa's selection as navy commander in chief was quickly approved by the non-Han Manchu rulers. However, his Islamic background presented problems with the Han Chinese officers, so much so that early in his assignment, Sa confided to Gillis the entire navy included only five or six officers upon whom he could depend.[14] Thus, it is not surprising to see Sa follow tradition by assigning family members to key naval positions.[15]

Still, when it came to naval reform, Sa possessed a great deal of integrity and idealism. For instance, upon assuming control of the navy, he openly opposed large-scale purchases of warships from the West, preferring to limit such acquisitions to a few cruisers for training and gunboats for river and coast security. Such a philosophy, however, brought Sa pressure from foreigners and Chinese alike, who saw further naval purchases as stepping-stones to power and wealth.

Captain Sa Zhenping (1900). Sa served the Chinese navy for nearly seventy-five years. Trained at both the Fuzhou Naval Academy and Britain's Royal Naval Academy, Greenwich, he was the epitome of the Western-trained Chinese naval officer. Note that the traditional gentry jacket has been slightly altered with captain's stripes. Sa is also wearing his British-designed and manufactured Imperial Chinese Navy sword. (Courtesy of Captain E.B. Larimer, U.S. Naval Historical Center, Washington, DC.)

CHINA'S NAVY AND THE DOLLAR DIPLOMATS

Sa's assumption of the duties of commander in chief coincided with the era of dollar diplomacy in China, when most Western nations and Japan vied with each other for influence and control in Chinese affairs. In the postwar period China's navy remained an especially attractive target for armaments salesmen as well as those who sought lucrative trade advantages. Sa soon found himself courted by Europeans, Americans, and Japanese, each of whom wanted to acquire a foothold in China's navy. It was the era of the Open Door, which allowed for equal opportunity for the trade of all nations.[16]

From 1906 to 1907, events in Europe and Asia conspired to upset the delicate balance that had existed between the naval powers in Asia. Japan had stunned the world by defeating Russia, and England was sending many of its Asiatic fleets to Europe to offset German naval expansion. The resultant shifts in power caused the growth of considerably more antagonism between the previously "friendly" Asian rivals.

JAPANESE INFLUENCE

As early as 1905, when speculation began as to the rebuilding of a new Chinese navy, the Japanese were busy trying to gain a controlling position. In an article in the *Japan Mail* in 1905, a Japanese writer paid great tribute to the pre-Yalu Chinese navy, Li Hongzhang, and the "gallant" Admiral Ding. He reported: "There must still be in China many naval men who received a good training at the old naval academy, for only ten years have passed since the Yalu and Weihai [battles] extinguished the Beiyang squadron. Perhaps some of these will be employed in the newly expanded institution, but the evident impression is to have a staff mainly of Japanese." He went on to belittle the Western naval advisors that China had formerly employed, and added that, if given the funds, Japanese assistance would produce efficient naval personnel for China.[17]

Many Chinese were susceptible to such Japanese blandishments. They had been quite impressed by Japan's naval defeat of Russia at Tsushima in 1905, and saw Japanese naval assistance to China as an opportunity to get from under the yoke of European commercialism. Thus, it is not surprising that in 1907 and 1908 China began to do business with the Japanese shipyard at Kawasaki by accepting the delivery of four torpedo boats.

By 1909 Japanese naval influence had increased even more. At that time eight Chinese naval officers were sent to the Naval Gunnery School at Yokosuka, and an agreement had been worked out between Tokyo and Beijing whereby a select number of Chinese midshipmen would be admitted annually to Japanese naval schools. The first Chinese officers to study in Japan attended the Yokosuka school for six months and then attended torpedo and technical schools for another six months. This was followed by six months of practical training aboard Japanese training ships cruising in Chinese and Korean waters. Following this eighteen-month course of instruction the officers returned to China for further assignment. Within two years the number of Chinese officers studying in Japan had increased considerably. A total of eighty-nine officers were then in Japan, with twenty-three aboard the training ship *Tsugaru*, thirty-three in the Naval Gunnery School at Yokosuka, and the remainder under instruction at the Japanese Mercantile Marine Academy.[18]

There were problems with Japan's naval aid, however; for, during this same period, Japanese mining interests led to the discovery of rich deposits of phosphorite on several islands in the South China Sea.[19] These islands, still the subject of much controversy, are identified by their more familiar Western names: Pratas Reef, the Paracels, and the Spratly Islands. In 1907 Admiral Sa was granted approval by the emperor to send a naval expedition to these islands to survey and reclaim them for the Chinese government. In

1909 and 1910 China issued annexation announcements for each of the islands. In the face of China's determination to retain control over the islands, the Japanese removed their men and equipment.

Sa used the island controversy to advance another idea to the court. In 1909 he proposed and received approval to send a ship on an annual cruise of the South China Sea to maintain contact with overseas Chinese on these islands as well as others residing in various southeast Asian nations.

GREAT BRITAIN

British interest in the Chinese navy was greatest among those representing various shipbuilding firms. They were a disparate lot. For example, there was a British commander by the name of Heugh who retired in China, hoping to win a lucrative contract for the shipbuilding firm of Beardmore.[20] He traveled constantly up and down the coast, inspecting prospective naval-base sites and visiting various Chinese naval officers. After several years of being wined and dined, Heugh quit in disgust at having accomplished nothing.

A notorious shipping agent was Edmund Backhouse, who represented John Brown and Company. He was both a clever charlatan and a brilliant Chinese language scholar. Backhouse had excellent connections with the Manchu court, and from 1909 to 1911 he traveled about with albums containing illustrations of ships he hoped to sell to China.[21]

Another player was the ubiquitous William Tyler, who attempted to ingratiate himself with Admiral Sa. Tyler tried to become the secretary of the Chinese navy in 1906, a position he hoped would allow him to share power with Sa as head of the navy. Tyler also believed it would permit him to deal with they Royal Navy on an Admiralty-to-Admiralty basis. Sa saw through Tyler's scheme, however, and made the Englishman his personal secretary with no power. Tyler was mortified and later described Sa as a man whose "judgements were vagaries" and whose ideas "were as intangible as nightmares."[22]

One of the most blatant examples of the British attempt to gain influence in the Chinese navy occurred in 1909 during a visit to England by Sa and the Manchu prince, Zai Xun. The latter, who was the brother of the prince regent, had been appointed in July 1909 to be co-president with Sa of a commission to undertake plans for the reorganization of the navy.[23] Before their recommendations were approved, however, the court ordered them to undertake a year-long world tour to observe foreign navies. While in England, both men were subjected to lavish parties by shipbuilders and government officials. But the most open attempt to curry Chinese favor was the knighting of Sa Zhenping by King Edward VII.

THE UNITED STATES

No one was more aggressive in pursuing Chinese naval contracts than the Bethlehem Steel Company. Besides employing the U.S. naval attaché, Commander Gillis, as its representative, the firm also pressured the U.S. minister to China, William J. Calhoun, to persuade the Chinese to visit the United States. In September 1910 Zai Xun and Sa, together with a considerable retinue of officials, arrived in San Francisco for a two-week visit. Bethlehem and others spared no cost in entertaining the Chinese. They even arranged for Zai Xun to meet President Taft in the Blue Room, where a state dinner was held in the prince's honor. Meanwhile, Sa was treated to tours of Annapolis, West Point, New York, and the Brooklyn Bridge.[24]

Upon their return to China, Sa and Zai Xun were filled with energy and grand plans. The admiral ambitiously launched a new series of surveys in search of suitable ports for the navy, which at the time possessed an unimpressive total of 45,000 tons. He prepared a set of plans to survey more than twenty-five sites stretching from the Gulf of Zhili to Hainan Island.[25]

During his visit to America Zai Xun had signed a contract with Bethlehem. It contained nine articles of agreement and reflected the Chinese government's intent to expend 25 million taels on naval improvements to be carried out by the Bethlehem Steel Company. Included in the contract were the following agreements:

1. Bethlehem would receive 2 million taels for improvement of existing gun and arsenal facilities or construction of new facilities, as designated by the Chinese government.

2. Two million taels would be spent on Bethlehem's improvement of existing port facilities or construction of new dockyards.

3. The remainder of the money would be spent on construction of new vessels and guns, to be decided by the Chinese government.[26]

Bethlehem also agreed to secure the training of Chinese naval officers and midshipmen aboard U.S. warships. Furthermore, Bethlehem promised to obtain permission from the U.S. government to admit Chinese students and officers to the naval schools and academies of the United States.

THE CHINESE NAVY REFORM COMMISSION

The Bethlehem contract was consummated concurrently with the proposed establishment of a Chinese naval ministry and the promulgation of new naval regulations in late 1910.[27] These efforts had begun nearly two years earlier when, by imperial edict, a commission for the reorganization of the navy had been set up. Sa and Zai Xun had been appointed the co-presidents of the commission, and in July 1909 their recommendation for the temporary Navy Council had been approved. The council, with six departments, represented the initial step toward organizing a ministry patterned after similar foreign naval offices. The departments were (1) Jiyao Si—Department of Urgent Affairs; (2) Chuanzheng Si—Construction Department; (3) Yunchou Si—Department of Naval Tactics; (4) Chubei Si—Department of Communications and Accounts; (5) Yiwu Si—Medical Department; and (6) Fawu Si—Department of Naval Law.[28]

In October 1909 final recommendations were submitted to the court. They included the establishment of a national navy and naval ministry that would be controlled by the central government. They also suggested that the Board of Finance and the provincial viceroys raise 38 million taels (22.8 million dollars) to support the navy. Of this total, 18 million taels would be needed to defray initial expenses. Two million taels would be required for maintenance costs. Establishment of dockyards and schools would cost 1.5 million taels. The purchase of three cruisers, two training ships, two torpedo boats, and one large oceangoing war vessel (specification unidentified) would amount to 16.5 million taels.[29]

The memorial went on to state that while a national navy was "prerequisite to national strength," the question of finances continued to make the chances for the creation of a navy remote. Of the twenty provinces polled, sixteen reported they could raise 11,340,000 taels, but that they would require an extension of time. It was also requested that the matter be held over until a method for raising the funds could be devised. Four provinces protested their inability to assume any responsibility for financing the navy.

It was not before the fall of 1910 that the first recommendation was approved. At that time, Sa and Zai Xun submitted their final recommended plans for a naval ministry. On 9 February 1911 these plans were officially approved. But it was too late. China was soon in revolution and most warships would defect to the side of the revolutionaries.

Before discussing the navy's role in the revolution, it is important to examine the navy ministry plans. Although the plans fell through, the final commission report submitted by Sa and Zai Xun demonstrated a keener grasp of the fundamental doctrine and psychology of Western naval systems than had any previous Chinese naval reform movement.

General Considerations

In general the navy ministry plan was too elaborate and would have been too expensive to maintain. The important problem of finances, moreover, was not addressed.

The plan stressed the need for a national navy and called for the promotion and selection of officers to be handled at the central level. While such idealism was admirable, it seemingly ignored the continued existence of the Fujian naval clique. Nearly every major warship was still commanded by Fujianese, and most departments within the existing command structure were dominated by Fujian officers.

Although a wide variety of detailed responsibilities were spelled out in the plan, it did not address the matter of fleet organization. Hence, while the navy ministry was a modern organization on paper, the fleet structure remained closely tied to the traditional imperial system.

Balance of Power

The plan made no concessions to the provinces in the matter of operating provincial fleets. The need for water-police units to maintain security in the estuary and upper river regions was recognized, but such duties were to be handled entirely by the navy. The plan stated that the primary responsibility of the chief(s) of the navy ministry was "to be in charge of affairs concerning the executive department of the National Navy, in supreme command of the Navy, its personnel and everything pertaining to the Navy and all the provincial navies. . . . "[30] In other words, provincial maritime viceroys would no longer be able to deal directly with the imperial court on matters relating to maritime or naval affairs.

RECTIFICATION OF WEAKNESSES

The plan did attempt to correct serious weaknesses in the navy. For example, it called for a department of naval education that would stress the examination, selection, and advanced training of officers. It also recognized the need for both line and staff officers and a thorough overhaul of the naval school system. Significantly, the plan also called for the continued practice of hiring foreign advisors and sending midshipmen abroad for study. Officer and enlisted pay was to be increased and corrupt practices were to result in censure or dismissal.

FUNCTION OF OFFICES

The plan contained many detailed regulations designed to manage the technical aspects of training. Most were quite advanced even by today's standards. For example, regular reports were to be required listing the results of gunnery drills, maneuvering practice, and fire drills. A bureau of tactics was suggested, which, among other things, would develop wartime telegraph codes, standard shipboard command procedures, and flag and light signals. There was also to be a bureau of general statistical accounts, responsible for compiling statistics on nearly every facet of shipboard operations and shore management. Unfortunately, these modern offices were impossible to man, and would only have served the Chinese as ultimate goals.

STANDARDIZATION OF EQUIPMENT

The plan recognized the long-standing problem of trying to standardize China's ships and equipment. There were regulations that called for a single bureau to be charged with purchases and construction. Repair and machinery standardization was also urged, and a system of hull inspection was included.

THE NAVY'S ROLE IN THE REVOLUTION, 1911–12

Ironically, as final approval was being given to the navy ministry plan and as the Chinese government was concluding the Bethlehem Steel navy contract, the nation was split by revolution. No less than ten days after the Bethlehem agreement was signed and only three weeks short of imperial approval to move forward with the formal establishment of the navy ministry, revolutionary army units captured the key Yangzi River city of Wuhan. At the head of the revolutionary military government was Li Yuanhong, a former naval student and protégé of Admiral Sa. Li had been dragged from hiding under his bed and presented with a choice of death or leadership of the rebel forces.[31] Li chose the latter, but kept looking for someone else to take command.

When word concerning the fall of Wuhan reached Beijing, Admiral Sa, in Shanghai, was ordered to take the combined Nanyang-Beiyang Fleet up river to quell the disorder. Except for the few Manchus in Sa's command, most of his officers and crews openly sympathized with the revolutionary government. Moreover, upon his arrival at Wuhan on 25 October, Sa received a letter from Li Yuanhong imploring the admiral to take over leadership of the revolutionary forces. In the letter Li asked Sa: "Who is willing to be the Manchus' slave to the detriment of one's own brothers? . . . I swear allegiance and [am] determined to restore this territory to the Han Chinese."[32]

According to a contemporary Chinese naval historian, Li's appeal to the admiral's nationalism was for naught, because Sa's heritage was Semu. Members of the Sa clan, in fact, had always supported the dynasty and were close cousins of the Manchus. Hence, no amount of urging would have swayed the admiral to forsake the Manchu regime.[33]

On 27 October Sa ordered his fleet to proceed to Wuhan and bombard the revolutionary forces. As his ships slowly made their way toward the city, they came within range of the revolutionary's shore artillery. Inexplicably, the rebels held fire, permitting the warships to get into firing position. At 0930 Sa opened his bombardment and the effect was deadly. His shots hit with alarming precision and the revolutionists retreated in haste. The imperial forces took courage and soon gained the upper hand.

Aboard ship, feelings were running high as undertones of mutiny spread. Apprised of this, Sa elected to bluff by departing the area and turning the fighting over to the imperial army units ashore. Beijing denied him this move, however, and directed Sa to return and continue the bombardment the following day. The admiral stalled and used the presence of foreigners ashore as an excuse not to renew firing.

Perhaps emboldened by the lack of warship action, the revolutionaries launched a counterattack against the imperial troops ashore. As the fighting intensified, Li Yuanhong once again sent a message to Sa urging the admiral to take command and lead the revolution. Part of Li's entreaty reads as follows:

> To such a person as Admiral Sa with worldwide fame and noble principles, we humbly submit this letter asking him to read it and consider it with patience and wisdom. China is now in a critical position. The people have shown great enthusiasm and determination for the overthrow of the Manchu yoke and to gain back their independence. . . .
>
> Again, Sir, perhaps you will hesitate to join the Republicans when you think it ungrateful to turn disloyal to the Manchus, and it might be that you will think you have derived much benefit from the Manchus, but, Sir, the benefit which seems to be derived from them is in reality obtained indirectly from the Han people, who are the source of all wealth, prosperity and official honour. Moreover, your duty, Sir, is to profit the many, not the few, to save the people, not to destroy them, to help your own race and not the alien [obviously Li was unaware of Sa's family background], and to stand by the righteous and not by the wicked. The Manchurian yoke has the barrier against the growth and development of the Han people. It is the Manchus who would not send many students abroad at an earlier date in order to acquire Western civilisation and education. It is the Manchus who will not put the returned students into proper position. It was the Manchus that

roused the Boxer Revolt, which has weakened the Empire and made it poor. And it is the Manchus who are misappropriating the loans from Foreign Powers. They have squandered the funds from the imposition of taxes for their private sensual pleasures, such as the construction of parks and the building of beautiful residences. They have encouraged squeezes, practised villainies, sold offices and brevet ranks, and demoralised the Customs. They have decided cases unjustly. . . .

Therefore, Admiral, we appeal to your general sympathy and wisdom and plead for the safety and welfare of four hundred million souls for the free growth and development of the Chinese, who, if allowed to be free, are bound to make a wonderful contribution that will go to enrich the civilisation of the whole world. If you would disarm your gunboats and cruisers and steam up to Wuhan, all the people in these three cities will be enraptured to welcome you with wild enthusiasm and intense honour.[34]

Sa's reaction to this letter was never recorded, but its well-publicized contents did have an important impact upon the fleet. On 12 November 1911 Chinese officers and crews mutinied and overpowered the few Manchus and loyalists remaining on board. Sa's flagship was observed to haul down the Dragon Flag and run up a white one. Meanwhile, Sa abandoned ship and eventually made his way down river to Shanghai where he took refuge in the British consulate.

In one respect, the navy's defection was predictable, for most of the rebel forces were made up of southerners; men of the largely Fujian-dominated fleet required little urging to throw in with southern Cantonese leaders who were determined to force the Manchus from power. It now remained to be seen whether the navy of the Republic would assume important responsibilities in modernizing China or whether it would reinforce its recent image of weakness and ineptitude.

CHAPTER 10

DISSENSION AND DECAY, 1912–37

 In the aftermath of the Chinese revolution, political and military affairs became entwined in a successive series of internal power struggles. Despite its many weaknesses, the imperial form of government had provided a stable, monolithic structure upon which all Chinese institutions had been dependent. The navy was no exception. Now it found itself intimately involved in sociopolitical experimentation as three contending groups formed the basic nuclei around which the Chinese power struggles revolved: the radical revolutionists led by southern and Hawaii-reared Dr. Sun Yat-sen; the constitutionalists, who desired to maintain a reformed version of the imperial government; and the militarists, who were the most pragmatic of the three groups but who inclined toward rule by warlord and gun.

Some scholars have rightly dubbed this period the Age of Confusion. Despite all the talk of reform and republicanism, the objectives of the revolution were hardly recognizable after the Manchu overthrow. Lawlessness was the order of the day. Canal and irrigation waterways quickly decayed, leading to floods and famine. Food transport became erratic for lack of an efficient coastal grain-transport fleet.

Meanwhile, intellectuals left government and retired to a life of academe, creating a void that could be filled only by military men and assorted bureaucratic hangers-on. The gentry took their money out of the countryside and placed it in the better protected maritime cities. The peasants became leaderless and lacked funds.

It was not long before the internecine fighting split the nation into traditional geographic divisions. In the north, various military overlords joined together in the loosest of coalitions to back an endless series of parliamentary governments at Beijing—between 1912 and 1928 there were forty-five cabinet changes.[1] In the southern and eastern coastal regions, revolutionaries led by Sun Yat-sen continued to foment uprisings against the Beijing government. Their home base was at Canton, where Sun attempted several times to set up a military government and build an army capable of marching north to throw out the warlord government.

Canal workers in republican China. A timeless view of grain being shipped north. (Courtesy of U.S. Naval Institute Photographic Library.)

The navy quickly became mired in political and military power disputes. Coastal defense and piracy were forgotten issues as the navy struggled to survive. Soon officers and enlisted men alike were engaged in illicit activities, and ships frequently deserted to whomever was willing to pay wages and upkeep.

REPUBLICAN NAVY ORGANIZATION

In spite of its fragmented loyalties, the navy did initially retain a semblance of order and discipline. A promotional system remained in effect throughout this period, and although an officer might desert to another region, his name and lineal number was rarely removed from the navy list. Hence an admiral or captain in one fleet demanded and usually got equal pay and rank when he defected, and if he later chose to return to his original patrons, he was seldom punished.

Perhaps because of this, the navy continued to place more importance on position rather than rank. The commanding officer of a cruiser with the rank of captain was senior in authority and pay to many staff admirals. It is not surprising, therefore, that afloat commands were more highly prized and carried greater prestige than staff positions.

THE HAIJUN BU

In 1912 Sun Yat-sen approved a request by the navy to reorganize and name new officers to key positions. Chosen to lead the navy was Huang Zhongying, a politician and supporter of Sun's Kuomintang (Guomindang) party.

Others assigned to high positions were, for the most part, many of the same navy officers who had risen in rank under the Manchus. This continuity was soon apparent in the formation of the Navy Ministry (Haijun Bu), which reflected a strong Western bias and was organized along the lines proposed by Admiral Sa in 1909–10.[2]

THE FLEET ORGANIZATION

The revolution gave rise to one significant change. The traditional geographic fleet arrangement was discarded in favor of a functional alignment. On paper, at least, this change gave the navy the appearance of being national rather than provincial. There were three squadrons. The First Squadron was the primary coastal and ocean combat force, formed by a consolidation of the old Beiyang and Nanyang ships. The Second Squadron was a defense squadron stationed permanently on the Yangzi River. The Training Squadron was, as the name implies, a force to be used for training officers and enlisted men in all facets of shipboard duties.

WARSHIPS

The naval ships inherited by the Republic between 1911 and 1912 were small in number but not too badly outdated. The First Squadron had four cruisers, the *Haiqi*, *Haichou*, *Hairong*, and *Haichen*, each of which was in good working order. The Second Squadron contained mostly river gunboats; these, however, were old and of little value. The Training Squadron had the newest ships, for in 1912 China took delivery of three cruisers that had been contracted for and funded by the Manchus.

The Training Squadron's lead ship, the *Chenghe*, was built at Elswick and was 320 feet long, 2,600 tons, and mounted two 6-inch guns and four 4-inch guns as the main batteries. The second ship, the *Yingrui*, was an Armstrong-built cruiser configured like the *Chenghe*. A third vessel, the cruiser *Feiying*, was constructed in America by the New York Ship Building Company and patterned after the two British-built cruisers. In 1912 China also received three destroyers from Germany that had been contracted for by the Manchu government. These were the *Yuzhang*, *Xiaoan*, and *Jiankang*. Each was 390 tons and carried two 3-inch guns and two torpedo tubes. When new they could run at 32 knots at flank speed.

In 1912–13, China also ordered four cruisers to be built at the Austro-Hungarian shipyard Cantiere Navale Triestine, Monfalcone. Three units, 1,800 tons each, were equipped with ten 10.2-cm guns and torpedo tubes, and could steam at 32 knots. A fourth ship, a 28-knot, 5,000-ton cruiser, mounting four 20-cm guns, twelve 12-cm guns, ten 4.7-cm guns, and two 45-cm torpedo mounts, was also to be built. But these ships never reached China, for in May 1915 Italian Austria declared war on Hungary, and the shipyard was occupied for two years with the half-completed vessels suffering heavy damage from artillery firing.[3]

It would not be until the 1930s that China would add any major units to its navy. In 1931 and 1935, two 2,500-ton cruisers, the *Ninghai* and *Pinghai*, were received. The former was built in Japan at Kobe and the latter was constructed at the Jiangnan Shipyard in Shanghai.

SCHOOLS AND SHIPYARDS

In the period from 1912 to 1937, China maintained six naval schools and two shipyards that functioned on a sporadic basis.

FUZHOU

The most efficient naval school remained at Fuzhou. It operated throughout this entire period. According to Bao Zenpeng, the modern Chinese naval historian, the school was taken from navy control in 1913 and returned to the Fujian gentry to operate and finance.[4] The curriculum was much the same as that provided before the revolution, except that in 1917 the school added an aeronautics and submarine division which taught the theory of these emergent weapon systems. Later, in 1927, the division was closed owing to lack of funds. In its last year of existence, however, students did build four functional hydroplanes.

The Fuzhou Dockyard remained operational. Beginning about 1921 it was run by an M.I.T.–trained marine engineer, Ma Dejian. Despite the lack of modern machinery, Ma managed to keep the yard running throughout the period from 1921 to 1937. He did this because the dockyard, like the naval school, was a gentry enterprise, and Ma was able to levy taxes on nearby towns and villages to obtain operating funds. Ma also had another unique way of gaining revenue—he operated a semigovernment, semicommercial mint. Housed in old shipbuilding lofts, Ma's mint was capable of turning out some ten thousand Chinese copper pennies per day.

OTHERS

The old Huangpu, or Whampoa, school operated under primitive conditions, but until 1922 when it closed, it continued to teach courses in navigation, mathematics, Chinese literature, English, physics, chemistry, history, geography, and mine and torpedo theory. In 1924 the naval school was reopened by Chiang K'ai-shek as the Whampoa Military Academy. It was operated by Soviet advisors in the early period, and, as will be seen in the next chapter, it soon gained a reputation as a site for Communist intrigue. After Chiang broke with the Communists he kept the Whampoa Naval Academy operating. It did not close until 1939.

In 1912 a naval school for training radio operators was opened in Nanjing. Although it operated for only five years, it did manage to graduate 153 communicators.

The government sponsored a naval academy at Yentai, which was probably intended to be a northern counterpart to Fuzhou. When it closed in 1928, it had graduated 238 officers.

The facilities at Yentai were poor and the instructor staff was generally unprofessional. For instance, in 1926 the commandant was noted to spend most of his time at the races or at parties.[5] The lack of strong leadership at the school resulted in political agitation among the students. Most were sympathetic to the Kuomintang and participated in overt revolutionary activities. One student, who later became a confidant of Chiang K'ai-shek, formed a society dedicated to encouraging navy midshipmen to join the Kuomintang cause.[6]

The Qingdao Naval Academy was formed in 1923 by a Japanese-trained navy officer, Admiral Shen Honglie. Although a supporter of the Kuomintang, Shen, a northerner, was not fond of the Fuzhou-dominated navy. The academy at Qingdao was set up to train officers who would not be influenced by the Fujianese. Funds were provided by the Manchurian warlord, Zhang Zuolin, whom Shen served.[7]

The Naval Telecommunications and Mines Academy was established by Chiang K'ai-shek in 1933 at Nanjing. Chiang was president of the school, which, although it operated for only five years, graduated nearly six hundred officers and enlisted men.

The Jiangnan Shipyard was the most modern yard in China. Until at least 1926 it was managed by the Scottish engineer, Robert Mauchan. Enlarged in the 1930s, it was the only yard capable of building both merchant vessels and warships.

FINANCING

More often than not, the navy's biggest problem was finances. Many schemes were adopted to pay crews and keep the ships running. In certain areas customs fees obtained from merchant ships and coastal transport taxes (*likin*, or *lijin*) were used by the navy. The Navy Ministry also once tried to work out a deal with an American businessman calling for the establishment of a Sino-American fishing company. The revenues were to be shared by the American firm and the Chinese navy. The navy minister believed that if the fishing industry could be protected by the Chinese navy and thus put on a sound financial basis, then it could be used as security towards a loan for building ships in America for the Chinese. When the idea reached the ears of influential Japanese in Beijing, they raised a howl of protest and it quickly died.[8]

Beijing's fear of arousing Japan's ire also gave rise to student protests in early 1919, after the Versailles Conference confirmed Japan's claim to Shandong. The conference results set in motion a new spirit of Chinese nationalism. During the period of student unrest, known as the May Fourth Movement, the financial plight of the navy again made news. The *Peking Leader* published an article written by an anonymous naval student, who lamented at one point that the navy received only about 4.5 percent of the amount of funds appropriated to the army.

> Whether the policy of the Chinese Government of the last few years has been dictated by pure party interests or other questionable authorities to produce such prevailing deplorable conditions is beyond the judgement of ordinary persons. But the fact remains that since the establishment of the Republic, especially since 1915, the Chinese Navy has been living on appro-

priations equal to virtual starvation. It is, indeed, excruciatingly funny to see how the recent national budgets depict clearly the biased attitude of the Chinese Government towards her Army and Navy.*[9]

POLITICAL GROUPS IN THE NAVY

Strong words were not enough, however, for most senior naval officers could not even agree among themselves. In fact, they were loosely divided into three factions that were aligned with the stronger forces then vying for power in China. The strongest navy faction was the Fujian navy clique, primarily made up of opportunists and dilettantes who saw the navy as a stepping-stone to power. They dominated the navy at all levels and made Fuzhou and Xiamen their main centers of activity. The following official figures released in 1932 indicate the advantage enjoyed by Fujianese in the navy:[10]

Province	Officers	Petty Officers	Civilians	Other Ranks	Total
Fujian	710	253	372	5,079	6,414
Jiangsu	50	32	62	628	772
Guangdong	19	6	26	225	276
Zhejiang	20	16	49	129	214
Anhui	14	—	9	167	190
Guangxi	—	—	—	8	8
Yunnan	—	—	—	1	1

The second most influential faction in the navy was the strongly nationalistic revolutionaries who backed Sun Yat-sen. At the senior officer level these men were few in number, but there were several whose dynamic leadership was enough even to sway many of the Fujianese. Interestingly, few naval revolutionaries were from Fujian, although many had attended the Fuzhou Naval Academy.

The last group was composed of the few senior naval officers who favored a constitutional monarchy. These men were willing to serve, and indeed did serve, whomever held power. They wanted to turn China back toward imperial autocracy. Most were Fujianese who had risen in rank in the nineteenth century and come to be known by Chinese and Westerners alike as Old China.

The following provides an overview of the background and activities of several of the principal officers.

The Revolutionists

Admiral Cheng Biguang, like his patron, Sun Yat-sen, was born and reared a member of a gentry family in Guangdong Province. He attended the Fuzhou Naval Academy in the 1870s and was the commanding officer of the only Nanyang vessel to fight at Yalu in 1894, the gunboat *Guangbing*.

---

*The navy's expenditures totaled 9,379,506 dollars, while the army's were more than twenty times as great, totaling 207,832,480 dollars.

When China surrendered at Weihai, Cheng was ordered to represent the navy at the ceremony. At the signing of the Treaty of Shimonoseki, Cheng was so humiliated that he decided to support Sun Yat-sen, who was planning revolution in Canton in 1895. Cheng became Sun's agent in the navy, and was discovered attempting to induce the remnants of the post-Yalu navy to join Sun's revolutionaries. In late 1895 he escaped to Hong Kong, subsequently settling in Singapore. When Sun's first attempt at revolution failed, Cheng remained in hiding.

He finally returned to China and, although from Guangdong, was named director of the Fuzhou Dockyard. In 1909 he was made commander of the cruiser *Haiqi*. In 1910 to 1911 he sailed the *Haiqi* to England to represent China at the coronation of King George V. While he was gone the revolution took place. When Cheng finally arrived back in China he was chagrined to learn that a subordinate, Huang Zhongying, had been named navy minister.

Despite his disappointment, Cheng continued to strongly support Sun Yat-sen, even after the latter was ousted from power by the militarist, Yuan Shikai, in 1912. Although the revolutionists loyal to Sun attempted a counter coup, their efforts collapsed and Cheng was again forced to flee China in 1913. After an unsuccessful attempt to become emperor, Yuan Shikai died in 1916. Cheng was named navy minister by the new president of China, Li Yuanhong, the old Fuzhou Naval Academy graduate and reluctant hero of the 1910–11 revolution.

In 1917 the parliament dissolved. Cheng resigned and reassumed command of the *Haiqi*, which he sailed to Canton with Sun Yat-sen aboard. His action set off a mass defection of the First Squadron, which soon followed the cruiser to Canton. At the time Cheng declared:

> We came to Canton to be united with the provinces of the Southwest to uphold the Constitution. If we shall not achieve this goal, we shall sacrifice our lives for the cause. As a citizen, every one of us has a duty to denounce the wrongful actions of the Beijing government. The present Beijing government is a dictatorship under the name of republicanism. We in the Navy are determined to struggle for the return of true republicanism. We naval officers and men shall not rest until our lawful national assembly is reestablished.[11]

Cheng and the First Squadron set about helping Sun organize a military government at Canton in 1917. The admiral was subsequently rewarded by being named commander in chief of the combined forces in Guangdong—a somewhat dubious honor in view of the fact that Sun had few forces to command.

Another admiral, Shen Honglie, was one of the few Chinese from the interior to hold a high position in the republican navy. He was born in 1882 in Hubei Province, the son of a scholar. In 1905, upon graduation from Zhang Zhidong's Prussian-run Nanjing Military Academy, he went to Japan for six years of training at the Japanese Naval Academy.

In Japan Shen soon came into contact with many Chinese revolutionaries who were plotting to overthrow the Manchu dynasty. In 1906 he joined Sun Yat-sen's Tongmeng Hui (Common Alliance Society), whose fiery manifesto called for revolution and the establishment of a republic. Shen became the key leader in converting others. Very likely he met another young military officer also studying in Japan, Chiang K'ai-shek, who would later place Shen in positions of responsibility.

In 1911, at Wuhan, Shen took command of the fleet after Sa Zhenping fled and set about converting other junior navy personnel to the revolutionary cause. Subsequently, he captured Nanjing in the name of the revolution and was rewarded by being named navy chief of staff. He remained in Beijing for four years in various staff positions until 1916, when he was sent to England as a member of a Chinese war observation mission. He returned a year later.

When the Beijing government began breaking down Shen went north, where he served the Manchurian warlord, Zhang Zuolin, as an intermediary and arbiter with the Japanese in Manchuria. He was also given several important tasks to improve defenses in northeastern China.

When Japan attacked Mukden (modern Shenyang) in 1931, Shen returned to Qingdao, where he served as mayor until 1937. Later Shen served the Nationalist government as the governor of Shandong (1938–44), the minister of agriculture (1942–44), and the governor of Zhejiang (1946–47). He authored an interesting book in 1933 entitled *Border Defense and Navigation Rights in Manchuria.*

THE CONSTITUTIONAL MONARCHISTS

Sa Zhenping, Li Dingxin, and Liu Guanxiong were the three admirals who backed constitutional monarchy.[12] Their careers were quite similar. Each was a member of a Fujian gentry family; they were raised within several miles of each other; and they were nearly the same age. All attended the Fuzhou Naval Academy at the same time as well as the Royal Naval College in England.

Only one, Liu Guanxiong, played a significant role in the war of 1894. Nevertheless, they all rose to senior rank under the Manchus in the last years of the dynasty. Liu was also the only one who seemingly sided with the revolutionaries. It was soon evident that their true sympathies lay with Yuan Shikai. They supported Yuan's attempt to restore the monarchy and served in a variety of naval and civil positions under him.

When Yuan died, the three initially lost their positions in the navy, but during the warlord interregnum that ensued, they alternated as the navy minister. In this capacity, they exercised little real control over the three fleet squadrons and were content to play palace politics at Beijing, serving the various pretenders to power as well as consorting with the many foreigners who frequented the capital. They each faded from the political-naval scene in 1928, when Chiang K'ai-shek took control of the country.

THE OPPORTUNISTS AND DILETTANTES

This group of officers grew up after Yuan Shikai's death, when the nation came under warlord rule. Most were Fujianese who tried to live a life patterned after the traditional gentry style. For example, while China struggled for political survival under Yuan Shikai, these officers were bombarding the navy minister with requests that a naval officer's club be constructed at Fuzhou to commemorate Li Hongzhang, Zuo Zongtang, and Shen Baozhen as founders of the modern Chinese navy. In a memorial to Yuan Shikai, they proposed that the club be erected for navy officers and that "a garden should be laid out within the enclosure of the club premises, with flowers and shrubs to make the place attractive. After office hours, naval officers may gather together at this club for recreation and mutual fellowship. In the garden, a temple should be erected to the memory of Li Hongzhang, Zuo, and Shen, and dates be selected in spring and autumn upon which the Ministry of the Navy would offer sacrifices to the spirit of these founders of the Chinese Navy."[13] Ultimately, the club was built at Mawei near the site of the Fuzhou Naval Academy and became the scene for many splendid banquets.

Two prominent members of this officer type were Vice Admiral Yang Shuzhuang and Rear Admiral Chen Shaokuan. The former had become the virtual ruler of Fujian Province by 1924 and made his headquarters at Xiamen (Amoy). Although he was one of the few naval officers who had not been trained abroad, Vice Admiral Yang was comfortable with Europeans. As a result he was popular with foreigners. He was not liked by the Soviets in China, however. One reported that Yang was timid and addicted to opium; moreover, the Soviets suspected Yang of having embezzled millions of dollars.[14]

Rear Admiral Chen Shaokuan subsequently became Yang's successor as leader of the Fujian naval clique. He remained the commanding officer of the training cruiser *Yingrui* for nearly a decade, maintaining the ship in scrupulous fashion and throwing lavish wardroom parties for visiting European and American naval leaders.[15] He was trained at Greenwich and was proud of the fact that he was present at the Battle of Jutland as an observer. Unlike Admiral Yang, Chen was held in high esteem by the Soviets. One Soviet "agent," for example, reported to Moscow that Chen was "quite modern in his political convictions" because the admiral con-

The Chinese cruiser *Yingrui*. This 2,700-ton cruiser was built for the Chinese by Vickers in 1911. It was always well maintained and served as Admiral Chen Shaokuan's command ship for many years. (Courtesy of Mr. W.G. Kelly, U.S. Naval Historical Center, Washington, D.C.)

sidered his duty to be that of putting "the Chinese navy in order and thereby raising the general status of China."[16] Chen may have been flattered by such praise, for in early 1926 he gave the Soviets approval to form a politically oriented New Seaman's League. In the 1930s Chen succumbed to similar Japanese blandishments, which landed him in serious trouble with Chiang K'ai-shek.

SUN YAT-SEN AND THE NAVY

In 1917 the revolutionist, Cheng Biguang, inspired the First Squadron to go south and give Sun Yat-sen legitimacy in his drive to restore the constitution and bring republicanism to China. Cheng maintained strong support of the constitution, despite bribe offers and telegram demands from Beijing to defect. His fierce patriotism made him a marked man. On 26 February, en route home after dinner aboard one of his ships, Cheng was gunned down by several assassins.

The killing had a demoralizing effect on the navy and Sun's fortunes. Without strong navy support, Sun's credibility waned. He was soon forced to leave Canton as the military government dissolved. Naval officers, lacking Cheng's strong leadership and political support, began agitating for the ships to return north and reunite with the Beijing warlords. However, the fleet was induced to remain at Canton when Sun Yat-sen returned in May 1921 and reorganized the military government. Sun, in fact, was inaugurated by the military government as president of the Republic.

Upon his return to Canton Sun attempted to consolidate his forces, which had become dangerously fragmented during his absence. Among the actions he took was the immediate dismissal of many of the crewmen aboard the navy vessels at Canton. To ensure continued loyalty of his navy, Sun replaced these men with members of the Seaman's Union, a group whose cause Sun supported during strikes in Hong Kong.

Sun was faced with intrigue from several sides. He still had few troops and the balance of power lay with the local warlord, Chen Jiongming, who controlled the strong Guangxi military faction. As Sun tried repeatedly to form an army for his northern expedition, he was watched suspiciously by Chen. Finally, in June 1922, Chen became alarmed at Sun's growing power and ordered his troops to surround the presidential palace at Canton. Sun managed to escape to the *Haiqi*, then at anchor at the Canton bund.

LOYALTIES SEVERED: UPHEAVAL AT CANTON

The following little-known tale recounts Sun's attempt to maintain his credibility by using the navy as a political instrument against his rivals.[17]

On 16 June Sun responded to his ouster by carrying out a naval bombardment of Canton. At Sun's direction three gunboats steamed upriver from Huangpu past the bund and opened fire on the city. Many innocent civilians were killed and several foreign buildings were damaged.

Following two days of bombardment, the American vice-consul in Canton, Mr. J. C. Huston, determined that Sun must be sought out and convinced to put an end to the fighting. Accompanied by Captain G. M.

Baum, commander of the U.S. South China Patrol, Huston proceeded by speed launch to Huangpu, where he found Sun aboard the *Haiqi*. Confronting the Chinese leader, Huston angrily informed Sun that he was protesting the firing on American property at Canton.

According to Huston, Sun justified the bombardment with the statement that his ouster by Chen "was the biggest act of treachery and came as a complete surprise." Sun went on to demand that "the powers should intervene and punish the traitors. I barely escaped with my life [and] I bombarded the city as a protest and [I] will continue the bombardment tomorrow."[18]

During subsequent discussions, Sun agreed not to bombard the city in areas where civilians would be killed but rather to redirect his fire on military targets. Huston and Baum then departed the ships and returned to Canton.

Upon their return, Huston visited General Chen Yongshen, Chen Jiongming's son. The general, a Yale graduate who spoke English fluently, agreed to order his troops to refrain from firing on the gunboats and to transmit this message to Sun. Apparently this was done, for Sun's ship did not bombard the city the next day as promised.

During his conversation with Huston, Chen claimed that Sun Yat-sen had ordered the assassination of Admiral Cheng Biguang, and that the assassin had been rewarded with the directorship of a cement plant. According to Chen, certain officers within Sun's navy had approached him regarding terms, and it would be only a matter of days before they surrendered. Chen said that during the initial bombardment of the city, one of Sun's naval captains and his officers were forced to fire on the bund at gunpoint by crew members belonging to the Seaman's Union. The captain and others had informed Chen that they were not going to take part in any further bombardment of Canton.

Chen's assessment may have been exaggerated, but pressure was being exerted on the navy to end its support of Sun. Some of Sun's naval officers, in fact, had agreed to quit if the following conditions were met:

1. That the navy be nationalized and not subject to provincial or sectional authority

2. That the navy have a voice in national policies

3. That all officers and men be retained in the navy in their present status and personnel be paid monthly

4. That back pay be guaranteed

The stalemate dragged on. Finally, on 8 July, a ultimatum was sent to Sun demanding that he abandon Huangpu or surrender by noon the following day. When interviewed by an American Associated Press reporter on the ninth, Sun claimed no knowledge of the ultimatum. On the morning of the tenth, six of Sun's gunboats commenced laying heavy fire into the forts below Canton. Within two hours the fort's guns had been silenced and the ships made their way back up the Pearl River toward Shameen, the international settlement.

However, at least two other gunboats, the *Yongjian* and *Zhangfen*, had declared their neutrality and lay at anchor off Shameen. As Sun's units approached, both ships went to general quarters to prepare for action. Sun, on the *Yongfeng*, ordered his fleet of six ships to moor off Shameen. Shortly thereafter, a boarding party from the *Yongfeng* went aboard the *Yongjian* and *Zhangfen*. The crews were mustered and ordered at gunpoint to support Sun.

A day later, a general strike was called by all labor unions to enforce compliance with Sun Yat-sen's demands for reinstatement as president. All business came to a halt, stalemating the situation again. But not for long. Anti-Sun forces had taken Huangpu by 14 July, leaving Sun without a usable port facility. On the evening of the fourteenth, the *Yongjian* got under way and managed to escape to Huangpu, where its crew once again declared their neutrality.

The situation was becoming precarious—a mine had exploded alarmingly close to Sun's gunboat on 19 July. Despite his dislike for the British, arrangements were made for Sun to escape to Hong Kong aboard HMS *Moorehen* in August.

Neither the officers nor crew of the *Yongfeng* realized that Sun was escaping until the *Moorehen* departed. At that point, the ship's company took Sun's remaining staff members hostage, including Sun's son-in-law.

Dr. Sun Yat-sen aboard the *Yongfeng* (August 1923). Dr. Sun escaped from Canton in 1922 aboard this vessel, from which he commanded the navy against local warlord forces. His wife, Madame Soong Ching Ling, who died in 1981, stands at his left.

They demanded safe conduct from Canton as well as all back pay due them.

The commanding officer of the *Yongfeng* then forwarded a letter on behalf of his ship and the other vessels to the British consul general, holding him responsible for their demands. The Chinese officer threatened that if his demands were not met the ships would continue their bombardment of Shameen and Canton.

On 10 August arrangements were made for a conference between Admiral Dang Dingquang, Sun's navy minister, and the commanding officer of the *Yongfeng*. The captain and four crew members showed up at the fleet landing. Admiral Dang informed them that he was prepared to take back all of the ships' crews and that they would receive the same ration allowances granted them by Sun. However, they would be subject to Dang's orders and other officers appointed over them.

The contingent returned to the *Yongfeng* accompanied by Mr. Norman, Sun Yat-sen's American legal advisor. A long discussion ensued, and the delegation decided that since Admiral Dang was "a paper admiral," it must have assurance of an admiral in the regular navy, such as Admiral Wen Shude, who was in command of the neutral ships anchored in Deep Bay. If they could receive a letter of assurance signed by Admiral Wen and forwarded through the British consul general, they would accept the terms. Norman then contacted the British to have the letter drawn up and signed by the Chinese admirals Dang and Wen. Once that was done, the *Yongfeng* relaxed its activities.

On the following day Mr. Samuel Wong, a Chinese with an American passport who had been intimately connected with Sun Yat-sen, delivered twenty thousand dollars to the *Yongfeng* as partial payment of the crew's back pay. The hostages were then released and the officers agreed to submit to the orders of Admiral Wen.

This incident marked the end of the First Squadron's support of Sun and the revolution. In 1923 Admiral Wen took the vessels north to Qingdao, where he changed the name of the squadron back to the Beiyang Fleet and joined forces with the northern warlord Wu Beifu.[19] Meanwhile, the Second Squadron remained on the Yangzi River serving successive warlords. In Fujian the Training Squadron had become a semi-private navy that answered only to Admiral Yang Shuzhuang. This state of affairs existed until 1928, when Chiang K'ai-shek captured Beijing and set up the Nationalist government at Nanjing.

CHIANG K'AI-SHEK VERSUS THE FUJIAN NAVAL CLIQUE

Once the new government was established, Chiang encountered traditional problems with the navy. Although his conquest of China had resulted in the reunification of the three fleets, he found that the navy was once again firmly controlled from Fujian. In fact, the naval leadership had "sat out" the northern upheaval, waiting until the autumn of 1927 to extend tentative support to Chiang. When the generalissimo promulgated an outline calling for a new government system, the Fujianese were furious. Not only did the plan do away with the Navy Ministry, but it made the navy a department under the War Ministry.[20]

The Fujian navy clique viewed the system as an attempt to destroy their already weak political position, and they tried to counter the proposal with one of their own. This involved the traditonal method of drawing up an elaborate reorganization scheme. In 1928 the three leading Fujian admirals, Yang Shuzhuang (commander in chief), Chen Shaokuan (commander of the Second Squadron), and Chen Jiliang (commander of the First Squadron), submitted a plan calling for the expenditure of about 69 million dollars over two years to expand and improve the navy.[21]

Chiang K'ai-shek ignored the Fujian submission and in December 1928 slashed the navy's already austere monthly budget from five hundred thousand to two hundred fifty thousand dollars.[22] The Fujian naval leaders held a series of emergency meetings, where they decided to pressure Chiang by having the commanders of the First and Second squadrons submit their resignations.

The generalissimo could not afford to have the navy defect, so he used an old ploy to gain time. He authorized the formation of a Chinese naval mission to go abroad and "investigate naval conditions" in Japan, the United States, and Europe.[23] The mission was to be headed by a Fujian admiral, Tu Xigui, who, with the usual naval entourage, would be gone for about one year. Chiang promised that upon Tu's return he would review the admiral's recommendations and make necessary changes.

Obviously, Chiang K'ai-shek was stalling the navy while he tried to deal with more pressing problems. He still had to contend with several powerful warlords who continued to challenge his authority, and the Communists were beginning to reorganize under a new leader, Mao Zedong. Additionally, Japan was becoming aggressive in Manchuria, which it would seize in 1931.

In the face of these challenges, Chiang neutralized the one navy officer who could rally the navy against him, Admiral Chen Shaokuan. He approved the formation of navy ministry and brought Chen to Nanjing to organize it.[24] By this move, Chiang effectively kept Chen from having close dealings with the fleets.

Life at the capital soon became depressing to the fiery little admiral. He was given only eighty-six thousand dollars to operate the ministry, and fleet funds were similarly reduced.[25] In 1933 the three aging cruisers, the *Haiqi, Haichen*, and *Chenghe*, defected to the still semiautonomous provincial government at Canton. For two years the officers and crews engaged in piracy and smuggling activities, until Chen was finally able to muster enough power to force their surrender in 1935.[26] Naturally, upon the vessels' return to Nanjing, all was forgiven.

Chen also had other troubles in Nanjing. In 1933 impeachment charges were brought against him for supposedly having assisted Japanese expansion in Shanghai. The charges were subsequently dropped, but Chen's once promising career was badly tarnished. To make matters worse, Chiang K'ai-shek was openly challenging the Fujian navy clique; he rushed large numbers of naval cadets through his Nanjing academy and placed them aboard ships and on the navy staffs. In 1937 Chiang added insult to injury when he sent the admiral off to London to attend the coronation of King George VI. While Chen was in Europe, Japan and China went to war. Within several months nearly the entire Chinese navy had been sunk by Japanese air attacks. By the time Chen Shaokuan returned to China, his command no longer existed.

CHAPTER 11

THE NAVY AND FOREIGN RELATIONS, 1912–37: PART I

Internal bickering was not all that occupied the Chinese navy during this period. Relations with foreign countries engaged its attention as well. While the Chinese revolution had successfully thrown out the Manchus, other foreigners remained and continued to enjoy special privileges and the rights of extraterritoriality.* The principal foreign powers in China were Great Britain, the United States, Russia, Germany, and Japan. Each had vested interests on the mainland, which meant that they were often at odds trying to improve their political, commercial, and military advantages.

Subtle changes were at work, however. While China's government came close to disintegration, the Kuomintang party of Sun Yat-sen held out the promise of overturning unequal treaties. Sun's strong appeal to Chinese nationalism in the 1920s coincided with new attitudes in Europe and America that were critical of imperialism. (Asian regional powers, however, eyed China hungrily, as will be discussed in the next chapter.) Thus, just as Chiang K'ai-shek was succeeding in unifying China under the Kuomintang banner, other impressive gains were being made by the Chinese in reclaiming full autonomy.

China's struggle for autonomy and modernization was complicated by an endless series of internal and external conflicts over power and influence. China's navy, while a minor factor in internal politics, neverthe-

---

*Consciously or unconsciously, the Chinese thought foreigners acted like conquerors in a vassal state. China still lived in the shadow of humiliation cast by the zenophobic Boxer Rebellion of 1900–1901. The provisions of the Boxer Protocol, signed on 7 September 1901, included

1. The destruction of forts near Tianjin and the insurance of free communication between Beijing and the sea

2. The occupation by the powers of certain strategic points, including Tianjin, to ensure communication

3. Assent by the Chinese government to negotiations modifying treaties of commerce and navigation

4. Improvement of river channels leading to Tianjin and Shanghai

5. The transformation of the Zongli Yamen into the Ministry of Foreign Affairs, which would rank above all other Chinese ministries

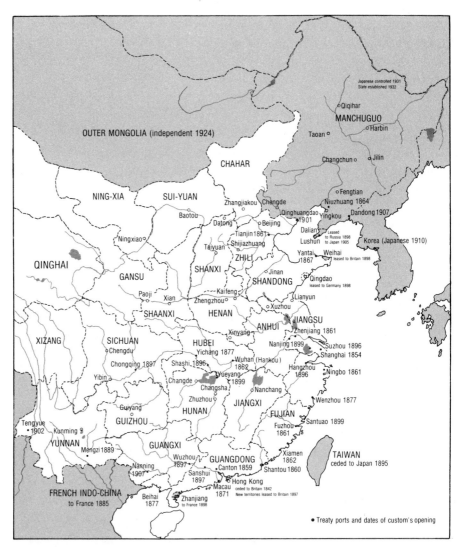

Foreign influences in China. This map shows the many areas of foreign encroachment in nineteenth- and early twentieth-century China.

less remained a principal focal point among all the antagonists. The adjective that best describes China's navy in this period is *potential*. As already seen, it possessed the potential for sustaining the revolution, and no matter how outmoded it was, naval power never failed to awe most Chinese.

Foreign investors and politicians were also attracted by naval potential. The Chinese navy offered the possibility of high-stakes contracts. It was also a force whose allegiance and influence might be useful to whichever foreign power was successful enough to win its support. As a result of this situation, several Chinese tendencies resurfaced. The proliferation of foreign armaments salesmen enabled the Chinese to manipulate contracts both for their psychological and material value; it encouraged as well a Chinese inclination to feign the promise of greater expectations. Also, the navy tried once again to seek quick results at the expense of practical, step-by-step development.

China's naval leaders, particularly those at the Navy Ministry, relished the game that ensued. Whether being courted by foreign armaments contractors or concocting endless schemes to rebuild the navy, the bankrupt admirals played marvelously well. They indeed were their fathers' sons, knowing fully well how to employ the age-old tactic of using foreigners to control foreigners.

GREAT BRITAIN

From 1912 to 1931, Britain's concessions in China were considerable. It maintained the leading position in shipping in Chinese trade; it continued to oversee the Maritime Customs and the Jiangnan Dockyard; it was first in Shanghai and the rich Yangzi Valley in business and banking; it possessed the island of Hong Kong, whose importance to Asian commerce grew steadily; and it still retained its leasehold on the ports of Weihai, Xiamen, and Jinjiang.

Britain's power in China was endangered, however. By the mid-1920s there was considerable anti-British sentiment, and both the Kuomintang and Communists fomented incidents in 1925 and 1926 that resulted in the boycott and seizure of British businesses. Clashes occurred and, in a conciliatory move, the British government gave up the aforementioned port leaseholds. By 1931 Great Britain's influence in China had eroded significantly as London's attention was becoming more and more occupied by events in Europe.

BRITISH CONTRACTS

In the years prior to World War I, Britain retained a strong interest in assisting the Chinese navy. John Brown and Company still had Edmund Backhouse lobbying in Beijing, and in 1911–12 the company engaged a Lieutenant Edward Boyle, RN, to be their agent in Asia. In January 1913 Boyle wrote the shipbuilding firm that China wanted to buy eight *Town*-class battle cruisers. Rumors of this had reached Tokyo and the Japanese were strongly opposed to such a sale.* Boyle urged the company to consider selling the Chinese a fleet of eight smaller seagoing vessels that would at least "enable the Chinese government to gain face and show the flag in ports where there are large Chinese communities who seldom if ever see a Chinese man-of-war."[1]

Although Boyle and Backhouse kept trying, only a few small contracts developed. A year later the *United Service Gazette* published a strong condemnation of China's hesitant naval policies that temporarily ended Britain's interest in aiding the Chinese navy.

> There could be no greater or more striking example of the shifting and uncertain nature of the policy of the Chinese Government, during the last 50 years, than the wobbling manner in which the affairs of its navy have been conducted by those in authority, whether under the Dynasty or under the Republic. Millions of taels have been absolutely wasted in the giving and subsequent cancelling of orders to build warships, provide naval works and equip naval bases. All nations which build ships have had a taste of the yellow man's shiftiness and untrustworthiness in nearly everything that concerns his fleet of warships. At least half-a-dozen missions of British naval officers and petty officers have from time to time been sent to the Far East to lick the Chinese Navy into shape and set up some sort of honest and reliable administration. They have one and all, in the end, come home discomfited. When the Republic was formed it was hoped by the best friends of China that honesty and straightforwardness might prevail. There may be a gain in this direction, but uncertainty and wobbling still form a part of their policy in handling their naval affairs. The mission which was engaged has not started, the order for the best part of the last batch of warships has been cancelled, and the money is to be spent on merchant ships, and all is once again weakness and confusion in the Chinese Navy. Contracts are being kept, as the President of the Republic promised they should be, but at a great sacrifice to the Chinese public. In fact, China appears to have yet to learn that she cannot become a big world power, in present conditions, unless she possesses a war fleet commensurate with her sea interests.[2]

THE TYLER EPISODE

The *United Service Gazette*'s words were a bit hypocritical in light of an episode involving the ubiquitous William Tyler.[3] Tyler had returned to his old job with the Maritime Customs, but he retained many close contacts in the Chinese admiralty. Tyler openly expressed admiration for Yuan Shikai, while dismissing Sun Yat-sen and the Kuomintang as a bunch of "agitators."[4] To Tyler the situation clearly called for Yuan to squash the political opposition, thereby enhancing Britain's trade position in China. Tyler's opportunity to involve himself in this troubled period came in 1913, during the so-called second revolution.

In the spring of that year, nationwide elections were held and the Kuomintang came away from the polls with a wide majority of seats in the house and senate. Such successes so upset Yuan Shikai that he took the

---

*In 1902 Britain and Japan had formed the Anglo-Japanese Alliance to thwart Russia. Three years later Tokyo and London renewed the alliance, which was to run ten more years. This was the cause of Boyle's concern for Japan's negative attitude in the matter of warship sales to China.

William F. Tyler. Mr. Tyler, a British subject, served the Chinese navy in various capacities from about 1893 to 1920. His adventures are detailed in a book aptly entitled *Pulling Strings in China*. (Courtesy of Constable and Company, London.)

drastic step of assassinating a potential rival. Additionally, he ordered his army and the navy south to reassert control over the provinces below the Yangzi River.

In Fujian Province, the military strongman, Sun Daoren, supported Yuan Shikai, but he remained at the same time a member of the Kuomintang, as did most of the military leaders who ran the surrounding southern provinces. When Yuan's forces clashed with the Kuomintang's army in July, Sun began to equivocate in his support of Yuan. Subsequently he declared his independence, along with several other southern provinces. This action triggered another break within the navy, whose main units were anchored near the Jiangnan Arsenal at Shanghai. These ships were commanded by Li Dingxin.*

* Admiral Li was a backer of the constitutional monarchists. He was born in Fujian in 1861 and attended the Fuzhou Naval Academy's English school. He then went to Greenwich where he stayed for six years. During that time he cruised aboard a British naval vessel to the Indian Ocean and the United States. Upon his return to China he was promoted to lieutenant and assigned to the *Dingyuan*, where he came to know William Tyler as a close friend. After the war of 1894, his career slowed until he became the chief of the Martial Law Department of the Navy Ministry in 1910. After the revolution he became commander of the Yangzi Squadron with the rank of rear admiral. Although an able and progressive naval leader, Li was ambitious and easily swayed by the power politics of the time.[5]

On 16 July 1913 Li called a meeting aboard the Chinese flagship at the Jiangnan Arsenal to discuss battle plans. The arsenal was thought to be in danger of being overrun by the anti-Yuan army, which was busy enlisting sympathy among the troops and sailors of Yuan's Beiyang forces at Shanghai. At the meeting Li was confronted by two commanding officers who placed their pistols on the wardroom table and declared that the navy ought to join with the Kuomintang in the attack on the arsenal. Li stalled. He realized that he was quickly losing control of the situation, since many crew members openly sympathized with the commanding officers' demands.

The next day, Li was contacted by Tyler, who had learned that something was brewing aboard the ships. He found out from Li that the situation looked grave and that, should the fleet defect, the Kuomintang would control the Yangzi River. Tyler then asked the admiral if money would help. Li claimed that "money would save any situation in China."[6] He informed Tyler that the Kuomintang was offering to pay the crews two months' worth of back salary. One million taels (six hundred thousand dollars) was the amount that Li estimated was needed.

Tyler immediately departed the ship and proceeded to the International Commission of Bankers, where he met with Mr. A.G. Stephen, manager of the Hong Kong and Shanghai Bank. After a long explanation of the situation, Tyler convinced Stephen to send a cable to the home office requesting funds be taken from customs revenue to pay off the crews.

The next day Tyler returned to the Jiangnan Arsenal, where he was briefed by R.B. Mauchan, the Scottish engineer-manager of the dockyard. Mauchan, a man of quick temper and little sympathy for the rebels, introduced Tyler to Admiral Zheng Rucheng, who commanded a force of marines protecting the arsenal. Zheng, who himself had no sympathy for the Kuomintang, was soon plotting with Tyler how to best use the money.

That afternoon Tyler met with Admiral Sir Thomas Jerram aboard HMS Newcastle. They were joined by the British consul general, who was greatly agitated by Tyler's bold efforts to buy off the Chinese naval fleet. Despite the official's forebodings, permission was given to Tyler to be the administrator of a fund that totaled two hundred fifty thousand taels. The next day the inspector general of customs wired Tyler that the latter was free to act at his own "discretion."

Tyler returned to the arsenal to meet with Zheng and Li. He told them that he had enough money to pay the wages and that a meeting must be called aboard the flagship to inform the crews and prevent the rebel officers from taking over the ships. He required both Zheng and Li to maintain a ledger of how the money was expended. In Tyler's words, "the scheme worked like a clock; there was never a hitch or a doubt."[7] The ships remained loyal to Yuan and the arsenal was saved from the Kuomintang, despite several weeks of shelling by the rebels. Tyler proudly recalled how he passed progress reports on the fighting to Beijing via Stephen. Rear Admiral Li was rewarded several weeks later with a promotion to full admiral.

THE BRITISH NAVAL MISSION, 1929–34

After 1911 small contingents of Chinese naval officers did continue to receive training in England. However, other events, including war and political change in Europe and the spread of warlordism in China, prevented the British from further serious wooing of the Chinese navy. In 1928, however, the reunification of the navy under the pro-British Fujian naval clique offered a new opportunity for the British, who were anxious to develop some rapport with Chiang K'ai-shek's newly formed Nanjing government. This suited the Chinese navy, which, as usual, was anxiously looking for foreign aid to refill its empty coffers and maybe provide some new ships. (Chiang K'ai-shek had cut the navy's budget severely during this period.)

Following a year of intense negotiation, an Anglo-Chinese naval agreement was concluded between Admiral Yang Shuzhuang and Sir Miles Lampson, the British minister to China. The pact included the following key provisions:

1. If China became engaged in hostilities against another power or powers, the members of the British naval mission could not be required to take part in any belligerent operations.

2. In the event of hostilities between China and any other country, the contract was to be terminated if either the Chinese government or British government requested it.

3. The British head of mission was to have direct access to the Chinese minister of the navy and act as his advisor on all matters connected with the mission and on any other matters as requested by the minister of the navy.

4. Twenty Chinese officers were to go to Britain for advanced naval training.

5. The Chinese government pledged itself to keep secret such confidential matters as the head of the mission indicated.

6. No British officer or rating, while in the service of the Chinese government, could be called upon actively to take part in the suppression of disorder or rebellion.

7. The Chinese government declared its intention in the near future to place substantial orders in Great Britain or Northern Ireland for the construction of ships for the Chinese navy.[8]

Although the British naval mission continued to function until 1936, nothing substantive resulted. In fact, British reentry into the Chinese naval-aid game may have been made only for intelligence-gathering purposes, for at that time Chiang K'ai-shek, who was no friend of the British, had begun hiring a number of German military advisors to help him deal with a succession of warlord and Communist rebellions.[9] As Chiang's army became more and more Germanic in its organization and operations, the British grew ever more curious. In fact, when Chiang expressed interest in purchasing German submarines and in 1934 hired a German naval advisor, the British decided to extend the naval mission's contract.*[10] Later the senior British advisor confided to the U.S. naval attaché that he was doing "about the same thing" as his German counterpart.[11]

THE UNITED STATES

United States policy toward China underwent two changes in the decade preceding the Chinese revolution.[12] In the early phase, U.S. Secretary of State John Hay created the Open Door, which was intended to preserve equal commercial opportunity in China although equal investment opportunity did not exist. Later, Philander C. Knox became the secretary of state. Being a practitioner of dollar diplomacy, he pressed hard for both equal commercial and investment opportunity, and offered little resistance to those who advocated the sale of weapons to the Chinese.

THE BETHLEHEM STEEL CONTRACT

During Knox's tenure as secretary of state, the Bethlehem Steel Company convinced the Chinese to sign the sizeable naval contract in 1911. The contract was not canceled when the Manchu government collapsed, and the story of Sino-American naval relations for the next two decades revolved around whether successive Chinese governments would honor the contract. Struggles between American interests precipitated anti-American sentiment among the British and Japanese.

The principal American agent representing Bethlehem's interest in China was Commander Gillis, the U.S. naval attaché. Gillis had been instrumental in gaining the 1911 contract for Bethlehem, an activity that required him to take a leave of absence from the U.S. Navy. Although the U.S. Justice Department deemed such practices unlawful, Gillis was recalled to active duty in 1912 and sent to Beijing as the assistant naval attaché. In addition to his normal duties, he also had instructions "to continue his assistance to American firms."[13] Two years later, Gillis officially retired but stayed on in China with six thousand dollars a year paid by a number of U.S. shipbuilding firms, including Bethlehem and the Electric Boat Company in Groton, Connecticut.

On 16 December 1913 the Chinese cabinet agreed to honor the 1911 Bethlehem contract. The American company sent its senior vice president, Archibald Johnston, to China work with Gillis. The two went to Fujian, where they visited with Admiral Liu Guanxiong. During the visit and subsequent tour of the Chinese coast, Johnston and Gillis discovered that the Chinese navy no longer wanted to order warships. Instead, they were interested in constructing a naval base. Working quickly, the Americans proposed two plans to Admiral Liu—one costing 20.7 million dollars and the other 46 million dollars. The proposal named Sansha Bay in Fujian

---

*The German naval advisor was Captain Ortwin Rave, an ordnance expert and specialist in coastal defense. Rave's activities included drawing up defense plans for the coastal areas around Nanjing, Shanghai, and Ningbo.[14]

Midshipman Irvin V. Gillis. Commander Gillis served as the first U.S. naval attaché in Peking from 1900 to 1912. He retired in China and pursued a career as a naval armaments salesman. (Courtesy of Mrs. Raymond Stone, U.S. Naval Historical Center, Washington, D.C.)

as the best site for a Chinese naval base, and requested that U.S. naval advisors be employed for the project to be successful.

Upon their return to Beijing in January, Johnston and Gillis encountered serious obstacles to the plan. No one could be found to finance the Chinese bonds being put up as security. Rumors were circulating about the Chinese negotiating with Britain for naval advisors (China feared a Japanese backlash if it employed American naval advisors).[15] Moreover, Gillis and Johnston were shocked to learn that the Chinese were having cruisers built in Austria-Hungary.[16]

Gillis believed that Britain was behind most of Bethlehem's contract problems. When Johnston returned to the United States, Gillis wrote to him that the British would "exert themselves more than ever to do us in the eye if they can."[17] His suspicions were temporarily forgotten when World War I broke out. The Bethlehem contract was temporarily suspended by the U.S. Navy Department and the State Department.

FURTHER NEGOTIATIONS

However, in January 1915 the Chinese again whetted Gillis's interest. They approached him with a proposal for the United States to sponsor

Chinese officers to go to America and observe the manufacture and operation of submarines. By the summer, Gillis had arranged for the Electric Boat Company to host a Chinese admiral, Wei Han, and thirty Chinese officer-students at New London, Connecticut.*

One modern scholar comments that, upon his arrival, Wei Han "delighted company officials by announcing that China needed a fleet of two hundred submarines."[18] Such comments did indeed greatly excite Gillis and the Electric Boat Company. The U.S. Navy Department also began to seriously study the advantages of training the Chinese. Soon Secretary of the Navy Josephus Daniels approved Chinese training aboard U.S. submarines. He extracted from the Chinese a promise that any classified information acquired during their training would not be divulged to any other foreign navies.

At this point serious discussions got under way with the Chinese for the purchase of U.S.-built submarines. Bethlehem Steel also reentered the picture because it worked closely with the Electric Boat Company on submarine construction. Bethlehem's president, Charles M. Schwab, informed Wei Han that he would assist in the process of financing a Chinese purchase of about twelve vessels. Schwab next obtained a tentative agreement with the National City Bank in San Diego to loan China the money without collateral. This amounted to some 6 million dollars loaned against unsecured Chinese bonds. Electric Boat was wary of Japanese reaction, however, and the firm considered a "back-door" plan whereby Chile would order the submarines and then deliver them to China.

All this maneuvering was for naught when Yuan Shikai attempted to restore the monarchy. As the political situation deteriorated in China, the various parties to the submarine scheme began to lose interest until finally, in 1916, the idea was dropped.

One last effort was made by China and the United States to conclude a mutual naval arrangement. In 1921 the new Chinese navy minister, Li Dingxin, notified Gillis that China again wanted to discuss the 1911 Bethlehem contract. When word reached Washington, the U.S. State Department acted strongly in opposition to the idea. John V.A. MacMurray, the chief of Far Eastern Affairs, sent a memo to his superior, U.S. Secretary of State Charles Evans Hughes, stating his case.

> The Chinese Navy is scarcely a serious Governmental Department; it is very largely the perquisite of a small group of officials from Fujian Province, who have no purpose—no conception, indeed—of making it a national service. They have in the past given contracts and other favors, on terms profitable to themselves, to various nationalities in turn; and have later sought by creating issues among the several interested powers to evade fulfillment of the obligations they entered into as inducements for making such agreements.[19]

---

*Wei Han's background and career differed somewhat from those of the high-ranking Chinese naval officers so far introduced. Born in Fuzhou, he attended the Fuzhou Naval Academy's French school and studied at Cherbourg in 1878. After two years he went to Germany to observe the construction of the *Dingyuan*. By 1887 he was in charge of construction at the Fuzhou Dockyard. Thereafter, as an engineer-admiral, he held posts at various dockyards and arsenals. Fluent in English and French, he was promoted to vice admiral in 1912.[20]

CONSEQUENCES OF THE WASHINGTON CONFERENCE

Despite MacMurray's criticism, secret negotiations did proceed once again. The talks were slow, however, and dragged on for three years. One reason for caution centered around the Washington Conference of 1921, which produced a series of settlements having important naval implications in the Pacific. These included

1. The abolishment of the Anglo-Japanese Alliance.

2. A naval agreement that limited capital ship construction to a 5:5:3 ratio for Britain, the United States, and Japan. An important proviso was that America and Britain agreed to no further development of naval bases east of Singapore or west of Hawaii.

3. Japanese agreement to withdraw from Shandong and the northeast Asian mainland, including eastern Siberia. An exception was Korea.

4. A Nine-Power Treaty that recognized the Open Door and the territorial and administrative integrity of China. Future conferences were to be convened to discuss abrogation of the treaty system in China.

On the surface these agreements were favorable to China, but other events spelled disaster for acquiring naval aid. A week after the conference adjourned, in February 1922, Admiral Li contacted the U.S. naval attaché in Peking to raise the question of whether the United States would build warships for China and train Chinese on American ships and in American schools. Thus, even in the face of the Washington Conference, Li blithely pressed for a U.S. commitment to aid the Chinese navy.

Together with Bethlehem, the U.S. General Board offered strong arguments in support of the Chinese, but the U.S. State Department remained adamantly opposed. MacMurray, for example, argued that "China was a country in turmoil and nearly bankrupt, and America had no business lending millions of dollars to provide funds for the naval clique to squander in playing for position with the strong military factions."[21]

The Chinese Navy Ministry was not unaware of the opposition in Washington, and took steps through American contacts in Beijing to assure the United States that China's intention was to create a credible navy for protecting foreign commercial interests. In a memorandum to Archibald Johnston, still the senior vice president at Bethlehem, the ministry admitted that the Chinese navy had "been drawn into politics," but that with foreign assistance the navy could again become an instrument for law and order under civil control.[22] The ministry did not address the question of ship construction by size and number, nor did it offer any further suggestions on how it was to be maintained.

While these exchanges were going on, the Chinese had no way of knowing that Secretary Hughes was acting to stop all foreign naval assistance to China. On 4 May 1922 Hughes sent the powers that had attended the Washington Conference a memoire that spelled out the Chinese request for naval aid through the Bethlehem contract. It stated that the United States had no intention of honoring this contract, providing the other powers agreed not to do the same if China approached them. Japan was again indignant over the reintroduction of the Bethlehem contract, claiming that such an action was not consistent with the Washington Conference. Within two months the powers agreed to an accord that forbade providing naval assistance to China.

The Chinese Navy Ministry regarded the American action as insulting and canceled all further negotiations. Gillis castigated the State Department's interference, calling it a "supine action" that deprived America of an "opportunity to control the Chinese Navy."[23] Indeed, the episode postponed attempts by the U.S. Navy to involve itself in Chinese naval affairs until after World War II.

CHAPTER 12

THE NAVY AND FOREIGN RELATIONS, 1912–37: PART II

Following the Opium War, Russian expansionism along China's northern borders resulted in several treaties that were disadvantageous to the Chinese. These treaties had certain maritime implications. For example, in the Treaty of Aigun in 1858, the Chinese yielded to Russian demands that China recognize the left bank of the Amur River as being Russian territory, while the territory between the right bank of the Wusuli (Ussuri) River and the sea was held to be common to each country. Two years later, Russia acquired this last property in the Treaty of Peking.

After the conclusion of the Sino-Japanese War of 1895, Russia colluded with Germany and France, depriving Japan of the Liaodong Peninsula. A year later, the czar obtained the right to construct the Chinese Eastern Railway through China's northeastern provinces of Jilin (Kirin) and Heilongjiang. This railroad served as a straight route connecting Chita, Russia, with Vladivostok. There was a problem with Vladivostok, however: heavy ice in the winter hampered merchant and naval operations. Thus, in 1898 Russia obtained a twenty-five-year lease of the Liaodong Peninsula and the right to build a railway from a point on the Chinese Eastern Railway to its newly acquired ice-free ports of Port Arthur (naval) and Dalian (merchant). The railroad was completed in 1902.

Following the Boxer Rebellion, Russia continued its expansion and seemed bent on annexing all of Manchuria. This led to a confrontation with Japan, which also had its designs on Manchuria. War broke out on 8 February 1904, when the Japanese navy delivered a surprise attack on Port Arthur. Subsequently, Japan destroyed Russia's Baltic Fleet in the famous Sea of Japan naval battle of May 1905.

The Treaty of Portsmouth, signed in September 1905, passed most of Russia's gains and claims in Manchuria to Japan.* The only thing Russia

*The principal provisions of the treaty were
1. The recognition of China's sovereignty in Manchuria
2. Russia's transfer to Japan, with the consent of China, of the lease of Port Arthur,

retained was de facto administrative control over the northern section of the Chinese Eastern Railway.

Japan's defeat of Russia was a bitter experience for the czar and a humiliation from which imperial Russia never recovered. Late in 1917 the Russian Revolution took place and temporarily paralyzed Russian activities in Siberia and north Manchuria. Once the Bolsheviks gained control and Soviet Russia was created, a new policy toward China was announced: the Soviets declared all prior czarist treaties to be null and void.

Two years passed. Then in August 1922 a Soviet envoy, Adolph Joffe, arrived in Beijing seeking to reestablish diplomatic relations. Rebuffed by the warlord regime, Joffe went south and met Sun Yat-sen. He won Sun's friendship when he agreed that Soviet-style Communism was not suitable for China and that Soviet Russia was supportive of Sun's goals of national unification and full independence for China.

Several months later the Beijing warlords welcomed the Soviets. A treaty was concluded calling for the resumption of relations and the withdrawal of Soviet troops from that region. The treaty recognized Chinese sovereignty in Outer Mongolia. Also, the Soviets recognized China's sovereignty over the Chinese Eastern Railway. The latter concession, however, was a moot point, for in 1922 the Manchurian warlord, Zhang Zuolin, had declared the autonomy of the three eastern provinces, a modus vivendi that the weak Beijing regime was forced to accept. In 1924 the Soviets recognized Zhang Zuolin's authority in Manchuria by concluding an agreement with the anti-Bolshevik warlord. The agreement with Zhang was essentially the same as that concluded earlier with Beijing. A main feature of the agreement was the recognition of equal rights of navigation on border rivers and maintenance of the boundary line.

THE NAVAL SEQUEL

As early as 1924 the Soviets began formulating plans to penetrate China's navy. No partiality was to be shown, either, as both Sun Yat-sen's Canton navy and the major forces subordinate to the northern warlords were to be targets of agitation.[1] The former navy was primarily manned by Guangxi and Guangdong natives whom Sun had recruited from the local Seaman's Union.

The Soviet scheme for the forces dominated by the Fujianese was outlined in a classified document taken by Zhang Zuolin's troops when they broke into the Soviet embassy in Beijing in 1927. The unidentified Soviet agent charged with infiltrating the Chinese navy reported, in part, as follows:

> Enlisted men on board the cruiser *Hairong* always display a *spirit of protest*, and we must admit that it is possible to put our expectations in this phenomenon. We positively must make use of the last incident with this

Dalian, and adjacent territory and territorial waters, and all rights, privileges, and concessions connected with or forming part of this lease

3. Russia's transfer to Japan of the railway between Changchun and Port Arthur and all its branch lines, together with all rights, privileges, and properties appertaining thereto

ship, in order to increase still more their power and resistance.* We have, however, to bear constantly in mind the fact that they set a great value upon the population of the province and therefore, in order to carry on the agitation work on board this ship, it is absolutely necessary to find for the purpose natives of their own province, i.e., Fujian. Recently *principles of a narrow patriotism* were very much in vogue among the personnel of the headquarters of the navy, and I consider this phenomenon as very dangerous and worth thinking about. In my opinion during the period when there are no military operations, it is necessary to carry on only a slow *agitation work*, and I consider that now our principal work must be in *the educational organs*, in order to create there sincere and steady elements. Special attention must be paid to the development of the nuclei of the "New Seaman's League" and the work must be started, first of all, in these nuclei. [Italics added by agent][2]

The Soviet agent's plan went on to give background details on all senior Chinese naval officers as well as judgments on whether they had Communist tendencies and could be influenced. The fighting ability and condition of each Chinese warship was carefully documented.

In this plan, the Soviet estimate of Sun Yat-sen's Canton navy reflected a feeling that political conversion would be difficult to achieve. For one thing, corruption was so rampant that most of the officers and crews were doing quite well by smuggling and taking bribes. One ship, the *Zhongshan*, was described as follows:

There is no "opening" through which it would be possible to approach the crew of this ship with political propaganda, because both soldiers and sailors are extremely ferocious and cruel in character and absolutely refuse to receive any political training. They are for the most part natives of Guangsi, and the spirit of "provincialism" is very strong in them. For many years they have been following the "path of counter-revolution." They took away opium, enriched themselves at the expense of the people, and there was hardly anything which they did not make use of, always for the purpose of "lining their own pockets." They gradually became rich men and with such men it is very difficult to talk about revolution. At present the Nationalist Government has to defray all the expenses in connection with the maintenance of this ship in silver dollars.[3]

Despite such gloomy estimates, the Soviets were able to infiltrate Sun Yat-sen's Canton government. In 1924 Sun founded the Whampoa (Huang-pu) Military Academy and appointed Chiang K'ai-shek his director. At the time, an accommodation had been reached between the Chinese Communist party and the Kuomintang whereby they closely cooperated in attempting to put together a military force capable of marching north and defeating the warlords. In fact, Zhou Enlai, one of the most important Chinese leaders in the twentieth century, was the deputy director of Chiang's political department. Foreign Communists also held important positions at Huangpu.[4] For instance, in the first several years of its opera-

*In 1924 a change of commanding officers on the cruiser *Hairong* led the Fujianese crew to mutiny because the new captain was from Jiangsu and "bullied" the enlisted men. The crew on the cruiser *Yingrui* mutinied in sympathy for the *Hairong*. A series of resignations and desertions by officers followed and the matter was cleared up only when a Fujianese captain took command of the *Hairong*.[5]

tion, Chiang K'ai-shek had a contingent of influential Soviet military advisors at Canton.

Included in the Soviet group were two naval advisors, Andrei S. Bubnov and an "Admiral" Smirnov. Known by his Chinese name Qisangke (Kisanke), Smirnov was a surly and argumentative individual who knew little about naval matters. A Soviet inspecting team later labeled Smirnov as a person not working "with a full sincerity for the benefit of the Chinese Navy."[6]

Chiang K'ai-shek intensely disliked Bubnov. The Chinese leader was most unhappy when Bubnov temporarily became head of the Soviet advisory group in November 1925.[7] Chiang, in fact, was beginning to suspect that the Soviets and Chinese Communists had more than cooperation with the Kuomintang on their minds.

The elevation of Bubnov led to the promotion of a Chinese Communist, Li Zhilong, to the head of the Canton navy. When Li attempted to cut back the navy's illicit smuggling operations, he may have unwittingly provided the opportunity Chiang K'ai-shek needed to severely limit Communist activities at Huangpu.[8]

As time passed, Li, Bubnov, and Smirnov were increasingly subjected to criticism by the navy at Canton. Many naval officers felt their jobs were in jeopardy as the Communists delved deeper into the navy's illegal activities.

Growing tension between the navy and Soviet mentors reflected general divisions of opinion at Canton. Rival groups abounded. After the Second National Congress of the Kuomintang in January 1926, leadership of the party was almost entirely in the hands of the Communists. Chiang K'ai-shek was now very much on his guard. On 16 February 1926 he removed all Soviets from their administrative posts. Ten days later he arrested the Chinese Canton garrison commander on charges of conspiracy with Bubnov.[9] When the left-leaning Wang Jingwei, Sun Yat-sen's successor, failed to take action against Bubnov, Chiang made up his mind to take control of Canton by staging a coup d'etat.*

At this point, the story of the coup d'etat becomes blurred. Apparently, on 18 March Li Zhilong, embarked aboard the *Zhongshan*, ordered the ship and a sister vessel, the *Baobi*, to get under way from Canton and proceed to Huangpu. Chiang K'ai-shek, in Canton, became extremely agitated when he learned of the unauthorized ship movement. According to Li, at about this same time Chiang learned that a Soviet military inspection team wanted to visit the *Zhongshan*. Thus, when Li phoned Chiang on 19 March, the generalissimo ordered him to return immediately to Canton so that the *Zhongshan* could be inspected by the Soviets.[10] Li's story is not consistent, however, for at that time Chiang had gone to see Wang Jingwei, to whom he made a plea for stronger action against the Communists. Chiang, in fact, was in no mood to receive visiting Soviet inspection teams. He made plans with two of his trusted army division commanders to take Canton by means of a coup the following day.

*Sun Yat-sen died unexpectedly on 12 March 1925.

That evening a tense Chiang K'ai-shek observed the *Zhongshan* tie up in front of the military officer's club at Canton with the crew apparently at general quarters. Chiang interpreted this as an attempt to kidnap him. He later wrote that he believed Li Zhilong and the Soviets intended to take him prisoner aboard the gunboat and sail to Vladivostok.[11]

There has been no evidence to substantiate Chiang K'ai-shek's suspicions about the kidnapping, but he did use the incident to justify the coup on the following day. The so-called March Twentieth Incident, in fact, was the beginning of the distintegration of the Kuomintang-Communist alliance. The final break would come the following year.

THE SINO-SOVIET CRISIS OF 1929

In the fall of 1929 a little-known naval engagement occurred on the Heilong (Amur) River between Chinese and Soviet riverine forces. The river action was part of a brush-fire border war between China and Russia that was precipitated when the new Chinese Manchurian warlord, Zhang Xueliang, tried to take over full control of the Chinese Eastern Railway.* The riverine action that resulted involved Admiral Shen Honglie, who was commander in chief of Zhang's Manchurian navy.

To the author's knowledge, details of the events have never been documented. The following description is a translated synopsis of a description provided orally by Shen Honglie to the Chinese naval historian Li Zhejin:

1. The Positions of the Chinese and Soviet Navies in the Battle of Dongjiang

The Jilin-Heilongjiang Defense Fleet of the Chinese navy had at that time the following vessels under my command: *Jiangheng* (displacement of 550 tons); *Liji* (166 tons); *Lisui* (170 tons); *Jiangping; Jiangan; Jiangqing;* and *Jiangtong.* At the time when the Russians launched the attack, I was on an inspection tour to the eight islands of Changshan at Bohai. When the news of the attack reached me, I immediately reinforced the fleet and ordered an alert. I then issued heavy guns and other military equipment. Along with other commanding officers, I then rushed to Harbin to conduct the battle in the front line on 9 August 1929.

The area around the junction of the Heilong, Sunghua, and the Wusuli (Ussuri) rivers was a marsh land. Chinese ships could use the shallow water area at any time but the [larger?] enemy's ships could not. The defense strategy was divided into two phases: defense on land and defense on the waters, with the naval vessels *Jiangheng, Liji,* and *Lisui* taking frontal positions. (The *Jiangheng* had the best firing power.) The other converted ships [merchant ships] were positioned in the junction area for reserve and defense. Heavy wooden guns were placed on board the ships *Jiangping, Jiangan,* and *Jiangtai* to fool the enemy. The junction was the first line of defense, equipped with torpedoes; obstacles were then placed in the rivers as the second line of defense. Sunken commercial ships were tied together to form a secret floating flotilla and hauled to the marsh land area to be hidden there to provide additional artillery strength. These concealed ramparts could be hauled to any place at will.

---

*Zhang Xueliang was Zhang Zuolin's son, who was assassinated in 1928.

The defense strategy on land was devised thus: The apex of the junction area could control the channel that the Russian ships used. This was to be achieved by having Chinese marines fire at them from the shore. In order to prevent surprise attacks by the enemy, a battalion of soldiers was positioned behind the river bank. Torpedo firing and observation stations were also constructed. The headquarters was established inside the town of Dongjiang. Russian planes were on reconnaissance missions during the war-preparation phase but the concealed ramparts were never discovered by the planes.

I then issued orders to be on constant alert and to fire back whenever the enemy attacked. The Russians, realizing their superior military strength, knew that our side would not be the first party to open fire. They were just anchored at the rivers and acted as if there was nothing going on. But our forces were constantly busy and on the alert, especially the sailors positioned in the marsh land area, for they were exposed to the bright sun and being attacked by mosquitoes and other pests. They wanted to attack the Russians and wished that the battle was over. However, they remained at their stations and waited.

2. How the Naval Battle Was Fought

On the morning of 12 October 1929, when the *Jiangsui* was sailing upstream toward the blockade line in the junction area, nine Russian vessels suddenly opened fire at the *Lisui*, and at the *Liji* and *Jiangping* anchored at the river. The *Jiangheng* had left its station for Fujing several days earlier. The bulk of the enemy's fire was aimed at the *Lisui*. The Russian planes were also attacking the *Jiangan* and *Jiangtai*. Because the Russians did not respect our firing power, they remained at the same anchored positions, firing randomly at our ships. Then our vessel *Liji* signaled the entire fleet to weigh anchor and attack, concentrating all their fire on the Russian ships. Thus was the beginning of the Sino-Soviet naval battle. The disguised *Jiangan* was the first ship to get under way and sail slowly toward the Russian vessels. The captain of the *Jiangan* had already calculated the distance to the anchored Russian ships, and his first salvo killed the commander of the enemy forces, their chief of general staff, and the captain of the ship on which they were embarked. After further concentrated firing, the Russian ship began to sink. The other Russian ships did not even know where the Chinese firing was coming from. Three other enemy vessels inflicted heavy losses by our concealed ramparts and gunboats. Our forces put up a tremendously fierce battle.

The *Liji* fought for a long hour but was sunk. The *Lisui* was badly damaged and one of its big guns was destroyed; it left the firing line with serious damages. The other vessels, the *Jiangping*, *Jiangan*, and *Jiangtai*, were originally merchant ships and had weak firing power and could not withstand the enemy's frontal attack. The captain of the *Jiangtai* was killed. The *Jiangan* received a direct hit and exploded. The *Jiangping* received a direct hit on the engine area and after the crew abandoned ship, she sank. The badly damaged enemy ships and our damaged ships remained at the battle area; the other slightly damaged vessels retreated. Thus the naval battle at Dongjiang ended.

Shortly thereafter the enemy troops captured Sanjiangkou [the junction area]. However, the junction was mined by our forces, so when the Russians landed there, quite a few enemy troops were killed. The enemy spent more than a half a month clearing up mines.

On 29 October 1929, the Soviet army and navy, combined with the air force, attacked Fujin Xian [county] located up river. At 1600 of the same day, five enemy vessels attacked Fujin. I, together with several staff officers, then went on board the *Jiangheng* and rushed to repulse the attack. Soviet planes in groups of six also attacked us but none of the bombs hit the ship. We fired at the planes with our heavy guns.

On the next day, our army's front line was broken by the enemy and we had to retreat toward the line of our blockade. The Soviet vessels and the land forces attempted to launch a combined frontal attack at our line of blockade. But with strong fire from the *Jiangheng*, the enemy did not succeed. However, we finally used up all our ammunition and had to sink the blockade line to impede the enemy's approach. The Soviet army finally captured Fujin and the enemy navy also used light vessels to enter the line of blockade. The Soviet forces then withdrew from the junction area, taking with them food and supplies from the county.

As both sides were preparing for more and bigger attacks, the three powers, Great Britain, France, and the United States, sent a communiqué on 3 December to China and the Soviet Union for a cease-fire to work out a peaceful solution of the dispute. China, at the time realizing that her frontiers were in great danger because several of her strategic areas had been captured by the Russians, and because of Japanese agitation in southern Manchuria as well as the continuing civil war, accepted the three great powers' mediation. Sino-Soviet negotiations were held at Khabarovsk and a protocol was signed on 22 December to end this Sino-Soviet war.

The casualties of the battle at Dongjiang were as follows: (1) on the Chinese side: the captain of the *Jiangtai* was killed; more than a hundred officers and men of the other ships and of the army were also killed; the *Liji*, *Jiangping*, and *Jiangan* were sunk; and the *Lisui* was damaged; and (2) on the Russian side: one naval vessel was sunk, three severely damaged, and four slightly damaged; two aircraft were shot down also; and more than a hundred officers and men were killed.[12]

JAPAN

The Soviet episode at Huangpu and the fighting in Manchuria made one thing clear: Soviet Russia under Lenin and Stalin retained the imperialist ambitions of the czars in northern China. That fact was not lost on Japan, whose expansionist interests in the region remained only lightly disguised.

Much of the background to Japan's involvement in China during this period has already been introduced. However, several incidents are worth noting to show what role China's navy played in Japanese calculations.

In 1914, for example, the Chinese First Squadron became involved in a minor protocol misunderstanding with the Japanese navy that nearly drew China into a naval war with Japan.[13] The cruiser *Haiqi* had gotten under way from Shanghai and was en route to its operating area, where it was to conduct routine drills at sea. As the cruiser cleared the mouth of the Yangzi, it encountered a Japanese warship heading up river. In accordance with international convention, the Japanese rendered a gun salute to the *Haiqi* and the Chinese cruiser returned the honors. The commander of the First Squadron, Lin Baoyi, counted thirteen puffs of smoke and so returned thirteen gun salutes. Afterward the Japanese vessel signaled the *Haiqi*, asking how many salute rounds the Chinese had fired. When the Chinese signaled thirteen, the Japanese complained that they were insulted, for they had fired fifteen rounds. The Japanese nearly went to general quarters over the incident, but instead departed the area in anger. The affair was subsequently elevated to the diplomatic level at Beijing, and Yuan Shikai was forced to extend an apology to the Japanese. Yuan ordered the *Haiqi* to get under way, locate the Japanese vessel in Shanghai, and render a fifteen-gun salute. Lin Baoyi did as ordered but the Japanese did not return the salute. This humiliation became a frequent topic of conversation in the Chinese navy and remained a sore point for years.

At this same time, Japan disregarded China's neutrality in World War I and sent troops ashore in Shandong Province to take control of German positions. When no Western denunciation followed, Japan pressed its advantage by delivering the infamous Twenty-one Demands to Yuan Shikai. The demands were divided into five groups and concerned the following points:

1. The settlement of the Shandong region, which Japan had recently occupied.

2. Defining Japan's position in southern Manchuria and eastern Inner Mongolia. Japan intended to secure from the Chinese government full recognition of Japan's "natural" position in these regions. Included was a demand for China to grant Japan a ninety-nine-year lease of Port Arthur and Dalian.

3. Safeguarding Japan's interest in the Hanyebing Company, an iron development in central China with which Japanese capitalists were closely identified.

4. Upholding China's territorial integrity by not permitting China to lease or cede any harbor, bay, or island along the coast to any other foreign power.

5. Control over the Chinese government. China was to agree to exclusive employment of Japanese advisors in nearly all spheres of trade and military organizations, including the police, arsenals, arms buying, and the development of Fujian Province.

The Chinese attempted to stall Japan and released the secret document in the press, hoping that the Western nations would intervene. Despite verbal condemnations of Japan, no foreign power took any further action to deter the Japanese. Following an ultimatum by Japan to the Chinese government on 7 May, Yuan Shikai capitulated and accepted the first four sets of demands.

There were several immediate results of Yuan's capitulation. First, the Bethlehem Company's plans for the construction of a Fujian naval base were postponed indefinitely. This suited the Japanese because the fifth group of demands was intended to halt American naval penetration of the province.[14] Secondly, eight Chinese naval officers and midshipmen were sent to Japan for naval training in 1918.[15] (By 1920, however, the Chinese had only two officers in Japan for training.) Thirdly, Japan succeeded in having a small naval advisory group assigned to the Chinese navy to instruct in wireless and flag signals. In fact, this group attempted to introduce Japanese as the official language of the Chinese navy.[16] Lastly, the Japanese assigned a naval historian, the only person doing historical research on China's naval past, to the Chinese Navy Ministry.[17]

In the 1920s Japan's policies toward China softened. The main reason for this was the development of a Japanese foreign policy based on internationalism, where cooperation with other nations was espoused. An indication of Japan's mellowed approach was its disinclination to take retribution against China when Chinese nationalism led to anti-Japanese violence and boycotts.

FURTHER COMPLICATIONS

By the late 1920s, however, change was in the air. Japan underwent a cultural and economic metamorphosis that inspired a new spirit of militarism. Friction began to mount as the Japanese tightened their already firm control of southern Manchuria, a move which openly worried Communist Russia.

The threat of resurgent Japanese militarism was on Chiang K'ai-shek's mind in 1927. At a cocktail party in Shanghai he and Admiral Mark Bristol, commander in chief of the U.S. Asiatic Fleet, had the following exchange:

> CHIANG K'AI-SHEK: We know that Americans have always been our friends and your country is the only one which is our friend today, and which wishes to see us a united nation. All the others have something to gain by keeping us disunited. Japan is our greatest enemy. Japan and Russia are trying to unite against us, but we can handle them with America's friendship and moral support. We realize that America cannot take any aggressive action to support us. We feel, however, that Japan is trying and may succeed in misleading America—in getting her to take some action that will harm both China and herself. The China problem is a problem of the Pacific, and will be the subject of a war unless China becomes united and ceases to be the disturbed center which it has been for several years. I may be fanatical on the subject, but I feel convinced that unless we can solve our problem within five years a great war is likely to follow.
>
> ADMIRAL BRISTOL: I have no fear of this because I have faith in the Chinese leaders, that they will now see that they cannot accomplish anything by acting independently, and that they must unite. When once united your greatest troubles will be over. Also the nations of the world wish to see you united. Lately there has been a noticeable change in that respect on the part of foreign nations generally.

Chiang K'ai-shek also believed in employing foreign advisors. Later in the party, he and Admiral Bristol again chatted.

> ADMIRAL BRISTOL: What do you consider your greatest need?
> CHIANG K'AI-SHEK: Foreign advisors. We find we make faster progress with foreign advisors.
> ADMIRAL BRISTOL: Since it is China's problem I think it should be worked out by the Chinese so that, although it may be slower, it would be a Chinese product when finished. With foreign advisors you are likely to develop an unnatural growth. There is also likely to develop jealousy and suspicion among foreign nations.

> CHIANG K'AI-SHEK: China is too slow and the time is too limited for the Chinese to work out this problem. Unless we are able to accomplish it in five years, I believe that a war in the Pacific will result.
>
> ADMIRAL BRISTOL: I believe the Chinese can and will unite in time to prevent this.
>
> CHIANG K'AI-SHEK: Technical advisors are necessary. There are a great many technical problems which the Chinese are entirely too slow in solving.[18]

Chiang's prediction was quite accurate. China did not unite. Although no formal war was declared, Japan and China skirmished intermittently from 1927 to 1931. For example, the Japanese leasehold over Dalian and Port Arthur denied the Chinese effective use of their two best northern ports. In 1929, therefore, China tried to set up a competitive commercial port at Huludao in the northern end of the Gulf of Bohai (Zhili). Japan immediately objected and the project was canceled.

There were other complications as well. Japanese maritime industries were expanding. By 1929 Japan's merchant fleet was third in the world. In fishing Japan led all nations. To meet the needs of a rapidly expanding population, the annual catch had become equal to about one-fourth of the world's total.[19] Part of Japan's total was acquired at the expense of China. Sleek, efficient Japanese trawlers sailed the Yellow and East China seas. Chinese fishermen, handicapped by the lack of capital and modern equipment, grew indignant over Japan's poaching. By 1928 Shen Honglie had to assign units of the northern fleet to fishery-protection patrols during the fishing season.[20] These duties continued until at least 1936.

Exacerbating the situation was the influx of Japanese to the Liaodong Peninsula. At Dalian, in 1928, the Japanese population swelled to nearly two-thirds that of the Chinese, and a large, efficient Japanese fishing industry sprang up to feed the people.

Pushed out by the Japanese, Chinese peasant-fishermen resorted to piracy and prowled the coast in alarming numbers, looking for defenseless merchant ships or fishing junks. Their attacks increased rapidly in the late 1920s. Japanese ships were favorite targets. In 1932 Japan's government published a paper condemning Chinese piracy. The report included some statistics that listed successful pirate attacks against foreign coastal steamers in the range of 30 to 500 tons.[21] In the years from 1926 to 1931, twenty-eight Japanese steamers sustained successful pirate attacks, whereas only eleven Chinese steamers were attacked.

In 1937 the U.S. naval attaché in China reported a typical Chinese-Japanese fishing confrontation in the Yellow Sea.

> What might have been another incident for the Japanese was averted by the quick action of Captain Shi Yunzhang, of the Jiangsu water police.
>
> A Japanese fishing craft anchored outside Lienyun harbor, and attempted to fish in spite of strong protest from the Chinese fishermen. The delegation, which went on board the Japanese fishing craft to persuade the Japanese to withdraw, was roughly handled. At this treatment, the Chinese fishermen decided to adopt drastic action and the tension was only relieved by the prompt action of Captain Shi in pacifying the fishermen. Captain Shi then

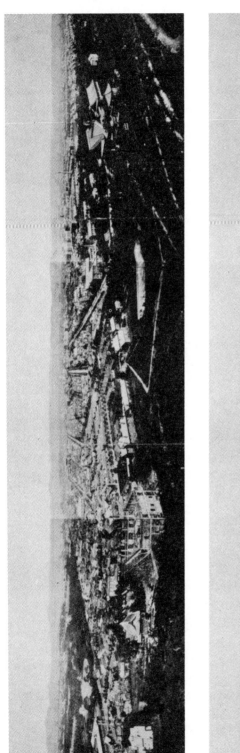

Japanese efficiency in north China. These two photos, taken twenty-one years apart, demonstrate Japan's tremendous expansion into China's Liaodong Peninsula. (*The Manchurian Yearbook*, Tokyo, 1931.)

boarded the Japanese fishing vessel and convinced the Japanese that they were in the wrong. They then weighed anchor and left.[22]

Other conflicts arose over the security of the Manchurian railroads. Tensions were running high by the summer of 1931, when a Japanese military officer was killed by Chinese troops in Manchuria. Several weeks later "mysterious" explosions rocked the South Manchurian Railroad at Mukden and Japan seized Manchuria.

The Chinese objected by resorting to anti-Japanese boycotts in the south. Subsequently, Japanese marines moved into Shanghai and gunboats shelled Nanjing. Although peace was restored in the spring of 1932, the situation never got better and war was formally declared in 1937.

During the five-year interval from 1932 to 1937, formal diplomatic relations, although strained, were maintained. Japan, in fact, began to take stock of its naval position in China. Two of its priorities included augmentation of the forces operating in Chinese waters and attainment of naval rapprochement with China. Japan resented British influence in China's navy and set about trying to counter it. In 1935 Rear Admiral S. Kobayashi, chief of the Imperial Japanese Personnel Department, went to Shanghai and offered the following three proposals to the Chinese:

1. The assignment of Japanese technical advisors to the Chinese navy

2. The assistance of Japanese naval forces in guarding the Yangzi and the south China coast

3. The use of Japanese steamers to transport anti-Communist Chinese troops engaged in bandit suppression[23]

China rejected the offers for two reasons: recent Japanese technical assistance had been poor, and the Chinese navy was plagued by mutinies, some of which were suspected to be Japanese inspired.

China had employed Japanese contractors to help build the new cruiser *Pinghai* at Jiangnan. Their presence, however, was the cause of friction. The Chinese had previously relied on Japanese engineers to supply three main engines for which the ship was designed, but the Japanese had provided only two outmoded reciprocating engines.[24] Moreover, just prior to launch, it was discovered that the wiring, junction boxes, and electrical fittings, which Japan had supplied and installed, would not stand up to weather and gunfire.[25]

The mutinies were the result of a general malaise that took hold of the Chinese navy. As noted earlier, the commander in chief of the navy, Chen Shaokuan, had been impeached in January 1933 on charges of having assisted the Japanese in 1932 when they put marines ashore in Shanghai.

Although Chen was eventually exonerated, the morale of the navy had been permanently impaired. In 1933 three aging cruisers, the *Haichen*, *Haiqi*, and *Chenghe*, defected from Shen Honglie's Qingdao command and went south to Canton, where they were welcomed by the warlord military commander and redesignated the Huangpu Squadron. The cruisers soon began to drain provincial finances, however. In an effort to prevent this and retain the crews' loyalty, officers and enlisted men were granted smuggling privileges by the warlord government. Very quickly the ships became floating centers for all kinds of illegal activity. Their success soon led the

Upper Yangzi River, Fengxiang Gorge. Cliff walls rise to 900 feet and frightening whirlpools abound. Here a U.S. Navy LSM traverses the famous gorge in 1946. (Courtesy of the U.S. Naval Institute Reference Library, Annapolis.)

provincial government to reexamine the arrangement. When it was decided to crack down, the ships once more defected, sailing back north in the summer of 1935.[26]

THE SINO-JAPANESE NAVAL WAR

On the eve of the second Sino-Japanese War in 1937, Chinese naval strength was negligible compared to Japan's. The bulk of the vessels were located on the Yangzi River and there were only 56,239 tons in all.[27] Vessels were classically arranged to defend the lower part of the Yangzi River at the Jiangyin forts and prevent the Japanese from advancing up the river to Nanjing. No effort was made to contest the Japanese navy at sea.

When fighting broke out in August at Shanghai, the Japanese undertook a heavy assault against the Jiangyin forts. The Chinese navy was ordered to move into a blockade line below the forts. For nearly fifty days the Chinese navy squadron gave the Japanese all they could handle. Despite constant air attacks, the *Pinghai, Ninghai, Yingrui,* and *Yatsen* (ex-*Zhongshan*) fought gallantly against overwhelming odds. Finally, on 23 September, the Japanese sent in successive waves of bombers that succeded in sinking the *Pinghai* and *Ninghai*. Still, the remaining ships continued to fight well, and it was not until December that the Japanese were able to break the blockade.

The Chinese navy did not quit, however. A gunboat force of some eighteen ships sailed up river to Matang in Anhui Province and established another blockade. They continued to fight and hold portions of the Yangzi until 1940, when the remaining ships were scuttled near the Yangzi Gorges at Yizhang in Hubei Province. At that time Chiang K'ai-shek ordered the Navy Ministry dissolved.

CHAPTER 13

TARNISHED TRADITIONS, LEND-LEASE, AND CIVIL WAR, 1944–49

 The war with Japan and the Communists prevented Chinese Nationalists from undertaking any naval rebuilding plans until 1944. However, the Kuomintang did manage to operate a makeshift naval academy in the mountains near Chongqing (Chungking), the Nationalist wartime capital. The director of the school was the irrepressible Admiral Chen Shaokuan. By 1944 a small group of two hundred officers had received rudimentary training. Chen successfully petitioned Chiang K'ai-shek to allow the navy to recruit one thousand enlisted men to form a nucleus in the postwar period.[1]

However, even at this early stage serious problems were developing. Chiang's suspicion of Chen and the pro-British Fujian naval clique resurfaced at this time. The generalissimo began to move officers loyal to his own Huangpu military clique into the navy hierarchy. This set off a great deal of political intrigue and dissatisfaction within the navy at a time when Chiang sorely needed loyalty and dedication.

THE U.S. OR BRITISH SYSTEM?

One of the points of contention between Chiang K'ai-shek and Chen Shaokuan was the latter's insistence on reestablishing close Sino-British naval relations. The admiral wanted to send his newly formed naval contingent to England for training and also acquire some warships from the British. He believed that after the war the British navy would again be the dominant naval force in the Pacific and renewed ties would be to the Chinese navy's benefit. Chen was particularly mindful of the British naval system, which placed great emphasis on line-officer predominance.[2] It was also a system founded on ceremony and ritual, which harmonized with Chinese Confucian instincts.

On the other hand, Chiang's small cadre of naval advisors was counseling a system built along American lines. They believed that Britain was an "aging lion," and that the United States would be preeminent in Asia after Japan was defeated.[3] They also considered the British naval education system to be rather incomplete, because crews were not sufficiently trained in various areas and not enough responsibility was given to senior enlisted men. They pointed out that the American naval system, after all, had shown itself to be superior to the Japanese in the various naval engagements of World War II.

Additionally, some of Chiang's naval strategists believed that Sino-American naval cooperation was necessary to counter potential Soviet naval expansion in the Pacific. While stressing mutual cooperation between China, the USSR, and the United States, they did not forget that, with the Yalta Agreement, "the Soviet Union took over the southern half of Sakhalin Island and the Kuriles from Japan. She also acquired special privileges in Dalian and Port Arthur from China through the same pact. Thus her position in the North Pacific is considerably strengthened." Going further they stressed the following to the generalissimo:

> The Kuriles are worth special attention. They are the gate to northern Japan. Japan acquired them from Russia through the Russo-Japanese treaty of 1875. Composed of 47 big islands and 164 small islets, the Kurile group stretches for 700 miles like a chain of stepping-stones. The retaking of the Kuriles and the southern half of the Sakhalin Island by the Soviet Union has made the Okhotsk Sea a Soviet navy lake. Its military value is especially great. The Kuriles will be a fortress to check the rise of Japan. The threat to the Soviet naval bases along the Maritime Province and the Okhotsk Sea is removed, and the Soviet Union's position in the Pacific is greatly elevated. In studying naval relations in the Pacific, this new factor, namely, that the Soviet Union is no longer isolated from the Pacific, must not be overlooked.[4]

THE U.S. ATTITUDE

Within the U.S. Navy there were several senior officers who advocated reequipping and training the Chinese navy. In late 1943 their proposal gained the attention of Admiral Ernest J. King, who forwarded it to Secretary of the Navy Frank Knox for consideration. King's memorandum, which also was sent to the Joint Chiefs of Staff, recommended that fifty Chinese naval officers and five hundred enlisted men be sent quarterly to the United States for naval training.[5] Once a solid nucleus was trained, King recommended that destroyers and other smaller combatants be made available to Chiang K'ai-shek to carry the naval war to the Japanese. King's proposal was subsequently denied, however. Its disapproval was due largely to the European lobby in the U.S. Navy, which believed that American naval interests in the postwar period should focus on the Atlantic rather than on the Pacific.[6]

THE BRITISH ENTRY

Owing to this initial U.S. disinterest, Chiang subsequently gave Admiral Chen approval to explore a British-sponsored training program. By late 1945 Chen had succeeded in getting London's authorization to accept 18 officers and 117 enlisted men for naval training in England.[7] The British government also agreed to turn over a number of ships to the Chinese, including one corvette, eight torpedo boats, one cruiser, two submarines, and one destroyer escort. The rate of turnover of the ships was contingent upon the speed with which the Chinese naval personnel were trained.

By January 1946 enough Chinese sailors had been trained to take command of the corvette, HMS *Petunia* (renamed the *Fubo* by the Chinese). The event, as it was highlighted in the Chinese navy's periodical, *Zhongguo Haijun* (*China's Navy*), is recorded here because of an ironic, tragicomic perspective.

> The presentation ceremony for the *Fubo* took place beside HMS *Renown*. The *Renown* is a 35,000-ton battleship, while the *Fubo* is only a 1,400-ton patrol gunboat corvette.
>
> . . . The ceremony took place at 1000 on 12 January 1946. Important officials were dispatched by China and Britain to take charge of the ceremony. The Chinese government was represented by General Gui Yongjing, then head of the military mission to Britain. The British government was represented by Admiral Sir C.E. Kennedy. Admiral Kennedy arrived first, followed by General Gui five minutes later.
>
> . . . When the ceremony was over, those in charge went on board the *Renown* for a party. A certain British naval officer said apologetically to General Gui at the party, "From outward appearance the ship given to China is a bit old."
>
> General Gui said, "If the ship is still so old when it arrives in China, it will be our fault."
>
> The local English evening papers carried the news of the whole ceremony with the full history of the ship. The ship was named the *Petunia*, launched in 1940, has a cruising record of 150,000 miles, took part in the Atlantic and Mediterranean battles and the landing on France. After reading the papers, one of the sailors said jokingly, "Britain is not giving us a good ship; she is giving us a history."[8]

Interestingly, one of the first operations carried out by the ex-British ship was the reoccupation of the Xisha (Paracel) and Nansha (Spratly) islands. In October and November 1946 a Chinese naval squadron visited these islands and assisted in setting up radio and meteorological stations.[9] Upon his return to Canton, the Chinese squadron commander announced: "The Xisha and Nansha Islands have always been our territory. They were occupied by the Japanese during the war. Now that we are victorious naturally we have to have them back."[10]

THE UNITED STATES RECONSIDERS

Britain's involvement in Chinese naval affairs and the focus on the Pacific island campaigns served to rekindle American interest in aiding the Chinese navy. In the spring of 1945, just as Germany surrendered, the United States approved the transfer to China of two destroyers, four minesweepers, and two patrol craft escorts. All of these ships were taken to Miami, Florida, for refitting. The Chinese, in turn, sent one thousand officers and enlisted men to the U.S. Naval Training Center in Miami for a one-year concentrated training program in preparation for sailing the ships back to China. In addition, forty-nine officers were sent to Swarthmore College for general training. Upon graduation twenty-five went to Annapolis and twenty-four to M.I.T. for specialized technical training.

Transfer of warships to China (October 1945). Admiral Thomas C. Kinkaid, commander of the U.S. Seventh Fleet, officiated at the ceremonies. Accepting the ship was Admiral Chen Shaokuan (center), the leader of the Fujian naval clique for nearly twenty-five years. On the left is Rear Admiral Sa Zhenping, who lived to be ninety-two years old. (Courtesy of the U.S. Naval Historical Center, Washington, D.C.)

One year later the United States decided to expand its naval assistance program in China and established a small U.S. Navy training group at Qingdao. In 1947 American naval involvement again increased with the creation of the Joint U.S. Military Advisory Group (JUSMAG) at Nanjing.[11] Included in the JUSMAG organization was the U.S. Navy Advisory Division, which oversaw the Qingdao training group and two new naval assistance groups at Shanghai and Canton. The Shanghai group was to assist the Chinese in modernizing the Jiangnan Shipyard, while the Canton group was to advise the Chinese on anti-piracy and anti-smuggling operations in the Pearl River area. The JUSMAG also managed the transfer of more ships to the Chinese, including eight LSTs, six LSMs, seven LCIs, three LCTs, twenty-five LCMs, and twenty-five LCVPs.[12]

The U.S. decision to increase its naval presence in China was based partly on renewed Soviet activities in northeast China. The Japanese surrender on 14 August 1945 had caught the Chinese Nationalist government unprepared to follow up by reestablishing Nationalist authority over north China. Instead, the Chinese Communists, with the help of Soviet-captured Japanese weapons, began to make immediate geographic and military gains in the north.

Furthermore, on the very day of the Japanese surrender, the Nationalist government, represented by Dr. T.V. Soong, the premier and foreign minister of China (and Chiang K'ai-shek's brother-in-law), concluded the Sino-Soviet Treaty of Friendship and Alliance in Moscow following several weeks of secret negotiations with Stalin and the Soviet foreign minister, Molotov. The treaty pledged mutual respect for each country's sovereignties and mutual noninterference in their internal affairs. From a naval standpoint, the treaty committed China to declare Dalian a free port, "open to commerce and shipping of all nations."[13] Both parties agreed that the port would be administered by the Chinese. However, China consented to lease half of the port facilities to the Soviet Union. Additionally, China agreed to the joint use of Port Arthur and extended the boundary of that area farther than the United States expected. Within nine days after the treaty was signed, the Soviet army occupied both ports and began moving transport aircraft and combat Yak fighters onto the undamaged airfields located in that area.

By late 1945 Chinese Nationalists were increasingly preoccupied with the advances being made by Communist forces in the north. The U.S. Navy thus found itself becoming directly involved in the expanding civil war. The Nationalist armies required sea transport to the northern front, and the only available forces were the American naval units operating in Chinese waters at the time.

The White House, through the Joint Chiefs of Staff, quickly directed General Albert C. Wedemeyer, the China theater commander, to commence planning for the following major U.S. Seventh Fleet actions:

1. The U.S. Seventh Fleet would immediately establish its presence and control in the Yellow Sea and Gulf of Bohai.

2. The Seventh Fleet would undertake the sea lift of several Nationalist armies from southern China to the Shandong and Liaodong peninsulas.

3. The Seventh Fleet would transport the U.S. Marine III Amphibious Corps from Okinawa to the landing sites at Taku, Tianjin, Qinhuangdao, Yantai, and Qingdao.[14]

The directive, however, was couched in language that conflicted with the sort of tasks being levied. "All provisions [of this directive] . . . apply only insofar as action in accordance therewith does not prejudice the basic principle that the United States will not support the Central Government of China in a fratricidal war."[15]

GUERRILLA WAR AT SEA

The directive was anticlimactic, for to most Americans in China the Nationalist position was fast deteriorating. George C. Marshall had unsuccessfully tried to create a coalition government between the Communists and the Kuomintang. When he departed China in January 1947 major fighting erupted in the north. The Communists soon gained the upper hand. As their control tightened, they commenced a series of water-resupply activities in the Gulf of Bohai and northern Yellow Sea. Within weeks most of the sailing junks and small motor vessels in the region were controlled by the Communists.

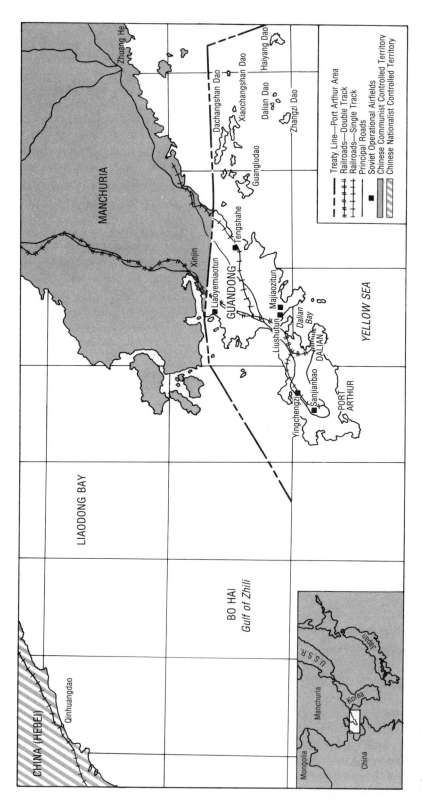

This map shows the considerable area of Chinese territory reclaimed by the USSR in a secret 1945 agreement with Chiang K'ai-shek's Nationalist government.

As pressure mounted inland, the Nationalist navy became heavily engaged attempting to blockade sea-lanes between the Liaodong and Shandong peninsulas. Regular patrols were set up in this area to inspect vessels operating between the Dalian–Port Arthur complex and the ports on the northern coast of Shandong. Soon the Nationalist patrol captured a number of junks ferrying Communist troops, guns, and ammunition. The Communists, however, sailed mainly at night, and by day would anchor in the Communist-controlled Changshan Islands, which stretched across the entrance of the Gulf of Bohai.[16] The number of Nationalist vessels was insufficient to enforce a total blockade of the area, and Communist sea traffic continued to increase in 1947.

The Nationalists were considerably hampered in their blockade efforts by the Soviet refusal to allow commercial or naval vessels to enter Dalian, which resulted in a U.S. protest to the Soviet Union about the continuing closure of the port. The Soviets pointed out that the Sino-Soviet agreement stated that, in case of war, the port was to come under control of the military regime that governed the Port Arthur naval base. The Soviets added that since the war with Japan had not been terminated, there being no peace treaty, Dalian would remain closed and continue to be administered by the Soviet government.

Aside from the technicalities contained in the diplomatic texts, the Soviets had other reasons for keeping Dalian closed. According to U.S. Navy intelligence reports, a Communist naval academy had been established in 1946 under the titular administration of Li Lisan, the veteran Communist politician and sometime foe of Mao Zedong.[17] Li had spent most of the war in Moscow, returning to northeast China in August 1945 as political advisor to Lin Biao. The Communist naval academy, in fact, was divided into two schools, with officer training conducted at Dalian and enlisted personnel assigned to a school located at Jiamusi, on the Sunghua River in northeast Heilongjiang Province. The Chinese Communists ordered the nucleus for their navy to be selected only from the most intelligent Chinese youths, all of whom had to be party members in good standing. The curriculum, managed entirely by Soviet naval advisors, called for a two- to three-year course of study with particular emphasis on espionage. The latter course was intended to train personnel to be smuggled into the Nationalist navy for subversive activity.[18]

By the fall of 1947 Li Lisan had been relieved by Zhang Lianrui, a defector from the Nationalist navy. Zhang, a navy commander and former commanding officer of the *Zhongjian* (previous U.S. LST 716), had been arrested by the Kuomintang Qingdao Garrison Command in April 1947 for stealing money allotted to pay the salaries of Nationalist navy personnel. Zhang had apparently hidden the money and bribed police guards in Qingdao to allow him to escape. When Zhang reached Communist territory, Lin Biao, seizing upon Zhang's naval experience, named him to replace Li Lisan.[19]

Within a year the naval academy graduated three hundred midshipmen from the school. Many received training aboard Soviet submarines operating from Port Arthur. It is very likely that the cruises aboard these ves-

sels—the U.S. naval attaché in Nanjing estimated that the Russians operated as many as eighteen submarines in Liaodong waters—permitted
Chinese Communists to observe Nationalist surface patrols and carefully
note their operating routines.[20] With such information, junk-resupply
activities could proceed with little risk of detection.

As Communist pressure in the north increased, even the Qingdao naval
complex began to experience threats from the sea. On 15 July 1948, sixty
Communist junks landed undetected southeast of Tangkou airfield at
Qingdao; guerrillas successfully blew up the reservoir, causing considerable disruption in the area.[21] Protected by the Soviet presence in the
Dalian–Port Arthur complex, the Communists also constructed motorized junks for daily shuttle runs across the straits to the Shandong Peninsula; with these junks they transported food, ammunition, and supplies.
By the summer of 1948 Communist vessels no longer practiced deception
and openly flew black flags.[22]

NAVAL REORGANIZATION AND LEADERSHIP CHANGES

As the civil war spread to the sea, the Nationalist navy grew at a rapid rate,
reaching twenty-nine thousand officers and men by 1947. This growth
necessitated new organizational and leadership changes, which in turn
reopened old clique wounds.

ORGANIZATION

In 1946–47, the Nationalist navy underwent two major organizational
revisions. The first, which went into effect in early 1946, established a
Department of Naval Affairs (DNA). The DNA was one of the departments
subordinate to the army-dominated Board of Military Affairs. It therefore
had little real power; tactical command of the ships was in the hands of the
army chief of staff. The fleets, in fact, retained the old prewar organizational structure, with two oceangoing squadrons, the First and Second
squadrons, and the Yangzi River Squadron. Additionally, a small Guangdong Province Squadron was created whose headquarters was at Canton.[23]

The establishment of JUSMAG at Nanjing did help the Chinese navy
regain some autonomy in 1947. At that time U.S. Navy advisors were
instrumental in changing the DNA into the Navy Headquarters (Haijun
Silingbu), which in turn became the mirror image of the then-standard U.S.
Navy Headquarters organization. The fleet arrangement remained the
same except that the Transport Squadron was added, which was responsible for shipping supplies to the other squadrons.

LEADERSHIP AND CLIQUES

The *Zhongguo Haijun* (the Chinese navy periodical) was used by Chiang
K'ai-shek as a sounding board for ideas and problems. Thus, when an
article appeared criticizing the navy's past educational system, it represented an attempt by the generalissimo to root out the old naval cliques. In
part the article stated the following:

Because of the quasi-feudalistic conditions of the Chinese society, the naval education system was not unified, and naval officers were too much affected by sectionalism. For instance, naval officers trained before the war by the Qingdao, Huangpu, and Fujian academies would not cooperate or coordinate with one another. Frictions and conflicts were frequent, and the navy itself was neglected.[24]

Chiang's main target was the Fujian clique in general and Admiral Chen Shaokuan specifically. He was determined to break their hold on the navy by filling the important positions with men loyal to him. Thus, in late 1945 he ousted Chen Shaokuan from the navy and replaced him with General Chen Cheng, a close confidant. The move caused extreme upset in the navy as the general began replacing Fujianese officers with officers from other provinces. Very soon Chen found himself heading a navy in a state of near mutiny. By 1946 the general was able to rid himself of the problem by convincing Chiang K'ai-shek to give the troublesome job to another army man, Lieutenant General Gui, the aforementioned military attaché to London.

Gui was a competent, hard-working infantryman who was determined to set a new course for the navy. One of his first acts was to establish a revised promotion system styled on the U.S. Navy, where promotion depended upon daily performance and fitness reports.

Gui encountered immediate resistance from the Fujianese. His chief of staff, Rear Admiral Zhou Xianzhang, went to great lengths to annoy the general. For example, when Gui decided to issue naval uniforms to all military personnel under the control of Navy Headquarters, Zhou objected, stating that only genuine naval officers who had undergone rigid four-year training should be permitted to wear the uniform.[25] This obvious slight to Gui, an army man, only aggravated the schism within the navy. Gui reacted by wearing his army uniform and maintaining the army rank structure within his staff. He also continued to replace Fujianese with graduates of the Qingdao Naval Academy.

CORRUPTION

General Gui had other more serious problems. His navy men were underpaid and at the mercy of China's postwar inflation. The actual rate of exchange on the black market reached four hundred thousand Chinese dollars to one U.S. dollar. Thus, by the spring of 1947 a seaman apprentice's monthly take-home pay amounted to about sixty U.S. cents.*

In this situation participation in corrupt practices was absolutely necessary for the survival of one's family. In southern China, where pressures from the Communists had not reached extreme proportions, corrupt practices within the Guangdong navy provided the clearest examples of Chinese navy involvement in smuggling and piracy.

---

*The U.S. naval attaché, Nanking, recorded that the navy's authorized budget for 1947 was 836,987,150,000 Chinese dollars.[26]

In July 1946 the Guangdong Navy Office of the Special Delegate of the War Ministry was comprised of one thousand enlisted men and a staff of twenty officers headed by Rear Admiral Liu Yongkou. Admiral Liu's responsibilities included the overhaul and subsequent activation of captured Japanese vessels. His mission was to create a river defense fleet for precautionary measures on the numerous rivers around Canton. In conversations with U.S. Navy representatives in the area, Admiral Liu had intimated that, except for a group of two hundred sailors recently sent to Qingdao for training, his men had not been paid in three months. Admiral Liu went on to state that "we are quite prepared to eat very little, but the engines of our ships require a regular amount of food and it cannot be cut down." Admiral Liu added that under the present chain of command he was responsible to Marshal Zhang Fakui, the old warlord and present head of the Chinese Nationalist Second Front area. Liu said that the movement of his ships was subject to the orders of Marshal Zhang and the fleet's only source of fuel was from Zhang's Army Headquarters.[27]

Admiral Liu's apparent outspokenness regarding the command arrangement under which he operated may have stemmed from his knowledge that he was in trouble with Nationalist military authorities. Several months later he was arrested on charges of abuse of powers and improper exercise of duties by illegally using his ships for smuggling.[28]

If honest Nationalist military authorities thought that the example of Admiral Liu would discourage other naval officers from participating in illegal smuggling and piratical activities, they were to be disappointed. By mid-1947 piracy and smuggling had achieved such a degree of legitimacy that the Canton area sponsored competitive firms that guaranteed their work. In the Sanpu District a Cooperative Smugglers Union openly advertised that it smuggled for profit and was able to move ten thousand catties of foodstuffs on a daily basis. Rumors abounded that the heads of the three largest smuggling rings were the wives of the three leading military and civil leaders in the Guangdong region.[29]

The remedies attempted by the DNA to correct the malpractices within the Guangdong navy only deepened the rift between contending factions. Chiang K'ai-shek replaced Admiral Liu with Captain Zou Yi, who, although a southerner from Jiangsi Province, was a personal friend of General Chen Cheng. He therefore was regarded with deep suspicion by the remaining officers of Admiral Liu's staff. Captain Zou became even more unpopular when he arranged for his cousin, a navy commander, to be transferred to Canton as a member of his staff. Subsequently, he arrested most of Liu's staff and replaced them with officers loyal to him.[30]

Meanwhile in the north, at Nanjing, the recently arrived squadron of eight ships from Miami, it had been discovered, had a considerable amount of smuggled goods aboard. Three Shanghai newspapers reported that the ships had arrived with four Lincoln automobiles, gold watches, fountain pens, cosmetics, and cigarettes as part of their cargo.[31] General Gui immediately relieved the squadron commander, Admiral Lin Zun, and two ship commanding officers of their commands. He replaced Lin with the commanding officer of the Shanghai Naval Base, Captain Wei Qimin. One of the ship commanders, Xu Heng, who was involuntarily retired, later confided to the assistant U.S. naval attaché in Canton that the whole incident was manufactured by Captain Wei as a way of gaining command of the flotilla.[32]

Because of this atmosphere of rancor and recrimination, it is difficult to determine whether any naval faction would have carried out honest programs. Perhaps the most honest assessment was provided by two junior naval officers who were trained in America and returned to China with the Miami squadron. The two informed an American naval advisor that the situation aboard the ships was far from harmonious. "It was a great mistake to send us to America! We received $200 per month while there but upon our return we got $30. But more important, in the United States we understood what a democratic country really is, and now when we come back to China it is a bad dream." They went on to tell the American that during the return voyage senior Chinese officers had openly transported several U.S.-made automobiles to be sold in China for private profit. Moreover, several officers misappropriated mess funds so that "only one or two of the ships had decent chow, the rest of [the crews] ate like coolies!"[33]

The American sat in silence as the two went on to comment that most junior officers in the Chinese navy had no faith in the honesty or capability of their superiors, whom they collectively called Old China. "The enemy," they said, "was not the Communists but 'Old China.'" They explained that Old China was associated with widespread corruption and irresponsibleness, and that most senior naval officers belonged to the group. They added that the newly acquired vessels could not be properly maintained due to the lack of spare parts. "Whatever you give us," they said, "will be squeezed, what is left will be allowed to fall apart, and anything that can be used will be used for the wrong purpose."[34]

Maladministration within the Chinese navy quickly affected operations afloat, and on 19 March 1947 the navy suffered a major tragedy when the *Fubo* was sunk off the Fujian coast. The ship was night steaming in heavy merchant-shipping sea-lanes and collided with a Chinese merchant vessel. She sank almost immediately, with only one officer surviving out of a crew of one hundred thirty officers and men. A court of inquiry determined that although the commanding officers of both vessels had been negligent, the officers of the *Fubo* were primarily guilty of following poor navigational practices.

The problem of corruption within the Chinese navy continued to plague Gui, who had been appointed a vice admiral by Chiang K'ai-shek. During the first six months of 1948 he was frequently tied down investigating cases of corruption. In March 1948 the former commanding officer of the Chinese Naval Training Center at Qingdao, Captain Lin Xiangguang, was arrested on charges of graft and corruption. Vice Admiral Gui suspended Lin from duty and sentenced him to one year in prison. Captain Lin, however, was not without influence, having served on Chiang K'ai-shek's personal staff; he was a close friend of Chen Cheng. Captain Lin appealed, and was afterward exonerated and released.[35]

The situation remained as bad when the commander of the newly designated Fourth District Naval Base at Canton was arrested on charges of smuggling. The officer, characterized by a U.S. naval advisor as an "intellectual virgin—he hasn't had an idea yet," had been operating LSMs between Yulin on Hainan Island and Canton, ferrying illegal goods.[36]

THE WATER POLICE

Navy corruption in south China forced Chiang K'ai-shek to attempt to deal with smuggling and piracy through the creation of a civil agency. He authorized his wealthy brother-in-law, Dr. T.V. Soong, to establish an independent water police force in Canton in 1948. Having already been appointed by Chiang as director of the Guangdong provincial headquarters, Dr. Soong, in the manner of a traditional naval patron, set about purchasing ships and organizing his revenue guards as the nucleus for a civil water police. Immediate conflict arose between Dr. Soong and the navy, since it was Soong's position that the proposed provincial water police would assume the exact same duties previously assigned to the navy. Furthermore, Soong's proposal undercut the customs' responsibility for smuggling. Soong's ideas clearly envisioned a police organization with national powers greater than any other law-enforcement agency.

In May 1948 his water police was established under the name of the Provincial Police and Pacification Department. It was given broad responsibilitiés. However, high government officials and navy officers expressed strong opposition to Soong's organization. His enemies claimed "that the formation of the Provincial Water Police was just an excuse for Soong's attempt to strengthen his own power in South China at the expense of the government."[37] As a result, almost as quickly as it was begun, Soong's water-police concept lapsed into dormancy. By the fall of 1948 the Fourth District Naval Base at Canton was actually operating the water police, although it nominally remained a civil organization under the Provincial Police and Pacification Department.

FURTHER COMPLICATIONS

Ashore, at Chinese Navy Headquarters, army dominance remained a significant factor as Huangpu army officers headed the Bureaus of Personnel, Supply, and Procurement. Admirals of the Fujian clique headed the other four bureaus: Maritime Affairs, Operations and Plans, Organizational Training, and Technical Affairs. Fujian power remained substantially diluted, however, since most subgroup heads represented a cross section of other army or navy cliques. For example, in the Bureau of Maritime Affairs, Commodore Ouyang Bao, a native of Fujian and a graduate of Britain's Royal Naval College, was requested to operate his intelligence group with three Huangpu army officers and one navy lieutenant commander who was a member of the new Qingdao naval clique.[38]

Afloat, the problem of control was considerably more complicated. In November 1948 the Chinese Navy Headquarters created a Headquarters Squadron, which was composed of the two major combatants, the cruiser *Chongqing* (previously HMS *Aurora*) and the destroyer *Lingfu* (previously HMS *Medip*), and the landing ships previously assigned to the Transportation Squadron. All these ships were under direct operational control of the Chinese Navy Headquarters. They represented a roving force whose location depended upon contingencies of the moment or the whims of Vice Admiral Gui. Interestingly, this squadron also contained the only tankers and repair ships in the Chinese navy, so that all of the other combat squadrons remained dependent upon the Chinese Navy Headquarters for timely logistics support.[39]

There had been attempts by the Kuomintang government to improve the pay system within the military, and the navy's newly adjusted pay tables did appear to be significantly better. For example, the pay for a navy captain had risen from 33 to 118 dollars per month. An ensign's pay increased from 15 to 55 dollars. Enlisted pay also showed an increase, except that a seaman's pay remained miserably inadequate, with apprentices receiving only 4 dollars per month.[40] Despite these increases, cost of living in China had accelerated proportionately, and it was still necessary for a professional navy man to seek alternate ways to earn money in order to maintain his family.

If these moves by Vice Admiral Gui were intended to stifle criticism of his leadership, they were not successful. One Chinese navy officer was quoted as saying:

> Staff and supply officers are mostly army officers in naval uniform, who know nothing about naval requirements. The shore-based officers are very stingy and indulge in red tape, to the disgust of the professional navy men. The officers ashore are inefficient and corrupt. It is bad enough for a navy to be headed by a professional soldier, and the situation is not improved by having landlubbers as naval paymasters and supply officers.[41]

DEFECTIONS

The arrival of the *Chongqing* had produced a wave of enthusiasm among the crowds of Chinese officials who watched her moor at Nanjing on 14 August 1948. Nearly every high-ranking Chinese naval officer assigned to Chinese Navy Headquarters visited the ship that day, as Vice Admiral Gui proudly showed off the expensive 5,000-ton warship. The *Chongqing* was nearly 500 feet long and carried six 6-inch guns, six 21-inch torpedo tubes, and numerous antiaircraft 40-mm and 20-mm guns. She could steam at flank speed of 32 knots and had a radius of 12,000 miles at economical speed. She had cost the Chinese government nearly ten million pounds sterling to train its crew and prepare it for delivery to the mainland.

If Gui was placing his hopes in stemming Chinese junk traffic in the northern Yellow Sea and Gulf of Bohai by using the heavily armed cruiser, he was to be sadly disappointed. When she and the *Lingfu* arrived in Hong Kong on 29 July 1948, immediate personnel problems developed. Nearly one-third of the engineering ratings aboard the cruiser jumped ship within twenty-four hours after it docked. These men were former merchant marine sailors who had been inducted into the Chinese navy with a contract that guaranteed them a higher wage than that received by engineers of corresponding rate in the regular navy.[42] The ill-will created by this situation, coupled with stricter rules on earning extra income, led to their unhappiness and subsequent desertion. Thus, when the *Chongqing* sailed into Nanjing on 14 August, her engineering department stood a two-section, or port-and-starboard, watch—a nearly impossible situation if the large warship was to be maintained in a high state of readiness.

Nevertheless, the *Chongqing* was a symbol of Chinese power. Gui declared to a group of naval personnel in Nanjing that "the Navy would never surrender to the Communists." He added that "even if all the ships were lost and all river defenses broken, he himself would still fight up and down the Yangzi on board the cruiser."[43] As the Nationalist military situation grew bleak in late 1948, Gui's words began to ring true.

Although the *Chongqing* had very little preparation and additional training, her visit to Nanjing was shortened and she was directed to proceed to the Gulf of Bohai at the head of a three-ship task force. Her mission was to provide gunfire support to the Nationalist armies that were being rapidly pushed toward the sea along the Zhili and northern Shandong coasts. During September and October the *Chongqing* engaged the Communist shore batteries around the northern ports of Huludao, Yantai, Yingkou, and Qinhuangdao.

During these operations, Chiang K'ai-shek spent time aboard the cruiser observing the worsening military situation along the coastal plains. When Huludao fell to the Communists in November 1948, the *Chongqing* returned to Shanghai.[44] Within three weeks the key city of Xuzhou fell, endangering Nationalist forces on the Shandong Peninsula and bringing Communist armies ever nearer to Nanjing and Shanghai. As military disasters began to accumulate, the Nationalist retreat increased in intensity. On 21 January 1949 Chiang K'ai-shek retired as president of the Republic and Li Zongren, the vice president, was designated to run the central government. Within two weeks Beijing fell to the Communists. Kuomintang government offices were transferred to Canton as the Communist Third Field Army began its buildup along the northern bank of the Yangzi River.

During this period, the Chinese Naval Training Center at Qingdao became isolated. Members of the U.S. Navy Advisory Division and the Chinese naval units assigned to the navy base began to withdraw, moving to Taiwan and Xiamen.

Meanwhile, the *Chongqing* returned to Shanghai. The situation aboard the cruiser was far from good, for the crew had not been paid since December. Adding to their discontent was the fact that the ship had been designated to hold and guard five hundred thousand silver dollars.[45] The money had been given to Vice Admiral Gui by Chiang K'ai-shek as an emergency fund, and Gui had entrusted the sum to the *Chongqing*'s Fujianese commanding officer, Captain Deng Zhaoxiang, for safekeeping. At this time Deng was discomfited to learn that he was to be relieved by a close friend of Vice Admiral Gui, Captain Lu Dongge. Most of the ship's officers, including Deng, were members of the Fujian clique and were unhappy with the appointment of Lu.[46]

In this atmosphere of uncertainty, a small group of crewmen began making plans to desert. The leader of the group, Wang Nishen, had joined the Communist party before going to England. While in England he had managed to convince about ten other crewmen to join the party, and with this small nucleus a Communist cell had been formed. As the Nationalist situation deteriorated, a "liberation committee" was established to promote mass desertions among the crew. By late February the committee had drawn up an elaborate plan designed to take control of the ship.[47] Word of their plans had apparently leaked out, for Vice Admiral Gui learned that subversive agents aboard the ship were planning to kidnap him and make off with his silver emergency fund.[48]

On the evening of 24 February, Wang Nishen passed the word to his fellow conspirators that someone had uncovered their plan and they must seize control of the ship before they were arrested. They opened up the small arms locker, passed out the weapons, and proceeded to round up all the officers. They forced Captain Deng to the bridge and ordered him to get the ship under way. Deng strongly objected at first. He was given two hours to make up his mind. If he didn't comply, the mutineers threatened, they would blow up the ship. At about 0300, Deng agreed to get the ship under way, and she departed her anchorage with all lights darkened.[49]

Once at sea the liberation committee issued a pamphlet to the crew which informed them that they were headed north to turn themselves over to the Communists in order "to seek democracy and freedom." Sailors were then permitted on deck. Immediately, the mutineers found that much of the crew did not favor the defection scheme, since their families were still living in Nationalist territory. An anti-revolution group was formed by ten officers, who threatened to retake the ship. Within forty-eight hours, however, the ship put into Yantai and the Communist conspirators distributed all of the silver dollars, with recruits receiving 250 dollars and veterans 450 dollars. Engineers were given 550 dollars each. For the moment this move succeeded in keeping the crew satisfied.[50]

While at Yantai, however, some anti-revolutionists continued to argue in favor of retaking the ship. Yantai, in fact, was under Communist control and the mayor came aboard to talk to the crew and persuade them to go ashore. On 2 March 1949 Nationalist reconnaissance aircraft located the ship, and the crew became quite uneasy over the prospect of being attacked. In the afternoon Nationalist bombers made their first attempt to sink the ship. The anti-revolutionary element handed an ultimatum to the liberation committee, saying that if the ship was not allowed to get under way by 1600, then they would get her under way themselves. The liberation committee signaled the Communist authorities ashore to send troops aboard to assist in putting down the rebellious sailors. This was done and the ship got under way for Huludao.[51]

A day later the Chongqing arrived at the port. She was immediately boarded by several thousand Communist troops. The ship remained there for nearly three weeks, while Communist political officers busily reorganized the crew. On 19 March Nationalist planes arrived and again attempted to bomb the ship. The crew demanded to be put ashore, but the Communists forced them to remain at their stations in the event of another attack. It came the next day and several near misses resulted. Finally, on 21 March the *Chongqing* was struck by a bomb in the stern. Most of the crew abandoned ship. The Communist military authorities issued instructions to have the ship scuttled. All vital equipment was heavily greased and much of the armament removed. Finally, the ship was sunk and the crew was taken ashore to be reformed as units within the People's Navy.[52]

Meanwhile, in the south, the Chinese Navy Headquarters was in turmoil over the *Chongqing* incident. Vice Admiral Gui had at long last realized the truth, that the lack of unity in his command would cause even more ships to defect. Accordingly, he called a meeting of his commanders and admitted to errors in judgment, particularly his failure to stem the corruption within the bureaus headed by army officers. He promised that reforms would be carried out immediately.

Gui's confession came too late. Communist forces were already preparing to cross the Yangzi and capture Nanjing. When the Communist army did finally establish a beachhead on 20 April 1949, Gui ordered Lin Zun, the "rehabilitated" Miami squadron commander, to take the Second Squadron up the river in an attempt to stop the Communist crossing. Gui promised Lin a decoration, a financial reward, and an appointment to the post of deputy commander in chief of the navy if the operation was successful. Lin invited Gui to accompany him, but the latter refused.[53] Faced with possible annihilation, Lin consulted with other officers in his squadron and decided it was useless to attempt to run the Communist gauntlet. Consequently, the entire squadron, consisting of one destroyer, three destroyer escorts, one patrol gunboat, five landing ships, and eight smaller auxiliaries, defected.

CHAPTER 14

IN THE IMAGE OF TRADITION: THE CHINESE NAVY, 1949–55

 If the Chinese had hopes that the new Communist regime spelled an end to centralized, bureaucratic, and authoritarian government, they were to be disappointed. Although Mao Zedong and his followers produced a revolution, they did not succeed in changing the basic system of government in China. Instead, they chose to pattern a system after Stalin's Soviet model, which was also centralized, bureaucratic, and authoritarian.

Another yardstick for measuring Mao's revolutionary success is how he handled naval and maritime development. If he had chosen to assume maritime security responsibilities aggressively by employing the navy, it would have been revolutionary by recent Chinese standards. But the trend of naval development under Mao Zedong bore marked similarity to the continental tradition. The Chinese Communist leadership was made up of people who sprang from the peasantry and had little formal education. They were trained guerrilla fighters, experts at riverine warfare, with no knowledge of navies and maritime matters. They would stand as a substantial obstacle to naval reform.

MAO'S NAVAL GOALS

In July 1949 Mao addressed the first session of the National Political Consultative Conference and announced the new goals of the Chinese People's Liberation Army (PLA). "Our national defense will be strengthened and we won't permit any imperialist to encroach any more upon our territory. Based on the gallant and tested People's Liberation Army, the people's armed forces of ours must be maintained and developed. We shall not only have a powerful army, but also a powerful air force and a powerful navy."[1]

Mao's early endorsement for building a navy was predicated on several maritime threats: the Nationalists still occupied many offshore islands and Taiwan; Chiang K'ai-shek's navy controlled the mainland sea-lanes from Shanghai southward; and the U.S. Navy, together with other Asian

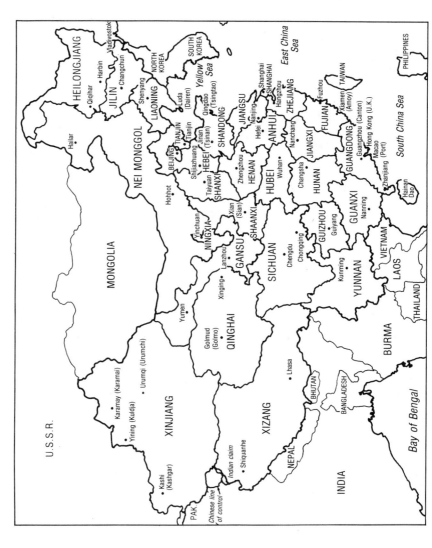

People's Republic of China.

"collaborationists," could easily mount an amphibious counterattack against the mainland.

The latter possibility became a most serious matter to Beijing when the Korean War erupted less than a year later. The setbacks and tremendous losses suffered by the North Koreans during the summer of 1950, including the U.N. army's advance toward the Chinese frontier, forced the Chinese into crossing the Yalu River in October of the same year. The Chinese action led to a U.S. naval buildup in the western Pacific that soon encircled the mainland at sea. The U.S. Seventh Fleet operated without challenge in the Yellow and East China seas, which prevented Mao from taking Taiwan. The Taiwan Strait "blockade" was established by President Truman when he announced the following in June 1950:

> The occupation of Formosa by Communist forces would be [a] direct threat to the security of the Pacific area and to the United States forces performing their lawful and necessary functions in that area.
>
> Accordingly, I have ordered the Seventh Fleet to prevent any attack on Formosa. As a corollary of this action I am calling upon the Chinese Government on Formosa to cease all air and sea operations against the mainland.[2]

COASTAL-DEFENSE BUILDING, 1950–53

Mao cared little about the sea. In fact, he was a staunch continentalist, much in the tradition of the nineteenth-century conservatives. His reputation had been made by the success of his protracted "people's war," and his armies consisted largely of politically minded guerrillas. Armies, in fact, were Mao's principal forces. The navy was seen as an expendable force used to defend the immediate coastal zone. Hence, there was no inclination on the part of Mao and his guerrilla-warfare adherents to develop a navy that could be employed for purposes beyond the protection of short-range aircraft based ashore.

THE QUEMOY DEBACLE, 1949

The first hint that the PLA was sadly deficient in naval power came in October 1949, when Communist assault forces were unable to defeat a small—an estimated fifteen thousand troops—but determined Nationalist garrison on Quemoy (Jinmen Island). The PLA hastily organized a junk assault force made up of about thirty thousand soldiers. On 25 October the attack was launched from Xiamen, about five miles distant. Throughout the day Nationalist defenders kept up a torrid fire against the overloaded junks attempting to land on the island. Communist corpses began to litter the beaches. Meanwhile, Nationalist aircraft were hurriedly dumping thousands of gallons of gasoline on the water near the beach and setting it afire. Hundreds of Communists troops struggled to swim through the inferno, but most burned to death.[3]

When it was successful in landing on one beach area, events proved disastrous for the PLA. The area happened to be in close proximity to the two Nationalist tanks. Communist infantry were helpless against the tanks and their armor. The 37-mm cannon and machine guns accounted for extensive casualties as Communists attempted to fight their way past the tank position.

By 27 October the Communists had pulled back. The Quemoy defeat effectively blunted further attempts to achieve a final victory over the Nationalists, giving rise to the two-China stalemate that so complicates China policy today. Moreover, the successful Nationalist defense cast doubt on the PLA's invincibility and reinforced the view in Beijing that coastal defenses needed to be greatly strengthened.

THE NATIONALIST NAVAL THREAT

The Chinese Communists had good reasons for rethinking their naval policies in the early 1950s. Despite President Truman's early admonition to the Nationalists to refrain from sea action against the mainland, the Nationalist navy dominated the central and southeast China coastal area and constantly harassed Communist coastal shipping. For example, Communist fishing fleets were often attacked by Nationalist naval vessels, which outgunned any of the armed and motorized junks that the Communists sent as escorts.

Also of concern to the Communists was the activity of Nationalist guerrillas and regular forces operating from some thirty-two Nationalist-held islands stretching from the northern Zhejiang coast to Quemoy. From these vantage points Chiang K'ai-shek's naval forces effected a partial closure of the ports of Wenzhou, Fuzhou, Shantou (Swatow), and Xiamen.[4]

Nationalist naval activity in the Taiwan Strait inconvenienced Communist commercial traffic. From 1950 to 1953, there were ninety incidents of Nationalist interference with international shipping destined for ports of the People's Republic of China (PRC). Two-thirds of those incidents involved British ships and prompted Great Britain to file numerous protests with the Taibei government. The Nationalists, in fact, had promulgated an executive order in 1950 that tasked the navy and air force to interfere with Communist water communications.[5] The order was an obvious violation of the U.S. neutralization policy (not recognized by the Nationalists) and became an added embarrassment when British merchant ships were openly intercepted, detained in Taiwan ports, and their cargoes confiscated.

The Nationalists also carried out guerrilla raids against Communist-held islands. For example, on 11 October 1952 five thousand Nationalist regulars and guerrillas raided Nanri Island, off the southern coast of Fujian. During seven hours of fighting, the Communists sustained 250 troops killed, 300 wounded, and 720 prisoners taken of the 1,300 troops assigned to the island. The Nationalists held the island for three days before withdrawing.

All of this activity prompted the PRC government to brand the United States a protector of Nationalist aggression. Communist propaganda repeatedly demanded the withdrawal of the Seventh Fleet from the Taiwan Strait.[6]

Rhetoric alone, however, would not solve the PRC's problems in the Taiwan Strait. It was obvious that an efficient coastal defense force was needed. Mao now took an active role in redefining the navy's responsibilities. On 4 December 1953 he directed the navy's mission to concentrate on the three following strategic goals:

1. Eliminate Nationalist naval interference and thereby insure maritime safety in navigation and transport
2. Participate in the recovery of Taiwan at an appropriate time
3. Oppose imperialist aggression from the sea[7]

Mao's strategic naval tasks were important to the new naval leadership, for they provided them with visibility in Beijing and the necessary high-level backing to improve the navy. However, with few reliable warships available, the Chinese initially had to restrict their activities toward improvement of beach and shore defenses. A massive effort was begun that bore strong resemblance to coastal-defense projects of China's dynastic past.

THE HAIFANG POLICY REVISITED

The traditional sea-defense line for Beijing and the industrial northeast underwent considerable modernization. Repair of facilities and coastal batteries was carried out from Shanhaiguan, where the Great Wall meets the sea in the Bohai Gulf, to Qingdao on the Shandong Peninsula.[8] This effort included the fortification of all defensive positions around Qingdao and the islands located in the sea approaches to that port. Such an undertaking entailed the strengthening of coastal forts with reinforced concrete capable of withstanding a near miss by 1,000-pound bombs. In the Qingdao area alone more than sixty-eight of these forts had been built by 1952.

In the east China region similar projects were under way by 1950. One defense effort involved the construction of a 250-mile, 10-foot-wide communication trench paralleling the southern bank of the Yangzi River from Wusong to Jiujiang up river. Along the trench, a machine-gun position was built every several hundred meters, and an artillery position was located every 1,000 or 2,000 meters. A similar trench was constructed along the coast south of Shanghai for about 200 miles. The Fujian coastal beach was honeycombed with emplacements for various types of weapons, communication trenches, and obstacles. In the large cities such as Fuzhou, defense works for street fighting were built at main points in the suburbs and inner city. At Xiamen, across from Quemoy, about two thousand reinforced concrete bunkers were built around the island at intervals of 15 meters.

The south China coast was similarly strengthened. Paralleling the Pearl River, artillery positions were formed inland along three lines. Forts were constructed on all of the major offshore islands stretching from Shantou to the Gulf of Tonkin.[9]

In each coastal province militia divisions were formed, numbering about six to seven thousand men per division.[10] These local forces received basic infantry training and eventually shared garrison- and local-defense duties within a given province.

Augmenting the coastal-defense system were Communist communications and observation posts, built everywhere along the coast. Radar and radio had replaced the ancient beacon fire system used by the traditional *wei-suo* surveillance posts. Equipped with surface-search and air-defense radars, these posts played an important role in coastal surveillance.

The Chinese Communists openly published their accomplishments as early as 1954, when Nationalist and Communist warships carried out a series of sea skirmishes. The PLA Zhejiang Front Command was noted commending subordinate posts for their "highly responsible and selfless work which resulted in supplying the commanding organ timely and accurately with information about enemy movement, a great part in ensuring victory in every combat."[11] As late as 1971 Chinese press and radio reports described the ten-year hardships endured by a PLA Jinan garrison company. This company, assigned to an island in the Yellow Sea in 1961 to erect an advanced coastal-defense site, was "warmly hailed by the people as a brilliant company which defends the sea frontier."[12] Some of the missions of other posts had expanded by the 1970s to include antisubmarine warfare. For instance, an official 1976 press release extolled the activities of a Paracel Island observation post whose alert radar operator had detected an "enemy submarine" operating in his surveillance zone.[13]

In the early period such naval craft as were available were used for coastal patrols, but because of Nationalist naval superiority they did not operate far at sea. Regular patrol operations, in fact, were confined to coastal waters around Shanghai, where the ships could be protected by land-based artillery.

NAVAL ACTIONS, 1953–55

From 1950 to 1953 the Korean War received the full attention of the Chinese Communists, but as peace talks resumed in 1953, PRC military leaders began to refocus their attention on the recovery of offshore islands still in Nationalist hands. These islands represented three strong points ranging from the Dachen Islands, about one hundred miles southeast of Shanghai, to Quemoy in the south. The central strong point was located at Matsu Island. As stated earlier, these three island areas effectively sealed off the sea approaches to Communist ports in Zhejiang and Fujian.

Until 1953 the Communists had made no effort to retake these islands, but they were incited to action by President Eisenhower's State of the Union Address on 2 February 1953, in which he announced that the U.S. Seventh Fleet would no longer prevent Nationalist attacks against the mainland. In less than three months of Eisenhower's announcement and during the period when Korean peace talks resumed, the Communists undertook a series of island assaults designed to weaken the Nationalist's northern stronghold near the Dachen Islands. On 29 May 1953 Communist troops were ferried to two islands, Beijishan and Dalushan, where they quickly defeated the small Nationalist guerrilla garrisons. Nationalist forces made a desperate attempt on the nineteenth and twentieth of June to recapture Dalushan, but in two savage assaults they were repulsed by stronger Communist forces. The Dachen Islands now were in jeopardy as the Communists readied Beijishan and Dalushan as staging areas for an assault against the larger islands.[14]

The Nationalists again attempted to take advantage of Eisenhower's deneutralization order. In July 1953 they carried out a large raid against Tongshan Island near Shantou. On the sixteenth paratroopers and marines numbering some sixty-five hundred troops, with about twenty-five vessels and fifty fighter aircraft in support, landed on the island. The paratroopers were immediately caught in a murderous Communist crossfire. The marines could not move far beyond the landing beach, since the Communists sent massive reinforcements across the shallow channel that separates the island from the mainland. By midnight of the second day the Nationalist forces were compelled to withdraw, having remained on the island for forty-four hours of a planned three-day occupation.

These activities forced the PRC into adopting a more active naval policy that presaged new island assaults then being discussed by the Communists. Beginning in February 1954, PRC patrol craft began to exhibit more aggressiveness in their persecution of Nationalist guerrilla activity. In the early morning of the twenty-fifth, two Communist patrol craft intercepted three Nationalist guerrilla junks loaded with assault troops some thirty miles at sea. One junk was sunk and the other two were forced to flee the area.[15]

In May 1954 Nationalist vessels operating from the Dachen Islands encountered still more aggressive resistance by the Communist navy. On successive days Nationalist warships (PGMs) were taken under fire by more than twenty Communist patrol craft operating in the area.[16] Nationalist ships sustained only minor damage, but the action reflected stepped-up Communist naval activity in the Dachen region.

From the standpoint of morale, the biggest naval disaster to befall the Nationalists during the struggle for the offshore islands occurred on 14 November 1954. Shortly after midnight on that date one of the largest naval combatants possessed by the Nationalists, the destroyer *Taiping*, was seriously damaged by a Chinese Communist torpedo boat. She sank while being towed by another Nationalist destroyer escort. The *Taiping*, a well-armed vessel, was on a routine patrol between the Nationalist-held Dachen and Yushan islands. She was steaming some ten to twelve nautical miles east of a Communist-held island and more than twenty miles from the mainland when attacked. Apparently, two Communist P-4 torpedo boats approached from the east at high speed and were within 3,400 yards of the *Taiping* before the captain was alerted. Several minutes later, as the boats were taken under fire, they launched their torpedoes and one struck the *Taiping* amidships. The main engines were out of commission and the ship began to flood. She sank six hours later, after attempts were made to take her in tow by a sister vessel.[17]

In the several months that followed, PRC torpedo boats stepped up their operations against Nationalist naval patrols. In January 1955 two Nationalist PGMs were attacked in separate actions, resulting in one vessel sunk and the other heavily damaged. During one of these actions, the attacking PT boats apparently hid themselves in a concentration of fishing junks and dashed from this cover to surprise the unfortunate Nationalist PGM—a strategem later extolled in the Communist press as an example of guerrilla warfare at sea.[18]

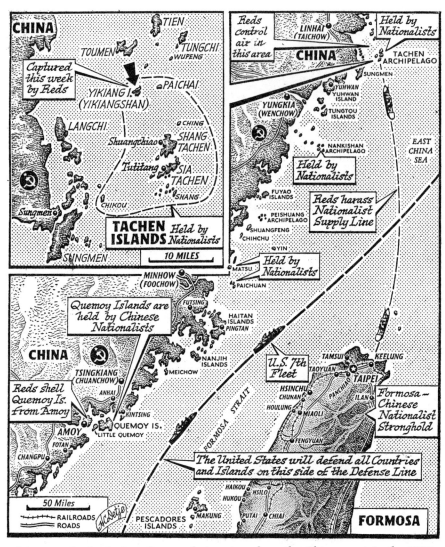

This map clearly depicts the naval situation along the China coast in the 1950s. (The *New York Journal American*, January 1950.)

Air attacks against the Dachens also increased in intensity, culminating in a well-executed Communist assault against Yijiang Island and the upper and lower Dachen islands on 18 January 1955. On the tenth air attacks had been concentrated in the upper Dachen Harbor, which resulted in damages to four Nationalist warships. Subsequently, the Nationalist navy withdrew to the south, thus isolating the islands for the Communist amphibious assault that followed.

On the morning of the eighteenth, Chinese Communist fighter aircraft commenced a series of sorties against Yijiang Island, which included horizonal- and dive-bombing operations. Two hundred and fifty sorties were executed. This was followed up by four hours of artillery fire from nearby islands and supplemented with naval gunfire support. When this barrage was lifted, Chinese Nationalist defenders observed a landing force approaching the island. The force, estimated at two regiments, was embarked aboard conventional landing craft and motorized junks. During the landing ground artillery support was lifted and PRC soldiers came ashore under cover of naval bombardment. Air attacks were halted during the landing, although air cover was maintained over the island. By night-fall the island had been secured, and the PRC naval infantry cleaned up small pockets of resistance.[19]

The significance of this assault was the Communists' demonstrated capability to conduct and coordinate a joint amphibious operation. Although the numbers of units and personnel were small, the Chinese Communists could no longer be considered a guerrilla-warfare force inca-pable of mastering the intricacies of air-, land-, and sea-combat operations. The successful assault resulted in Nationalist withdrawal from all but two islands, Matsu and Quemoy.

THE NAVAL MODERNIZATION DEBATE

The subsequent PRC naval successes against the Nationalists in the mid-1950s represented a significant milestone in the life of the Communist navy. The navy reflected a willingness to adopt Western-style tactics and employ proven assault techniques and equipment. A champion of the new attitude was the high-ranking PRC general and minister of the Chinese Public Security Forces, Lo Ruiqing. Lo, about whom we will hear much in later chapters, was quoted by his critics as considering the Maoist "pro-tracted-warfare" strategy outmoded and stating that "now conditions are different and the only method to be used is that of blocking the seas. With new technical equipment any invading enemy can be annihilated on the sea, in the air, or at the base from which it launches its attack."[20]

Lo's statement is important, for it highlighted the argument then begin-ning to surface regarding military (and economic) modernization. In many ways the debate closely resembled China's modernization debates of the nineteenth century. On one side there stood the advocates of professional military, economic, and technological systems. They favored a forward defense strategy based upon a strong deterrence system, emphasized mili-tary professionalism rather than ideological training, and urged the im-portation of necessary technology and Soviet advisors to make China competitive with other world powers. As far as a navy was concerned, the maritime supporters wanted a naval force that could operate beyond the protection of forts ashore—perhaps not a blue-water fleet, but at least a force that could perform limited blue-water operations and reestablish Chinese naval control over adjacent territorial seas.

On the other side were the ideologists, the guerrilla-warfare advocates, the xenophobes, the continentalists, the traditionalists. They favored a strong, conventionally armed land force that would fight a classic "peo-ple's war." They mistrusted foreign techniques and favored a path of self-reliance that minimized the importation of foreign technology. They retained an almost mystic belief in Maoist military doctrine and promoted the continued development of a highly politicized revolutionary guerrilla army. They were coastal-defense adherents who still followed the brick-and-mortar strategy of *haifang*.

The question thus was framed: How would the Chinese resolve this latest "struggle between two lines" and how would the struggle affect ideological purity and technological priorities?

CHAPTER 15

MODERNIZATION: SINO-SOVIET NAVAL COOPERATION, 1950–59

The maritime advocates wasted little time convincing Mao to seek naval aid and advice from the Soviet Union. By 1951 it was noted by U.S. intelligence experts that the USSR had a large contingent of naval advisors in China to assist and advise on the development of the Chinese navy.[1] Other maritime-associated technicians arrived in China, provided for under the terms of pacts signed by Mao and Stalin at Moscow in February 1950. Some of those agreements had important naval implications.[2] For example, the Soviets agreed to the reversion of Dalian to Chinese administrative control as well as the termination of dual (Sino-Soviet) control over Port Arthur in favor of the Chinese. These agreements were contingent upon the signing of a peace treaty with Japan or the arrival of the end of 1952, whichever came first. A month later, in March 1952, three more agreements were concluded, one of which provided for shipbuilding and ship-repair assistance.

The impact of the Soviet naval advisory group in China was soon evident in official statements by PRC naval leaders. At a ceremony in November 1951, Wang Hongkun, deputy commander of the Chinese navy, stated: "The Soviet Navy is an example for the Navy of the Chinese people and is the direction of construction of the Chinese People's Navy. We should learn from the great Red Navy in order to speed up the building of a powerful people's Navy."[3]

Mao, whose attention was consumed by the Korean War, may not have been too busy to notice the possibilities of Sino-Soviet naval cooperation. In February 1952 he visited his new Beijing Navy Headquarters, where he inspected its officers and received briefings on the navy's organization, facilities, and weapons. Following the briefings, Mao sat down with his naval leaders and undertook a study to "work out a long-term plan for the development of the Navy."[4]

ADMIRAL XIAO JINGGUANG

Before discussing the details of Mao's long-term naval plans, it is important first to describe the man he selected in 1950 to lead the navy, Admiral Xiao Jingguang.

Admiral Xiao was a contemporary of Mao and had attended the same school, although they were not classmates. In 1920, at the age of eighteen, Xiao became involved in revolutionary activities in Changsha, Hunan. Soon he was selected to attend a Russian-language school in Shanghai, which was being administered by Mao. Within months of his arrival in Shanghai, Xiao joined the Socialist Youth League and the Chinese Communist party. From about 1922 to 1924, Xiao studied in Moscow. Upon his return to China he became a military instructor-student at Chiang K'ai-shek's Whampoa (Huangpu) Military Academy. When the Kuomintang split with the Communists in 1927, Xiao returned to the Soviet Union, where he spent three more years as a student.

Xiao's career suffered a temporary setback in 1933, when he refused to attack Nationalist-held cities—a tactic then favored by the Communists but criticized by Mao, who was also out of favor. This refusal resulted in Xiao's arrest by Zhou Enlai, who at the time was the Communist party's senior military leader. Xiao's sentence of five years in prison was overruled by Mao when the latter returned to power. Xiao took part in the Long March and held many important military posts through 1949. His fluency in Russian undoubtedly was a factor in his being named chief of naval operations in 1950.

Xiao had other qualifications. He was an excellent administrator and manager, as well as a staunch Maoist who could be counted upon to adhere to whatever line the chairman espoused. The admiral exhibited characteristics that closely resembled the traditional idealistic senior commander: he was a loyal continentalist who strongly believed that coastal defense of the homeland was paramount.

FACILITY MODERNIZATION

A top priority in the PRC navy's long-term plan was the rapid modernization of naval bases and shipyards. Such projects required extensive Soviet aid and technology. By the early 1950s Sino-Soviet "friendship associations" were located in each of the key maritime cities.[5]

In north China the Dalian–Port Arthur complex was the most modern facility. At Dalian piers were enlarged to accommodate oceangoing vessels, and warehouse and storage space was expanded to handle several hundred trainloads of cargo. New anchorages were built inside three breakwaters, which could comfortably anchor forty to fifty vessels in the 5,000- to 10,000-ton range. The existing dry docks and double-track railroad, which served the Dalian naval repair facility, were also refurbished. All of the old shop facilities were modernized and soon able to carry out repairs of destroyer-size warships. By 1953 the Dalian facility was producing small gunboats.[6]

The modernization of facilities at Dalian–Port Arthur was accomplished undoubtedly as a direct result of a modification of the 1950 Sino-Soviet Treaty. In September 1952 Zhou Enlai traveled to Moscow and signed a new agreement that extended Soviet occupation and control over Port Arthur indefinitely.[7]

Meanwhile, at Qingdao, work progressed on the shipyard and ship-works, where many facilities left by the United States remained intact. Over 120 major repair machines were operational by 1953, and repair of vessels up to 5,000 tons could be efficiently carried out.

The real center for naval shipbuilding remained at Shanghai. A torpedo factory and naval arsenals were refitted, as was the major repair and shipbuilding facility at Jiangnan. In 1953 Jiangnan possessed three large dry docks and six 500-ton platforms. Eleven shops were operational, including a machine shop, fabricating-plate shop, blacksmith shop, electric shop, welding shop, assembly shop, carpenter shop, and forging shop.[8]

By late 1955 plans were completed for the opening of the PRC's first shipbuilding college at Shanghai. The school was to be modeled after the Leningrade Institute of Shipbuilding. It consisted of five departments specializing in the construction, dynamics, electrical engineering, machine building, economics, and organization of the shipbuilding industry. The college was the responsibility of the First Ministry of Machine Building. Seventeen laboratories were being outfitted and a curriculum was drawn up that included evening classes for shipbuilding and machine workers. Concurrently with this effort, the China Shipbuilding Association was formed in Beijing. As an important subagency of the First Ministry, it was charged with organizing shipbuilding personnel and experts in China to engage in academic and theoretical research activities. The association began to collect, collate, and disseminate standard naval science and technical books used in other countries.

Shanghai (1956). A new orderliness prevails in the once boisterous and bawdy city. (Courtesy of the U.S. Naval Institute Reference Library, Annapolis.)

In south China shipbuilding and naval-facility reconstruction progressed at a much slower pace. Facilities at Canton, Huangpu, and Hainan
Island remained in generally poor condition. This was largely due to the
Nationalist blockade of the Taiwan Strait, which required the Communists to emphasize the construction of a strong shore-based line of defense.
Money and manpower, for example, were allocated to protect Canton's
vital railway connections rather than to improve shipyards and naval
facilities. The old shore batteries along the Pearl River were also a top
priority—fortifications were repaired and refitted with Soviet long-range
heavy guns.[9]

NAVAL WEAPONRY

In the early 1950s the Soviets began supplying China with naval hardware
of varying sophistication. In 1951 the Chinese received their first naval aid
from the USSR with the delivery of fifty P 4 motor torpedo boats. These
vessels made up the major offensive striking force of the PRC. Two years
later, in 1953, the Soviet Union delivered one M-class short-range submarine and, in the spring of 1954, three S 1-class submarines were turned
over to the Chinese. Between 1954 and 1956 the USSR gave the Chinese
four *Gordy*-class destroyers, six *Kronstadt*-class submarine chasers, and
two T 43-class minesweepers.[10]

Besides deliveries, the Soviets provided active support to the Chinese in
the building of new warships. With Soviet help the PRC was producing
small district patrol craft (YPs) by 1953. Nearly one hundred of these were
constructed between 1953 and 1955. Each was about 80 to 90 feet long and
displaced about 60 tons. All were diesel powered and armed with 37-mm,
20-mm, and .50-cal machine guns.[11] More ambitious naval construction
programs were begun at Shanghai in 1955. With Soviet assistance, four
modern *Riga*-class escort destroyers were under construction at Shanghai's Hudong Shipyard. Also, construction plans were begun at Shanghai
for the building of modern, conventionally powered W-class submarines,
Kronstadt-class ASW craft, T 43 minesweepers, and the new class P 6
motor torpedo boat.[12] All were of Soviet design.

Mao's fascination with China's new naval projects could be seen in his
several visits to the fleets between 1953 and 1958. His first visit, in
February 1953, took him aboard some of the old escorts captured by the
PRC in 1949. For nearly four days he stayed aboard the ships, chatting with
crews and observing various exercises. At the end of his first visit, Mao
took note of the complications involved in shipboard operations and said
to the crews that "it is necesssary to learn from the advanced experience of
foreign countries."[13]

In 1956 Mao visited the Jiangnan Shipyard, where China's first W-class
submarine was nearing final construction. While aboard the submarine, he
was briefed as to its capabilities and escorted on an inspection of the vessel.

Two years later Mao went aboard a torpedo boat and witnessed sea
trials. He expressed his amazement at the ship's speed and requested the
commanding officer to operate the vessel at flank speed. Upon debarking

Sino-Soviet naval cooperation (1956). In June 1956, units of the Soviet Pacific Fleet make an official visit to Shanghai. Pictured here from left to right are Xu Jianguo, vice-mayor of Shanghai; Vice Admiral Dao Yong, commander of the Chinese East Sea Fleet; and Vice Admiral V.A. Chekurov, commander of the Soviet Fleet. Note the Chinese naval uniform and rank designations, which were done away with in 1965. (Courtesy of the U.S. Naval Historical Center, Washington, D.C.)

Mao once again paid homage to technology, remarking to the builders that it was important for China to train its own technicians and "master advanced technology so as to build still larger vessels."[14]

TECHNOLOGY, TRAINING, AND PROFESSIONALISM

The call for advanced technology was spelled out at the Eighth Party Congress in 1956 when a Chinese spokesman stated: "In leading scientific work, the Party should rely on scientists to the fullest extent. Modern sciences are finely divided into various fields. Only the specialists know the fine points of a certain field of science. When we have scientific problems, we must learn humbly from specialists."[15]

Two years later the Academy of Military Sciences was established under the directorship of Marshal Ye Jianying. At the inaugural cere-monies, Ye was quoted as saying that the new academy "should make full use of the latest scientific and technical developments and carry out research in a planned way, combining the advanced Soviet military sci-ences with the concrete situation in China, so as to accelerate the mod-ernization of the army."[16]

One of the first indications of Chinese determination to modernize their military establishment along Soviet lines came in February 1955. At that time the Regulations on the Service of Officers were adopted. As one scholar noted, these regulations "fundamentally altered the informal, egalitarian and 'democratic' nature of the Chinese Communist Officer Corps as it had been molded during more than two decades of revolutionary warfare."[17] At the same time that the regulations were promulgated, the Chinese announced the establishment of conscription laws, which did away with the volunteer army system that had existed until then.

The impact of the new regulations and laws on the navy was significant. In September 1955 ranks were conferred on military personnel. Thirty-two ex-army leaders received the rank of rear admiral or above (there were three admirals, nine vice admirals, and twenty rear admirals). The next four years would see nine more flag officers promoted, of which at least seven were guerrilla veterans of the Long March.

The regulations also included important provisions for the selection of personnel for officer training, with emphasis on technical abilities. Graduates of technical academies could receive a direct commission, while military-academy graduates could be given non-commissioned-officer or petty-officer status if their technical performance was not high enough. Promotions were to be heavily dependent upon professional competence, and time limits were set for advancement. Pay and allowance provisions were also included in the regulations.

For enlisted personnel, the regulations also led to the establishment of a rating or specialty structure. Over ninety different specialties were identified, most of which required technical training. The emphasis on naval technical training was clearly manifested in April 1956, when a movement was launched to create "master technicians" for the navy. A year later it was reported that these efforts had led to the selection of more than six thousand technicians, whose ratings covered the spectrum from electronics and engineering to weapons repair and radio operators. The drive to develop naval technicians was enunciated by the *Qingdao Daily* when it declared that "the study of military skills and techniques has become the rage" in the navy.[18]

The emerging naval air force was not immune to the concerted effort to master technology. In 1955 a conference of naval aviators was convened in Beijing. They declared their objectives to be the strengthening of training, the continuation of studies, a swift mastery of flying techniques, and the continued effort to build a professional naval air force.[19]

Concurrently with the establishment of the professionalism program, the navy set up a naval schools system, since in 1950 the only trained pool of naval personnel in China were ex-Nationalist defectors. The Chinese Communists exercised little hesitation in employing those officers as instructors or using enlisted men for technical duties.

The best source of trained manpower was to be found among the U.S.- and British-trained crew of the *Chongqing*. These men, who numbered about three hundred, were taken to Andong in 1950, where they underwent a heavy indoctrination program. They read the works of Mao and the Communist version of *A Brief Modern History of China*. Finally, they were given forty days to write their autobiographies and self-criticism. Afterward they were examined, and those who passed were to be assigned to various naval schools and facilities for further training. A *Chongqing* sailor, who underwent this program and later defected, reported that the British-trained Fujianese captain, Deng Zhaoxiang, proved to be an outstanding success among his Communist captors and "was graded 'A,' indicating his great endeavour in learning the Communist theories."[20] The sailor's observations were accurate—in 1977 Deng was named deputy commander of the PRC's North Sea Fleet, the Communist version of the imperial Beiyang navy.[21] This was a remarkable case of survival, for in 1953 Deng supposedly "still enjoyed his cup to tea in the afternoon in good British tradition, considering himself 'British Navy.'"[22]

Other ex-Nationalist naval officers seemed to survive their indoctrination equally well. By 1959 several were still on active duty and assigned to responsible positions. At that time Captain Deng was the chief of staff of the Qingdao Naval Base, and Captain Lin Zun, the former Miami squadron commander, had been promoted to rear admiral and was a deputy director of a naval school at Nanjing. Commander Chen Jingwen, former executive officer of the *Chongqing*, was the assistant director of the gunnery school at the Nanjing school.

Significantly, the Fuzhou Naval Academy had not been reopened. Instead, the two most important naval academies established by the Communists in the early 1950s were at Dalian and Nanjing. The former was initially under the direct management of the Soviet navy, and its four-year curriculum was geared toward technical subjects. Standards were very high, with students selected from the best-educated youths from the cities. The Soviets brought in good equipment and set up efficient classrooms.

The situation at Nanjing was considerably different. Very little equipment was available and space was at a premium, as the Communists jammed some three thousand students into the first class. Most of the recruits, former members of the Thirtieth and Thirty-fifth Communist armies, had no experience with naval operations. Classes were conducted by ex-Nationalists on a variety of subjects, including gunnery, radar operation, signaling, and minesweeping. Upon graduation the personnel were assigned to ships in the East China Sea Fleet. There were about three Communists to every Nationalist aboard these vessels, with the Communists being assigned to the senior positions (there were about four hundred ex-Nationalist sailors assigned to the East Sea Fleet).[23]

By 1956 PRC naval schools had expanded to at least twenty-five facilities of varying size and emphasis. Training was becoming much more professional. For example, in 1955 a college for senior officers was established in Nanjing, and students were reading a translated version of Mahan's *The Influence of Sea Power Upon History*. The curriculum at the school was divided into junior- and senior-officer training, with the juniors taking a four-year course and the seniors assigned to a two-and-a-half-year course. Foreign languages were taught, along with courses on navigation, meteorology, logistics (supply), communications, engineering, strategy, and tactics.[24]

At Dalian the naval academy continued to operate with a four-year curriculum. By 1956 the courses of instruction provided student training in several specialties: general line (surface), submarine, and aviation.

Basic enlisted training was carried out at schools located within their respective fleet geographic regions. Presumably, graduates were to be assigned to the fleet in which their school was located—a practice not unlike that carried out in the imperial and republican navies. The training itself lasted six months, with the first three devoted to mastering basic infantry skills and the last three spent on naval subjects. Students who demonstrated high technical proficiency were then sent to advanced schools.[25]

While the above descriptions are by no means exhaustive, they do demonstrate the emphasis being given to technology and technical training. Perhaps the best summary of these activities and the debt owed to the USSR was written in 1959 by Admiral Xiao Jingguang. His article, which appeared in a Soviet naval journal, left little doubt as to the elite status of the emerging PRC navy. It also paid respect to China's Soviet tutors.

> We overcame all difficulties and established our naval forces within a short time. The best fighting men and officers were transferred from the army to naval service, people who came from the workers and had high political consciousness and rich revolutionary experience. The beginning was difficult. Technical and special knowledge was lacking. Therefore, to raise the general education and technical level of the naval personnel became a task of primary importance. A movement to master technical equipment and for a growing number of specialists was launched in the navy. As a result, officers and sailors, by continuous study and improvement mastered naval science. The scientists and young representatives of the revolutionary intelligentsia which were sent by the party and the government to the navy played no small role in the training of personnel and the construction of the navy. . . .
>
> The development of the Chinese Navy is inseparable from the fraternal aid of the Soviet Union. At a time when our industry was still weak and our science and technology comparatively backward, the Soviet Government, the CPSU, and the entire Soviet people rendered us selfless aid.[26]

While the foregoing clearly demonstrated the ambitious nature of the PRC naval training system, the proliferation of schools was reminiscent of what happened in the late nineteenth and early twentieth centuries. The PRC system, like its forerunners, lacked coherence. The various schools and academies had different methods of instruction and were not coordinated with one another in operations or in technical knowledge. The only thing keeping the various training programs from collapsing was the presence of Soviet advisors.

PRC NAVY ORGANIZATION

Although the relationship between the Chinese and Soviet navies was a close one, it had little impact on China's naval organization. The organizational blueprint that was followed had been spelled out by Mao in 1945, when he commented upon the virtues of the PLA. At that time he stated: "This army is powerful because [of] its division into two parts, the main forces and the regional forces with the former available for operations in any region whenever necessary and the latter concentrating on defending their own localities and attacking the enemy there in cooperation with the local militia.[27]

While Mao's organizational scheme was created for conditions of a people's war, its application to the Chinese navy and resemblance to traditional Chinese naval systems was unmistakable. For example, the main forces closely resembled the Manchu Banner Army, which operated across provincial boundaries, while the regional forces were similar to the Army of the Green Standard, which defended specific provincial geographic areas.

Within the PRC navy, Mao's organizational concept was soon implemented. One Chinese admiral explained the naval organization as being entirely founded on the army system.

> Our Navy is built on the basis of the ground forces of the PLA. . . . There are no better conditions for building our navy than the solid foundation laid by the PLA. Such a foundation has obviated the method of trial and error, or at least minimized the errors, in the building of our navy, which is being built successfully in accordance with the glorious tradition of the PLA.[28]

Although the above quote had political implications, it did accurately reflect Chinese intentions to organize the navy along army lines. Hence, by the mid-1950s naval organization began to take a form that was decidedly traditional. Its major elements are described in the following sections.

THE NAVY HIGH COMMAND

The PRC Navy Headquarters was created in 1950 and operated fairly autonomously during the early growth period. However, as was so often true in the imperial and republican periods, it remained subordinated to an army-dominated command system. Thus, for operational matters, the Navy Headquarters reported to the General Staff Department. This important department, in turn, took its orders from China's national command authorities: the chairman of the Chinese Communist Party (CCP), the Party Central Committee (or its designated representative, the Politburo), and the Military Commission of the CCP. If events so dictated, these authorities could bypass middle-echelon commands.

One of the middle-echelon commands that played a command-and-control role in the navy was the Military Region Command. Patterned after the traditional provincial system, it had thirteen military regions (two were later abolished). Headed by military region commanders, these areas become important in wartime situations when the normal command-and-control systems are jeopardized. The commanders, like old-time viceroys, have authority over all units assigned to their regions, including naval units.[29] Tactics employed would be of the guerrilla-warfare type. The military region commander is expected to defend his geographic region indefinitely without orders from high authority.

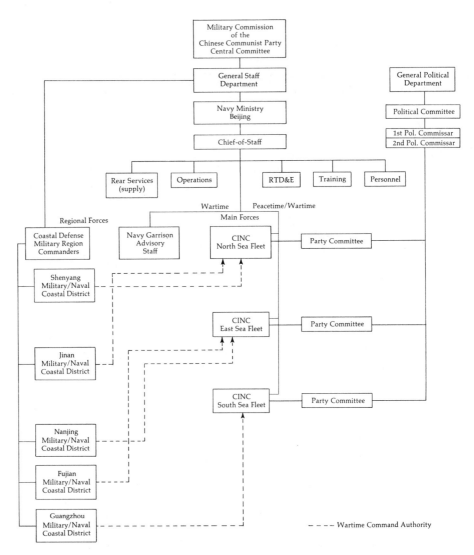

PRC Navy organization. The PRC Navy remains greatly decentralized. (Courtesy of the U.S. Naval Institute Press, Annapolis.)

THE FLEET SYSTEM

By 1955 the PRC had adopted the three-fleet system, similar to the fleet arrangement proposed by Zuo Zongtang in 1880. These fleets were the North Sea Fleet, whose region covered the Yellow Sea and Bohai Gulf areas from the Korean border to the Shandong-Jiangsu provincial boundary; the East China Fleet, from the Shandong-Jiangsu boundary to Guangdong Province; and the South Sea Fleet, whose area extended from the Fujian-Guangdong boundary to the Vietnamese border, including Hainan Island. The headquarters for the three fleets were in Qingdao, Shanghai, and Zhanjiang, respectively.[30]

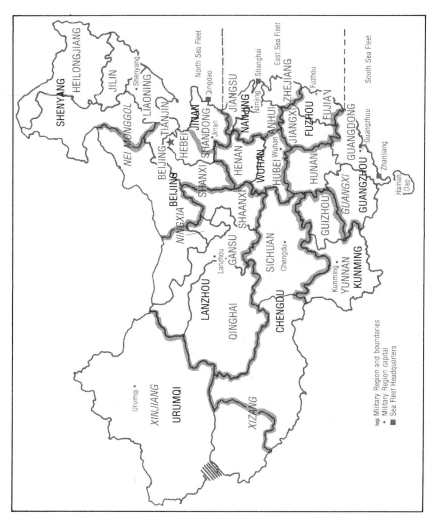

PRC military regions and naval fleets.

Organizationally, the fleets were formed in a manner closely styled after the past. For example, there were main forces, or *zhuli jun*, composed of units which could operate at a distance from the coast or perform intrafleet operations. The units consisted of submarine and large surface combatants (destroyer escorts and above). Later, Mao's *zhuli jun* were also designated to perform special assignments such as supporting missile tests at sea.

THE REGIONAL (COASTAL) DEFENSE SYSTEM

The PRC Regional Defense System also retained traditional features similar to the *zhenshu jun*. It was composed of several interlocking elements whose chains of command were not always restricted to the navy. For example, at sea there evolved two distinct coastal defense forces: the Public Security Force (PSF) sea units (similar to Soviet MVD or coast guard units, as well as the traditional Chinese water police), and the naval district defense units (similar to the traditional provincial navies).

The PSF sea units were formally established in 1955, when conscription laws stated that officers of the "seaborne Public Security units" could hold ranks equivalent to the navy, that is, ensign through vice admiral.[31] These units were entrusted with "watch-dog" responsibilities over ports, estuaries, rivers, and fishing fleets. The latter responsibility often took them to sea at greater distances than the navy, which placed the PSF in a coastal-defense or territorial-sea-defense role.*

The naval-district-defense units were formed from smaller vessels, such as torpedo boats and various classes of patrol craft, which had limited sea-keeping capabilities and endurance. They defended local geographic coastal areas, often seaward extensions of the military districts. Thus, as in the past, these craft retained a definite command relationship with the shore coastal-defense system, the third element in the PRC defensive arrangement.

Like coastal defenses in the imperial system, the shore coastal defenses integrated army units and certain specialized naval elements. For example, major coastal—and inland—cities had special garrison forces assigned to them for defense. The navy and air force had elements subordinate to the garrisons. The navy also played a significant role in manning the previously described communications and observation-post system—an obvious throwback to the imperial early-warning system.

Another continuity between the Communist and imperial systems was the large number of ships assigned to the East Sea Fleet. Many were charged with protecting the Yangzi River, for Mao was quite mindful of the fact that in order to control the mainland he needed to control the Yangzi.

---

*The first of the PSF's coastal-defense functions was carried out in 1956, when the PSF minister, Lo Ruiqing, noted that Japanese fishermen, legally fishing in authorized zones 50 to 60 nautical miles from the PRC coast, were being harassed by his seaborne units. Accordingly, he admonished his PSF sailors to "rigidly adhere to our country's foreign policy of peaceful coexistence in the intercourse with our neighboring nations, and resolutely oppose 'big nation chauvinism,' respect the people of other nations, and adopt a friendly attitude toward them."[32]

The Chinese Communist island campaigns of the 1950s also high-lighted the need for further development of naval infantry. However, not one single reference to such a force has ever been noted in the Chinese Communist press or provincial radio broadcasts. In 1958 a Communist naval-officer defector reported that although plans for a marine corps had been initiated, by 1953 they had apparently been abandoned.[33] Analysis of amphibious actions in the 1950s indicates that Soviet-type naval-infantry units, made up of regular PLA infantry personnel, were used for the offshore island campaigns. After the campaigns ended, the units were subordinated again to shore-based armies.[34]

The final element of the regional-defense system is the naval air force. Development of the PRC naval air force began in late 1951, when Soviet air advisors recommended to the Chinese that a naval air force be established. Their recommendations, as advanced to the Chinese, included the Soviet concept that a naval air force primarily should be a defensive force used to control the coast. Its secondary role would entail offensive operations, albeit limited by the range of shore-based aircraft. Thus, in 1952, in accord-ance with the terms of the Sino-Soviet Treaty of 1950, Soviet instructors and technicians began to create a Chinese naval air force made up of aircraft provided by the USSR.[35]

The missions of the naval air force were spelled out by its first com-mander, Vice Admiral Dun Xingyun, on 8 October 1956, when he stated: "The Chinese Navy Air Force has begun to shape up as a combat force. We have fought cooperatively with our brother force in liberating Yijiang Island and the Yushan Islands. We have accomplished our missions of protecting the sea routes and fishing fleet, and of defending our territorial air [space]."[36]

Subordinated to the air force, the PRC naval air force was eventually formed into three air divisions—each corresponding to a fleet region. The pilots initially underwent fifteen months of academic and technical train-ing before being assigned to a division.[37] Three basic types of aircraft were flown by naval air pilots: Soviet piston, twin-engined TU-2s; MIG-15 jet fighters; and IL-28 twin-jet bombers. By 1958 the naval air force increased its order of battle from some 80 aircraft to an estimated 470 planes—an order of battle similar to the present and changed only by the introduction of newer (but same model) aircraft.[38]

THE PRC SHORE COMMAND

The PRC shore command included the previously described schools sys-tem, a rear services (logistics or supply, medical, ship repair, finance, and petroleum), and an operations department. The navy published a naval newspaper that printed stories of navy men as well as passed along in-formation of national significance. There was also a political department, which, as will be seen, played a key role in navy affairs.

NEW STRATEGY CONSIDERATIONS, 1955–60

China's first military modernization program inevitably led to modifica-tions in its strategic thinking. By the mid-1950s many military leaders privately were doubtful of the Maoist "man-over-weapons" principle. They found a champion in Marshal Peng Dehuai, who became the powerful minister of National Defense in 1954. A tough, crusty battlefield commander, Peng led the struggle to modernize China's armed forces in the late 1950s, but was purged in the process. Among many charges later levied against him was that he stressed technology over politics in the navy. He was quoted as stating, "As there are no forests, mountain ravines, green curtain of sorghum fields and no masses at sea, people's war and such stuff are outdated."[39]

The above quote is somewhat misleading, for early in his term as minister of defense, Peng still spoke of the ability of China's vast manpower to survive an American atomic attack. Peng, in fact, still believed that China's ability to survive was proof that a "people's war" was still a viable option in the atomic era.[40]

Peng, however, did admit that the rapid changes being made in military technology required China to adjust its policies to one of "strategic defense against any possible sudden attack from the imperialists."[41] By 1958 Peng was stressing the importance of studying modern military science, strategy, and weapon systems. He also pressed for the development of scientific and technical knowledge. Such programs were to be closely patterned after the Soviet Union's own emerging strategic-force concepts.

Peng's pressure to modernize the military had strong support within the PLA. In the post–Korean War period, many Chinese army commanders believed that large-scale guerrilla tactics were ill suited to long-range artillery and advanced air power. They had statistics to back their argument—it was estimated that UN armies in Korea had accounted for more than nine hundred thousand Chinese killed or wounded. Moreover, the Chinese commanders discovered that the typical PLA soldier was not technically proficient to operate various Soviet-supplied equipment. These arguments were strong ones, but the professionals failed to reckon with the strength of the traditionalists, who had begun to counter the emphasis being placed on the imitation of foreign military systems.

CHAPTER 16

IDEOLOGY VERSUS TECHNOLOGY, 1956–59

Despite the disastrous casualties suffered in Korea, most Chinese ideologues retained a fierce belief in the Maoist people's war. They had faith that if an enemy invaded China, its communications would be severed and supplies reduced by guerrilla warfare. Under these conditions, the enemy would withdraw.

The ideologues, like their nineteenth-century ancestors, did not understand seapower. They viewed attempts to build a large seagoing force as expensive and alien to the idea of a people's war. They also were wary of repeating the past mistake of casting the navy in a foreign mold. Thus, as soon as Soviet assistance began to endanger Chinese independence, it had to be curtailed.

COMPLAINTS OF THE IDEOLOGUES

Some ideologues, in fact, charged that building a navy along Soviet lines and with Soviet aid would doom China to having a navy that could not be depended upon in time of war. The ideologues' chief policy instrument, the CCP, had a number of complaints.

THE PORT ARTHUR–DALIAN TRANSFER

To most Chinese, the port treaties with the Soviet Union continued to be a source of embarrassment, for they represented "neo-extraterritoriality." Although the Chinese story of how the ports were subsequently returned to China is unavailable, Nikita Khrushchev's memoirs provide some details of the Soviet version. His account, in fact, shows that the Sino-Soviet partnership was quite tense, particularly as it affected naval relations. Khrushchev recounts the 1954 meeting between himself and Mao, where the USSR agreed to return the ports to China in May 1955. The Russian premier states that Mao, while strongly desirous of reacquiring the ports, did not want the Soviets to leave abruptly, claiming that the United States might take advantage of such a move and attack China. Khrushchev writes

Khrushchev writes that he countered Mao's argument by pointing out that the Soviet navy could still provide adequate protection from Vladivostok.[1]

Khrushchev's reporting of Mao's concern over a rapid Soviet withdrawal is likely exaggerated. The reason that the Chinese were upset may have been related to the Soviet refusal to leave behind much of the ports' defensive weapons. Khrushchev writes that, during the 1954 talks, Zhou Enlai approached him and asked whether the Soviets would consider leaving their heavy artillery in Port Arthur without compensation. The Soviet Premier responded to Zhou as follows:

> Comrade Zhou, please understand the awkward position in which we find ourselves. We haven't yet recovered from a terribly destructive war. Our economy is in shambles, and our people are poor. We'd be happy to sell you this artillery for a low price, but we simply can't afford to let you have it for nothing. Please try to see our side of the question.[2]

THE ROLE OF THE COMMISSAR

Another problem that surfaced during this period was the attempt to downgrade political commissars in the navy. In the early years of the PRC navy, a ship's captain could issue no order unless it was first approved by the commissar. The apparent power of Chinese political commissars was nothing new; they were generally held in high esteem and respected for their combat knowledge. After all, most Chinese political officers had matured in an era of war and participated in many combat actions. Thus, as far as the navy was concerned, the commissar was as qualified as the commanding officer to lead in combat.

The Soviet system, however, differed from the Chinese. After the Russian Revolution, commissars had been installed aboard Soviet ships to oversee ex-czarist naval officers. They lacked naval experience and their presence was resented. About 1924 the Soviets began to evolve their system of one-man command, where responsibility for combat and ideological training was supposedly vested in the commanding officer. While CCP organizations and commissars remained part of the shipboard organization, by World War II it was clear that the commanding officer decided the type and content of political training.

Based upon later denunciations of Marshal Peng Dehuai (and presumably others), there seems little doubt that he attempted to adopt certain features of the Soviet system for the Chinese military. Within the navy, his supposed disdain for politics and commissars and support of technology became a frequent point of criticism among ideologues who opposed the military modernization programs. He allegedly declared that "in battle the Navy relied upon the tonnage of its vessels, the calibre of its guns and the slide rule."[3] Later, Peng was accused of stating that the Maoist principle of building the army politically did not apply to the navy. In fact, Peng's strong stand on modernizing the fleets technologically was one of the reasons he was purged in 1959. In addition to other charges, he was accused of having abolished the system of political instructors in certain naval squadrons.[4]

THE PAY SCALE

The ideologues were concerned with other side effects of the modernization program. For example, the technological needs of the navy led to an imbalance in the military pay scale, where navy men were better paid than their counterparts in the army. The following is a comparison of a naval officer's monthly pay with that of an officer in the ground forces (in U.S. dollars circa 1957):[5]

Rank	Pay (Army/Navy)
Second Lieutenant/Ensign	20/31
First Lieutenant/Lieutenant Junior Grade	24/36
Captain/Lieutenant	29–33/52
Major/Lieutenant Senior Grade	39–44/60
Colonel/Captain	62–64/128

The navy also received criticism for extravagance in its messes. A rear service officer wrote in the *Liberation Army News*: "For a time, coffee was served at every meal and milk was taken every day and no fish heads or meat skins were eaten. The supply standard was apparently so good for naval ships that not all the money could be spent, even though the mess was amply supplied with chicken, fish, meats, eggs, rice, and wheat flour."[6] The article goes on to state that naval personnel assigned to duties ashore were still drawing sea rations and sea pay and had been able to save several hundred yuan of their food allowance after several months ashore.

DISCONTENT WITH TRAINING

Other problems were beginning to appear in the Chinese press. As early as October 1956 the first reflection of dissatisfaction showed up in a *Liberation Army News* article in the form of a complaint by a navy captain. The captain, a post-graduate naval student at the PLA's Nanjing Military Academy, indicated that while much had been learned from the naval experience of the USSR, not enough was being done to fully develop the spirit of independent thinking and flexibility in applying the Soviet experience to actual conditions in China. He cited several examples of teachers leaving no room for student questioning, as well as teaching materials that were incompatible with current Chinese naval capabilities. For instance, he went on, "when marine battles are categorized, and when it is known that some types of battle cannot be carried out by our naval force, the teaching materials failed to mention this point in clear terms."

Another issue raised by the captain was the stifling of student creativity. For example, he noted that a student could only use one of the many types of submarine patrolling methods. "Consequently, the students could only devote their energy and time to guess what the teacher had in mind and they had little or no time to concentrate their efforts on studying the conditions and ponder on the employment of military power. Lastly, the important stage where students must be trained to command troops in battle was always neglected."[7]

THE PARTY'S RESPONSE

Concern over the proper direction of the navy, coupled with a budget pinch, produced a politically inspired retrenchment policy in the navy in 1957. A campaign was launched to conduct thrifty training and ensure that a policy of expenditure curtailment was carried out. At the large Qingdao naval complex, officers and men were encouraged to adopt measures to save fuel oil. One measure the main force units came up with was the reduction in time needed to prepare a ship for sailing. Shortening the preparation period to 90 minutes, the base commander reported, could save one ton of oil each time that a vessel got under way. He went on to report that the various economy measures cut the total expenditure by 28.5 percent as compared to 1956, and amounted to a savings of 980,000 yuan (431,000 dollars).[8]

Steps were taken to counter the growing Soviet influence as well. One way this was achieved was the reorientation of the navy toward "supporting the masses" in the manner of the army. It was made mandatory for the navy to participate in national construction projects. Accordingly, sailors freed from training became engaged in auxiliary production. In Qingdao in 1957, navy men were reported to have raised a total of 551 head of pigs, sheep, and cattle and cultivated 1,059 acres of land capable of producing 150,000 pounds of grain and 200,000 pounds of vegetables. Sailors devoted more than 11,000 working days to fishery co-ops. During the peak of the wheat harvest, 5,000 officers and men were mobilized at the Qingdao Naval Base, contributing 18,000 working days to the harvest.[9]

The CCP also made other gains. In early 1957, when a conference of navy activists was convened, Admiral Su Zhenhua, newly elevated to the position of first political commissar of the navy, laid great stress on opposing doctrinairism and formalism in the navy.[10] The *People's Daily* quickly followed with an editorial summarizing the Navy Activists Conference on 12 March 1957. It never mentioned Soviet assistance, but glamorized the navy's role in promoting agricultural production and economy in operations, and in encouraging inventions or recommendations by sailors that had resulted in savings to the government, such as refitting old torpedoes in stock into training torpedoes. The editorial emphasized "that the People's Navy must continue to manifest the glorious traditions of the People's Liberation Army . . . and the spirit of devoting their service wholeheartedly to the people should be manifested . . . and the political awareness should be elevated."[11]

Another article appeared in the *People's Daily* on 30 July 1957, written by Vice Admiral Zhou Xihan, chief of staff of the PLA Navy Headquarters. It too reflected growing CCP pressure. While he paid lip service to Soviet assistance and Marshal Peng Dehuai's "correct" appraisal of the modernization of the armed forces, Zhou clearly struck at the central issue in his concluding remarks.

> First of all, the Party's absolute leadership of the Navy must be strengthened. This leadership is the soul of the people's armed forces. They will be lifeless as soon as they are deprived of this leadership. The rightists, always

on the lookout for trouble, understand this quite well, for they have been trying to remove the Party's leadership from the armed forces. . . . The highly class-conscious members of the Navy fully realize that the Party's leadership of the people's armed forces is absolutely necessary and that if it had not been for the Party there would have been no people's armed forces. . . . Had it not been for the leadership of the Communist Party, no such results would have been possible, and there would have been no such People's Navy as the one we have now.[12]

In summary, there was an obvious attempt in 1957 to bring the navy back into the revolutionary fold, through a reidentification with Maoist doctrine and at the expense of reducing naval training and naval professionalism. This was evident when the disagreement over the proper development of the navy reached its zenith in late 1958. At a debate at the Dalian Naval Academy, certain Chinese naval leaders contended that, unlike the army, the navy had neither experience nor foundation, which therefore must be imported from abroad. A *Liberation Army Daily* article reported the vigorous response by the political cadres present.

> Could we really say that the navy and the other branches of service have been built up without foundation? No, these services were built on the foundation of the Army. . . . Based on his personal experience in revolutionary combat and on [the] basis of the dialectical materialist viewpoint, Chairman Mao set out the basic strategy and tactics for the people's revolutionary warfare. . . . These principles apply not only to the Army but the Navy. . . . Over the past eight years our Navy has been built on the framework of our Army under the direction of Mao Zedong's military thought. How can we say that we have no foundation?[13]

The article went on to point out that the central issue was not that of naval experience or foundation, but rather whether the correct method of study was being applied. It stressed that there were two methods, one being "the unity of study with practice," the other "mechanical copying." The latter was considered mere plagiarism, as it discounted actual conditions of a country's natural and physical qualities. The political cadres reiterated that Mao's ideas differed fundamentally from those of the "dogmatists," since they were formed according to the actual situation and not on the advice of foreigners. In summarizing, the political cadres strongly urged naval representatives to remember the following:

> The key to a correct study method and to the elimination of dogmatism lies in cracking down on superstition and the downfall of slave ideology. The way we deal with the masses and with reality is the touchstone. . . . In the past, by relying on the masses and by insisting on practice we defeated the reactionaries in China and abroad and obtained a great victory. At present in the modernization of our armed forces, we should follow the same principle. If only we can rely on the masses and base everything on reality, we will surely work out something which is suitable. . . . A good example was set up by a submarine school in writing its textbook. The principle it followed was: "theory is derived from practice, and skill is acquired through toil." Since the officers and enlisted men are toiling and practicing every day, they will create

something of their own. *All superstition concerning foreign superiority, blind relief in rules and orders and in copying from others represent slave ideology. We must bring about the downfall of slave ideology.* [Italics added][14]

CAUSE AND RESULTS OF THE MATSU-QUEMOY ATTACK

Mao and the CCP had other internal problems to contend with in 1957 and 1958. In May 1957 the Hundred Flowers Movement was launched by Mao, which encouraged intellectuals, scientists, and artists to exercise complete freedom of expression. Within weeks forums were organized throughout China and criticism of the state was rocking the Communist leadership. One prominent Beijing editor proclaimed, "I believe a party that guides a people is not the same as a party that possesses a people; the public supports the Party but the members of the public have not forgotten that they and not the Party are the masters of the nation."[15]

In such an atmosphere of "blooming and contending," the movement soon spread to workers, peasants, and students. Demonstrations increased in frequency in June and slogans welcoming Chiang K'ai-shek and the Kuomintang appeared. Mao and the CCP stopped the campaign in late June and commenced a counteroffensive. Purges followed and mass arrests occurred under the guise of the Anti-Rightist Campaign. The CCP's response could be readily discerned in articles such as one that appeared in July 1958 in the *People's Daily*. It reported as follows:

> Facts prove that the Party is perfectly capable of controlling the vital issues of scientific development. It is precisely in these issues that we must ask the Party to lead. . . . In order to improve leadership the Party leaders in scientific institutions should make a serious effort to study science. Ignorance is not to be feared; reluctance to learn is. The more one knows, the more concrete, more timely, and more accurate one's leadership will be. For the sake of the Party, one must make a tremendous effort to study hard. After three to five years of determined effort, one is bound to know something about a branch of science. *If more time is given, it is not impossible that certain Party workers may become scientists themselves. Science represents knowledge. It is not something mysteriously unknown.* The reason why science was regarded as a mystery during the past is that certain bourgeois scholars had deliberately mystified it. Another reason is that in the minds of some comrades, the difficulty of studying science was overrated. [Italics added][16]

Mao's next effort was directed at improving the struggling Chinese economy. In the spring of 1958, he implemented the Great Leap Forward, a labor-intensive campaign aimed at developing industry and agriculture. Mao's efforts almost caused the state's economic planning and administrative functions to collapse. Simultaneously, the People's Commune Movement was launched, which restructured the old collective system into communes, where membership was to be united under a coordinated command to improve such economic sectors as agriculture, local industry, fishing, and forestry. The movement, however, was far from coordinated; tools and experienced personnel were in short supply. The harvest began to fail and the grain supply was disrupted. By August 1958 Mao and his supporters were under considerable pressure from opponents to end these disruptive policies.

It is this writer's opinion that Mao temporarily halted criticism of his internal economic and cultural policies by creating a crisis in the Taiwan Strait. One hundred eighty MiG fighters were deployed to the Fujian Military Region on 1 August 1958.[17] Army troops numbering nearly three divisions were moved to Fujian from neighboring military regions. Several Shanghai-based PT squadrons were shifted to the Quemoy region via railway, thus rapidly and unobtrusively altering the naval order of battle at the so-called Fujian Front.[18] Although the first air clashes occurred on the fourteenth near Matsu, the shelling of Nationalist islands did not commence until the twenty-third. It lasted until 5 October. The Communists lobbed nearly four hundred fifty thousand shells against the Nationalists— an amount equal to nearly 10 percent of the artillery stockpiled in the PRC. That there was no attempt to launch an amphibious assault lends credence to the theory of a hastily organized feint intended to draw attention away from internal political and economic problems. The Communists did suffer some embarrassing tactical losses—nearly forty MiGs were destroyed versus four aircraft losses to the Nationalists. The Communists also had five PT boats sunk, while the Nationalists sustained no naval losses.[19]

There was another more important loss to the Chinese Communists, however. The offshore island crisis contributed directly to a seemingly irreversible break in relations with the Soviet Union. According to Khrushchev, who was in Peking from 31 July to 3 August 1958, Mao informed the Soviet leader that China was contemplating an attack against Taiwan.[20] When President Eisenhower declared on 27 August that the United States would not "desert responsibilities or standards . . . already made regarding Taiwan and the offshore islands," Khrushchev became apprehensive, thinking that the Chinese may have gone too far.[21] He also discovered that Mao seemed unconcerned at the prospect of a nuclear war. This attitude, more than any other, caused the Soviet leadership to reassess its policy of military assistance to China.

The PRC also lost whatever small gains had been made regarding freedom of movement in the Taiwan Strait. As a result of the crisis, the U.S. Seventh Fleet increased its naval units in the Taiwan Strait. The force totaled some sixty warships, including the carriers *Essex* and *Midway* and the cruiser *Los Angeles*. Smaller ships also began escorting Nationalist convoys to the offshore islands. The PRC response was the issuance of a declaration extending China's territorial waters from 3 to 12 nautical miles, which applied to the coastal islands, Taiwan, the Pescadores, and all other islands claimed as Chinese territory.

THE MOSCOW-BEIJING JOINT NAVAL COMMAND

With the cessation of the Soviet conventional submarine program in 1958 came the development of nuclear submarines. The change was a tremendous one for the Soviet navy, and required the Kremlin to rethink its naval support plans. One concern to the Soviet leadership was the creation of a submarine communications system that could maintain contact with the new long-range nuclear vessels then being designed. They now were desirous of negotiating an agreement with China permitting the placement of a communications facility on Chinese soil. Additionally, the Soviets wanted to consummate a new agreement that would allow Russian naval units to use Chinese ports for refueling, repairs, and shore leave.[22]

To some Chinese leaders, who wanted nuclear weapons and continued Soviet technical aid, the Soviet naval requirements seemed ideally suited for reciprocity. The Chinese, in fact, had already received plans for the new Soviet missile submarine, the G-class SSB. They had also been given plans for the Soviet R-class submarine, which was intended to replace the W-class. Additionally, the Soviets had probably provided blueprints of the 20-nm STYX missile and the new *Osa/Komar*-class craft which was to carry that weapon. Before the Chinese could develop these ships and weapons, however, more Soviet assistance and better relations were required.

It was not to be. Before the island crisis, during his visit to Beijing, Khrushchev had approached Mao with the Soviet proposal, which called for the establishment of a joint Sino-Soviet naval command. Mao opposed the plan. Khrushchev, however, said that Chinese submarines could use the Russian port of Murmansk if the Soviets could use Chinese ports.[23] Mao was less than impressed with this offer and remained adamantly opposed to reopening Chinese ports to the Soviets. According to Khrushchev, Mao's stubborness was due to the Chinese leader's suspicion that such a scheme smacked of extraterritoriality. In 1964 this version was confirmed to a visitor from Japan by a Chinese spokesman, who said: "In 1958 the Soviet Union brought up the subject of forming a combined fleet of China and the Soviets along the coast of China and proposed the erection of Loran C electric wave [navigation] bases jointly by China and the Soviets on Chinese national territory. This proposal was their attempt to get control into their hands. China rejected this: It defended its independence."[24]

Less than a year after Khrushchev's visit, the Sino-Soviet schism crystallized. Withdrawal was partly a result of the PRC's refusal to accommodate Moscow's naval plans. That the break undoubtedly hurt Chinese naval research and development was spelled out in the *People's Daily*. The Soviets "suddenly and unilaterally decided to withdraw all their experts . . . tore up 343 contracts and supplementary agreements concerning the experts and annulled 257 items of scientific and technical cooperation. After that they heavily slashed the supply of whole sets of equipment and crucial parts of installations."[25]

Difficulties in the PRC navy immediately followed. In May 1960 U.S. intelligence reports told of accidental submarine sinkings and unrepaired vessels in the East Sea Fleet. The Chinese confirmed these reports in a series of secret papers later released by the U.S. State Department. While figures were deleted by the Chinese, the description alone highlighted the seriousness of the situation.

> The present training program is troubled by a comparatively important problem; it is the conflict between the training and the maintenance of the equipment and materials. Especially this is true in the technical branches of service of the Ground Force, Navy and Air Force. There is x percentage of the vessels and ships of the Navy to be repaired. A tactical hard-core Navy unit, the 1784th Army Unit, of the East [China] Sea Fleet originally had xx ships, and now only xx ships are operational; the 1385th Army Unit originally had xx ships, and now only xx ships are operational and cannot be submerged.[26]

U.S. intelligence reports also told of a general slowing of naval construction in the several years following the Sino-Soviet break. For example, it took more than a year (1960–61) for two W-class submarines to completely fit out, although the hulls had been finished months before.[27]

The resurgence of the ideologues set in motion a new series of struggles between continentalists and maritime advocates. The conflict once again required the navy to develop within the confines of a self-strengthening movement. Help from foreigners was not tolerated, and naval modernization was to be accompanied by an appropriate amount of political indoctrination.

Related to this "red-versus-expert" problem was the question of strategy, for China was again confronted with continental and maritime adversaries. Without a strong navy, would tradition again prevail? That is, would China seek accommodation with her maritime foes (the United States and Japan) and meet her continental adversary (the Soviet Union) with force?

CHAPTER 17

OLD TRADITIONS, MODERN PRACTITIONERS: COASTAL CONTROL AND THE MARITIME MILITIA

 Only two of Mao Zedong's military-naval entities, the main and regional forces, have been examined. Before addressing their further development in the turbulent decade of the 1960s, it is essential that Mao's third military element, the militia, be discussed, for shortly after the "liberation" of the continent, the Communists made it clear that the traditional Chinese concept of a militia was integral to their plans to consolidate control over the mainland. They defined the militia as follows:

1. It is the military force of the masses, whose members are not disengaged from their civilian employments; its units are made up of producers—the working people—bearing arms; and its organization, combining labor power with armed strength, is at once military and civilian in character.

2. It is organized on a voluntary and democratic basis; its daily life is ordered on the principle of democratic centralism; and its leading members at all levels are, in general, elected democratically.

3. It is an armed organization which has the character of the entire people; it is a vast organization whose many members are scattered widely throughout the villages and cities and engaged in many occupations.[1]

Like all dynasties before them, however, the Communists faced severe problems trying to implement the militia system among the skeptical, sometimes corrupt, and mobile coastal population. In fact, peasant fishermen had not played any significant role in the Communist militia system up to 1950; they had been either under Kuomintang or Japanese control during the previous twenty-five years. Now, however, they were going to be exposed to the Communist indoctrination process and transformed into both a coastal and maritime militia.

PRC CONTROL SYSTEMS

During the first several years of Communist rule, thousands of Chinese boat people fled to Taiwan, Hong Kong, and southeast Asia. An example reflecting the magnitude of the problem of organizing the boat population was given in a New China News Agency (NCNA) news release of 23 July 1951. It indicated that only 47,500 junks and crews out of 510,000 in the Canton area had been successfully organized into fishing collectives. The article stressed four things that required remedial attention. The first three were concerned with combating feudal attitudes, improving wages, and increasing the catch. The last laid stress on "strengthening of measures for education of the fishing folk in patriotism, the extension and consolidation of their organization, and their mobilization for assistance to national defense works."[2]

The news release highlighted the Communists' problem of organizing and controlling fishermen and other boating peoples. In order to gain ascendency over this traditionally independent segment of the population, the Communist government would have to administer strong doses of political indoctrination and exercise stringent organizational control.

ORGANIZATION

In 1950 the PRC found its coastal fisheries in disarray, able to provide only marginal food supplies in the immediate coastal areas. Salt was in short supply and no refrigeration existed. Moreover, boats, nets, and other assorted equipment were antiquated. As a result, fish consumption was restricted to communities along the coast. Nearly one-third of all fish caught in Chinese waters was either consumed in Shanghai or shipped up the Yangzi River. The Communists also inherited the sizable smuggling and pirate organizations left behind by the fleeing Nationalists.

The first step taken by the PRC was to dismantle the traditional port-marketing system and organize all coastal boating peoples into production units or fishing collectives. Working outward from the shore, the Communists divided the broad continental shelf into three main types of fishing zone.

1. Beach and estuaries—in this zone people were permitted to use sampans or small scows to harvest mollusks, crustaceans, seaweed, and miscellaneous invertebrates such as sea urchins and jellyfish.

2. Immediate coastal waters to 20 miles offshore—here traditional sailing junks and other small hand-powered boats fished seasonally for the major fishes such as croaker, cod, hairtail, and shrimp.

3. Offshore 20 to 300 miles—initially, only a small government fleet of large power vessels was available to the Communists to carry out this fishing, and it had to compete with the larger, more efficient fishing fleets of Japan, Taiwan, and Hong Kong.[3]

Ashore, the Communists standardized fishing ports into major and minor centers and designated distribution, marketing, and supply ports. The Bureau of Aquatic Products was established and assumed responsibility for setting catch targets as well as formulating saltwater fishing policy.

Once the paper-organization process was finished, the Chinese undertook the more difficult task of indoctrinating and organizing the numerous fleets. The system they set up was not innovative. In fact it was nearly identical to the group-responsibility and mutual-guarantee systems used by the Manchus in the eighteenth and nineteenth centuries. For instance, the Communists had at least two members of a boat family live ashore, and strict regulations were promulgated that required junks to obtain permission to sail. Additionally, fishermen and water-transport workers had to file trip schedules and account for all personnel aboard prior to clearing port. As in the Qing system, boats were organized into sections of ten vessels. Members of each section were held responsible for defections or illegal activities of any vessel in their section. In the case of fishermen, all boats in a section were required to maintain contact while engaged in fishing.[4]

Despite these precautions, in late November 1952 more than three thousand persons defected en masse aboard some four hundred junks from the Zhongshan District in Guangdong Province to Hong Kong. As a result of this flight, political vigilance was tightened in each coastal province and the Sea Coast Department was set up to direct the political organization aboard fishing boats. At least one reliable CCP member was embarked aboard each major fishing vessel and a member of the Young Communist League went aboard the smaller vessels. Based upon personal interviews with defectors, one scholar found that the Sea Coast Department consisted of eight men. He was informed that "under a department head and deputy, there was one 'custodian,' who also acted as a statistician, and five staff members."[5] Beyond this, the department had no other staff or forces of its own located in the coastal areas, but rather worked through regular CCP channels and the PSF.

Ashore, the central government established fisherman's collectives in the larger fishing centers. Each collective had a chief supervisor and a CCP cadre assigned as a deputy. One of their chief responsibilities was the screening of fishing-license applicants to ensure that the applicant had properly registered the names of his shore-based "guarantors." A report was then submitted to the local CCP branch headquarters for approval.[6]

One of the licenses, issued in 1951, came into American possession. Its issuing authority was the Haidao Branch Bureau, Pearl River Area, Guangdong Province. The preamble illustrated the maritime-defense function that fishermen were directed to serve—"strengthening National Defense, preventing raids and infiltration"—and ended with the following admonition: "If it is discovered that some other vessel is violating the regulations contained herein, the fact must be revealed and reported to an office of this bureau. A suitable reward will be given when the offender is arrested. Offenders will be punished according to the degree of their offense."[7]

The regulations required the junk master to register his vessel, obtain a license, and obtain an arms license if arms were to be carried. The regulations strictly forbade piratical operations, smuggling, the evasion of duty, the housing of prostitutes, gambling, and opium smoking.

The effectiveness of the campaign to control coastal fishermen was best illustrated on the Shandong Peninsula, where both farmers and fishermen formerly had banded together, committing acts of piracy during the two decades preceding the Communist takeover of the mainland. By April 1956 the Communists had established 787 fishing collectives, involving nearly seventy-six thousand households, which represented nine-tenths of the Shandong fishermen.[8]

INNOVATIONS

Other programs were launched to gain the confidence and cooperation of the fishing fleets. The central government set up loans from government banks for the repair and enlargement of the fleets, and incentives like marine insurance were added in the event of boat damage.[9] The government also built motorized trawlers and installed radio transmitters aboard the larger units.

Schools were set up by the PLA to teach coastal peoples to read and write. They were also assisted in rehabilitating their villages and improving their living conditions through reclamation projects and the erection of medical facilities. Such tactics gradually paid dividends: by the mid-1950s the pirate menace was nearly ended. Many fishermen lived ashore, organized into collectives. Their cooperation in the Communist militia effort to make the coast safe was praised as follows: "The fishermen on the islands and along the coast also ardently love and support their own military units. The fishermen often voluntarily helped the PLA arrest pirates, offering clues concerning the pirates. They defend their own happy life and the Coast of the fatherland shoulder to shoulder with the military units."[10]

A number of administrative changes took place between 1954 and 1958 that affected the development of the maritime militia. Fishing collectives were transformed into state fishing corporations and fishing communes. This transformation brought about a new division of effort between state and provincial authorities.

For example, twelve state fishing corporations were established along the coast. There were three major corporations corresponding to the three sea areas: the Luda Corporation—Yellow Sea; the Shanghai Corporation—East China Sea; and the Nanhai Corporation—South China Sea. The remaining nine minor corporations, nominally under provincial control, were located at traditional minor-marketing posts, such as Tianjin, Qingdao, Fuzhou, and Beihai.[11] Together these corporations possessed the bulk of China's trawlers and seiners. They were assigned sea-fishing responsibilities from the 20-nm zone up to longitude 124° east.[12] They also possessed processing and cold-storage facilities ashore and handled the distribution of their catch through state-managed markets. Twenty percent of the annual catch was gotten by the corporations.

Fishing close to the coast, which accounted for the remaining 80 percent of the catch, was carried out by fishing communes located in the more than 140 coastal counties. Members continued to fish in the traditional manner. Most lacked modern vessels and facilities. In fact, even today, they still must salt and dry their catch at sea, lest it spoil en route to market.[13]

By 1959 it appeared that the Chinese Communists had accomplished what few governments before them had been able to do. China's fishing

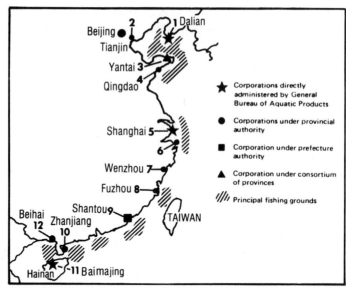

1. Luda (Dalian) State Fishing Corporation, Liaoning Province Fleet: at least 150 trawlers and seiners; estimated annual catch: 80,000 metric tons; 2. Tianjin State Fishing Corporation; 3. Yantai State Fishing Corporation, Shandong Province Fleet: approximately 100 trawlers; estimated annual catch: 50,000–60,000 metric tons; 4. Qingdao State Fishing Corporation, Shandong Province; 5. Shanghai State Fishing Corporation Fleet: at least 200 40-meter trawlers of 600 hp, and 50 15-meter seiners; estimated annual catch: 130,000 metric tons; 6. Zhoushan State Fishing Corporation (based in Shenjiamen), Zhejiang Province; 7. Wenzhou State Fishing Corporation, Zhejiang Province; 8. Fuzhou State Fishing Corporation, Fujian Province; 9. Shantou State Fishing Corporation, Guangdong Province; 10. Zhanjiang State Fishing Corporation, Guangdong Province; 11. Nanhai (South China Sea) State Fishing Corporation (based in Baimajing), Hainan Island, Guangdong Province Fleet: at least 60 trawlers; number of seiners unknown; estimated annual catch: 30,000 metric tons; 12. Beihai State Fishing Corporation, Guangxi Autonomous Region.

(Information contained on this graphic reprinted with the permission of *The China Business Review*, Washington, D.C.)

fleets had undergone a complete metamorphosis and a vast network of effective controls had been established that reached down to the individual level. In terms of production the statistics were impressive: in 1959 China ranked second in the world among fishing nations.[14]

The initial success of the ocean fishing industry led to mistakes, however. Many productive inland ponds were destroyed as farmers were encouraged to fill them in and concentrate on growing grain. The state fishing corporations arbitrarily fixed prices and quickly undermined the enthusiasm of the profit-minded communal fishermen. Additionally, equipment modernization and the emphasis on increasing the catch soon proved disastrous. For example, shrimp became seriously depleted in the Yellow Sea and some popular types of carp disappeared entirely from large rivers.[15]

COASTAL DEFENSE AND RELATIONS WITH THE NAVY

Foundations for the maritime militia became more firm, as some boats were armed and actively participating in reconnaissance duties, filling the void of a Chinese navy that was only beginning to take shape. At a fishing exhibit in Shanghai the following was reported:

> The fishermen along the coast, taking fishing nets in one hand and rifles in the other, keep a vigilant eye open for enemies who dare to invade. Many fishermen have trained themselves as militiamen and some have captured armed agents sent by the U.S. Chiang espionage organization to carry out sabotage activities on the mainland. In this way they are also making a contribution to their country's defense.[16]

Further evidence of the close relationship of the maritime militia with the PRC navy is furnished in the message of appreciation extended to the Naval Commands of the Chinese People's Liberation Army on 31 December 1957 by the Bureau of Aquatic Products. "Our fisheries were often disturbed by the enemy.... Safety in fishery operations was impossible but for the protection of naval units."[17] The message also expressed gratitude for gifts from navy units of such items as radio sets and signaling lamps. It is significant to note that Rear Admiral Yuan Yelie was identified as vice minister of the Bureau of Aquatic Products in May 1960, after previously being assigned as vice commander of Navy Headquarters in Beijing in 1957.

Close coordination between the fishing militia and the navy was reflected in a statement made by the chief of staff of the Military Affairs Commission, General Lo Ruiqing, on 15 May 1961, when he said: "Our Navy has two ships engaged in fishing over 70 nautical miles off the coast. One of them had an accident, and the other was not able to send the message to headquarters. Finally, the sailors asked the civilian fishing boats to report the situation to the local authorities, who forwarded the message to the navy. Only then did we find out about their plight."[18]

Even in battle, where main-force naval units were committed, the peasant fishermen played an active role. During a skirmish with the Nationalists in the 1950s, a Communist torpedo-boat flotilla received orders to ambush and attack a Nationalist ship that was operating in the area. To reach the Nationalist vessel, the Communist PT boats had to pass close to Kuomintang-held islands. The problem of how to get the torpedo boats by the islands undetected was solved with the cooperation of the fishermen. They concealed the PT boats within a large force of fishing junks. Several junks then assumed patrol and reconnaissance duties while the torpedo boats lay at anchor. Once the Nationalist ship was located, the torpedo boats struck from the fishing fleet and severely damaged the Nationalist vessel.[19]

The extent to which the Chinese relied on the maritime militia for early warning and armed resistance at sea became even more significant following the Sino-Soviet split in 1959. In the aftermath of the Soviet exodus, the Chinese main-force navy had begun to experience a great many materiel and training problems. To overcome this, Marshal Ye Jianying, a prominent member of the powerful Standing Committee of the Military Affairs Commission, provided a report on 22 June 1961 on the problems of military training. In that report he recommended that navy men be assigned to

Maritime Militia, Tonkin Gulf (1969). A study in contrasts. Here an armed fishing junk watches the USS *Bon Homme Richard* (CVA 31) during the Vietnam War. (Courtesy of the U.S. Naval Institute Reference Library, Annapolis.)

mechanized junks for fishing expeditions "so as to toughen those who are prone to seasickness and to have more experience in navigation."[20] Quite obviously, then, while the main forces trained and economized, the burden of coastal defense remained the responsibility of the peasant fisherman.

More recently, the Chinese have used the maritime militia as an instrument for carrying out foreign policy. In the spring of 1978 more than two hundred deep-sea fishing craft appeared off the PRC-claimed Diaoyudai Islands—known as the Senkaku Islands in Japan, who also claims them—southwest of Okinawa. Their presence upset relations between China and Japan just as the two nations were preparing to sign a peace and friendship treaty. For over four weeks fishermen circled the barren islands, taunting Japanese patrol craft by waving signs claiming Chinese sovereignty. It is still unclear why the Chinese fishermen did this. The incident caused Japan to seriously reappraise the islands' ownership and value, as well as weigh the importance of going ahead with the treaty planning. In the end the ships were ordered home and the treaty signed, but not before Japan concluded that the territorial question regarding the islands would be an important issue in future relations with the Chinese.[21]

In conclusion, one vital point stands out in regard to the peasant-fisherman maritime militia: since 1949 it has played a much more dynamic role than its continental counterpart. The inland militia since that time has been the object of a number of campaigns designed either to downgrade its importance or give it strong CCP support. However, support is given usually for economic and political reasons alone. On the other hand, the peasant-fisherman militia operates on that uncertain frontier beyond the coast, which gives its activities a more active military flavor. It would be fallacious to dismiss the militia's wartime potential to carry out various missions such as minesweeping, minelaying, supply lift, reconnaissance, or foreign-policy activities.

CHAPTER 18

SELF-STRENGTHENING AND THE STRATEGY DEBATE, 1960–65

The five-year period following the formal break in relations between China and Russia was pivotal. The Chinese not only faced problems with their Soviet "lend-lease" weapon systems, but the nation experienced a general economic depression brought on by Mao's Great Leap Forward policies. It was both a period of strain and a period of debate as various CCP and PLA factions argued over how to achieve Chinese strategic goals. These goals were concerned with (1) how to assure national security, (2) how to attain great-power status, (3) how to achieve unification (that is, recover Taiwan and other regions), and (4) how to promote revolution and socialism in the world.

The basic issue was familiar by now—whether or not to imitate foreign technologies and strategies. On one end stood Chinese leaders of various backgrounds and ideological persuasions. They believed that attainment of China's strategic goals could not be accomplished without renewed Sino-Soviet unity and the further input of Russian technology. In the center there was a latent group that discarded the Stalinist economic model. They believed that, if modernization were to be sucessful, China could not afford to ignore the technical know-how of the West. On the other end were the ideologues who opposed importation of technology from outside China. Chinese naval development depended upon how these opposing factions would compromise on the issues.

LIN BIAO AND THE NAVAL RED-AND-EXPERT POLICY

The man charged with overseeing the next phase of China's naval modernization program was the new minister of National Defense and senior vice chairman of the Military Affairs Commission, Marshal Lin Biao. A participant in the Long March, Lin had fought in many campaigns and been wounded several times. Of all of China's senior military leaders, he was the one most trusted by Mao. His appointment came as no surprise to the CCP and military hierarchy. Lin was not a political novice, for, while he had many enemies, he possessed the politician's instinct to survive when major issues were at stake.

Mechanical failures then rampant in the navy forced Lin to review technological priorities. Some naval leaders wanted to follow up on their Soviet-style missile-submarine program. They pointed out that the Soviet navy was already placing missile-equipped G-class diesel and H-class nuclear submarines in serial production. Naval developments undergoing subtle change in other parts of the world did not escape the attention of these leaders.

At the same time, Lin was faced with accommodating the arguments of the ideologues, who viewed most new concepts as revisionist. They wanted to use China's vast manpower to fight an invader in a protracted struggle inside Chinese borders. Under such conditions, the navy was a minor factor, clearly limited to its traditional coastal-defense mission of local guerrilla-style interdiction operations.

Initially, at least, Lin Biao chose a course of action that seemed to mollify both groups. He would press for the further development of a technically proficient naval force, but one that emphasized "politics in command." Such a course was risky, and in order to carry it out Lin needed the complete cooperation of the naval leadership. To insure that cooperation, he used his own men to infiltrate the navy. For example, between 1960 and 1964, a new group of officers was promoted to navy flag rank. Of thirty identifiable officers, at least nine were ex-members of Lin Biao's old Fourth Field Army: three were appointed to high political and military positions in the South Sea Fleet; four were assigned to similar positions in the East Sea Fleet; and at least two were in the Beijing Navy Headquarters. One of the latter admirals, Li Zuopeng, a long-time Lin protégé, would become both the navy's deputy commander and "first political commissar." Admiral Xiao Jingguang retained his position as chief of naval operations, perhaps because he had served for many years under Lin during the civil war.[1]

Another old Lin associate, Vice Admiral Fang Qiang, was named to head the Sixth Ministry of Machine Industry, formed in 1963. (The ministry was charged with merchant-ship and naval-combatant design and construction.) Fang's credentials remain somewhat obscure. In the 1930s he had considerable combat duty. In 1942 he studied at the Red Army University in Moscow, possibly specializing in engineering. He commanded the PRC South Sea Fleet in 1952–53 and later was a deputy commander of the East Sea Fleet.[2]

DEVELOPMENTS DURING THE EXPERT PHASE

Fang's appointment and the creation of the Sixth Ministry were apparently manifestations of Lin Biao's desire to move on boldly with naval research and development projects, for despite political opposition, the navy did begin to move ahead in both theoretical and practical programs.

The most ambitious project undertaken during this period was the study of nuclear propulsion and the development of a model of a teardrop-shaped nuclear submarine hull. This effort, carried out at the Shanghai Jiaodong University, involved highly theoretical research. A report of these studies appeared in the Chinese-language periodical, *Zhongguo Zaochuan (Chinese Journal of Shipbuilding)*, in April 1965. Both the articles and critiques, which were appended, displayed a keen awareness of experiments then being carried out by Western and Soviet experts.[3]

Other theoretical studies during this period showed the same knowledge of sophisticated Western and Soviet research and development. For example, in 1963 the Shanghai Shipbuilding Society published a series of articles with excellent bibliographies on the following advanced subjects: linearized theory for two-dimensional, fully cavitated hydrofoils; maneuverability of jet-propulsion ships; forecasting methods for performance curves and points of variable working conditions of the turbine supercharged two-stroke diesel engine; theory and analysis of vertical-blade propellor characteristics; a new method for approximate calculation of viscous resistance on a ship with a smooth hull; and viscous resistance of a body in a fluid during oscillation.[4]

The Chinese concentrated their engineering efforts on research of British Napier and West German Junker four-shaft engines.[5] These engines, capable of large power, were nonetheless lightweight enough for installation in torpedo boats and hydrofoils. Lin Biao apparently approved of continued research on these engines, which had begun in the late 1950s. By the early 1960s, research at various Shanghai shipbuilding design institutes was moving ahead in the study of engine vibrational and dynamic characteristics and hydrofoil static characteristics.[6]

Considering China's naval defense needs, there appeared to be good reason for the increased emphasis on theoretical research. Based upon the construction seen a few years later, it seems likely that both Mao and Lin Biao intended to pursue a modified Soviet-style naval construction program. Obviously relying upon Russian plans left behind during the 1950s, the Chinese pressed ahead in limited production of submarines and small surface combatants. For example, nine more W-class submarines were launched between 1960 and 1964, and by late 1964 a follow-on prototype, a replica of the Soviet R class, was in production.[7]

Both the R and W classes served to potentially extend China's offensive naval capability. The R class, for example, has about a 7,000-nm range and a 35- to 45-day fuel capacity. The older W class has about the same range and fuel capacities. Both classes must snorkel at regular intervals, and when running on the battery submerged, their speed over long distances is greatly reduced. However, for Chinese shallow-water coastal-defense operations, where neither endurance nor speed are factors, both the R- and W-class submarines are ideally suited to carry out local interdiction missions. From a conventional-weapons standpoint both classes possess formidable capabilities. Each carries eighteen to twenty 533-mm torpedoes, and during the attack phase these submarines can reach submerged speeds up to 15 knots for short distances.[8]

The Soviets also left behind the blueprints for a conventionally powered missile submarine, the G class. The Chinese wasted little time constructing a prototype, launching one in 1964 at Dalian. The submarine was designed to carry three surface-to-surface missiles (the SS-N-4 Sark). Each missile had an approximate 600-km range. The submarine had to surface during the launch phase. But the development of the G-class weapon system was another matter. The Soviets had not been very accommodating about giving the PRC missile blueprints, and the Chinese are still trying to perfect missiles for this one, their only missile submarine.[9]

Chinese studies did lead to success in the construction of smaller coastal combatants. By the late 1950s the first hydrofoil, the *Huchuan* class, appeared. Capable of speeds up to 55 knots in calm seas, these ships carry two torpedo tubes, four 127-mm guns, and have an estimated 500-nm range. Serial production of the *Shanghai*-class patrol craft also increased significantly during the early 1960s. These ships, of which four types now exist, average 128 feet in length and carry a variety of small guns. Some have torpedo tubes and all carry depth charges. Most can be quickly refitted to carry mines.[10]

Significantly, the PRC naval planners made no effort to design or construct any new amphibious warfare vessels. Rather, the Chinese went to great lengths to keep their older LSTs, LSMs, and LSILs in good running order, but as will be seen later, these vessels were used as much for auxiliary or civil purposes as they were for military operations.

NAVY OPERATIONAL TRAINING

The PRC navy also implemented a monthly training program that required ship crews to train at an exhaustive rate. Described in 1961 as "intensive practice in the harbor and qualitative practice at sea," the navy commenced a monthly training cycle where officers and enlisted rates were divided into training sections.[11] For several days each week, "blackboard" workshops were conducted in which planned activities for at-sea training were carefully outlined to each training section. The remainder of the week was spent at sea, with vessels getting under way early and returning to port at night. While at sea, each training section apparently rotated through the basic shipboard routine, so that each became proficient in deck, engineering, navigation, and weapon drills. Thus, each man was qualified to perform basic responsibilities in every department.

Finally, a monthly at-sea program was carried out with a specialized type of training that required extended sea time. Ships were instructed to exercise intensively at high-seas navigation and conduct periodic inter-fleet transits. Also, ships were directed to carry out collective training while at anchorages. There was apparently little deviation from the highly stereotyped system, and ship's crews continually retrained in accordance with the monthly program.[12] To ensure further continuity, both officers and enlisted men remained assigned to ships for many years.

CHINESE NAVAL EXPANSIONISM?

Although the PRC seemed content not to exacerbate naval relations in the Taiwan Strait, it was making tentative moves in other regions of the

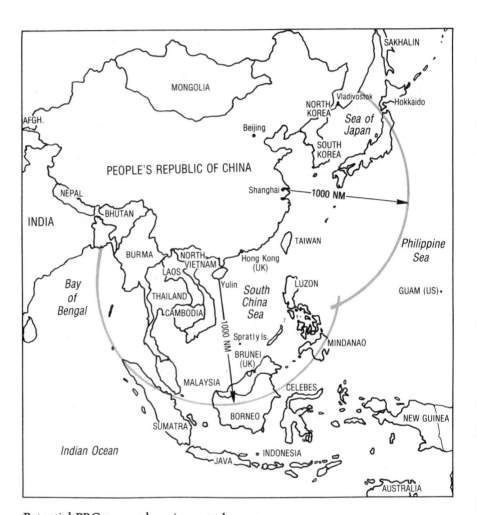

Potential PRC navy-submarine patrol areas.

PRC submariners in readiness drill. China's navy men train at an exhaustive rate. Here, sailors assigned to two R-class submarines dash aboard ship for drills. (Courtesy of the U.S. Naval Institute Photographic Library, Annapolis.)

world that had naval implications. During this period some Western press releases hinted at possible Chinese naval expansionist policies.

One ocean area that figured prominently in the accounts was the Mediterranean. There Albania, who had sided with China against Soviet revisionists, began receiving the attention of Chinese naval advisors. In 1961 the Soviet navy had a fleet of twelve W-class submarines stationed in the Albanian port of Vlona. When Moscow and Tirana broke off relations that year, the fleet was ordered home as part of the withdrawal of Soviet military aid to the Albanian "political deviationists."[13] Albanian authorities opposed the departure of these submarines, and fighting broke out as the Soviets attempted to leave the port. Eight submarines forced their way past the naval blockade, but four were captured by the Albanians. However, Soviet sailors had removed several vital engine parts and destroyed other key control devices. Albania subsequently requested Chinese submarine experts to come to Vlona and put the ships back into working order. Chinese technicians arrived in 1962–63; officers and crews followed shortly thereafter. According to Italian accounts, by 1965 the submarines had been refitted, but their operations were under the complete control of Chinese crews, who were carrying out training operations in the southern Adriatic.[14]

It is not known how long the Chinese continued to operate these vessels for Albania. However, for the ensuing decade of close Sino-Albanian relations, the Chinese probably made good use of these ships for training their own crews in deep-water operations.

THE RED PHASE

As mentioned previously, Lin Biao intended to consolidate political control over all elements of the military. A campaign was launched in November 1960 that directed thorough background investigations and purging, if necessary, of military personnel involved in critical functions.

Within the navy, fleet-level political commissars were exhorted to "learn from the Army" and sharpen their technical skills in order to gain the confidence of the navy rank and file. The commissar was directed to improve ideological training among the crew, while at the same time he was to avoid acquiring the image of a watchdog by strengthening his technical expertise.

By 1961 the influence that political commissars had in naval affairs was significant. They wielded considerable command authority aboard ships. In this regard, commissars took complete control of shipboard routines related to the crews' duties, including ideological education and supervisory work in matters ranging from navigation to safety. Evidence of this is contained in a series of secret documents that reached the West. One article described how "Warship 703" (probably an LST) had safely sailed thirty-five thousand nautical miles from 1955 to 1960. The ship had completed training for more than seventeen hundred midshipmen and participated in maneuvers at sea with other fleet units more than one hundred times. The fact that the ship was able to perform all its missions safely was attributed to CCP control exercised aboard the ship.[15]

The article goes on to report how the ship's CCP branch carried out certain operational functions that would normally be performed by the navigational department on a Western ship.

> Whenever preparing for a mission, the Party branch always made a study of the mission and took all necessary measures for safety. For example, they were supposed to go to the maritime area of Zhoushan Island, Zhejiang, in 1959 without previous experience of visiting the area. The Party branch called a special meeting to make a study of safety measures to be adopted, as the sea currents of Zhoushan were complicated by many narrow channels of navigation and the Party branch had no materials on hand with regard to this area. After their arrival at Zhoushan, they made a further study of the navigation conditions of the area and obtained some directions and assistance from the base; consequently they were assured of safe navigation.[16]

The engineering article also reflects the naval commissar's commitment to be as well versed in shipboard operations as his army counterpart was in military tactics and strategy. Commissars formulated four points of care to be heeded by the engineering department: (1) to test the temperature of the bearings, (2) to listen to the sound of different sections, (3) to look carefully at the readings indicated in instruments, and (4) to take careful note of the odor of the machines.[17]

The real essence of the article, however, was that the CCP had complete authority to train new personnel in all facets of day-to-day operations. The captain and other department heads were essentially watch standers. On the previously described voyage to Zhoushan Island, both the captain and the chief navigator remained on the bridge throughout the voyage, continuously rotating watches. The organizational and psychological aspects of shipboard life remained in the hands of the political commissar.

So Chinese shipboard routine had a political nature. The commissars prided themselves on their frequent inspections and criticisms. A typical routine included holding departmental meetings twice a month and squad meetings weekly. For the purpose of carrying out safety measures and making timely inspections, the entire ship's company held meetings periodically.[18]

THE PROBLEMS OF POLITICS

The navy's indoctrination campaign was not without problems, however. Some commissars were conscientious to the point of over zealousness. For example, Lin Biao had initiated a program with the rating of "four-good units" and "five-good sailors." These were designations of political excellence for ships and individuals who promoted political unity, livelihood, and military skills and tactics. In order to qualify for the "four-good" designation, a division had to be good (1) in political and ideological work, (2) in the "three-eight" work style, (3) in military training, and (4) in arranging daily life. In 1963–64 naval conferences began to play up these designations. A naval air unit, for example, was cited for "careful political and ideological work as well as achieving a safe flying record." A signalman was praised for his political fervor by manning a remote island lighthouse for twelve continuous years.[19]

On those ships and individuals who had difficulty attaining these awards, however, there was considerable pressure brought to bear by the embarked commissar. A case in point was a W-class submarine that failed to be rated a "four-good" unit in 1961. For a whole year following this failure, the commissar called an endless series of crew meetings to determine the "cause of the backwardness" and to study ways to catch up with more efficient sister ships. Eventually, the enlisted members began to speak out and criticize the officer corps, indicating that the latter refused to listen to suggestions made by the crew. The commissar apparently took the officers to task and demanded closer cooperation between them and the crew. When training at sea, the captain and executive officers were required to "regularly and promptly submit problems concerning tactical direction to the Party Branch Committee for discussion." Subsequently, whenever a training period was concluded, both the officers and enlisted men had to hold a meeting at which they were to criticize themselves publicly and compare themselves with one another.[20] Through this method of coercion, the submarine subsequently won the "four-good" honor in 1962.

Schools were most susceptible to the imposition of political ideas, which complicated the process of teaching necessary tactical and technical skills. For example, in 1963 the training of "barefoot" torpedo-boat commanders at "thatched hut" naval schools was extolled by the CCP as an excellent example of revolutionary practices. From 1963 to at least 1969, one of these schools, constructed of bamboo and grass and located in the mountains, provided training for many torpedo-boat commanders destined for duty with the PRC South Sea Fleet.[21]

Sometimes CCP recommendations could become physically and materially destructive. For instance, a coastal PT-boat squadron, prompted by the CCP, undertook an open-ocean mission in 1963 that resulted in serious damage and personnel injuries. The incident was described in a Chinese press release as follows:

> In the winter of 1963, the unit received a distance navigation talk, which entailed sailing long distances on the high seas. According to bourgeois and revisionist theories, PT boats can only work along coastal waters, since they are not equipped or built for deep-sea navigation; such a task as sailing the high seas was deemed impossible. Nevertheless, after careful ideological preparation initiated by the unit's party committee, the mission was successfully carried through, despite heavy winds and high seas that tossed the boats around and inflicted damage and injury to the vessels and men.[22]

The CCP controlled personnel assignments and applications for party membership, which hindered the development of technical expertise. Because it was often suspicious of the emergent naval technocrat, the fleet's political department sometimes relegated Western or Soviet-trained officers to minor posts.[23] It also kept others from joining the CCP, which was a sure method for shortening careers.

RETURN TO LAND RECLAMATION

In the summer of 1962, evidence appeared that the PLA was again attempting to bring naval officers and enlisted men into closer contact with the masses by putting them to work ashore. An article reported that several thousand sailors of the East Sea Fleet worked at a huge land reclamation project for seven months on Chongming Island, the large delta at the mouth of the Yangzi River. The sailors cleared nearly 7,000 acres of land and assisted in planting soya beans, maize, cotton, and wheat.[24] This enormous undertaking also included the construction of a large dike and the creation of new river channels for irrigation.

The article revealed another interesting thing about these navy men: "Seventy percent of the men of the reclamation unit were educated youths from urban areas who newly joined the Navy and who seldom took part in heavy manual labor in the past, especially in agricultural production work."[25] Quite obviously, the fact that nearly three-fourths of this single navy unit was youthful and educated demonstrated that expertness was not being totally neglected.

THE GREAT STRATEGY DEBATE, 1964–65

Due in no small part to impractical political measures, signs of strain were developing between the "reds" and the "experts." Despite the concentrated involvement of the CCP in military affairs, there still existed a powerful group that emphasized military professionalism at the expense of political training and argued for a forward-defense strategy based upon a strong deterrence system. The leading spokesman for this group was General Lo Ruiqing, who had become Lin Biao's chief of staff.

Lo had been a professional political commissar as minister of Public Security, a job requiring excellent administrative skills as well as a knowledge of internal and external security affairs. Thus, while not a professional soldier in the purest sense, Lo did represent that special breed of Chinese commissar who could appreciate and manage the difficult interface between ideologue and technician. For example, he was most conscientious about levying and enforcing crew proficiency-training policies. Once such policy dealt with submarine crew rotation. He apparently made it mandatory that, any time a submarine crew had 30 percent of its billets manned by new recruits or non-qualified personnel, the submarine had to undergo extensive underway training before it could participate in local patrol duties.[26]

As early as 1962, Lo may have begun to doubt the PRC's ability to defend itself against foreign aggression. In that year a series of events seem to have pointed toward a serious reassessment of China's military, economic, and foreign-affairs policies. Reports out of Taiwan indicated general unrest on the mainland. Stories circulated containing statistics of counter-revolutionary activities, as well as numerous cases of robbery, arson, murder, and armed insurrection. Some of the Nationalist propaganda was undoubtedly true, for by April thousands of refugees began to filter out of southern China to Hong Kong. Concurrently with this activity, the Nationalists stepped up their raids against the mainland, causing Beijing to deploy a large number of aircraft and army units to Fujian. In June the Communists again began to shell Quemoy. This elicited a reaction from the United States, who promised to "take necessary action to assure the defense of Taiwan and the Pescadores" if the PRC were to take "aggressive action" against Matsu and Quemoy.[27]

By this time the United States was fending off the USSR in the Cuban missile crisis; the Chinese delivered a thinly veiled attack against Khrushchev's retreat, calling it another "Munich."[28] The Chinese became embroiled with India, fighting a six-week war in October and November over disputed border regions. Although activity in the Taiwan Strait and Sino-Indian border soon cooled down, the war of words between Moscow and Beijing was just heating up. In the months that followed, the Chinese frequently denounced the Soviets, promising that the PRC would expose those modern revisionists who betrayed Marxism-Leninism. The PRC attacked revisionism as the main enemy of the world Communist movement.

In the eyes of some Chinese leaders, including General Lo, the PRC rhetoric was misdirected, particularly in light of the events after August 1964, when the situation in the Tonkin Gulf brought about the introduction of more than one hundred thousand U.S. troops into Vietnam. This was followed by B-52 strikes against North Vietnam in February 1965. With the threat to China's southern flank increasing daily, Lo and others reexamined China's strategic capability and came away nervous about what they found: China had only detonated its first nuclear device in October 1964, and the sole delivery system available to the PRC consisted of a few outdated IL-28 *Beagle* light bombers. These aircraft could carry one nuclear bomb about 1,100 miles on a one-way trip. Meanwhile, the lone Chinese G-class submarine, still in a sea-trial status, had no SLBM capability, and the newly established PRC Second Artillery, a force similar to the Soviet strategic rocket forces, had no weapons.[29]

Faced with these uncertain conditions, Lo published an article in the *Peking Review* in May 1965, in which he expressed great alarm over U.S. intervention in Vietnam. He advocated a forward-defense strategy whereby Chinese forces would be sent to Vietnam to fight with the North Vietnamese against the United States. To do this, what Lo appeared to propose would require normalizing relations with the USSR and the formation of a front for unified action. Lo also argued that the PRC armed forces should begin stressing military training and devote less time to political matters.[30] According to statements critical of him, published during the Cultural Revolution, Lo favored the continued development of nuclear-missile capability as well as general modernization of conventional weapons and forces. Lo's major sin, however, was his recommendation to do away with the Maoist protracted-warfare strategy and replace it with a strategy requiring intensive development of strategic deterrence systems.[31]

Lo also pressed for a more aggressive show of force in the Taiwan Strait; he was later accused of directing PRC naval vessels to extend their combat operations beyond local waters. He was reported to have ignored the chain of command by ordering the Fujian Military Region commander to attack Chinese Nationalist vessels on the sea. Lo was quoted as telling the Fujian naval forces that they could "on their own initiative attack the enemy; in order not to waste any opportunity, strike first and report later."[32] In fact, on 13 November 1965, eight small PRC naval units and two larger Nationalist units fought a fierce two-hour sea battle near Quemoy. Both sides lost several warships; the Nationalists lost the largest ship, a minesweeper.

The incident led to Lo's purge two weeks later. It is interesting that four days after the incident Lin Biao proclaimed the sinking of the Nationalist minesweeper "a result of . . . giving prominence to politics, firmly carrying out the instructions of the Central Committee of the Chinese Communist Party and the Committee's Military Affairs Commission."[33] Six months later Lo would be accused of ignoring higher authorities in ordering the Fujian naval actions. A work group of the CCP Central Committee, in obvious refutation of Lin Biao's statement above, reported the following:

Concerning the question of struggle against the enemy in xx [Fujian] along the coast, Chairman Mao, the Party Central Committee, and the Military Affairs Commission all repeatedly and clearly pointed out that the struggle in the Taiwan Strait was not only a struggle against bandit x [Chiang K'ai-shek], but more importantly a struggle against U.S. imperialism; not only a military problem, but more importantly a political problem. Therefore all military actions against bandit x [Chiang K'ai-shek] should be considered in terms of politics, military strategy, and all other aspects and then decided by the Party Central Committee according to its understanding of the requirements of the overall situation. No person should take his own stand or act lightly without due consideration or without getting authorization from the Party Central Committee. Lo Ruiqing, without asking Chairman Mao, the Party Central Committee, or the Military Affairs Commission for instructions, all by himself brashly instructed xx [Fujian] Military Region that from x day x month on they should fight on the sea.[34]

These statements are interesting for several reasons. First, they clearly show that the CCP was directly involved in the naval strategy decision-making process and, at least in the case of the Taiwan Strait, had the final say on tactics to be used in that potentially explosive area. Secondly, the statements reflect the deep rift between the PLA's military and political factions over how the CCP was to exercise control over the military. Lo had major disagreements with the PLA political faction over the general military organization system. He was later accused of wanting to merge some military regions while expanding the number of main-force military units and downgrading the militia.[35] Lo also wanted to centralize military command and control. Although most of his proposals were logical, they met with little success. One reason for his failure was that such a system would have weakened the power of military region commanders, a degradation they would not stand for.

Since many of his criticisms struck at the very heart of Mao's military theories, Lo Ruiqing's outspokenness could not go unanswered. The task of responding fell to Lin Biao, who, while perhaps in agreement with some of Lo's comments, nevertheless had to defend the Maoist line. Lin rallied support from among the PLA's political faction, the Military Region Command, and the CCP Central Committee. He and his supporters counterattacked by publishing articles that presumably set forth the majority view.

Significantly, Lin chose Admiral Li Zuopeng to make the first response. Li's article, entitled "Strategically Pitting One Against Ten, Tactically Pitting Ten Against One," was a rehash of Mao's protracted-war theories. It refuted Lo Ruiqing's adventurism in dealing with the U.S. invasion of Vietnam, stating that China must be prudent and not "advanc[e] in a reckless way." Admiral Li also criticized people who "wanted to engage the enemy [the United States in Vietnam?] now." Instead Li counseled that China and Hanoi should use guerrilla tactics and concentrate superior forces "to destroy the enemy forces one by one." According to the admiral, this method would be the most "effective way of fighting to change the situation in which the enemy is strong while we are weak."[36] Interestingly, only ten days after Li's exposition was published, ranks and insignia were formally abolished in the PLA. This event seemed to signal the triumph and the strength of the PLA political faction, for the armed forces were now being required to reidentify with the pre-1955 informal, egalitarian military system.

Five months later, Lin Biao jumped into the fray with his own article, "Long Live the Victory of People's War," an important policy statement that attacked the adherents of professionalism and nuclear-deterrence strategy. Lin also indirectly expressed anti-Soviet sentiment by restating the historic PRC position on self-reliance. Referring to the protracted Civil War period, Lin wrote that "the problem of military equipment was solved mainly by relying on the capture of arms from the enemy, though we did turn out some weapons too. . . . Foreign aid can can only play a supplementary role." Lin seemingly closed the door on any further detente possibilities with the Soviets by labeling absurd the assertion that "China's victory in the war . . . was due entirely to foreign assistance."[37]

Lin went on to reemphasize Mao's protracted-war theories, cautioning that the United States was stronger than China at the present time. He attacked those who "assert that nuclear weapons and strategic rocket units are decisive . . . and that a militia is just a heap of human flesh." He left no doubt, too, as to China's position vis-à-vis Vietnam.

> Revolution or people's war in any country is the business of the masses in that country and should be carried out primarily by their own efforts; there is no other way. . . . If one does not operate by one's own efforts . . . but leans wholly on foreign aid—even though this be aid from socialist countries which persist in revolution—no victory can be won, or be consolidated even if it is won.[38]

The Lin Biao–Lo Ruiqing strategic debate highlighted the inability of the ideologue and technician to work in harmony. What had started as an attempt to meld theories and systems ended in alienation, acrimony, and a reaffirmation of technological and political isolationism.

The debate provided a proper backdrop to the next phase of Chinese history—the Great Proletarian Cultural Revolution (GPCR). During the GPCR all political, economic, and military institutions came under the attack of a new generation of revolutionaries. In many ways, the GPCR would resurrect the worst of Chinese traditions—the belief in Chinese political centrality, cultural superiority, and economic self-sufficiency. As it had in the past, such thinking inevitably stifled naval development.

CHAPTER 19

THE NAVY AND THE GREAT PROLETARIAN CULTURAL REVOLUTION, 1966–68

 The Lin Biao–Lo Ruiqing strategic debate was the manifestation of a larger power struggle, one that pitted ideologues against emergent neo-maritime advocates. The latter were led by the old Communist cadre, including men such as Liu Shaoqi, who had been elected Mao's successor in 1959, and Deng Xiaoping, the general secretary of the CCP and a standing member of the Politburo (along with Liu). Both of these veteran leaders viewed China's destiny to be dependent upon more intellectual freedom and human or cultural rights; de-emphasizing domestic and foreign class struggle; improving the economy by adopting "capitalist" wage and material incentive programs; imitating or borrowing from foreign technology; creating a strong and effective collective-leadership system rather than relying on an individual dictatorship; and stressing the development of a modern military force. Liu and Deng also favored the improvement of China's navy and merchant fleet by purchase or charter. They felt that, unless China modestly copied foreign designs and production techniques, any large-scale maritime building program was unattainable.

These were the "gray" issues that became sharply focused in the summer of 1966, when Premier Zhou Enlai clearly expressed the seriousness of the situation. He defined the struggle as one where "the Chinese wanted to liquidate entirely by this 'cultural revolution' all the old ideas, the entire old culture, all the old habits and customs created by the exploiting classes in the course of thousands of years of poisoning people. . . . We want to create and form in the ranks of the broad masses of the people the new ideas, the new culture, the new habits and customs of the proletariat." Zhou added that the "main cutting edge of this cultural revolution is turned against a handful of bad elements that are waging dirty anti-Communist activity under the cover of a false communism."[1]

Although Zhou's remarks were not intended to incite the Chinese into open violence, only three months passed before pro-Maoist Red Guards, primarily made up of middle-school students, were welcomed by the high leadership in Beijing at a mass rally. More than one million Red Guards were on hand to celebrate the Great Proletarian Cultural Revolution. At this rally Liu Shaoqi seemed to have lost much influence—his name appeared well down the list of those in attendance. Conversely, Lin Biao emerged as Mao's new heir apparent, appearing second on the list after Mao.

Within two weeks, law and order began to break down throughout China as Red Guard activity became more violent. Private homes were ransacked, stores raided, and many people were made to stand public trial. Others were subjected to public beatings or humiliated by being forced to carry signs denouncing themselves.

Soon, however, Red Guard activity encountered a popular backlash. As early as August and early September 1966, resistance groups began to form in a number of cities. Open fighting soon broke out, but the Red Guards still continued to receive prestigious support. For example, on 4 September Beijing Radio broadcast a report indicating that the Red Guards had designated Lin Biao as their leader. Meanwhile, Madame Mao, who now was a deputy head of the Central Committee's Cultural Revolution Group, began to appear at the Red Guard rallies urging further revolutionary action.

By January 1967 it became clear that Mao's opponents were rapidly losing ground. Any hope that the anti-Maoists might have had regarding PLA assistance was dashed when Mao and the Central Committee approved a decision that virtually gave Lin Biao complete authority over the PLA. Madame Mao was rewarded (or rewarded herself) with the appointment as advisor to a new committee charged with directing the PLA. Soon thereafter, news leaks indicated that Liu Shaoqi had undergone public humiliation and been forced to make self-criticisms. Other leaders were similarly attacked and coerced into public confession. Purges ensued.

Amid reports of stepped-up fighting and the defeat of some Red Guard elements, the Military Affairs Commission published an order that permitted the PLA to intervene in the local GPCR. In many cities pro-Maoist vigilante organizations sprang up. Red Guards forced the creation of revolutionary rebel committees, which replaced the traditional CCP municipal committees and People's Councils. Fighting and general disorder intensified, and by February 1967 the PLA began to assume greater police duties in quelling disturbances. Such intervention was required because transportation was being hindered, spring planting was behind schedule, and many government institutions were being hampered in their daily operations.

In the summer of 1967 a significant rebellion at Wuhan took place. PLA units assigned to the Wuhan Military Region openly opposed pro-Maoists and arrested two important envoys sent from Beijing to mediate the conflict. They were released only after Zhou Enlai personally intervened by flying to Wuhan to confer with the military region commander.

Renewed fighting ensued and more important leaders were purged. All of this activity finally resulted in nationwide intervention by the PLA. By early 1968, arrests of Red Guards began in earnest while the army attempted to restore order. A year later disruption had run its course. Many changes had occurred. Among them were

1. The denouncement of CCP control and the concurrent assumption of control by the PLA over nearly all political, economic, industrial, and educational institutions.

2. The purging of many powerful opponents of Mao. In some cases the loss of their leadership and administrative skills spelled disaster for their respective organizations.

3. The ascendency of a new leadership element—the so-called radicals or ideologues. They represented technological isolationism, were strongly anti-Soviet, and favored the doctrine of the people's war.

4. The forfeiture of the police-keeping function to the PLA by a heavily purged Public Security Force.

5. A badly tarnished image abroad as well as a xenophobic foreign policy.

6. The collapse of the school system, which would take more than ten years to rebuild.

THE NAVY ENTERS GPCR POLITICS

In the early days of the GPCR, the navy continued to train at an accelerated rate, but the renewed emphasis on political instruction caused serious rifts in the PRC naval leadership. These strained relations had their genesis during the Lin Biao–Lo Ruiqing controversy and involved the navy's first political commissar, Admiral Su Zhenhua.

Early in his career, Su came under the influence of the tough pragmatist, Deng Xiaoping. Appointed to a regional military staff position in 1949 under Deng, Su was chosen to accompany the latter to Beijing in 1953. Neither man returned to his provincial post. Su was named the navy's deputy political commissar in that same year. Thereafter, his career was quite successful. The rank of full admiral was conferred upon him in 1955 and he was selected to alternate membership of the Central Committee in 1956. One year later, he was appointed the navy's first political commissar.[2]

Su's policies were aimed at improving the marriage of the red and the expert. He was instrumental in carrying out the carefully conceived red-expert programs in the early 1960s, but appeared more inclined toward professionalism and technology. He was an excellent politician, however, and could seemingly manipulate ideological affairs to meet more practical goals.

A good example occurred in early January 1966. At that time the PLA General Political Department carried out a series of meetings designed to ensure that the gun would "always [be] in the hands of the most reliable people." Several orders were generated calling for the military to stress politics, increase political and ideological activities, develop more Maoist programs, emphasize the CCP's leadership, and stress the PLA's responsibility for carrying out CCP policies and principles.[3]

Concurrently with this latest effort to reinforce the CCP's leadership position, Admiral Su, together with his Navy Party Committee, developed a naval campaign that seemed to support these latest CCP requirements. The campaign called for the emulation of a PRC naval hero, Engineman Mai Xiande.

The chronology of events in the Mai campaign began on 11 January 1966. At that time the PRC press printed the first of many stories about Mai, a naval hero wounded in the August 1965 Nationalist and PRC naval clash. According to the stories, Mai was an engineman assigned to a PRC torpedo boat that participated in the attack against a Nationalist warship. He had been wounded early in the battle but remained at his post, keeping the engines running throughout the fight. According to the press releases, Mai's heroism was largely owing to his being "armed with Mao Zedong's ideas," a condition that makes all men "brave and unafraid of death."[4] Shortly thereafter, the New China News Agency, quoting Mai's commanding officer, countered Su's subtle technical and professional line by reporting the following:

> In sea battles, bourgeois navies emphasize the tonnage of their naval craft and the caliber of their guns. The people's navy of the PLA, in line with the revolutionary spirit, makes a practice of going into combat on its own— having the daring to risk their lives in fighting the enemy at close quarters and take captive enemy fighters at close range. By adopting these combat tactics contrary to conventional methods of fighting employed by bourgeois navies, as many instances prove, small gunboats have torpedoed and sunk large U.S.-made naval craft of the Chiang bandit gang. How deplorable it is for bourgeois overlords to be so ignorant of this seemingly unheard-of approach to naval warfare. Let us tell you: This is known as destruction before construction—the revolutionary way of demolishing the old and establishing the new in every possible way.[5]

On the surface, at least, the Mai campaign seemed well tailored to satisfy the CCP's own political-reinforcement campaign. As time went on, however, it became evident that Su paid only lip service to politics, laying stress on professionalism and technical proficiency. Once this was discovered, Su and his second political commissar, Vice Admiral Du Yide, were purged.

Outwardly, at least, Su was identified as a member of the He Long clique. Marshal He was a respected old-time army leader and vice chairman of the Military Affairs Commission. A strong proponent of professionalism and military training, he was not happy with the development of the GPCR. Reportedly, he was upset over the fact that operational training was being degraded by the emphasis on ideology.[6]

For the time being the purge of the professionals ended any overt moves to counter the escalating involvement of the military in the GPCR. And lest there be any doubters, the CCP, in October 1966, published the following exhortation regarding the navy's political responsibilities: "The current GPCR is advancing victoriously in the direction pointed out by Chairman Mao. We must be one with the masses and thoroughly expose, criticize and repudiate the bourgeois line, make a clear sweep of its influence, and resolutely defend the proletarian revolutionary line represented by Chairman Mao, so as to carry through the GPCR to the end."[7]

The statement that clinched the navy's entry into the GPCR was carried in the same article. Admiral Wang Hongkun, long-time deputy commander of the navy, "speaking on behalf of the PLA navy," announced that "all commanders and fighters [i.e., officers and enlisted] of the navy . . . should respond with the greatest resolution and enthusiasm to the great call issued recently by Chairman Mao: 'You should put politics in command, go to the masses, and be one with them and carry on the GPCR even better.' "[8]

THE NAVY VEERS LEFT

Su Zhenhua's replacement was Admiral Li Zuopeng, Lin Biao's protégé and veteran army commander. Li wasted no time in ensuring that the navy would respond to Mao's "great call." A series of political campaigns were implemented, all designed to bring the navy into line with leftist policies.

One of the first radical activities involving the navy centered on Macao. In November 1966 Chinese Communists in that city organized a series of riots forcing the Portuguese to take strong preventive measures. During the fighting that ensued, a number of people, including many Chinese, were injured. Beijing protested in December. On 5 December four Chinese gunboats of the South Sea Fleet anchored off Macao. As tension continued to mount in January, fourteen more PRC gunboats alternately patrolled Macao's inner harbor. The situation finally cooled and the gunboats returned up river, but the PRC had served notice that it would use its navy, albeit in a local coastal situation, to confront another nation over what China perceived as a territorial or national-security interest.

This display of Chinese gunboat diplomacy was consistent with the xenophobia and political trouble, then rampant in China, that affected the rest of the navy. Concurrently with the Macao gunboat episode, East Sea Fleet headquarters personnel in Shanghai were meeting to affirm that fleet sailors, "while serving at various posts, . . . are keeping a close watch on the situation of the GPCR movement, which is sweeping across the country and rocking the whole world, resolutely standing on the side of the revolutionary leftists and vigilantly defending the GPCR."[9] A similar statement was issued several days later by the North Sea Fleet headquarters.

The fleet's pledges to support the left may have been issued as a result of problems being encountered in proximity to some naval bases. For example, on the Zhoushan Islands, the home port of many ships, thousands of farmers and fishermen had attacked Red Guards, and the involvement of naval shore personnel probably became a matter of concern to Beijing. The same chaotic conditions existed in Qingdao, Dalian, and Lushun (Port Arthur). In March 1967 the situation became so bad in Qingdao, the location of the North Sea Fleet headquarters, that shore-based naval units were ordered to intervene in local factories to assist "in the struggle against a counterrevolutionary organization."[10] At other large ports navy men were also filling in on the wharves as longshoremen to move cargo that was backlogged. Shipyards also required the assistance of navy men to carry out even routine repairs and construction work.[11]

Adding to the frustration of naval commanders who viewed such non-military activity as disruptive, Mao at this time urged the shortening of military education at training schools. He expressed the view that if the illiterate soldiers of the Red Army could defeat the Kuomintang's military-staff college graduates, then schooling could be shortened. Mao added that he thought it unnecessary to stay in military schools for too long.[12]

Mao's views were quickly accepted. One of the first naval-training policies to succumb was Lo Ruiqing's submarine policy of 30 percent non-qualified crewmen to 70 percent qualified crewmen. It was replaced by a new and dangerous system that approved the deployment of sub-marines to local operating areas with as many as 80 percent of the crew newly assigned. The basic training period for submarines, in fact, was reduced by half and the time previously devoted to torpedo-target practice was cut by two-thirds.[13] Another important change, implemented in 1967, altered the terms of enlistment. Naval personnel were required to serve only three years if on shore duty and four years if afloat (as opposed to the flat five-year term reported in 1961).[14]

THE WUHAN UPRISING

In July 1967 the so-called Wuhan Uprising occurred. It was strongly rem-iniscent of turbulent events of bygone days that required the government to send gunboats up the Yangzi River to quell disorder. As a prelude to this affair, many military region commanders had received sharp criticism from Madame Mao and the radicals for their lack of revolutionary zeal. One commander, General Chen Zaidao, did not appreciate such criticism. He ordered his troops to take action against the leftists in his command city, Wuhan, which produced a key turning point in the GPCR.

Lin Biao reacted swiftly. He sent a telegram to Wuhan ordering Chen's dismissal and sent extra-regional troops to Wuhan to restore order. Inter-estingly, five gunboats of the East Sea Fleet were sent up the Yangzi to assist in quelling the mutinous troops and anti-Maoists. According to Japanese accounts, the East Sea Fleet headquarters issued a warning against the counterrevolutionary elements in the Wuhan Military Region.[15] This was followed by a joint order, issued by Mao, Lin Biao, and the CCP Central Committee to the East Sea Fleet headquarters, directing the immediate dispatch of naval units up river to Wuhan.[16] Their mission was to support and provide protection for the radicals. Once at the city, this was accomplished by converting the ships into floating propaganda class-rooms. During the three-month deployment, the squadron conducted countless open houses for the leftists. At least one ship acted as a radio-broadcast facility after the main radio stations in Wuhan were destroyed by anti-Maoists.[17]

During the Wuhan affair, another naval purge seemed to demonstrate that some admirals, at least, viewed conditions with distaste. In August Admiral Dao Yong, the long-time East Sea Fleet commander, disappeared from the navy rolls. His purge coincided with the issuance of the unusual joint order mentioned above.[18] It is probable that Admiral Dao was not an enthusiastic supporter of the left—when the first call came to send ships to Wuhan, he may have been less than cooperative.

The Wuhan incident caused an intensification of internecine fighting in China. Many Red Guards were armed and violent criticisms of prominent figures continued to increase. By September the nation was in a state of near anarchy. That month finally saw a decision made that began to turn the situation around. Mao announced his "great strategic plan" ordering the PLA to take charge and discipline extreme leftists. Madame Mao joined in and publicly denounced indiscriminate criticisms and fighting. Red Guards were forced to return to their homes and forbidden to use force in imposing their views on opponents. Thus, temporary order was restored in China as the various factions prepared for the next round in Mao's plan.

OTHER NAVAL PURGES

There were other naval purges during 1967 for which the reasons remain obscure.* In Beijing, Admiral Zhang Xuexi, the son of the infamous northern warlord Zhang Zuolin, was purged from the position of the PRC navy's chief of staff. Two deputy directors of the navy's Political Department, Admirals Guo Bingkun and Hu Pengfei, disappeared. Kang Zhiqiang, director of the PRC's Naval Institute, was purged, as was a North Sea Fleet political commissar, Admiral Lu Renlin. A South Sea Fleet commissar, Fang Zhengping, was also a political casualty. Finally, three admirals assigned to civilian institutions were purged: Admiral Beng Deqing, the vice minister of the Ministry of Communications, Admiral Yuan Yelie, the deputy minister of the Bureau of Aquatic Products, and Admiral Fang Qiang, minister of the Sixth Ministry of Machine Industry.

The purge of Zhang Xuexi demonstrated the vicious nature of the struggle. Opposed to the move to radicalize the Navy Headquarters, Zhang was criticized by Madame Mao at an enlarged meeting of the Navy Party Committee. Subsequently, he was charged with being anti-Maoist and placed in solitary confinement. After four years of continual persecution his health failed. He died in 1970, still a prisoner.[19]

* The following is perhaps the best description of the reasons for naval purges:
Recently, the Red Rebel joint headquarters, an organ directly subordinate to the PLA naval headquarters, held a large-scale meeting to discuss the study and application of Chairman Mao's article "On the Correct Handling of Contradictions Among the People." The meeting was attended by Xiao Jingguang, Wang Hongkun, and other PLA naval leaders. At the meeting, the participants exchanged experiences in establishing the absolute authority of Mao Zedong's thought in their minds and strengthening the revolutionary spirit of the proletariat. By correctly handling the contradictions among the people, the proletarian revolutionaries of the PLA naval headquarters in the past year have gradually been united with more than 95 percent of the masses and cadres of the PLA Navy and dealt merciless blows to the handful of party persons in authority taking the capitalist road.
During the meeting, the participants came to realize that the revolution should be pursued bearing in mind its overall needs, not their personal likes or dislikes, and that the hoodwinked masses should be united to fight against the most dangerous enemies.[20]

Of all of the navy's purges, the best publicized was the one involving Fang Qiang.[21] Admiral Fang, who was charged with naval construction and research and development, became linked with the Liu Shaoqi purge. Based upon criticisms levied at the time, Liu and Fang supposedly wanted to maintain reliance upon the European ship-charter system for the transportation of goods to and from China. They urged China to begin buying more merchant vessels rather than attempt a full-scale effort to duplicate foreign shipbuilding technology. They also proposed that the necessary technology be imported so that the shipbuilding industry could avoid unnecessary and expensive mistakes. Their arguments were obviously embarrassing to their leftist opponents, for during the GPCR only five small merchant vessels had been built.

Liu's and Fang's problems extended to the management of shipyards too. In the Shanghai yards radical power was greatest. Early in the GPCR, revolutionary committees were established in the shipyards and many old-line managers were thrust aside in the fierce political infighting that ensued. They were replaced by undereducated radical workers who had nothing but disdain for technocrats.

In the summer of 1967 Liu and Fang also came under heavy criticism from navy leftists for wanting to deemphasize naval construction in favor of economic interests. They were castigated by a group of South Sea Fleet political activists for apparently ignoring "the aggressive nature of imperialism." According to Liu's opponents, his ignorance of this basic tenet would lead to naval warships being converted into "fishing boats and

PRC Navy in the cultural revolution. Sailors of the East Sea Fleet are being exhorted to "overthrow those in power within the party taking the capitalist road."(SOVFOTO.)

merchant ships," thus freeing naval personnel to "engage in [the] maritime industry." The activists went on to criticize Liu for stressing technology. He was accused of spreading "such nonsense as 'you should pay more attention to technique and study it well.'" The leftists also emphasized that while Liu attempted to stress technique, "he never said a word about the importance of living study and application of Chairman Mao's works and the necessity to put politics in command."[22]

The technology arguments also impacted upon the research, design, and production elements within Fang's Sixth Ministry of Machine Industry. He and others were attacked for lauding the "bourgeois reactionary technical 'authorities'" and slandering the working class as "not understanding production techniques and factory management." Hence, they stood accused of advocating a policy that stressed "letting specialists run the factories."[23]

THE IMPACT ON SHIPBUILDING

Such disagreements created serious political and technical problems in the shipyards. At the Hudong Shipyard in Shanghai, which produced both merchant freighters and naval combatants, a power struggle of significant proportion took place in 1967. Rebel groups composed of Maoists and anti-Maoists sprang up. For nearly six months these groups vied for leadership in the shipyard. The anti-Maoists apparently pressed for a more rational management approach to research, production, and construction that required learning certain Western methods. Their approach also required the disestablishment of redundant research-and-development organizations and the reassignment of older technicians to top management and production positions. The Maoists opposed these proposals as being counter to Mao's principle of self-sufficiency. By the end of December the struggle had become so severe that the shipyard was virtually closed down. Subsequently, a naval unit was sent into the yard to stabilize the situation.[24]

The impact of this political turmoil on Hudong's ability to produce ships was both immediate and lasting. For example, the shipyard encountered many problems in its attempt to manufacture a heavy, super-charged 12,000-hp diesel engine for a new-class commercial coaler of 16,000 gross tons. Beginning in 1967, the Chinese began experiments to build a reverse-gear system for the engine—a reasonably easy process for Western engine makers. The Chinese, however, took four more years and some twelve hundred factory test runs before all of the problems were solved; they eventually were forced to purchase Swiss-made Sultzer engines to use as a guide in correcting design errors.[25] There were also problems with diesel-crankshaft design at the Shanghai Iron and Steelworks. In 1968 it took two months to manufacture one crankshaft.*[26]

---

*On 22 September 1968 *Renmin Ribao* reported that the Hongqi Shipyard in Dalian took eighteen months to complete a single 8,820-hp diesel engine. It was reported that parts had to be collected from more than two hundred different facilities around the country. An earlier news report from the same paper also indicated that the navy had to be called in to help out.

Other problems showed up in the incompleteness of building ships and lack of machine tools for building engines. What evolved was a seriously inefficient "jury-rig" system. Foreign visitors to Shanghai noted that a 140-meter-long ship had been extended 25 meters by using an attachment made of waste material. Meanwhile, the stern of the ship under construction was submerged at high tide and work could be performed only during low tide. Additionally, the visitors noted that some engine milling was being done by hand.[27]

This kind of technical deficiency obviously impacted upon naval construction as well. For example, during the GPCR China produced only about sixteen major combatants—an estimated twelve R-class submarines and four Jiangnan frigates, a new class of vessel similar to the Soviet Riga class. The Chinese did continue to build small combatants in substantial numbers, including missile craft and hydrofoils, but these vessels, which already had prototypes built prior to the GPCR, did not require a further high level of construction skill or technological know-how to produce.

"SAILING THE SEAS DEPENDS ON THE HELMSMAN"

In late November 1967 a congress of more than four thousand naval activists took place in Beijing. This event signaled a sharper veer to the left as the GPCR entered a new phase. Mao, Lin, Zhou, and Madame Mao received the delegates. Lin Biao took the opportunity to write an inscription for the participants. "Sailing the seas depends on the helmsman; making revolution depends on Mao Zedong's thought."[28] Hailed as a slogan for all naval commanders and fighters, the inscription also seemed to clinch Lin Biao's bid to control the navy. In one of the decisions reached at the congress, the activists pledged "to put Vice Chairman Lin's great inscription into effect [and requested] that [naval] party committees and branches at all levels conscientiously study, give prominence to, and carry out Vice Chairman Lin's instructions."[29]

One of Lin's instructions seemingly reinforced the coastal-defense strategy. The delegates declared themselves ready to "launch resolute struggles against the bourgeoisie reactionary military line of the counter-revolutionary revisionists Peng Dehuai and Lo Ruiqing, arm all naval commanders and fighters with the invincible thought of Mao Zedong, and build the navy into a strong naval 'wall of defense.' "[30]

Lin's protégé, Admiral Li Zuopeng, spoke at the congress and left little doubt that loyalty to Lin and Mao was the order of the day. He said that "Vice Chairman Lin Biao should be the example for the commanders and fighters in the navy . . . [and] the navy should closely follow Chairman Mao's great strategic plan, fulfill [its] tasks of 'helping the left, helping industry and agriculture, exercising military control, and giving political and military training' in a better way . . . and build the navy into a mighty sea fortress."[31]

Despite the heavy emphasis on politics, professionals were represented at the congress whose vocal support for combat readiness and forward defense was still discernible amid the political rhetoric. "We pledge . . .

that we shall always be combat ready; advance wave upon wave, and annihilate the enemy. . . . Should the enemy come from the sea, we will make him lose his life in the water."[32]

The professional naval line, in fact, reappeared in an unusual article released in December 1967—concurrently with the PLA's move against the ultra-left and its assertion of military control in nearly all spheres of industry, agriculture, education, and politics. The article headline bragged, "Follow the Course Indicated by Chairman Mao and Build the World's Strongest People's Navy."[33]

Although the article was overwhelmingly political in tone, its point was that the PRC navy should develop rapidly and reexamine traditional coastal-defense ideas. The author, a political commissar of a torpedo-boat flotilla, stated flatly that "only by resolutely and courageously advancing along the red course opened by Chairman Mao, the great helmsman, is it possible to build the world's strongest navy—the PLA Navy. . . . We know that the navy which Chairman Mao instructed us to build must be a people's navy preeminent in the world in its purpose of carrying out the political tasks of revolution and powerful enough to defeat imperialism." He concluded that "in our lifetime we must bring to a close the era when imperialism reigns supreme over all the oceans of the world."[34]

As usual, however, such strong words were accompanied by careful reverence of Mao's strategic and tactical thinking on people's war. The reader was enjoined "to refute the theory that weapons, foreign stereotypes and experts are all powerful." Instead, Mao's teachings were used by the author to create a guerrilla-warfare-at-sea scenario. "Rely on the masses of the people, make best use of the sorghum fields at sea—the reefs, islets, cold, fog, and waves—and bring into full play the tactics and strategy of people's war." The commissar then gave an interesting example of how such tactics and deception were used by his torpedo-boat flotilla to attack the Nationalists in a bygone naval battle.

> Lying in ambush among the reefs in the darkness of the night, [we] suddenly appeared out of nowhere to inflict heavy damage on big enemy ships. Under cover of heavy fog, [we] launched surprise attacks on enemy harbours and anchorages, making the enemy ships scatter in confusion. Displaying much ingenuity, [we] would creep up close and then suddenly board enemy ships and capture them. [We] used hand grenades and other explosives, forcing enemy crews to surrender en masse. . . . One night we received an order to ambush and attack an enemy ship. In order to reach it from our base, we had to pass through a narrow strait less than two nautical miles away from an enemy-occupied island. The problem was how to get our torpedo boats through undetected. Our fisherman brothers thought up a good method. The fishing boats concealed us on our voyage through the enemy-occupied area. They surrounded us when our torpedo boats dropped anchor and they did patrol and reconnaissance duties for us. When our torpedoes struck out of the blue, the enemy had no idea where the attack had come from.[35]

Such public allegiance to the Maoist people's-war doctrine was obviously wise politics for the navy. It not only provided the navy with

The Great Helmsman. This oil painting of Mao Zedong on a warship was used in the early 1970s to demonstrate China's renewed interest in maritime affairs. (Painted by the art workers of the navy of the Chinese People's Liberation Army.)

visibility among the ideologues, but also kept it from becoming too embroiled in the political infighting that coincided with the last stages of the GPCR.

Beginning in March 1968, several more important purges occurred within the military as the leftists launched attacks against "right opportunism." This last surge of leftist activity resulted in renewed fighting that lasted until midsummer. These events provoked Mao so much that he angrily informed revolutionary representatives that they had disappointed him and the workers and army men of China. Mao again was forced to order the army to take charge and ensure public order.

It remained for one final issue to be resolved that ultimately gave the army complete control of the nation while temporarily destroying the CCP apparatus. This was the drive to complete the establishment of the twenty-nine provincial and metropolitan revolutionary committees. Until early 1968, only nine of the committees had been formed, but with Lin Biao in nearly full control of the country, the remainder were quickly established. All but three were chaired by senior military personnel.

The navy weathered these final months of the GPCR in seemingly good political style. In February 1968 a meeting of East Sea Fleet naval personnel and high-ranking political leaders was held in Shanghai to commemorate the fifteenth anniversary of Mao's first inspection of the fleet. The keynote speaker was Zhang Qunqiao, a member of the powerful Shanghai Municipal Revolutionary Committee. Zhang would subsequently be identified as one of the members of the notorious Gang of Four. Accompanying him was Admiral Wang Hongkun, the navy's second political commissar and leader of the navy's own cultural revolution group. Wang's power in the navy had been confirmed when the purged Admiral Su Zhenhua was accused of being a member of Peng Dehuai's faction and charged with trying to overthrow Wang's leadership in the navy.

In his address Zhang invoked Mao's old inscription, "In order to oppose imperialist aggression, we must build a powerful navy." He added that "this great program, drawn up by Chairman Mao, [was] now being carried out and great successes have been achieved in building our navy." Meanwhile, Admiral Wang left no doubt as to who was in charge when he solemnly pledged that the navy would "follow the brilliant example set by Vice Chairman Lin Biao to hold aloft the great red banner of Mao Zedong's thought."[36]

In early spring a navy spokesman, writing for the *Liberation Army News*, reinforced Mao's man-over-weapons philosophy when he criticized Lo Ruiqing's military line. According to the navy man, Lo "actively spread the reactionary absurdity of giving first place to military training and technique in opposition to Chairman Mao's line of building the army on a political basis."[37]

Finally, in June and July the navy convened a series of conferences in Beijing attended by those officers and enlisted men who were members of the navy's "four-good" companies (divisions). At the opening of the June conference, Admiral Wang once again addressed the representatives, stressing that the purpose of the conference was to mobilize the navy behind Chairman Mao's great strategic plan for all-round victory in the GPCR. Wang, as if warning the representatives, stated that the navy would be modeled along army lines, which emphasized building on a political base. He went on to paraphrase Mao. "Correct political and military lines do not emerge and develop spontaneously and tranquilly, but only in the course of struggle." The "four-good" campaign, Wang said, was used by the navy "to wage a sharp struggle against the bourgeois reactionary military line," and it had successfully "smashed all the attempts at interference and sabotage made by the counterrevolutionary revisionists Peng Dehuai and

Lo Ruiqing." Wang exhorted the conferees to continue pressing forward with the "four-good" campaign while putting political work first. In his final remarks it seemed that basic military training and combat readiness were regarded as tertiary; Wang reminded the representatives to "grasp revolution and promote production and other work and preparedness against war."[38]

It is worth noting that this conference lasted well into August, indicating that there must have been serious disputes or more than minimal dissent over the problem of politics versus technique and training. For example, in July conferees spent considerable time discussing political-commissar activities within the fleets. One deputy commissar was singled out and criticized for his lack of contact with naval enlisted engineering personnel.[39] Other groups discussed how Mao's thought, if properly studied, could be applied to solving technical problems. For example, CCP members of a W-class submarine told how auxiliary-men, buoyed by Mao's thinking, repaired a snorkel valve during a storm. The same group recounted how the submarine, while on local patrol, managed to use the technique of dead reckoning over a few-days period while refraining from exposing the ship to obtain a celestial fix.[40]

In early September, as the conference was finally drawing to a close, both Mao and Lin received the naval delegation. They highlighted the importance of politics in military matters. In a final effort to emphasize the political nature of the navy, Admiral Li Zuopeng spoke. He pointed out that the representatives must "make the navy a great red school of Mao Zedong's thought, and accomplish all the glorious tasks set for the navy by the proletarian headquarters headed by Chairman Mao and with Vice-chairman Lin Biao as its deputy leader."[41]

RESULTS OF THE CULTURAL REVOLUTION

If the GPCR was intended to reinforce technological isolationism, to lay stress on coastal defenses, and to emphasize politics at the expense of operational training and strategic weapons development, then it accomplished its goals.

TECHNOLOGICAL FAILURES

In the navy the process of technical innovation and advancement was politicized. Automatic credit was extended to ideas and innovations by low-ranking, nontechnical personnel. Some of these ideas were subsequently harmful. For example, CCP committees selected crewmen from ships assigned to flotillas and formed small, independent ship-repair facilities. Whenever a ship was in need of repair, a repairs committee was established from among the facility workmen and the crew of the vessel under repair. The committee was responsible for approving the cost of repairs, disbursements, and determining what repairs were necessary.

Emphasis was put on self-help and "jury rigging"; engineers and technicians were denigrated. A calculated lawlessness ensued as rules and procedures were held up to ridicule—"Repudiate the philosophy of the compradore and foreigners' slave who slavishly copy foreign regulations on repairs to vessels."[42] Thus, throughout the GPCR, vital ship-maintenance policies became a succession of mass tidal waves based upon the confrontation between those who favored technical standardization and those who saw it as anti-Maoist.

As a result, there were no innovative technological breakthroughs during the GPCR. The G-class submarine, commissioned in late 1964, remained weaponless. The problem with SLBM testing stemmed partly from political struggles within the Seventh Ministry of Machine Industry, responsible for missile and rocket research and development. The fighting between the two rival groups within the ministry became so severe that in April 1968 Zhou Enlai had to intervene to achieve order.[43] The struggles may have also resulted in the cancellation of the development of a cruise missile intended for the Chinese W-class submarine. There were reports that the Chinese were preparing to arm their submarines with the Soviet Shaddock SS-N-3 anti-ship missile (400-nm range and 2,000 pounds of explosives or nuclear warhead), but the development of these missiles never materialized.

The combatant vessels that did get built during the GPCR were duplicates of previous ship classes and most were small, conventionally armed coastal-defense units. The only new ship class that was added to the fleets was the *Jiangnan*-class frigate, and it was not armed with missiles. Five were commissioned during the GPCR, but it took nearly two years to launch the two lead vessels whose keels had been laid in 1965. The Chinese were able to construct and launch their first prototype missile craft, which were imitations of the Soviet *Osa*- and *Komar*-classes and armed with a Styx SS-N-2 missile. Hydrofoil serial production was also achieved during this period, but the small number of vessels constructed indicated that experimentation was still going on. The best efforts could be discerned in the R-class submarine construction, which began serial production as 9-12 units were built from 1966 to 1968. The *Shanghai*-class PTF construction was the most prolific: between sixty and ninety units were completed between 1966 and 1969.[44]

Compared with the three-year period preceding the GPCR, the naval-building results were impressive, but they were still primarily based upon 1950s technology. Integrated technology advanced while other, especially ancillary, technology remained outmoded or naive. The story of the submarine that did not surface to obtain a fix indicates that the Chinese possessed no periscope sextant device. Submarines used open-flame oil stoves for cooking, which made submerged operating conditions hazardous. The Chinese also seemed unmindful of keeping their submarines as quiet as possible. The R class, for example, had devices topside and free-flooding ports along the hull casing, making it rather noisy when submerged.[45]

OPERATIONAL TRAINING

Operational training suffered greatly during this period. It might not un-justly be characterized as unimaginative and repetitive. Typical of the time-consuming events that took place during the training cycle were the incessant mobilization meetings. These affairs, which threatened to turn the navy into a force of stereotyped Maoist automatons, were described as follows:

> The mobilization meetings before a fleet sails, meetings to discuss the tasks or sum up experience before and after a [naval air] flight, and all the administrative, party, and youth league meetings became meetings to ex-change experience in the creative study and application of Chairman Mao's works. Naval units hold such meetings to exchange experience in which a hundred and even a thousand people, including both navy men and civilians, participate, with leading cadres taking the lead in the exchange of experience.[46]

Perhaps the best insight into how the GPCR degraded navy operations is provided by an incident that occurred in December 1967. At that time, the USS Banner (AGOR 1), a sister vessel of the Pueblo, was operating near Shanghai, about 25-nm east of the Zhoushan Island area, in international waters. During testimony at the Pueblo Court of Inquiry, convened by the U.S. Navy in January 1969, the ex-commanding officer of the Banner, Commander Charles R. Clark, described Chinese attempts to interfere with his vessel. He testified that "the Chinese, on one occasion, did have some small fishing boats that encircled me, and at one point I felt that they were trying to take us under tow or something on that order. They got as close as five yards. Two of the fishing boats had larger guns than we did, but I felt that, while our guns were smaller, we could have possibly fought them off with what we had."[47] Unlike the North Korean navy's aggressive pursuit of the Pueblo a month later, the Chinese response in this circum-stance was quite restrained and apparently did not involve the navy.

When contrasted with the Pueblo episode, the Banner's activities must have given some PRC leaders cause for concern. Indeed, Lo Ruiqing's case for an active navy must have been considerably strengthened when the leadership saw that the coastal region was defended only by the maritime militia. Additionally, some Chinese naval leaders could point out that the South Sea Fleet was still weak and lacked any large combatant vessels, including submarines. This was embarrassing, too, especially when the United States was stepping up operations in Vietnam and roaming the South China Sea and Tonkin Gulf with little concern for China's small coastal combatants.

PURGES

High-ranking purges in the navy were small in comparison to those in the PLA, which suffered hundreds of disappearances and demotions. Only eleven top admirals can be identified as purge victims. But this was enough to keep the navy in line with whatever policy was being promoted. Addi-tionally, it is likely that many pro-left enlisted men were inducted into the

The maritime militia, East China Sea (1979). Here an armed Chinese trawler watches the Soviet carrier *Minsk* pass through the East China Sea. (Courtesy of Ltjg Joseph F. Beuchard.)

navy during this period, something that would have important implications in the future.

In summary, the GPCR's general effect on the navy was to render it catatonic. It did not progress, but seemed to go into a state of suspension while political tumult swirled about it. This would cost the navy valuable time in its modernization programs. It would also stunt the growth of many in the officer corps who believed the radical slogans that said nothing could be or should be learned from "bourgeoisie navies."

CHAPTER 20

THE EMERGENCE OF NEW STRATEGIC RELATIONSHIPS, 1969–72

 The convulsions of the GPCR had barely ended when China again found itself enmeshed in a border quarrel with the USSR that threatened to spill over into a bigger and more serious confrontation. On 2 March 1969 Soviet and Chinese border guards clashed on the Wusuli (Ussuri) River. The object of the fighting was a 1.5-mile-long island named Zhenpao by the Chinese and known to the Russians as Damansky. During the fighting, a large number of persons from each side were killed or wounded. Both Beijing and Moscow issued strong letters of protest and the Soviets bluntly stated that future reckless and provocative actions by the Chinese would be answered by strong measures. The Chinese, meanwhile, responded with equally strong notes, saying that if the Soviet government persisted in causing armed confrontation, it would be met with resolute counteraction.

In the months that followed the Chinese and Soviets continued to exchange bitter insults over the incident. Small skirmishes broke out in various border areas, including the area as far west as Xinjiang Province. The Soviet response was to deploy large numbers of ground-force units into the common border regions; the total subsequently reached an estimated forty to fifty divisions. This led to Chinese charges that the USSR was installing launching pads for nuclear missiles along China's Soviet and Mongolian borders "for use against China."

Meanwhile, China's fear of being encircled by "imperialists" was bolstered by the escalation of U.S. military action in Vietnam. Lin Biao, who had pressed for a lesser Chinese role in that region, may have begun to have second thoughts. American bombing strikes had been initiated over North Vietnam, and by mid-1968 the total number of U.S. military personnel in Vietnam had reached more than five hundred thousand troops. This, coupled with frequent reports of U.S. spy-plane shootdowns over China, Chinese protests over such flights, and U.S. naval activity in the South China Sea, seemed to produce paranoia in Beijing among Lin Biao and his followers. Despite the serious situation with the Soviet Union, there was an upsurge in news articles condemning the United States as an aggressor whose actions still posed the greatest threat to China's security. While this was not a new attitude on Lin's part, his views regarding defense and people's war seemed to shift slightly. He now believed that the development of modern weaponry was critical to China's survival, since she faced the USSR to the north and the United States to the south.

Perhaps the best confirmation of Lin's attitude change is in the increase in PRC defense spending that occurred between 1964 and 1970. During those years, the defense budget rose from an estimated 5.5 billion dollars (about 7.9 percent of the GNP) to about 12–13 billion dollars (about 10 percent of the GNP) in 1970. Naval weapons development received heavy emphasis.[1] Planning for a nuclear submarine moved from the blueprint stage to the assembly line. Meanwhile, conventional-submarine construction trebled in annual production rate—from an estimated two units per year to six per year from 1968 through 1974. The slow-moving surface-warfare programs also received greater emphasis in this period. Three more *Jiangnan*-class frigates were launched in 1968 and 1969, bringing the total number to five. The Osa and Komar missile-craft production rates underwent a dramatic increase in 1969, as both types were built at a rate of about ten vessels per year. This indicates that missile production problems probably had been overcome in the trouble-plagued Seventh Ministry of Machine Industry. A new class of destroyer, the *Luda*, was also being built in Dalian at the Hongqi Shipyard in late 1969. The first of this class was launched in 1970; six more followed through 1975. This vessel was China's best technical effort to date—it resembles a Soviet *Kotlin*-class destroyer that carries six anti-surface missiles. It also has a fair antisubmarine capability. PRC research and development institutes were also busy designing several new classes of frigates, the first of which would be commissioned in 1973–74. One of these, the *Jiangdong* class, would be armed with experimental surface-to-air missiles. The Chinese also had a massive rehabilitation and overhaul program approved for the four old

Luda-class guided missile destroyer. These warships have excellent sea-keeping qualities and enable the PRC navy to exercise more regional influence in Asia. (Courtesy of the Department of Defense, Australia.)

Soviet *Gordy*-class destroyers, which would result in the replacement of the torpedo tubes with missiles in 1971.

During this period, the Chinese also made several other decisions that showed a new appreciation of naval strategy. One centered on the naval buildup of the South Sea Fleet, a move that was important if the Chinese were to establish any kind of naval credibility among the various nations and navies either adjacent to or operating in that region. Several years later, in 1975, the PRC military attaché to London confirmed to the editor of *Jane's Fighting Ships*, Captain John E. Moore, RN, that Lin Biao had oriented China's naval building program toward an expansionist policy.[2]

FOREIGN POLICY AND THE NAVY, 1969–71

Concurrently with the naval developments within China, there was a renewal of Chinese contacts with the outside world. Most of the PRC's foreign relations were designed to counter Soviet activities, primarily among Third World nations. Some of the Chinese moves had naval implications. The PRC began to give the navy a role in carrying out Chinese foreign policy—particularly in two areas, state-to-state diplomacy and military-aid programs—in the following places.

ALBANIA

China's relations with Albania warmed considerably when the latter withdrew from the Warsaw Treaty Organization a month after the USSR invaded Czechoslovakia (August 1968). Mao, Lin Biao, and Zhou Enlai immediately followed up with a joint message to the Albanian leadership congratulating them for striking "a heavy blow to the Soviet revisionist renegade clique." The note also contained a warning that if the "Soviet revisionists and their lackeys ever dare to touch Albania in the slightest, nothing but a thorough, ignominious and irrevocable defeat awaits them."[3]

The Chinese took immediate advantage of the split in November 1968 by dispatching a military mission to Albania headed by Marshal Huang Yongsheng, chief of the PLA General Staff. Accompanying Huang was Vice Admiral Wu Ruilin, a deputy commander of the PRC navy. Wu's presence indicated that a new naval-assistance pact was probably negotiated. Developments in Albania shortly after the visit tend to corroborate this. Chinese naval advisors began to assist the Albanians in shoring up that nation's coastal defense with missiles and guns. The main emphasis was put on the Albanian naval base at Saseno, which was strengthened by the Chinese as a preventive measure against a Soviet naval attack.

TANZANIA AND PAKISTAN

The Chinese-Tanzanian naval connection actually began in 1964, when the two countries signed an economic- and technical-aid agreement containing provisions for military assistance. One year later the Chinese assumed responsibility for a marine-police-unit training program and made Tanzania a gift of four 20-ton patrol boats to initiate the program.

The Chinese were thought by some Western observers to have undertaken certain projects in Tanzania in exchange for a facility at Dar Es Salaam that would support a PRC missile instrumentation ship as well as other ICBM test facilities.[4]

The overthrow of East Pakistan and the creation of Bangladesh in 1971 dealt a blow to whatever future plans the Chinese may have had for using the former East Pakistani port at Chittagong. In 1970 China concluded an arms agreement with Pakistan that made provision for China to supply the Pakistanis with naval hardware.* A visit by the Pakistani navy commander in chief, Vice Admiral Muzaffar Hasan, to Peking on 25 September 1970, was made probably for the purpose of consummating the naval-aid agreement. Since that time, Pakistan has received assorted naval aid, including *Shanghai*-class gunboats and *Huchuan*-class hydrofoils. Additionally, the Chinese have hosted several Pakistani naval visits, which have included tours of PRC naval vessels and facilities by Pakistani naval students and instructors. In turn, PRC military and naval delegations have spent time in Pakistan touring that country's naval bases.

SRI LANKA AND NORTH KOREA

In 1971 China again was reported to be conducting talks with the Sri Lankan government in regard to leasing the ex-British naval base at Trincomalee for use in the servicing of naval and merchant ships. The Sri Lankans indicated that they would favor such an arrangement if the port were restricted to merchant ships.[5] The naval portion of the agreement was never consummated, but the Chinese maintained interest, for in 1976 and 1977, China and Sri Lanka exchanged high-ranking naval visits.

Fear of Soviet influence in Korea also moved the Chinese to strengthen military relations with North Korea. In September 1971 a new Sino–North Korean military-aid agreement was signed in Beijing. Unlike a 1961 agreement, this one called for the provision of PRC naval aid to North Korea. Within several years the Koreans were receiving Shanghai patrol boats and several R-class submarines. The exchange received its final stamp of approval in April 1972 with the visit to North Korea by Admiral Xiao Jingguang.

THE NINTH PARTY CONGRESS

Border tension with the USSR and the decision to modernize coincided with one of China's major political events, the convening of the Ninth Party Congress in Beijing in April 1969. Preparations for the congress had begun in late 1968, and as the results would show, it was used as a stepping-stone to power for Lin Biao's military group and the politically oriented radical faction. For example, of the 170 full members and 109 alternates named to the Ninth Central Committee, 45 percent (74 full members and 55 alternates) were PLA representatives. The remainder

---

*There was also an agreement for Chinese road builders to repair and modernize the old silk route from Xinjiang into Pakistan.

were about evenly divided between "revolutionary cadres" (28 percent, 58 full members and 19 alternates) and "revolutionary masses" (27 percent, 38 full members and 35 alternates).

The new Politburo was also surprising, for only nine members from the pre–Cultural Revolution period survived. Of the twelve new members, only one had ever been a member of a past politburo. Madame Mao was new, as was Lin Biao's wife. Two Lin protégés, Admiral Li Zuopeng and air force General Wu Faxian, respectively the navy's first political commissar and the air force commander, were on the Politburo. Both also were full members of the Central Committee. Li's ascendency also vividly demonstrated that the navy's position of first political commissar was more important than that of "chief of naval operations."Admiral Xiao, although a full member of the Central Committee, was junior to Li Zuopeng.

Seven other admirals besides Xiao and Li were named to the Central Committee (two as full members and five as alternates). Before the GPCR, only Xiao had been a member of the Central Committee. The two additional full members were Wu Ruilin, an operations-oriented admiral and a deputy commander of the navy, and Wang Hongkun, the leftist second political commissar of the navy. The alternates consisted of two political officers, Admirals Zhang Xiuchuan and Liu Haotian, the director of the navy's Political Department and the East Sea Fleet political commissar, respectively. There were two operational officers, a Beijing-based deputy commander, Admiral Zhao Qimin, and the North Sea Fleet commander, Yi Yaocai. A revolutionary cadre, Shu Jicheng, was the fifth naval representative.

THE OPPOSITION STRIKES BACK

The ascendency of Lin Biao and his followers to power in the wake of the Ninth Party Congress threatened many disparate groups in China. A backlash developed that led to an attempted coup and eventually cost Lin his life. Three main policy disputes brought Lin and his group into direct confrontation with other powerful leaders.

SERVICE RIVALRY, REGIONALISM, AND TECHNICAL IMPORTATION

The first policy dispute centered on old problems: service rivalry and regionalism. The new technology required by the navy, the air force, and the special weapons forces increased their share of the defense budget, which in turn significantly cut into the army's traditionally larger apportionment. Included in the service budget questions was the problem of satisfying the powerful military region commanders, many of whom were strong advocates of people's war and therefore supportive of continued development of conventional weapons. To understand the influence these men wielded, one need only review their positions and time in office: by 1970 three of the most powerful commanders, Chen Xilian, Yang Dezhi, and Xu Shiyu, had held power in the Shenyang, Jinan, and Nanjing military regions for eleven, twelve, and sixteen years, respectively.

Friction over the new defense technologies, together with their costs and potential dependency upon foreign imports, finally broke out into the open in 1971. Several articles appeared that strongly criticized the emphasis being devoted to electronics (missiles, modern weapons, forward defense, limited blue water) over that of the iron and steel industry (guns, conventional weapons, people's war, coastal defense). One article, published in the *People's Daily* in August, stated the following:

> Electronic technology is a new technology used in developing the national economy and national defense industry. Together with atomic technology and jet-engine technology it is generally regarded as a criterion used to measure the development level of a country's industry. However, advanced and special technology is one thing, while the foundation and center are another. The two cannot be mixed together . . . [and] the various branches of industry in China, including the electronics industry, must be developed proportionately and in a planned way. However, only the iron and steel industry should assume a leading role.[6]

Traditional regional prejudices were still around as well. In 1976 the New China News Agency republished Mao's 1956 treatise, "On the Ten Major Relationships." In that article, it was pointed out that Han Chinese chauvinism still existed. Moreover, there were still contending groups at the local level who objected to the concentration of power within the central government.[7]

POLITICAL VERSUS MILITARY TRAINING

The second policy problem, created by the excesses of the GPCR, was that of increased nonmilitary duties acquired by the PLA following its intervention in internal political struggles. The refutation of Lo Ruiqing's submarine training policies discussed in the previous chapter was a good example of inefficiency created on board PRC vessels. As far as the military professionals were concerned, the reduction in active-duty time initiated in 1967 was another bad policy decision. These decisions, as well as other political demands, were considered intolerable by many military leaders in the face of the massive Soviet buildup on China's northern borders and U.S. activities in Vietnam. These threats demanded a return to a more professional, nonpolitical posture. The navy, in fact, seemed to take such a course of action in 1969. Analysis of media reports in that year shows a marked reduction in naval political activities as compared to the previous three years.

THE REEXAMINATION OF CHINESE FOREIGN POLICY

The most significant policy dispute centered on a new and daring foreign-policy maneuver being contemplated by Zhou Enlai and apparently approved by Mao. It involved putting a stop to the dual-adversary strategy and seeking detente with the United States. It meant that China would continue to view the USSR as the primary threat to her national security.

Lin Biao and his followers took strong exception to this endeavor. From 1969 to 1971, occasional news articles appeared that strongly criticized

Japanese and U.S. naval activities in Asia. In fact, shortly before Dr. Henry Kissinger's first trips to China in 1971, which laid the groundwork for President Nixon's 1972 visit to China, articles began to appear pointing out U.S. and Japanese naval threats. In one, the U.S. Seventh Fleet was depicted as "an important tool for U.S. imperialism in pursuing its policy of aggression and war in the Far East and Southeast Asia." The article went on in stronger tones to describe the U.S. naval threat to China as one that had continued for twenty years. Broadcast in Chinese for internal consumption, it stated in part the following:

> Since 1950 U.S. imperialism has forcibly occupied our territory of Taiwan, making trouble in the Taiwan Strait and threatening us from time to time. The Seventh Fleet has helped the Chiang bandits send armed special agents to harass our coastal areas. It has more than once dispatched naval vessels and planes to violate the territorial waters and air space of Korea and China for espionage activities. During the war of aggression against Korea, its vessels and planes wantonly bombed Korea and slaughtered the Korean people. In the course of the war of aggression against Vietnam, it has been deployed in the Gulf of Bac Bo [Tonkin] to carry out frantic war provocations against North and South Vietnam. It has sent warships to North Vietnamese waters to bombard the DRV. . . . The United States vainly attempts to rely on an imperialist "gunboat policy" to intimidate the people of various countries. However, the peoples of various countries are not in the least afraid of such tactics. They have long since shattered U.S. imperialism's naval and air superiority. The blood debt owed by the U.S. Seventh Fleet to the peoples of various Asian countries will sooner or later be settled.[8]

Lin Biao also had other subordinates out castigating the United States. His chief of staff, General Huang Yongsheng, gave frequent speeches that were much more anti–United States than anti-Soviet.

The criticism of Japan was equally strident. Beginning in May 1971, a number of articles appeared that took issue with Japan's claims to the Senkaku or Diaoyudai Islands northeast of Taiwan. Subsequent articles blasted the Japanese Maritime Self-Defense Force for carrying out joint service exercises that the Chinese claimed were "directed at [a] new war in Asia."[9] Also, in late May Japanese authorities were strongly criticized for "Navy Day" celebrations that the PRC claimed were held for the purpose of recalling to the Japanese public the "strength of the Imperial Navy." The article ends with the following statements:

> It is noteworthy that the Japanese reactionaries distributed among the participants of the ceremony anti-China gramophone records made by the Japanese National Rural Village Broadcasting Association. Entitled "How to Deal With Japan-China Relations," these records contained vicious utterances such as that one must not forget [that] the presence of the U.S. Seventh Fleet is meant to prevent China from liberating Taiwan by force, [and] that "peace in the Taiwan Straits has great impact on peace in Japan." These statements were copied from the Japan–United States joint communique.
>
> Eisaku Sato, Yasuhiro Nakasone and their ilk have long regarded the Pacific Ocean as "the sphere of Japanese life" and they have clamored that the "air superiority and sea supremacy" around Japan must be ensured. The

series of activities carried out by the Japanese reactionaries around the "Navy Day" are a vivid illustration that the United States and Japanese reactionaries are making preparations for new aggressive war.[10]

LIN AND THE ABORTED COUP

The issues described above were extremely important ones, for their resolution would test the strength of the various factions vying for power in China. Lin Biao's faction, while in apparent control, was isolated because of its Beijing-based membership. And in an amazing show of resiliency, the CCP, led by Zhou and several powerful anti-Lin military region commanders, formed a coalition with Madame Mao and her left-wing Cultural Revolution group. The pressure they were able to generate against Lin was apparently so great that it forced him into contemplating a coup that included a plot to assassinate Mao.

The plot was found out, and in September 1971 the major conspirators attempted to flee China in an air force Trident VIP aircraft. It crashed in Outer Mongolia. Subsequent news reports stated that at least nine bodies were found, some of which had bullet wounds. A crisis atmosphere gripped all of China, and Chinese leaders shuttled in and out of Beijing during the month that followed. The seriousness of this epidode can be judged by the fact that the PLA air force was grounded for some thirty days and the October First National Day celebrations were cancelled.

Within several weeks of the incident, the outside world began to learn that a high-level purge had occurred. In addition to Lin Biao and his wife, the PLA chief of staff, the commander of the PLA air force, the first political commissar of the navy, Li Zuopeng, and the director of the General Logistics Department of the army were gone from view. Their purges led to a temporary leadership vacuum within the PLA as well as a serious reexamination of the entire spectrum of internal and external Chinese policies. And, as in the past, such a process had important implications for the navy.

CHAPTER 21

POLITICAL OPPOSITION AND THE ASCENDENC OF THE MARITIME SPIRIT, 1973–77

 In the wake of the Lin Biao affair, the prag-
matists, led by Zhou Enlai, had to make
several moves in order to broaden and consolidate their power. This had to be done
quickly, for China's government and economy were drifting. Some were
also concerned over Lin's military spending program, which had more than
doubled between 1968 and 1971, with the majority of the increase being
spent on a variety of naval, air, and missile construction and research
programs.[1] Zhou Enlai's solution was to reemphasize firm management
throughout all spheres of the Chinese government, including the military,
and the obvious move entailed bringing back large numbers of experienced
civilian and military officials who were purged during the GPCR.

One of the first experienced and skilled military administrators to be
"rehabilitated" was Su Zhenhua, the former naval first political commissar and an advocate of a strong, professional navy. Su's political skills and
broad knowledge were desperately needed by both central-government
leaders and the growing navy to manage an imminent shift toward an
outward, maritime strategy.

THE SOVIET NAVAL THREAT

The first challenge for Su was to reassess the Soviet naval threat, a process
that required deemphasizing the United States and to a lesser extent Japan
as the principal naval "villains" threatening China. Of strategic significance and of particular importance to China were the Soviet navy's
Indian Ocean activities, which had begun in 1968 and were steadily increasing in scope and intensity. Shortly after Lin Biao's death, the Chinese
began to condemn this naval activity loudly as an example of "social
imperialism." The first barrage was launched in late December 1971 and
appeared in the strongest of terms in an article entitled "Soviets Step Up
Expansion: Aggression in Indian Ocean."

Since Brezhnev came to power, Soviet revisionism has tried to seize the right to use the naval bases and the ports of certain countries on the shores of the Indian Ocean through providing "economic aid" and "military aid" and other baits.... Since 1968, Soviet fleets have "visited" almost every country along the Arabian Gulf, Gulf of Aden, West Indian Ocean and Red Sea. Soviet naval vessels disguised as fishing boats and electronic spy ships as tugs or oceanic scientific research ships were often sent to certain countries along the coast of the Indian Ocean to engage in the criminal activities of stealing military and oceanic information.... A formation of cruisers of the Soviet Pacific Fleet showed up in the Indian Ocean and carried out a military exercise in 1971. Bragging about the expansionist activities of Soviet revisionism, Sergey Georgiyevich Gorshkov, commander in chief of the Soviet navy, said, "Ships of the Soviet navy sail in the Atlantic, Pacific, and Indian Oceans...wherever it is required by the interests of our country's security."[2]

One year later the Chinese anti-Soviet-navy campaign continued to escalate. Articles reiterated the "imperialistic" tendencies of Soviet naval policies.[3] The articles appeared more frequently, despite rumored Soviet attempts in 1971 to seek a nonaggression treaty with China to deny the use of nuclear weapons to each in the event of war.

Chinese criticism of the Soviet Union and its naval aims continued unabated until August 1973. Beijing was plainly concerned about the Soviet naval threat to Asia. Quoting from a Malaysian newspaper, the New China News Agency stated that the "'Asian collective security system' is part of the Soviet effort to expand its influence in the world. *It is aimed at encircling China*, bringing small nations under its control and contending with the United States for hegemony in Asia.'"[4] The article went on to cite, in lurid terms, many instances of Soviet naval expansionism and the continuous dispatch of warships to the Sea of Japan, the South China Sea, the Pacific Ocean, and the Indian Ocean.

In the UN the Chinese also carried out a strong attack against Soviet naval activities in the Indian Ocean. For example, from late 1971 to early 1974, China was an important factor in getting the UN General Assembly to adopt a resolution urging all states to accept the principles and objectives of a declaration labeling the Indian Ocean a zone of peace and condemning foreign naval presence in that ocean region.[5]

China also no longer had any compunction about citing Japan as a victim of Soviet naval aggression. In December 1973 Beijing quoted extensively from a conservative Japanese magazine that noted that the Japanese Defense Agency had observed "about twenty-five major Soviet warships moving in waters around Japan between March and May [1973]." The article also referred to the fact that the Soviet Union had secured rights to use some ports and establish bases in the Indian Ocean west of the Malacca Straits and along the Persian Gulf coast. The Soviets were also criticized for their unwillingness to return certain northern islands to the Japanese. The Japanese article went on to point out "that the Soviet Union has not yet gained secure naval bases in the waters east of the Malacca Straits, so it is desperately seeking ports and bases in this area to moor its warships."[6]

NAVAL AID AND NAVAL CONSTRUCTION

The Soviet naval threat led the Chinese to make two significant decisions. First, it was decided to increase naval aid to selected Third World nations to counter similar Soviet naval aid programs. The type of assistance was restricted mainly to the transfer of various classes of fast patrol boats. Interestingly, unlike the Soviets, the Chinese did not provide any missile gunboats to Third World countries.

Secondly, a decision was made to speed up naval construction of certain classes. For example, the R-class submarines doubled in numbers from 1974 to 1977, going from an estimated thirty-two vessels to over sixty by early 1978. The *Osa* and *Komar* missile-boat programs were increased around 1970 to a building rate of ten units per year. This rate has been maintained to the present. A new class of coastal-defense frigate, the *Jianghu*, was also approved for construction in 1973.[7]

Desmond Wettern, British naval correspondent for the *Daily Telegraph*, visited several Chinese naval vessels in 1980, including a *Jianghu* frigate. His observations are stated in part as follows:

> The main propulsion machinery is diesel, and the hull is flush-decked. There are two trainable SSM launchers forward and aloft the large square stack. The gun armament comprises two single manually loaded 100-mm. and ten 37-mm. mountings. Again, there was no provision on board for reloading the SSM launchers.
>
> The frigate's ASW weapons were two 12-barrelled MBU-2500A-type rocket launchers forward and an array of depth bomb launchers on the fantail. No electronic support measures or chaff launchers were seen. . . .
>
> The after end of the bridge was open, and there was no indication that the ship had a CIC. A "Top Bow"-type radar was fitted on a platform on the foremast with a navigation radar and what may be a "Post Lamp"-type target designation radar.
>
> Mine rails on the fantail and depth bomb launchers mean that VertRep by helicopter would not be possible except perhaps for very small loads. It was significant that . . . there appeared to be no provision for highline transfers of fuel or stores. This indicates that the "Kiang Hus" are essentially intended for coastal defense purposes, although diesel propulsion should give them greater endurance than the steam turbine-powered "Lutas."[8]

THE ADVENT OF THE LAW-OF-THE-SEA ISSUE

While the war of words over the Soviet Union's naval activities was continuing, Admiral Su had yet another issue on which he could broaden the case for a stronger navy. That was the Law of the Sea (LOS), which was beginning to gain in worldwide importance as a strategic issue. In fact, China's entrance into the UN in October 1971 was most timely, for it coincided with the growing debate of LOS issues aimed at new technologies. China now realized, for example, that oil workers could extract oil from wells drilled at great depths; mining experts had new equipment that enabled them to mine strategic minerals from the ocean floor; and fishermen could scoop vast schools of fish from the oceans with new suction

The new PRC *Jianghu* frigate. This new-class vessel was launched in 1975 and has a range of 4,000 nautical miles. Like the *Luda* guided-missile destroyer, the *Jianghu* gives the PRC navy added ability to operate beyond the immediate China coast. (Courtesy of the U.S. Navy.)

systems. By the time the UN got around to debating the issues, LOS had become the subject of strong debate and the world was divided into two camps, the haves and have nots. China and most Third World nations were in the second category; they remain arrayed against most of the industrialized nations, which are capable of tapping the ocean's resources.

The main issues still being debated include

1. The extent of sovereignty a coastal nation can exercise over its ocean frontage

2. The distance at sea that sovereignty extends for mineral and fishery resources

3. The question of rights to resources located under the "high seas"

4. The question of establishing a UN organization that could settle arguments and/or exercise management over sea resources

A glance at any map graphically demonstrates the importance of these issues to China, with its extensive coastline. In fact, even while these issues were being debated, the UN released a 1971 report dealing with an economic survey of Asia and the Far East, in which certain regions of the South China Sea were reported to have oil-bearing tertiary sedimentary rock.[9] It was surveys like these that significantly influenced Beijing's neo-maritime supporters. In 1971–72, if one were to apply the 200-meter-depth rule still used by the UN to establish a coastal nation's sea rights, then China had the rights to half of the Yellow Sea; nearly all of the East China Sea to Okinawa; the entire Taiwan Strait and considerable sea territory to the north, east, and south of Taiwan, if that island were considered to be a province of the mainland.

The Communist Chinese were also beginning to see potentially serious problems with regard to fishing rights, for modernization of the fishing industry had seriously depleted the once-rich coastal fishing grounds. This now required China to seek catches beyond the immediate coastal zones, bringing her into direct competition with other Asian fishing states.

While mineral prospecting was still some years away, the Chinese, in 1971–72, began to develop their offshore oil reserves. They carried out extensive sea surveys as well as undertook large-scale purchases of foreign seabed drilling ships. These activities soon paid off with the discovery of offshore oil deposits in the shallow Bo Hai Gulf and the South China Sea near Hainan Island. The Chinese attitude toward its oil potential and its importance to the nation began to be openly discussed during this period. China was not oil poor and she intended to lay heavy stress on future development. (In addition to oil, China's largest titanium deposits are located on the Guangdong, Guangxi, and Hainan Island coasts.)

MERCHANT SHIPPING AND PORT MODERNIZATION

Until 1971 China's merchant fleet and ports were sadly outdated. In fact, Beijing had only a little more than one million gross tons of worn-out vessels to service both coastal and international trade. China still was heavily dependent upon foreign charter vessels to move goods, and most ports used lighters to bring articles ashore.

A drastic change in direction was required if China was to reach an adequate state of maritime self-sufficiency. Thus, decisions were made to

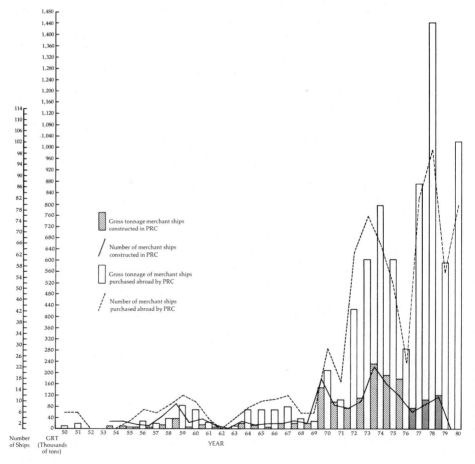

Growth of the PRC merchant fleet (1970s). (Data prepared from *Lloyd's Registry of Shipping*, London, 1980–81.)

purchase foreign vessels and modernize outdated port facilities. The results were dramatic. For example, from 1971 through 1976, China purchased 250 freighters, tankers, and bulk carriers amounting to 2.5 gross tons. Concurrently, 94 vessels (1,045,657 gross tons) of the same three types were constructed in PRC shipyards. Moreover, China remained the largest charterer on the London merchant-shipping market.[10]

Chinese ports and shipyards also began receiving facelifts. In five years, from 1973 to 1978, the capacity of major harbors was doubled and much new equipment added. For instance, Ro/Ro (Roll-on/Roll-off) vessels were introduced; container facilities were constructed; and computer-controlled loading and unloading systems were installed. China also secured membership in the International Maritime Satellite Organization (INMARSAT).

An unprecedented change was that by the late 1970s China was taking foreign orders for the construction of new ships by the Chinese. The deputy managing director of the China Corporation of Shipbuilding Industry, Wang Ze, noted in 1980 that China could produce about 800,000 deadweight tons annually, and that when new plans were completed, China would be selling 100–150,000 deadweight tons per year.[11]

There was much opposition to the decision to purchase merchant ships. For example, in 1974, two senior officials of the Ministry of Communications sailed to Europe on the maiden voyage of a purchased passenger liner. During the voyage, both were strongly criticized by others aboard the ship for "worshiping things foreign." They were also accused of "betraying the nation" in backing the acquisition of ships from the West. The two stuck to their decision, however, and argued convincingly that China's domestic shipbuilding industry could not possibly meet the demands for an ocean fleet and that the purchase of a number of ships from foreign countries was completely necessary.[12]

PRC-built merchant ship. Since the early 1970s, the PRC has concentrated on improving its coastal and international merchant fleets. This 16,000-dwt bulk freighter is representative of the type designed and constructed in China. It was built at the Shanghai Hudong Shipyard in 1980. (Courtesy of the U.S. Naval Institute Reference Library, Annapolis.)

The incident again highlighted the differences between the radicals and neo-maritime supporters, and it marked the beginning of the final showdown between the radical leaders and those who opposed them.

POLITICS AND THE PARACELS

The rise of the neo-maritime spirit coincided with the reappearance of Deng Xiaoping in 1973. Known as a tough, pragmatic individual devoted to the modernization of China, Deng cared little for radical politics, which kept his country backward. During the GPCR he had become identified with Liu Shaoqi, and together they had attempted to steer radical activities along a more reasonable course. Deng ran afoul of the radicals, however. They seized upon his pragmatism as a weakness and used his famous 1961 remark—"It doesn't matter whether a cat is black or white; any cat that catches mice is a good cat"—against him. Deng was purged in 1966. As with others, though, his administrative and managerial talents were sorely needed after Zhou Enlai managed to temporarily unify the various factions in 1971. Thus, in April 1973 Deng was renamed to the vice-premiership and designated a full member of the Tenth Central Committee. Later, in December 1973, he became a full member of the Politburo and was also appointed vice-chairman of the Military Affairs Commission. Significantly, he and Admiral Su retained a close personal friendship that had begun in the Long March era.

The timing of Deng Xiaoping's comeback coincided with a series of military reappointments apparently aimed at reducing the power of the military region commanders. This political maneuver was a most delicate one in view of the "king-making" status enjoyed by many of the commanders. As stated before, most of them had been assigned to a single military region since "liberation," and each had built up a loyal following based largely upon the traditional system of personal relationships. To Zhou, Deng, and others, the power of the military region commanders stifled further growth and modernization.

Deng's role in the reassignment process was based upon his own close personal relationship with many important military region commanders. His extraordinary abilities and contacts received their full play when all of them were shifted in December 1973. Their smooth reassignment seemed to assure Deng of the leading role in the post-GPCR period.

There was another delicate problem that probably required Deng's personal attention: the seizure of the Paracel Islands from the South Vietnamese. The timing of that incident in January 1974 was interesting, for it came when Deng was switching commanders around and its success risked a serious break with North Vietnam, who also claimed the islands. The Chinese had countered such claims in the media by frequently recalling Zheng He's expeditions, but the combined maritime issues then gaining wide attention in China likely moved her to use force.

On 11 January 1974 the Ministry of Foreign Affairs released a public warning to the effect that the PRC had indisputable sovereignty over the

Paracels, adding that the "sea areas around them also belong to China." The PRC spokesman also stated that the Chinese government would "never tolerate any infringement on China's territorial integrity and sovereignty by the Saigon authorities."[13]

Four days after the warning, the Chinese began to move their forces into position. According to South Vietnamese survivors, the Chinese naval force consisted of about eleven "warships" carrying more than six hundred amphibious assault troops. MiG fighters from Hainan Island, about 130 miles to the northwest, provided air cover. The Beijing version, which agreed reasonably well with that of the Saigon, stated that the trouble began about 15 January, when South Vietnamese ships attempted to displace Chinese fishermen from the islands. On the seventeenth several Chinese patrol vessels arrived, followed a day later by ten other warships. These ships were backed by the Hainan MiG fighters. The South Vietnamese navy had a former U.S. Coast Guard cutter, armed with a 5-inch gun, and four destroyer escorts (DEs), each armed with two 3-inch guns. They had no air support. (There were some U.S. reports that the South Vietnamese naval commander asked for air support from Danang, but he was turned down.)[14]

Within a day, the islands were in Chinese hands. The South Vietnamese lost one of the DEs. The *New York Times*, on 21 January 1974, reported that the DE was hit by a missile launched from a *Komar*, though the Chinese denied any such craft were present. Rather, the Chinese emphasized the "people's" participation in this fight by playing up the role of the fishermen-militia force also on the scene. Whatever the real tactics, the brief action vividly demonstrated that China would employ her fleet beyond the coasts to protect what she perceived as territorial and national interests.

It is instructive to look briefly at Chinese naval propaganda published immediately following the Paracels assault. It consisted of a twenty-page-long poem that emphasized the role of the "people's navy" rather than the evident action of a relatively modern, technical naval force. Part of the poem reads as follows:

> The young naval power of new China,
> The warships of the proletariat! . . .
> Sing for the fresh miracles created by the sea fighters of the motherland!
> Sing for the victory of the battle of self-defense that lasted no more than thirty minutes!
> The People's Navy of new China that took part in the action
> Has neither the so-called *Komar*-class destroyers
> Nor the so-called Styx-type guided missiles.
> We are the small fighting the big.
> The weak opposing the strong.
> And we have only begun to test our swords. . . .
> The People's Navy founded and commanded by Chairman Mao! . . .
> Making a sight of wonder and opening a new page
> In the annals of people's war on the seas.[15]

THE RADICALS ATTACK NEW NAVAL POLICIES

Despite naval success at the Paracels, Chinese radicals were beginning to have grave doubts about Deng Xiaoping. He shocked them by formally supporting peasant rights to have private farm plots, engage in sideline production, and be paid on the basis of work performed. It was too much for them, and from January to April 1975 they engaged in a counterattack, accusing Deng (not by name) of being a "capitalist roader."[16]

During this affair, Deng's close relationship with Su Zhenhua affected the navy, for the radicals took the admiral's new naval policies under attack. According to published criticisms, the radicals, led by Madame Mao, strongly opposed certain naval modernization plans and wanted to invest in more conventional weapons for the ground forces.[17]

According to subsequent reports, Madame Mao became greatly agitated in May 1974 when the PRC navy announced a uniform change—a change apparently approved by Mao and the CCP Central Committee.[18] This decision resulted in putting the navy back into a uniform style reminiscent of that worn in the 1950s period of professionalism. The new regulations saw officers and enlisted men wearing uniforms that differed considerably from the featureless Mao suits worn by army personnel. Officers such as Su Zhenhua were noted wearing a Western-style hat (with visor, chin strap, and gold star), a white blouse resembling the U.S. Navy's formal white tunic, and dark trousers. Enlisted men were seen, in summer, wearing a Western-style navy uniform replete with V neck and flap.

Madame Mao became so incensed over this style change that she supposedly sneered at the naval cadres who wore the new uniforms, calling them names such as "northern warlords," "Soviet revisionists," and "imperialists." Other radical leaders issued orders banning from the press and films any pictures of naval personnel wearing the new uniform.[19]

The radical attack against the navy finally culminated in Mao's having to step in and lend support. On 3 May 1975 a significant event occurred that would have a long-term impact on China's navy. According to news releases, Mao, at a high military meeting, clasped the hands of a high-ranking naval officer (probably Su Zhenhua), and told him "it was necessary to run the navy well." The officer was reported to have seized upon Mao's words as an opportunity to present the chairman with a new ten-year naval plan. Mao approved of it. The plan apparently proposed goals to be reached by 1985.[20]

The radicals strongly opposed this plan. Some came forward to advocate that defense money would be better spent on the army and the further development of shore-based strategic weapons. Shanghai strongman Zhang Qunqiao criticized the navy plan by stressing that the Chinese are continentalists. "Now the guided missiles are well developed. Installed on shore, they can hit any target, and there is no need to build a big navy."[21]

The latest naval-building debate was part of the larger controversy between Deng Xiaoping and the radicals, for the radicals undertook a political counteroffensive against Deng about this time. Two high-ranking radicals published articles in the CCP theoretical journal, Hongqi (Red Flag), in March and April 1975. They attacked the "bourgeois right," accusing "people like Lin Biao" of wanting to restore capitalism in China. This charge was aimed at Zhou Enlai and Deng, who by the summer of 1975 had prepared a series of papers calling for a plan to modernize China's industry, national defense, agriculture, and science and technology (subsequently known as the Four Modernizations).[22]

Regarding national defense, Deng apparently proposed a 30 percent reduction of China's military. He argued that such a reduction would permit concentration on industrial modernization that would ultimately provide China with nuclear weapons, modern communications, and improved logistical systems. As the argument goes, Deng intended to take the main cuts in regionally based local-defense armies, thereby continuing to strengthen central control over the main forces.[23] It was also rumored that Deng, or at least some influential moderates, were critical of the 1964 abolition of ranks, which they believed degraded the authority of senior officers. In this regard, Deng probably wanted to strengthen centralized command and control by introducing new telecommunications systems.[24] Interestingly, Lo Ruiqing was "rehabilitated" by mid-1975, and his reappearance coincided with radical criticism of Deng Xiaoping for placing too much emphasis on the importance of skill and equipment in war. Once again, the ideologues claimed that spiritual and political attitudes were most important, and that wars are won not solely with weapons but with correct political orientation and unbending will.

The decision that these policies were to be accomplished at the expense of ideology was to cause Deng and the moderates a delay in their bid to control China's destiny. In January 1976 Zhou Enlai died and Deng Xiaoping was again dismissed from office. A month later, the "Dengists" within the navy, particularly Su Zhenhua, came under attack by the radicals. Soon, a serious political struggle ensued among the navy's officer corps. Radical sympathizers in the navy were later accused of writing letters that framed moderates for political transgressions. Finally, the navy's leadership was attacked as "a restorationist clique."[25]

In May Deng's naval-building policies were again attacked in an article by a CCP committee group assigned to the large Hudong Shipyard in Shanghai. Using merchant-ship construction as an example, the group criticized Deng's modernization policy. They called it a "counterrevolutionary" effort to "oppose Chairman Mao's principle of maintaining independence and keeping the initiative in our own hands and relying on our own efforts" rather than "to develop industry by introducing foreign techniques and equipment." The authors went on:

> Take Shanghai's shipbuilding industry for example. Since we began to redouble our efforts to increase production in 1970, we have built one million tons of ships in six years, amounting to the total tonnage built in the seventeen years before the Cultural Revolution. In those seventeen years, only one 10,000-ton ship was built in Shanghai. Forty-four 10,000-ton ships have been built since the Cultural Revolution. This ironclad fact is a forceful criticism of the arch, unrepentant, party-capitalist-roader Deng Xiaoping's slavish comprador philosophy, which advocates reliance on foreign countries for industrial development. [The ship construction totals are factual.][26]

Less than a month after this criticism, the radicals were confronted with a visit by a senior Western military leader, General Guy Mery, chief of staff of the French armed forces. Among the military sites visited, the general also toured Shanghai, where he inspected East Sea Fleet units and was shown the Jiangnan Shipyard.

The Mery visit resulted in a wave of criticism by the radicals. Shortly after the French officer departed China, they published their sharpest attack against Deng's naval policies, comparing him with Li Hongzhang and Zeng Guofan, who, the radicals claimed, precipitated nineteenth-century naval failures.

> Li Hongzhang was a notorious representative of the advocates of foreignization. Of all his foreignization activities, the building of the Beiyang Navy lasted longest and was the most expensive.... However, what did they get after three decades? The people were more impoverished and the country became increasingly weaker and ever more colonized. Regarding the "armored vessels" bought and "new army" trained in accord with the line of worshiping things foreign and national betrayal, even Li Hongzhang could not but admit that they were of some use for suppressing bandits at home but could not be counted upon for guarding against the insults of foreign powers .... The Beiyang Navy was completely destroyed in the Sino-Japanese war of 1894. The defeat completely ripped off Li Hongzhang's veil of "self-improvement" and "guarding against the insults of foreign powers".... History is a mirror of reality.... What Deng Xiaoping advertises as "the most reliable" and "major policy" is nothing more than a refurbished version of Li Hongzhang's "self-improvement" and "enrichment" based on worshiping things foreign and showing blind faith in foreign countries. Like Zeng Guofan and Li Hongzhang, Deng Xiaoping is a 100-percent-pure advocate of foreignization.[27]

During this latest debate, the Chinese also played host to former U.S. Secretary of Defense James Schlesinger. He was allowed to travel into China's interior and see Chinese border troops in such remote areas as the Ili Valley. In a written summary of his trip, Mr. Schlesinger indicated that he suspected that there was some interest within the Chinese military establishment to acquire sophisticated weapons. He noted, however, that for diplomatic reasons such desires remained well hidden. According to Mr. Schlesinger, "If one talk[ed] in general to Chinese officials, one [heard] simply the standard line that weapons are not decisive, that Soviet tanks are 'tortoise shells,' that people's war is a sure defense, that if the Soviets were to invade they will be drawn in deeply and then will be encircled, and so on." Mr. Schlesinger added that he doubted that this type of patterned response revealed the true Chinese concern, but rather that "the military establishment [was] deeply aware of the growing power of Soviet armor, and of Chinese weaknesses in antiarmor." Regarding China's naval posture, Mr. Schlesinger opined that the Chinese recognized that "their own naval weaknesses in the Western Pacific [and] Soviet fleets moving down from Petropavlovsk or Vladivostok to Southeast Asia and the Indian Ocean are becoming an increasingly felt pressure."[28]

Considering the observations of visitors like Mr. Schlesinger and the increasing attacks on Deng Xiaoping's policies in the Chinese news media, it was obvious that a showdown was imminent. It came on 7 September 1976, when Mao Zedong died. His loss was profoundly felt, for he had long been the symbol of Chinese Communism—its founder, its teacher, omniscient theoretician, and military leader. The Chinese nation went into deep mourning, but his death seemed anticlimactic in light of the political reversals that soon followed. The radicals barely had time to observe Mao's passing before their four leaders were arrested. The incarceration of the so-called Gang of Four seemed to unleash much pent-up resentment, which led to other purges and "rehabilitations."* It also ushered in a new maritime spirit that bears strong resemblance to the attitudes of the past.

---

*A theoretical group in the PLA navy later noted that Madame Mao "has finally become something filthy and contemptible like dog's dung."[29]

CHAPTER 22

THE NEO-MARITIME SPIRIT: DIRECTIONS AND IMPLICATIONS

During the five-year period following the arrest of the Gang of Four, China experienced a tremendous maritime renascence. Along the coast and overseas, Chinese activities accelerated as neo-maritime advocates attempted to take control and redirect China's energies. The accomplishments to date have been remarkable. Several are highlighted to show the emphasis that the new leadership has placed on turning the nation seaward.

ACCOMPLISHMENTS

FOREIGN POLICY

The first of several dramatic changes occurred in 1978, when China normalized its relations with the United States and signed a peace and friendship treaty with Japan. Two years later China let the 1950 treaty with the USSR lapse and made no attempt to renew it. Then in June 1981 the United States agreed to sell weapons to China. These actions have led to a major shift in the east Asian balance of power, placing the Soviet Union at a disadvantage.

Moscow is clearly alarmed by a maritime-oriented China and has elevated her neighbor to second place on its threat list, making China equal to Europe (the United States obviously remains first). With increasing frequency, the Soviet Union has expressed concern over the rapid buildup of the PRC navy and its potential for conducting naval operations in the broader ocean areas.[1] The Kremlin views the Chinese moves as destabilizing and has acted to counter them by trying to contain and isolate China. One of the principal Soviet strategems has involved the strengthening of its Pacific Fleet and the establishment of a naval presence in the South China Sea.

The changes in east Asian relationships were accomplished without the PRC having to renounce its claims on Taiwan and the right to use force at some indeterminate future date. The ancient issue of "grand unification" remains a matter of simmering concern to the Beijing leadership, for as long as the island remains independent, the mainland government can be viewed by its subjects as weak and unable to unify the nation. But China's new maritime allies, Japan and the United States, do not want to see the PRC reestablish control over the strategically important island.

COMMERCIAL ACCOMPLISHMENTS

Chinese reemphasis on the maritime sphere has produced a number of dynamic changes, the most significant one being the dismantling and replacement of the Soviet economic model with a system that has strong capitalistic flavor. For example, China joined the International Monetary Fund (IMF) and World Bank in 1980. With the largest IMF quota among developing nations, she has obtained loans totaling nearly one billion dollars in 1981.[2] Other changes more directly associated with commercial affairs are as follows:

1. By early 1981 the PRC's ocean fleet was capable of transporting 70 percent of its contracted cargo, a remarkable achievement considering that it could haul practically nothing in 1970. Moreover, China's merchant fleet vaulted to a world rank of tenth in terms of tonnage in 1978.[3]

2. Many Chinese ports have undergone modernization. One hundred and thirty deep-water berths have been created and the use of containers has been introduced. By 1985 China is projected to be able to handle 700,000 teu (20-foot equivalent units), which compares with 1980 Hong Kong figures of 1.3 million teu.[4]

3. In Guangdong and Fujian the Chinese have reestablished special districts, reminiscent of the past, whose superintendents are authorized to compete for foreign investment without prior approval from Beijing.

4. In 1980 the China Shipbuilding Corporation began taking orders on ships and by early 1981 reached the saturation level on foreign orders for 10,000-ton vessels.[5]

5. The old Nanyang trade routes have been reactivated, and Chinese merchant ships are calling on Southeast Asian ports with increasing frequency. As many as five PRC merchant ships call at Singapore each day. Perhaps as a precaution, the Grand Canal has also been recently renovated. In 1978 the 600-km section from southern Shandong to Yangzhou in Jiangsu Province moved as much freight as the principal Chinese Tianjin-Peikou railway.[6]

6. The PRC redoubled efforts to improve its coastal and ocean fishing industries. New management techniques, modern equipment, and better ecological policies have been introduced. China's annual catch has improved; she concluded fishing contracts with Thailand allowing Thai fishermen to operate in China's claimed portion of the Tonkin Gulf. China, in turn, obtains a good profit from the Thais.

7. Since about 1974 China has been making headway in offshore oil exploration. It is estimated that, given the technology, the development of reserves in the north and south could double China's oil production by 1985–86 to an estimated 200 million metric tons annually.[7]

NAVAL ACCOMPLISHMENTS

The PRC's naval accomplishments are considerable as well. They include the following:

1. Today, in terms of numbers of major combatants, the PRC navy is the third largest in the world. It has more than two hundred missile craft and its SSMs are far greater in number than those of the United States. At any instant, the Chinese can put more than five hundred missiles to sea, albeit only as short-range extensions of shore-based coastal defenses.[8]

2. China now possesses more than one hundred conventional submarines, which could interdict sea-lanes in Malacca, the Philippine Sea, and the Sea of Japan without straining their propulsion systems.[9]

3. China's newer missile-equipped destroyers and frigates do have adequate ranges (2,500–4,000 nautical miles) for regional oceangoing operations and reliable geared-turbine engines. Each class has respectable acceleration characteristics and could be used effectively by the Chinese to maintain surveillance of, and if necessary to protect, offshore resources in the Yellow, East China, and South China seas.[10]

4. The Chinese have been able to launch a nuclear-powered submarine, indicating that their naval engineers can go from theory to production of sophisticated propulsion systems.

5. In the spring of 1980 China successfully tested its first ICBM, the CSSX-4. The rocket splashdown area was about 6,000 kilometers from the China coast on the equator and approximately 1,000 kilometers from the

The PRC satellite and missile-tracking ship *Yuanwang*. This vessel participated in the May 1980 ICBM tests conducted by the PRC in the South Pacific. Equipped with sophisticated missile-tracking radars, the *Yuanwang* deployed more than 3,000 miles from the mainland to monitor China's first successful long-range missile firing. (Courtesy of the Department of Defense, Australia.)

Solomon Islands. A Chinese naval task force was on site to observe and retrieve the missile. The ships replenished at sea and the crews apparently carried out their assignments in a professional manner.[11]

6. Professionalism, in fact, is being reemphasized throughout the navy. For example, in the South Sea Fleet, the Party Committee has lately been tasked with identifying all personnel who have received formal naval schooling, particularly those trained by the Soviets in the 1950s. Once identified, they are to be tested, and if found qualified in specialty areas, they are to be reassigned to key, responsible billets. A concerted effort is also being made to improve discipline within the navy as well as build up an awareness of modern weapons and tactics. Naval training has been reemphasized and senior officers have been directed to improve general administration and quality-control procedures. As an example of the changes in training, in 1981 the PRC navy's submarine school added courses on operational research, military science and technology, English, and underwater survival techniques.

DEFICIENCIES

Despite many accomplishments in the maritime and naval spheres, China's neo-maritime supporters remain constrained by technology and preoccupied with coastal defense. Their problems are numerous and readily identifiable.

PRC navy replenishes at sea. With little fanfare, the Chinese have launched a new-class replenishment oiler, the *Fuqing*. Here she demonstrates sophisticated refueling techniques with a *Luda*-class guided-missile destroyer. (Courtesy of the U.S. Navy.)

WEAPON SYSTEMS

According to a Hong Kong report, surface-to-air missiles installed on the *Jiangdong*-class destroyer have serious design and construction deficiencies. The report also indicates that China's one operational nuclear-powered submarine launched in 1974 has encountered severe technical problems. Other newer submarine classes have run into problems as well. The Hong Kong report indicates that the new generation *Ming*-class submarine, a conventionally powered vessel, has technical defects. Although launched in 1974 or 1975 as a new, "quieter" version of the reliable R-class, the *Ming* has yet to go into serial production.[12] There has been no secret about China's inability to develop an SLBM capability either. Fifteen years have elapsed since the launching of the PRC's single-missile submarine and a reliable missile system has yet to be installed.

ELECTRONICS

The Chinese have not developed any unique ship-borne electronics, but have relied upon duplicating the products of Western or Soviet research. Most of their radars, developed by the Soviets, have been in use for more than fifteen years. The Chinese apparently intend to continue this practice, as it gives them a great deal of confidence in their electronics. Like their weapon systems, however, it means that Chinese equipment is generally less advanced, and therefore probably less effective than the more modern systems used by China's potential adversaries.

WARSHIPS AND AIRCRAFT

More than half of China's navy is made up of small patrol craft that have poor sea-keeping qualities. Mine-warfare vessels are obsolete by Western standards, and most of China's auxiliary ships are vintage models acquired during the civil war. Amphibious warfare ships are quite old and inadequate to support a major offensive against Nationalist-held islands.

The Chinese naval air organization remains outclassed. It is equipped with about seven hundred obsolete aircraft, including 150 IL-28s, BE-6s, and TU-2s. There are substantial numbers of MiG-15, MiG-17, and MiG-19 interceptors, but they have no all-weather or antisubmarine-warfare capabilities. In 1974 the PRC did take delivery of several French-built Super-Frelon helicopters. Although intended for use as civil aircraft, they can be converted to an antisubmarine-warfare role.

MANPOWER, TRAINING, AND THE SHORE ESTABLISHMENT

While precise manpower figures are lacking, the PRC navy, including the naval-air arm, is estimated to have more than two hundred thousand officers and enlisted men. Enlistment in the navy entails a five-year obligation. There is a special incentive pay based upon longevity for submariners, flyers, and sea-duty personnel.

Like the imperial and republican navies, the PRC navy follows the practice of keeping many personnel semi-permanently assigned to the same billet. For example, commanding officers of warships can continue to serve in that position for many years. One torpedo-boat skipper captained his vessel for ten years.[13]

The Communist Chinese do rotate their enlisted men more often. However, reenlistments are restricted to the best qualified personnel. Thus, there is a constant input of "first-termers," which creates a huge training problem.

Tactical training remains somewhat primitive. For example, in 1977 a Chinese news release described submarine tactics as imitations of aerial combat; that is, two submarines were used in a wolf-pack-type attack against a single surface target. While one attacked the surface vessel, the other provided cover against a probable counterattack. Both submarines required extensive communications to coordinate the attack.[14] Such a compromising and uneconomic use of submarines probably indicates that, in the event of war in the near term, these ships would be used for coastal defense rather than for longer-range sea-denial tasks.

Part of the problem can be explained by the naval school system. As with civilian academic institutions, the naval schools were seriously disrupted for nearly a decade by the turmoil of the GPCR. The schools have a shortage of good technical instructors and training aids as well as basic equipment such as Xerox machines and textbooks. Additionally, the naval schools still suffer from tradition, being highly decentralized and lacking unity of instruction.

There are other inconsistencies. For instance, many patrol vessels do not have the ability to make fresh water and have to either return to port or be resupplied by water tenders while at sea. Nor are simple things like tide tables available for all warships. It has been reported that crewmen have to compile them by hand for use during operations.[15] Shipyards remain highly centralized and labor intensive. For example, a shipyard builds both the engines and forging propellers for vessels. Even armatures for small electric motors are produced at the yards.

Organizationally, the PRC navy's system is quite similar to the principal one used in the imperial period. It is dedicated to coastal defense and provides little opportunity for the development of expert high-seas officers and petty officers. The Beijing Navy Headquarters is still largely concerned with ceremonial duties, while the operational units perform roles that remain essentially provincial in nature.

The navy also continues to take an active part in production. Throughout 1980 and 1981, its ships and crews performed a variety of nonmilitary functions, such as guarding offshore oil rigs, laying civil-communications submarine cables, expanding fishing ports, and working as stevedores in various large commercial ports.

MERCHANT-FLEET WEAKNESSES

The PRC merchant marine has two basic problems. It lacks trained personnel and its main government organ, the China Ocean Shipping Company, is unfamiliar with international shipping practices. According to a Hong Kong newspaper, the Chinese must train nearly one hundred fifty thousand seamen and officers by 1990 in order to keep up with the requirements of their expanding operations and ship acquisitions.[16] Chinese equipment is also outdated, which slows loading and unloading of cargo. Unlike their ancestors, who were aided by the customs service, the present generation of coastal port administrators lacks effective maritime laws and regulations. Beijing has also been slow to respond to international conventions. As one Hong Kong observer wrote recently, "It was not until June 1975 that China acknowledged a revised version of the International Collision Regulations." Moreover, as of February 1980 China had "not acceded to the Hague Convention on the Carriage of Goods by Sea, the most important single document in international maritime law."[17]

DENG'S "CNO"

In February 1979 Admiral Su Zhenhua died, leaving the navy without an effective voice at the highest government levels (just before his death Su had become a full member of the Politburo as well as mayor of Shanghai). Xiao Jingguang, then age seventy-seven, continued to run the navy until the following month, when Deng Xiaoping replaced Xiao with Ye Fei.

Ye's assignment as both the navy's operational and political head was a surprise. Until his appointment he had no previous naval experience, although as minister of Communications from 1975 to 1979 he was associated with the continued buildup of the merchant fleet. Prior to that he spent six years out of power, having been purged in 1967 as "an agent of the Liu [Shaoji] and Deng [Xiaoping] clique."[18]

Ye is a Fujianese who remained in that province during the Long March. From 1941 to 1946, the war years, Ye was a brigade commander whose troops fought both the Japanese and Nationalists in many riverine actions along the Grand Canal and Yangzi River. After the mainland fell, Ye returned to Fujian where he quickly rose to become the Fuzhou Military Region commander from 1958 to 1960. Thereafter he served in a variety of political and civil jobs until his purge.

The choice of Ye can probably be interpreted as a move by Deng Xiaoping to steer the navy toward a modernization course consistent with the priorities of the Four Modernizations and to "reeducate" those officers and enlisted men who were promoted to responsible positions by the radicals.

NAVAL ARMS DIPLOMACY: THE NEW ERA

The Chinese Communists and the West have engaged in naval-arms diplomacy designed to familiarize navy personnel with new technologies as well as explore weapon-system purchases. Since 1976 China has hosted European naval delegations, including the visit of warships to Shanghai. Likewise, Chinese naval delegations have gone abroad once again to view Western naval installations. For example, in September 1979 a PRC naval group went to England and visited such places as Portsmouth, Devonport, Gosport, the Royal Naval College, and various ships. Less than a month later Premier Hua Guofeng visited the French naval base at Brest, where he inspected French naval facilities and was briefed by the commander in chief of the French Atlantic Fleet. Seven months later, Vice-premier Geng

Former President Carter aboard PRC R-class submarine. The PRC navy is not used as an instrument of diplomacy in the traditional Western sense: it maintains no naval presence overseas, nor has it carried out visits to foreign ports. However, it does host many foreign visitors. Here, Mr. Carter is seen touring a Chinese submarine in September 1981. Note the Chinese uniforms that Madame Mao once strongly criticized for being "bourgeosie" and "imperialistic."

Biao came to the United States and looked over American naval bases. He took a short cruise aboard the U.S. carrier *Ranger*, which particularly annoyed the Soviet Union.

Thus far, the Chinese have restricted their naval visits abroad to window-shopping and investigative talks. Money is the main reason why the PRC has not made any large purchases. The chief of the PRC Naval Foreign Affairs Bureau, Jiao Ai, stated that China is interested in acquiring advanced naval technology, but thus far "the price is too high." He was specifically referring to the British naval-armaments mission to Shanghai in September 1980. Jiao, at that time, said that English naval technology was too costly, but that China was talking with French, West German, and Italian manufacturers who were "also eager to sell equipment to the Chinese Navy."[19]

MARITIME STRATEGIC CONSIDERATIONS

China's renewed interest in naval armaments stems from a perception in Beijing that the Soviet navy is being used to pressure the Chinese into backing off from their maritime activities. The PRC leadership is particularly concerned with Vietnam-based Russian warships and aircraft operating in increasing numbers in and over China's sensitive southern maritime flank, the South China Sea. Deng Xiaoping has explained the Soviet activities as being part of the Kremlin's "dumbbell strategy."[20] As Deng sees it, the Soviet navy is bent on controlling the Pacific at one end and the Indian Ocean/Persian Gulf at the other. Joining the two regions is the critical bar of the Malacca Strait.

The Soviet invasion of Afghanistan in December 1979 reinforced the Chinese in their "dumbbell" assessment. China believes that the move into Afghanistan was the initial step toward the Soviet's ultimate seizure and control of the Middle East's oil centers. Secondly, China thinks that the Soviet Union, when ready, will drive southward through Pakistan to the Indian Ocean for the purpose of acquiring a warm-water port. According to Beijing, the Soviet navy can then control the Indian Ocean sea-lanes, strangling Europe and Japan. China also views the Soviet navy's presence in the South China Sea as an attempt to establish control over the Pacific approaches to Malacca as well as block Chinese territorial claims in that sea.[21]

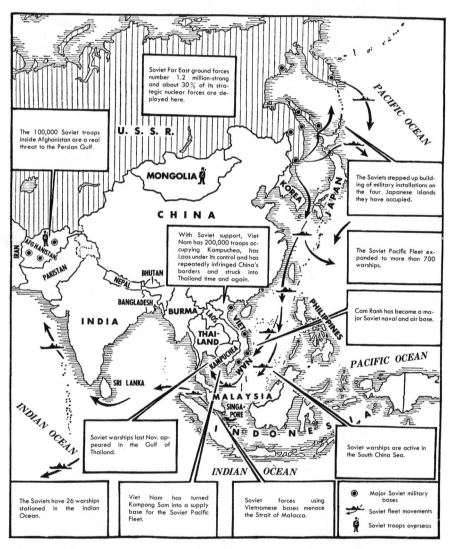

This schematic diagram demonstrates China's mounting concern over Soviet naval activity in Asia. (Diagram by Zhu Yulian in the *Beijing Review*, March 23, 1981.)

One important reason for Chinese concern over the Vietnamese-Soviet relationship is the matter of who controls offshore oil. The South China Sea is beginning to look like the site of a major oil source, which the Chinese are determined to have most of. Since the early 1970s Chinese seismic survey activity has confirmed the presence of large oil and gas deposits. Beijing has given other survey contracts to a number of U.S. firms.[22] It has been reported that at least twenty wells have been drilled in the offshore area near the Leizhou Peninsula city of Zhanjiang (headquarters for the South Sea Fleet).

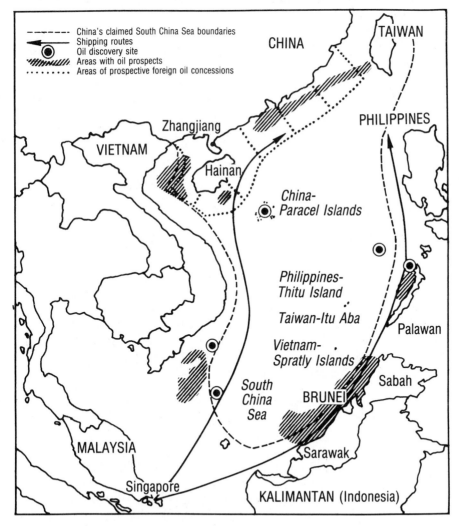

Nanyang today. China still has a great interest in the South China Sea. It claims certain islands and has made some oil discoveries.

Other oil activities are located near the central Gulf of Tonkin, which is close to Vietnamese claims. Hence, the question of sovereignty over various South China Sea islands has become a matter of serious concern between the two antagonists, Vietnam and China. The Soviets, in support of Hanoi, made the following accusation in February 1979:

> If we recall China's vast territorial claims on other countries, we can see more clearly the meaning of Beijing's attempt to strengthen its naval power. Everybody knows that the Beijing leadership has overtly and officially reasserted its claim on the South China Sea and the islands in this area, including islands claimed by the Philippines, Malaysia, and Vietnam. Some years ago, China encroached on the Hsisha [Paracel] Islands and China's ships have repeatedly intruded into Vietnam's territorial waters. . . . The Chinese rulers have great interest in the South China Sea because there is oil there. . . . But China now has little oil and it is looking for—and will seize—the oil-producing areas.[23]

The Chinese response has been to increase the frequency of their claims. Their latest statement, made on 30 January 1980, came in the form of a lengthy "white paper" whose title is self-explanatory: "China's Indisputable Sovereignty Over the Xisha [Paracel] and Nansha [Spratly] Islands."[24] It is reasonable to interpret the Soviet movement of warships into Danang and Cam Ranh Bay in 1979 as intended primarily to warn the Chinese not to attempt an assault on the Spratly Islands, specifically those occupied by the Vietnamese. The Chinese, not surprisingly, believe the opposite—that the Soviet naval presence in Vietnam is the first step toward an attempt to help the Vietnamese recapture the Paracels.

Without doubt, the sea areas adjacent to China are taking on increasing strategic importance, for they do serve as vital lanes for the expanding commerce of the Asia-Pacific region. The Chinese appear determined to meet Soviet assertiveness in the region with force if necessary, as well as to make good their claims to various island groups.

China, however, still counts heavily on the U.S. Seventh Fleet to monitor and deter the Soviet navy in the Pacific. It backs continued U.S. Navy presence at Japanese and Philippine bases, but has lately expressed alarm over America's weakened naval posture in the Pacific.[25] China also backs Japanese rearmament, and would support strengthening the Japanese maritime self-defense force in order to help protect the Indian Ocean–Malacca–Pacific commercial routes.[26]

AFGHANISTAN AND CONTINENTALISM

The Afghanistan invasion led the Chinese to make the following reassessments:

1. The international situation as a whole is considered extremely unstable, and the dangers of war between the United States and USSR are seen as rising. The Chinese believe that the Afghan events "show that 'detente' with the Soviet Union can never bring long-term stability to any particular region or country."[27]

2. Until Afghanistan, the Chinese judged that in the event of a war between the superpowers, the probability that either would attack the PRC was quite low. China has reassessed that estimate and now believes the threat to its security considerably higher.

3. At least in some of their public statements, the Chinese remain ready to challenge the Soviets, but want assurances that NATO, Japan, and the United States are similarly committed.

4. In the near term there is no likelihood of normalization of relations between China and the USSR. The chief commentator of the *People's Daily* recently concluded that "the ideological differences of opinion between China and the Soviet Union are irreconcilable. . . . I see no chance for a so-called reconciliation between China and the Soviet Union."[28]

Until Afghanistan, the Chinese believed that their present force levels were adequate to deter any potential aggressor and that increased expenditures on either nuclear or improved conventional weapons could be delayed. These policies are now under close scrutiny by the PLA.

It is an important debate because it again pits the army against the navy. Most army leaders see the Soviet border threat as the paramount problem; they are determined to strengthen ground forces at the expense of the emergent navy. For example, a 1980 essay in the *Liberation Army News* was openly critical of China's lack of adequate defense against nuclear attack. Among other things, it urged rapid development of tactical nuclear weapons.[29]

The essay also surfaced the old issue of internal security versus coastal security. This time the army has resurrected the 1874 debate to help its case. A March 1981 article leaves little doubt where emphasis should be placed in shoring up China's defenses.

> The so-called debate [1874] between "coastal defense" and "land border defense" . . . was a controversy over the major issue of whether it is necessary to defend the country's territorial integrity and to protect the fundamental interests of the Chinese nation. In essence, it was a struggle between patriotism and national betrayal. If the ideas of Li Hongzhang and company were adopted [i.e., coastal defense and navy building], the northwestern borders at that time would be in danger and, invariably, endless harm would [have been] done to our country.[30]

THE FUTURE

In many respects the PRC navy must solve the same problems that haunted Li Hongzhang one hundred years ago. The Communist leadership is still divided on the question of modernization and agreement on future navy building is lacking. Because of this, the navy finds itself at a critical crossroads, cautiously examining its alternatives.

For the moment its principal activities appear to be correctly concentrated on training and technical education. Unlike navies of the past, the PRC navy seems agreed on the need to acquire foreign technology selectively and at a moderate rate, concentrating on naval-maritime industries (shipbuilding, naval electronics, naval engineering, and the like); scientific research and equipment (SONAR, radar, naval missiles, torpedoes, and nuclear engineering); and naval-maritime literature. All these efforts will require naval scientists, officers, and midshipmen to have greater knowledge of foreign languages (especially Japanese and English), so it is expected that China will once again send naval personnel abroad to study modern naval techniques.

If tradition is overcome, this generation of naval officers can develop into a technically efficient group that is less involved in nationwide propaganda; they can expand their breadth of vision and sense of reality, thereby becoming an important force in the modernization process.

While this education proceeds, China will not undertake any highly sophisticated naval construction, continuing current programs at the same, or maybe a slightly accelerated, pace. Conventional submarines, missile craft, and small frigates will remain the basic naval units. While the improvement of technical capabilities is in progress, the navy will make radical changes in its organizational management and administration in order to cope with the demands of more sophisticated naval systems. Under these conditions, the CCP's hitherto strong role in naval affairs will probably decline.

Operationally, the navy will be employed periodically as a political instrument to exert limited pressure in sensitive adjacent sea areas such as

The new PRC *Dajiang*-class submarine support ship. This vessel carries two French Super Frelon helicopters and can steam at 20 knots. It displaces nearly 11,000 tons. (Courtesy of the Department of Defense, Australia.)

the South China Sea and possibly the Taiwan Strait. Given the current tension between Beijing and Hanoi, China faces pressure on her border that could result in naval action against Vietnam. This might involve making good Chinese claims on various South China Sea islands, especially those occupied by Vietnam in the Spratly Islands. Or China might conduct an extensive maritime resupply effort in support of guerrillas operating in the Kampuchean coastal zones. In the case of the Taiwan Strait, China will offset the withdrawal of troops and aircraft from the Fujian Military Region across the strait from Taiwan by improving her naval posture in that area. In this regard, Chinese naval activities in other claimed continental-shelf areas will increase in the East and South China seas, as will the number of destroyers, frigates, research vessels, and fishing fleets. On the other hand, the navy will not be present in areas such as the Diaoyudai Islands, where confrontation with Japan, a sorely needed economic partner, is possible.

Even with these moderate programs, the needs of the Chinese navy will remain controversial in military-budget deliberations. Growth will bring it into sharper competition for resources with the other military services and the civilian industrial sector. As past records indicate, China's navies have not been especially adept at maintaining constant growth or planned modernization programs. Much will depend upon the continuity of the current leadership of the neo-maritime advocate Deng Xiaoping.

Despite claims to the contrary, most Chinese leaders, including Deng Xiaoping, do not fully realize the magnitude of their tasks. They have not yet devised a clear plan or gained an effective consensus on how to proceed.[31] Until those important initial steps are taken, the navy's modernization plans must be sustained through a series of "quick-fix" programs. It is this kind of approach that has been debilitating in the past, for it requires the reintroduction of foreign experts and methodologies. The Chinese must come to terms with this problem or the current modernization program could meet the same dismal fate that its predecessor did in the late Qing period.

On the other side, the West, particularly the United States, now views China in a larger strategic context—as a valuable friend whose assistance is necessary to contain Soviet expansion in Asia. In these sensitive times, past mistakes cannot be repeated. The next moves must be precisely calculated, understood, and coordinated by all the principals. Regarding the specific issue of China and the sea, the players must ask themselves, How important is it, and what are the consequences of China's success or failure in its latest quest for maritime and naval power?

PRINCIPAL CHINESE DYNASTIES DISCUSSED

Names	Characters	Date
Qin	秦	221–207 B.C.
Western Han	西漢	206 B.C.–8 A.D.
Eastern Han	東漢	25–220 A.D.
Minor (Shu) Han	蜀漢	221–63 A.D.
Jin	晉	265–420 A.D.
Tang	唐	618–906 A.D.
Song	宋	960–1127 A.D.
Southern Song	南宋	1127–1279 A.D.
Yuan	元	1280–1368 A.D.
Ming	明	1368–1644 A.D.
Qing	清	1644–1912 A.D.

APPENDIX B

TERMS

Term	Characters	Term	Characters
Baochuan	寶船	Louchuan	樓船
Baojia	保甲	Nanyang	南洋
Beiyang	北洋	Neiluan waihuan	內亂外患
Bianqu	汴渠	Nianfei	捻匪
Dayi	大翼	Pianan	偏安
Da yitong	大一統	Shuilei	水雷
Danjia	蛋家	Shuishang yitiao long, lushang yitiao	
Danren	蛋人	chong 水上一條龍 陸上一條	
Folangji	佛朗機	Taiping	太平
Guandu shangban	官督商辦	Ting	鋌
Guomindang	國民黨	Wangdou	望斗
Haian	海岸	Woren	倭人
Haifang	海防	Xiao yitong	小一統
Haijiang fangyu	海港防禦	Yanhai yaosai	沿海要塞
Haijin dakai	海禁大開	Yuke	魚客
Haitan fangyu	海灘防禦	Yueren	越人
Hechuanzhan	河川戰	Zhongxue weiti xixue	
Huaqiao	華僑	weiyong 中學為體西學為用	
Jianbi quingye	堅壁清野	Zongbao	總保
Ketou	磕頭	Zongjia	總甲

GEOGRAPHICAL NAMES

Name	Characters	Name	Characters
Amoy (Xiamen)	廈門	Gansu	甘肅
Anhui	安徽	Guangdong	廣東
Annam	安南	Guangxi	廣西
Aomen (Macao)	澳門	Guangzhou (Canton)	廣州
Beijishan	北磯山	Guilin	桂林
Beizhili	北直隸	Haidao	海島
Bohai	渤海	Hainan	海南
Changchun	長春	Haishengwei	海參威
Chaozhou	潮州	Hangzhou	杭州
Chongqing	重慶	Hebei	河北
Dachen dao	大陳島	Heilongjiang	黑龍江
Dadengmen	大嶝門	Henan	河南
Dadu	大都	Hongqi (shipyard)	紅旗
Dakushan	大沽山	Huai	淮
Dalian	大連	Huaihe	淮河
Dalushan	大鹿山	Huangpu (Whampoa)	黃埔
Dinghai	定海	Hudong (shipyard)	滬東
Dongjiang	東江	Huizhou	惠州
Fengtian	奉天	Huludao	葫蘆島
Fujian	福建	Hunan	湖南
Fuzhou	福州	Hunghu	洪湖

Name	Characters	Name	Characters
Jiamusi	佳木斯	Shandong	山東
Jiangnan	江南	Shanghai	上海
Jiangsu	江蘇	Shantou	汕頭
Jiangyin	江陰	Siming	四明
Jilin	吉林	Tai	泰
Jining	濟寧	Taiping	太平
Jinjiang	晉門	Taiwan	台灣
Jinmen (Quemoy)	金門	Tanggu	塘沽
Jiujiang	九江	Tianjin	天津
Kaifeng	開封	Tongshandao	東山島
Lianjiang	連江	Weihai	威海
Liaodong	遼東	Weihe	濰河
Linqing	臨清	Wen	溫
Liuqiu	琉球	Wenzhou	溫州
Longqi	龍溪	Wuhan	武漢
Lushunkou	旅順口	Wusong	吳淞
Luzhou	鸕洲	Wusulijiang	烏蘇里江
Matang	馬當	Wuzhou	梧州
Mawei	馬尾	Xiamen	廈門
Miaodao	廟島	Xinjiang	新疆
Min	閩	Xisha	西沙
Minhe	閩河	Yaishan	厓山
Nanjing	南京	Yalujiang	鴨綠江
Nansha	南沙	Yangzijiang	揚子江
Nanridao	南日島	Yantai	烟台
Ningbo	寧波	Yijiang (shan)	一江山
Putian	莆田	Yingkou	營口
Qingdao	青島	Yizhang	宜昌
Qinhuangdao	秦皇島	Yunnan	雲南
Quanzhou	泉州	Yushandao	魚山島
Sanpu	三浦	Zhangzhou	漳州

Name	Characters	Name	Characters
Zhanjiang	湛江	Zhongtong	中洞
Zhejiang	浙江	Zhoushan	舟山
Zhenbaodao	珍寶島	Zhujiang	珠江
Zhili	直隸		

APPENDIX D

PERSONAL NAMES

Name	Characters	Name	Characters
Bao Zenpeng	包遵彭	Ding Ruchang	丁汝昌
Beng Deqing	彭德清	Dun Xingyun	頓星雲
Chen Cheng	陳誠	Fang Qiang	方強
Chen Jiliang	陳季良	Fang Zhengping	方正平
Chen Jingwen	陳景文	Geng Biao	耿飈
Chen Jiongming	陳炯明	Guangxu (emperor)	光緒
Chen Lanbin	陳蘭彬	Guan Yin	關音
Chen Lu	陳籙	Gui Yongjing	桂永清
Chen Shaokuan	陳紹寬	Guo Bingkun	郭炳坤
Chen Xilian	陳錫聯	He Long	賀龍
Chen Yongshen	陳永善	Hu Pengfei	胡鵬飛
Chen Zaidao	陳再道	Hua Guofeng	華國鋒
Chen Zuyi	陳祖義	Huang Huaixin	黃懷信
Cheng Biguang	程璧光	Huang Yongsheng	黃永勝
Chiang K'ai-shek	蔣介石	Huang Zhongying	黃鍾瑛
Chun, Prince	淳親王	Jianyan (reign)	建炎
Dao Yong	陶勇	Kang Zhiqiang	康志強
Deng Shichang	鄧世昌	Li Dingxin	李鼎新
Deng Xiaoping	鄧小平	Li Fengbao	李鳳苞
Deng Zhaoxiang	鄧兆祥	Li Hongzhang	李鴻章
Ding Gongchen	丁拱辰	Li Lisan	李立三

Name	Characters	Name	Characters
Li Yuanhong	黎 元 洪	Shen Baozhen	沈 葆 楨
Li Zhilong	李 之 龍	Shen Honglie	沈 鴻 烈
Li Zongxi	李 宗 羲	Shi Jinqing	施 進 卿
Li Zuopeng	李 作 鵬	Shi Lang	施 琅
Lin Baoyi	林 葆 懌	Shu Jicheng	舒 積 成
Lin Biao	林 彪	Soong, T.V.	宋 子 文
Lin Taizeng	林 泰 曾	Su Zhenhua	蘇 振 華
Lin Xiangguang	林 祥 光	Sun Tze	孫 子
Lin Zexu	林 則 徐	Sun Yat-sen	孫 逸 仙
Lin Zhiping	林 之 平	Tang Tingguang	湯 廷 光
Lin Zun	林 遵	Tianfei	天 妃
Liu Buchan	劉 步 蟾	Tian Xiong	田 雄
Liu Guanxiong	劉 冠 雄	Tu Xigui	杜 錫 珪
Liu Haotian	劉 浩 天	Wang Hongkun	王 宏 坤
Liu Kunyi	劉 坤 一	Wang Jinggong	王 荊 公
Liu Shaoqi	劉 少 奇	Wang Jingwei	汪 精 衛
Lo Fenglu	羅 豐 祿	Wei Han	魏 瀚
Lo Ruiqing	羅 瑞 卿	Wei Yuan	魏 源
Ma Dejian	馬 德 建	Wen Shude	溫 樹 德
Ma Huan	馬 歡	Wu Beifu	吳 佩 孚
Mai Xiande	麥 賢 得	Wu Faxian	吳 法 憲
Mao Zedong	毛 澤 東	Wu Ruilin	吳 瑞 林
Mo Zi	墨 子	Xining (reign)	熙 寧
Ouyang Bao	歐 陽 寶	Xiao Jingguang	蕭 勁 光
Pan Shicheng	潘 仕 成	Xu Shiyu	許 世 友
Pan Zhencheng	潘 振 承	Yan Fu	嚴 復
Peng Dehuai	彭 德 懷	Yan Zongguang	嚴 宗 光
Qi Jiguang	戚 繼 光	Yang Dezhi	楊 得 志
Qisangke	琪 桑 喀	Yang Shuzhuang	楊 樹 莊
Qing (prince)	慶 親 王	Ye Fei	葉 飛
Sa Zhenping	薩 鎮 冰	Ye Jianying	葉 劍 英

Name	Characters	Name	Characters
Ye Zugui	葉 祖 珪	Zhang Zhidong	張 之 洞
Yi Yaocai	易 耀 彩	Zhang Zuolin	張 作 霖
Yongle	永 樂	Zhao Qimin	趙 啓 民
Yong Wing (Rong Hong)	容 閎	Zheng Chenggong	鄭 成 功
Yuan Shikai	袁 世 凱	Zheng He	鄭 和
Yuan Yelie	袁 也 烈	Zheng Rucheng	鄭 汝 成
Zai Xun	載 洵	Zhou Enlai	周 恩 來
Zeng Guofan	曾 國 藩	Zhou Xianzhang	周 憲 章
Zhang Fakui	張 發 奎	Zhou Xihan	周 希 漢
Zhang Qunqiao	張 春 橋	Zhu Chengzu	朱 成 祖
Zhang Xiuchuan	張 秀 川	Zhu Qing	朱 清
Zhang Xuan	張 瑄	Zhu Yuanzhang	朱 元 璋
Zhang Xueliang	張 學 良	Zuo Zongtang	左 宗 棠
Zhang Xuexi	張 學 思		

OFFICIAL RANKS AND TITLES

MING DYNASTY

Title	Name	Characters
Regional commissioner	Du zhihui shi	都指揮使
Area commander	Zongbing guan	總兵官
Area vice commander	Fu zongbing	副總兵
Area assistant commander	Canjiang	參將
Mobile corps commander	Yuji jiangjun	遊擊將軍
Post commander	Shoubei	守備
Post vice commander	Qianzong	千總
Post assistant commander	Bazong	把總
Coastal patrol officer	Shaoguan	哨官

EARLY QING DYNASTY

Rank Equivalent	Name	Characters
Admiral in chief	Shuisi tidu	水師提督
Division (fleet) admiral	Zongbing	總兵
Commodore	Fujiang	副將
Captain	Canjiang	參將
Commander	Yuji	遊擊
Lieutenant commander	Dusi	都司
Lieutenant	Shoubei	守備
Lieutenant junior grade	Qianzong	千總
Ensign	Bazong	把總

LATE QING DYNASTY

Rank Equivalent	Name	Characters
Admiral	Zheng dutong	正都统
Vice admiral	Fu dutong	副都统
Rear admiral	Xie dutong	協都統
Post captain	Zheng canling	正參領
Commander	Fu canling	副參領
Lieutenant commander	Xie canling	協參領
Senior lieutenant	Zheng junxiao	正軍校
Lieutenant	Fu junxiao	副軍校
Midshipman	Xie junxiao	協軍校

REPUBLIC

Rank Equivalent	Name	Characters
Admiral	Shangjiang	上將
Vice admiral	Zhongjiang	中將
Rear admiral	Shaojiang	少將
Captain	Shangxiao	上校
Commander	Zhongxiao	中校
Lieutenant commander	Shaoxiao	少校
Lieutenant	Shangwei	上尉
Lieutenant junior grade	Zhongwei	中尉
Midshipman	Shaowei	少尉

PEOPLE'S REPUBLIC OF CHINA (1955–64)

Rank Equivalent	Name	Characters
Senior admiral	Dajiang	大將
Admiral	Shangjiang	上將
Vice admiral	Zhongjiang	中將
Rear admiral	Shaojiang	少將
Senior captain	Daxiao	大校

Rank Equivalent	Name	Characters
Captain	Shangxiao	上校
Commander	Zhongxiao	中校
Lieutenant commander	Shaoxiao	少校
Captain lieutenant	Dawei	大尉
Lieutenant	Shangwei	上尉
Lieutenant junior grade	Zhongwei	中尉
Ensign	Shaowei	少尉

ORGANIZATIONAL TERMS

Term	Characters	Term	Characters
Baihusuo	百户所	Yongying	勇營
Beiyang dachen	北洋大臣	Yunchou si	運籌司
Chubei si	儲備司	Zhenshu jun	鎮戍軍
Chuanzheng si	船政司	Zhuli jun	主力軍
Fawu si	法務司	Zongli yamen	總理衙門
Haijun bu	海軍部		
Haijun zong silingbu	海軍總司令部		
Hanglu si	航路司		
Jiyao si	機要司		
Lifan yuan	理藩院		
Nanyang dachen	南洋大臣		
Qianhu suo	千户所		
Sanbao taiqian	三保太監		
Shuishi yamen	水師衙門		
Shuishou jun	水手軍		
Suo	所		
Tongmeng hui	同盟會		
Tuanlian	團練		
Wei	衛		
Yanhai zhizhi shisi	沿海制置使司		
Yiwu si	醫務司		

SHIPS' NAMES

Name	Characters	Name	Characters
Baobi	宝 璧	Jiangshui	江 綏
Chaoyong	超 勇	Jiangtai	江 泰
Chenghe (Chao ho)	澄 和	Jiangtong	江 通
Chongqing	重 慶	Jiaoan	交 安
Dingyuan	定 遠	Jingyuan (Br.)	經 遠
Feiying	飛 鷹	Jingyuan (Ger.)	靖 遠
Fubo	伏 波	Laiyuan	來 遠
Fulong	福 龍	Liji	利 濟
Guangbing	廣 丙	Lijie	利 捷
Haichen	海 琛	Lisui	利 綏
Haichou	海 籌	Lingfu	靈 甫
Haiqi	海 圻	Ninghai	甯 海
Hairong	海 容	Pinghai	平 海
Haitian	海 天	Pingyuan	平 遠
Jiyuan	濟 遠	Taiping (Nat.)	太 平
Jiankang	建 康	Tongji	通 濟
Jianwei	建 威	Wannianqing	萬 年 青
Jiangan	江 安	Yangwei	揚 威
Jiangheng	江 亨	Yingrui	應 瑞
Jiangping	江 平	Yongfeng	永 豐
Jiangqing	江 泰	Yongjian	永 建

Name	Characters	Name	Characters
Yuzhang	豫章	Zhiyuan	致遠
Zhangfen	NA	Zhongjian	中建
Zhenyuan	鎮遠	Zhongshan	中山

BEIYANG NAVY, 1888: OFFICER DISTRIBUTION BY PROVINCE

Rank				Province					
	Anhui	Zhejiang	Zhili	Henan	Fujian	Jiangxi	Jiangsu	Guangdong	Shandong
Admiral	1				10			1	
Captain		1			5			1	
Commander	1				15			9	
1st lieutenant	1				9		2	6	
2nd lieutenant	1	2	4		10			4	
3rd lieutenant		1	1	1	18			3	
Midshipman	1		5		4	2		5	
Chief engineer					6			5	
1st engineer		1			17			5	
2nd engineer		1			14		2		
3rd engineer					2		1	3	4
Marine officers					5			1	1
Gunners			6		8				
Boatswains		1							
Totals	5	7	16	1	123	2	5	43	5
Percentage	2%	3%	8%	1%	60%	1%	2%	21%	2%

Source: The Imperial Chinese Navy List, Beiyang Squadron (Tianjin), 1888

WARSHIPS TRANSFERRED BY PRC TO THIRD WORLD NATIONS

Ship	Number	Years	Nation
Romeo (patrol submarine)	6	1973–75	North Korea
Komar (fast attack: missile)	4	1976	Albania
Hainan (fast-attack craft: patrol)	5	1976, 79	Pakistan
Shanghai (fast-attack craft: gun)	8	1967	North Korea
	6	1974–75	Albania
	2	1976	Cameroon
	3	1974	Congo
	6	1973–74, 76	Guinea
	12	1972–76	Pakistan
	5	1972	Sri Lanka
	3	1973	Sierra Leone
	7	1970–71	Tanzania
	8	1966	North Vietnam
Swatow (fast-attack craft: gun)	8	1968	North Korea
	14	1958, 64	North Vietnam
Huchuan (fast-attack craft: torpedo hydrofoil)	32	1968–71, 74	Albania
	4	1973	Pakistan
	4	1975	Tanzania
P6 (fast craft: torpedo)	6	1967	North Vietnam
P4 (fast craft: torpedo)	6	1965	Albania
Yulin (coast patrol craft)	4	1966	Congo
	3	1968	Kampuchea
	4	1966	Tanzania
Total	162		

STRENGTH OF THE PRC NAVY, 1980

Ships	*Number*
Destroyers	
gun	0
missile	11
Submarines	
attack	99
missile	1
Escorts	
gun/torpedo	49
missile	17
Patrol	
gun/torpedo	740
missile	215
Amphibious warfare	17
(+ 350 tons)	
Mine warfare	97
Auxiliary/Miscellaneous	500
Grand Total	1,746
Major Units Only	111
(destroyers/submarines)	

APPENDIX K

PARTS OF QING OCEAN-GOING JUNK DEFINED

Name	Characters	Meaning
Fengzhou	封舟	Official or blockade ship
Toujinding	頭巾頂	Topsail
Toupeng	頭篷	Foremast sail
Touqi	頭緝	Bowsprit sail
Toubo	頭樸	Spinnaker
Mianchaopai	免朝牌	Duty exemption notice
Pengku	篷褲	Foresail base
Ding	碇	Grapnel anchor
Dule	肚勒	Rudder bridle
Longgu	龍骨	Keel
Erliao	二繚	No. 2 winch
Daliao	大繚	Main winch
Pengqun	篷裙	Mainsail skirt or base
Dapeng	大篷	Mainsail
Chahua	插花	Tax [exempt?] ensign
Yitiaolong	一條龍	Dragon ensign
Shenqi	神旗	"Spirit" flag
Weisong	尾送	Mizen sail
Zhenfang	針房	Compass cabin
Shentang	神堂	Chapel
Jiangtai	將臺	Quarterdeck
Shendeng	神燈	"Spirit" light
Tielituo	鉄力柁	Ironwood rudder

SOURCE NOTES

CHAPTER 1. CONTINENTAL CHINA

1. John King Fairbank, *The United States and China* (New York: Viking Press, 1970), p. 19.
2. G. William Skinner, "Marketing and Social Structure in Rural China: Part I," *Journal of Asian Studies*, vol. 24, no. 1 (November 1964), pp. 5–10.
3. "Fishing Industry in Chekiang," *Chinese Economic Journal*, vol. 1, no. 5 (May 1927), p. 507.
4. Jung-pang Lo, "The Controversy Over Asian Conveyance During the Reign of Qubilai Qaqan, 1260–94," *Far Eastern Quarterly*, no. 13 (1953), p. 280.
5. Wei Tai, "Dongxian Bilu" [Jotting from the eastern side hall], late 11th century, chap. 7, trans. Joseph Needham, in *Science and Civilisation in China* (Cambridge: At the University Press, 1971), vol. 4, p. 311.
6. For an excellent overview of Confucian philosophy, see Frederick W. Mote, *Intellectual Foundations of China* (New York: Alfred A. Knopf, 1971).
7. A perceptive view of legalism is contained in Arthur Waley, *Three Ways of Thought in Ancient China* (Garden City, N.Y.: Doubleday and Co., reprinted by arrangement with Macmillan Co., 1939).
8. A detailed description of Confucian governmental management is contained in Fairbank, *The United States and China*, pp. 54–64.
9. On the Chinese written language, see John K. Fairbank, Edwin O. Reischauer, and Albert M. Craig, *East Asia Tradition and Transformation* (Boston: Houghton Mifflin Co., 1973), pp. 22–27.
10. For a discussion of the hindered development of science in China, see Fairbank, *The United States and China*, pp. 64–67.
11. George M. Foster, "Peasant Society and the Image of Limited Good," *American Anthropologist*, vol. 67, no. 2 (April 1965), p. 296.
12. Hsiao-tung Fei, "Peasantry and Gentry: An Interpretation of Chinese Social Structure and Its Changes," *American Journal of Sociology*, vol. 52, no. 1 (July 1946), p. 3. Also see Bernard Gallin, "Chinese Peasant Values Toward the Land," *Proceedings of the American Ethnological Society* (Spring 1963), pp. 64–71.
13. For an illuminating portrait of the concept of Chinese gentry, see Chung-li Chang, *The Chinese Gentry* (Seattle: University of Washington Press, 1955).
14. Hsiao-tung Fei, "Peasantry and Gentry," p. 2.
15. Ibid., p. 5.
16. Hsin-pao Chang, *Commissioner Lin and the Opium War* (New York: W.W. Norton and Co., 1964), p. 12.
17. All data on these eight organizations is taken from H.S. Brunnert and V.V. Hagelstrom, *Present Day Political Organization of China*, trans. A. Beltchenko and E.E. Moran (1912; reprint ed., Taibei: Ch'eng Wen Publishing Co., 1971).
18. Fairbank, Reischauer, and Craig, *East Asia Tradition*, p. 105.
19. Ouyong Xiu and Song Chi, "Xin Tang Shu" [New history of the Tong dynasty], ca. 1070 A.D., chap. 53, quoted in Needham, *Science and Civilisation*, p. 310.
20. T.F. Wade, "The Army of the Chinese Empire: Its Two Great Divisions, the Bannerman or National Guard, and the Green Standard or Provincial Troops," *Chinese Repository*, vol. 20 (July 1851), pp. 367–72.

21. The best delineation of these relationships and others is contained in Andrew J. Nathan, *Peking Politics, 1918–23* (Berkeley: University of California Press, 1976), pp. 50–55.
22. Ibid., pp. 51, 54.
23. Bao Zenpeng, *Zhongguo Haijun Shi* [A naval history of China], 2nd ed. (Taibei: Zhonghua Congshu, 1970), chap. 1, p. 6.
24. E. A. Kracke, Jr., "Region, Family, and Individual in the Chinese Examination System," in *Chinese Thought and Institutions*, ed. John K. Fairbank (Chicago: University of Chicago Press, 1957), p. 263.
25. An excellent treatment of the failure of the Chinese to reform is found in Mary C. Wright, *The Last Stand of Chinese Conservatism: The T'ung-Chih Restoration, 1862–74* (Stanford: Stanford University Press, 1957).
26. Thomas Taylor Meadows, *The Chinese and Their Rebellions* (London: Smith, Elder, 1956), p. 25.
27. Mao Zedong, "Problems of Strategy in China's Revolutionary War," *Selected Works of Mao Zedong*, vol. 1, p. 252, note 21. Also see Mao, "On Contradictions," ibid, p. 324.
28. An excellent account of this rebellion is contained in John Winthrop Haegar, "Between North and South: The Lake Rebellion in Hunan, 1130–35," *Journal of Asian Studies*, vol. 28, no. 3 (May 1969), pp. 469–88.
29. Yi-faai Laai, trans., "River Strategy: A Phase of the Taipings' Military Development," *Oriens*, vol. 5, no. 2 (1952), p. 309.
30. Ibid., pp. 313–14.
31. One of the best descriptions of the tributary system is contained in John King Fairbank, *Trade and Diplomacy on the China Coast* (Stanford: Stanford University Press, 1964), pp. 23–38. This is a paperback edition of the original two-volume work published in 1953 by Harvard University Press.
32. Cf. John King Fairbank, ed., *The Chinese World Order* (Cambridge: Harvard University Press, 1968), p. 11, and Fairbank, *Trade and Diplomacy*, pp. 34–35.
33. See Fairbank, *Trade and Diplomacy*, p. 8.
34. Mark Mancall, "The Ch'ing Tribute System: An Interpretive Essay," in *The Chinese World Order*, pp. 82–83.
35. Fairbank, *The United States and China*, p. 44.
36. Ibid., p. 29, and Chang *The Chinese Gentry*, p. 33.
37. Background on the population shift is given by Jung-Pang Lo, "The Emergence of China as a Sea Power During the Late Sung and Early Yuan Periods," *Far Eastern Quarterly*, vol. 14, no. 4 (August 1955), pp. 494–96.

CHAPTER 2. MARITIME CHINA

1. John King Fairbank adds that "these communities had been kept under control through their own headmen in their own restricted quarter, and trading operations had been supervised by Chinese officials" (*Trade and Diplomacy on the China Coast* [Stanford: Stanford University Press, 1969], p. 36).
2. "Fishing Industry in Chefoo," *Chinese Economic Journal*, vol. 2, no. 3 (September 1928), p. 813.
3. "Fishing Industry in Kiangsu," *Chinese Economic Journal*, vol. 3, no. 4 (October 1928), p. 836.
4. Barbara E. Ward, "A Hong Kong Fishing Village," *Journal of Oriental Studies*, vol. 1 (1955), p. 198.
5. "Commerce and Industry in Lungkow," *Chinese Economic Journal*, vol. 3, no. 3 (September 1928), p. 807.
6. According to Zheng Ruozeng, smaller coastal towns had a garrison called *xunjiansi* with several ships assigned for defense ("Chouhai Tubian" [Illustrated seaboard strategy], ca. 1562 A.D. [Library of Congress], chaps. 3–7).
7. "Fishing Industry in Kiangsu," *Chinese Economic Journal*, vol. 3, no. 4 (October 1928), p. 837.
8. "Fishing Industry in Chekiang," *Chinese Economic Journal*, vol. 1, no. 5 (May 1927), p. 502. Also see "Fish Trade in Foochow," *Chinese Economic Bulletin*, vol. 11, no. 342 (September 1927), pp. 142–43.
9. "Fish Trade in Foochow," p. 143.
10. Ibid.
11. Zheng Ruozeng, *Chouhai Tubian*, chaps. 3–7.
12. "Fish Trade in Foochow," p. 144.

13. See Yoshinobu Shiba, *Commercial Activities During the Sung Dynasty* (Tokyo: Kazama Shobo, 1968). The work is in Japanese; however, there is a most useful English summary.
14. John K. Fairbank, Edwin O. Reischauer, and Albert M. Craig, *East Asia Tradition and Transformation* (Boston: Houghton Mifflin Co., 1973), p. 136.
15. Hsin-pao Chang, *Commissioner Lin and the Opium War* (New York: W.W. Norton and Co., 1964), p. 6.
16. Dong Tiangong, "Taihai Jianwen Lu" [Record of things seen and heard in the Taiwan Sea], ca. 1751, trans. L.C. Thompson, "The Junk Passage Across the Taiwan Strait: Two Early Chinese Accounts," *Harvard Journal of Asiatic Studies*, vol. 28 (1968), p. 190 fn31.
17. Ho Ke-en, "The Tanka or Boat People of South China," F.S. Drake, ed., *Symposium on Historical Archaeological and Linguistic Studies on Southern China, South East Asia and the Hong Kong Region* (Hong Kong: Hong Kong University Press, 1967), pp. 120–23. The full Chinese text of this paper is in *Journal of Oriental Studies*, vol. 5 (1965), pp. 1–39.
18. Barbara E. Ward, "A Hong Kong Fishing Village," *Journal of Oriental Studies*, vol. 1 (1955), p. 214.
19. Ibid., p. 195.
20. A good description of the *baojia* system is contained in T'ung-tsu Ch'u, *Local Government in China Under the Ch'ing* (Stanford: Stanford University Press, 1969), pp. 150–54.
21. Ibid., p. 150.
22. For the coastal *baojia* organizational aspects, see Wei Peh T'i, "Internal Security and Coastal Control: Juan Yuan and Pirate Suppression in Chekiang 1799–1809," *Ch'ing-shih wen-t'i*, vol. 4, no. 2 (December 1979), pp. 86–89.
23. For example, see U.S. Navy Archives, "Red China's Coastal Fishing Fleet," *Office of Naval Intelligence Review*, declassified (June 1954), pp. 227–30.
24. Cf. Jung-pang Lo, "The Emergence of China as a Sea Power During the Late Sung and Early Yuan Periods," *Far Eastern Quarterly*, vol. 14, no. 4 (August 1955), p. 493, and George A. Ballard, *The Influence of the Sea on the Political History of Japan* (New York: Dutton, 1921), pp. 25–27.
25. Jung-pang Lo, "China as a Seapower," p. 493.
26. Jung-pang Lo, "The Controversy over Grain Conveyance During the Reign of Qubilai Qaqan, 1260–94," *Far Eastern Quarterly*, no. 13 (1953), pp. 263–64.
27. Much of this section is based on Jung-Pang Lo's "Controversy over Grain Conveyance," pp. 263–85.
28. Professor Lo provides an interesting translation of a Yuan record, the "Ta Yuan Haiyun Ji" [Records of maritime transportation of the great Yuan], in ibid., p. 265.
29. Quoted from Hu Jing, "Ta Yuan Haiyun Ji," chap. 1, p. 26.
30. See Jung-pang Lo, "The Controversy over Grain Conveyance," p. 284.

CHAPTER 3. CONTINENTAL AND MARITIME IDEOLOGIES IN CONFLICT: THE MING DYNASTY

1. Su Chung-jen, "Places in Southeast Asia, the Middle East and Africa Visited by Cheng Ho and His Companions," *Symposium on Historical Archaeological and Linguistic Studies on Southern China, Southeast Asia and the Hong Kong Region*, F.S. Drake ed. (Hong Kong: Hong Kong University Press, 1967), p. 199.
2. John K. Fairbank, Edwin O. Reischauer, and Albert M. Craig, *East Asia Tradition and Transformation* (Boston: Houghton Mifflin Company, 1973), pp. 179–80.
3. Ibid., p. 180.
4. Wang Yi-t'ung, "Official Relations between China and Japan, 1368–1549," (Cambridge, Mass.: Harvard-Yenching Institute Studies, vol. 9, 1953), pp. 2, 20. See also L. Carrington Goodrich and Ryusaku Tsunoda, *Japan in the Chinese Dynastic Histories* (South Pasadena, 1951), p. 112.
5. Jung-pang Lo, "The Decline of the Early Ming Navy," *Oriens Extremus*, no. 5 (1958), p. 160.
6. Fairbank, Reischauer, and Craig, *East Asia*, p. 195.
7. Ibid., p. 196.
8. See quote in ibid., p. 197.
9. Ibid., p. 266.
10. Ibid., pp. 201–2.
11. Joseph F. Fletcher, "China and Central Asia, 1368–1884," in *The Chinese World Order*, John K. Fairbank, ed. (Cambridge, Mass.: Harvard University Press, 1968), pp. 209, 219.
12. Ibid., pp. 209–10, 349.

13. Lo Hsiang-lin, "Chung-kuo min-tsu shih" [History of the Chinese tribes] (1953), ref. in Su Chung-jen, "Places in South East Asia," p. 198.
14. Fletcher, "China and Central Asia," p. 218; p. 359.
15. Fairbank, Reischauer, and Craig, East Asia, p. 201.
16. Fletcher, "China and Central Asia," p. 206.
17. Fairbank, Reischauer, and Craig, East Asia, p. 197.
18. Ibid., p. 266.
19. Fletcher, "China and Central Asia," pp. 210–16; p. 36.
20. Lo Hsiang-lin, "Chung-kuo min-tsu shih," in Su Chung-jen, "Places in South East Asia," p. 198.
21. "Ming Shi Lu" [Veritable records of the Ming dynasty], ca. 17th century (Library of Congress), chaps. 20–116. These official histories show that the Chinese constructed 2,149 vessels over a sixteen-year period.
22. Zhong Tingyu et al., "Ming Shi" [Ming dynasty history], ca. 1739, chap. 304, p. 26.
23. G.R.G. Worcester, The Junks and Sampans of the Yangtze (Annapolis: Naval Institute Press, 1971), pp. 162–67; pp. 187–94.
24. Joseph Needham, Science and Civilisation in China (Cambridge: At the University Press, 1971), vol. 4, p. 479 ff.
25. Bao Zenpeng, Zheng He Xiaxi Yangzhi Baochuan Kao [A study of the treasure ships used by Zheng He on the western sea voyages] (Taibei: Zhonghua Congshu, 1961), pp. 25–26.
26. See Ma Huan, Ying-Yai Sheng-Lan [The overall survey of the ocean's shores], trans. and ed. J.V.G. Mills (Cambridge: At the University Press for the Hakluyt Society, 1970), pp. 27–31.
27. Shen Juo, "Mengchi Bitan" [Dream pool essays], ca. 1086, chap. 24, pp. 6a–b, trans. J.J.L. Duyvendak, China's Discovery of Africa (London: Arthur Probsthain, 1949), p. 19.
28. Personnel, watchstanding, and navigation information is contained in Mills, Ying-Yai Sheng-Lan, pp. 306–8. Water mirrors, known as shuijing, are discussed in Xie Jinluan, ed., Taiwan Wenxian Congkan [Taiwan literature collection] (Taibei, 1962), trans. from the 1807 version, pp. 27–38.
29. See Mills, Ying-Yai Sheng-Lan, pp. 306–8.
30. Su Chung-Jen, "Places in South East Asia," p. 198.
31. Duyvendak, China's Discovery of Africa, p. 27.
32. A detailed description of Ma Huan's life can be found in Mills, Ying-Yai Sheng-Lan, pp. 34–37. Also see Su Chung-Jen, "Places in South East Asia," p. 201.
33. Mills, Ying-Yai Sheng-Lan, pp. 22–27.
34. Hsu Yun-ts'iao, "The Revamping of Oceangoing Sea Routes Made in the Yuan and Ming Dynasties and Repercussions in Southeast Asian History," Chinese Culture, vol. 19, no. 3 (September 1978), p. 52.
35. Hsu Yun-ts'iao, "The Revamping," p. 52.
36. Information contained in this paragraph is recorded in greater detail in Mills, Ying-Yai Sheng-Lan, pp. 22–27.
37. Ibid., p. 10.
38. Su Chung-Jen, "Places in South East Asia," p. 201.
39. From Ma Huan's account in Ying-Yai Sheng-Lan, trans. Mills, p. 100.
40. Ibid., p. 102.
41. Ibid., p. 114.
42. Ibid., p. 113.
43. See C.W. Nicholas and S. Paranavitana, A Concise History of Ceylon, (Colombo: Ceylon University Press, 1961), pp. 303–8.
44. Mills makes this point in his introduction to Ying-Yai Sheng-Lan, p. 13.
45. Ma Huan, Ying-Yai Sheng-Lan, pp. 154–59.
46. Ibid., p. 104.
47. Needham, Science and Civilisation, pp. 479–80.
48. Ming Shi Lu, chap. 1, p. 9, ref. in Jung-pang Lo, "Early Ming Navy," p. 158.
49. Jung-pang Lo, "Early Ming Navy," p. 160.
50. Ibid., p. 163.
51. Ibid., p. 151.
52. Ibid., p. 162.
53. Ibid., p. 156.
54. Duyvendak, China's Discovery of Africa, p. 27.
55. Zhang Tingyu, Ming Shi, p. 12.
56. Tsunoda and Goodrich, Chinese Dynastic Histories, pp. 116–7.
57. L. Carrington Goodrich, A Short History of the Chinese People (New York: Harper and Row, 1943), p. 195.

58. Excerpt from Fan Ji's memorial in 1426, trans. by Jung-pang Lo, "Early Ming Navy," p. 167.
59. Shen Shixing, ed., "Da Ming Huidian" [History of the Ming administrative statutes], ca. 1587, 5 vols. (Taibei, 1964).

CHAPTER 4. EMIGRATION, SMUGGLING, AND PIRACY

1. Gu Yanwu, *Tianxia Junguo Libing Shu* [China description and travel], (Chengdu, 1823), vol. 9, p. 32a.
2. "Luzhou Xianzhi" [Gazeteer of Luzhou prefecture], Wanli edition (1563–1620), chap. 2.
3. This policy is discussed in Lawrence D. Kessler, *K'ang-Hsi and the Consolidation of Ch'ing Rule, 1661–84* (Chicago: The University of Chicago Press, 1976), p. 41. The best detailed description is in Xie Guozhen (Hsieh Kuo-chen), "Removal of the Coastal Population in the Early Tsing Period," trans. by Chen Tongxie (Ch'en T'ung-hsieh), *Chinese Social and Political Science Review,* vol. 15, (January 1932), pp. 559–96.
4. An excellent description of emigration is contained in Victor Purcell, *The Chinese in Southeast Asia* (London: Oxford University Press, 1951), chap. 3.
5. Ibid., pp. 234–5, 238.
6. Quoted in ibid., p. 585 fn3.
7. "The Overseas Chinese," *Far Eastern Economic Review* (June 16, 1978), p. 21; David Jenkins, "Indonesia: Too Many Wongs and Lees," p. 22; and Peter Fish, "Children the Key to Thai Integration," p. 23.
8. C.R. Boxer, *The Great Ships from Amacon* (Lisbon, 1959), pp. 179–81.
9. "Ming Shi Lu" [Veritable records of the Ming dynasty], chap. 16, quoted in Chan Cheung, "The Smuggling Trade," *Symposium on Historical Archaeological and Linguistic Studies on Southern China, Southeast Asia, and the Hong Kong Region,* ed. F.S. Drake (Hong Kong: Hong Kong University Press, 1967), pp. 223–7.
10. Chan Cheung, "The Smuggling Trade," pp. 224–5.
11. Hsin-pao Chang, *Commssioner Lin and the Opium War* (New York: W.W. Norton and Co., 1970), pp. 19, 97.
12. Ibid., p. 19.
13. "Modernization's Black Side," *Far Eastern Economic Review* (April 4, 1980), p. 115.
14. Xu Kuanhow, "Yapian Huohua Chushi" [The early history of the opium evil in China], *Takung Pao* (February 19, 1937), p. 3.
15. "Problems of Strategy in Guerrilla War," *Selected Military Writings of Mao Tse-tung,* English edition, (Peking: Foreign Language Press, 1968), p. 170.
16. See, for example, Kwan-wai So, *Japanese Piracy in Ming China During the Sixteenth Century* (East Lansing: Michigan State University Press, 1975), p. 28.
17. Xie Guozhen, "Removal of the Coastal Population," p. 564.
18. Charles Q. Neumann, *History of the Pirates Who Infested the China Sea from 1807 to 1810* (London, 1831), pp. 14–15.
19. "Ming Shizong Shilu" [The veritable records of the reign of Shizong of the Ming dynasty], pp. 10–11b.
20. Li Chien-nung, *The Political History of China, 1840–1928,* trans. by Ssu-yu Teng and Jeremy Ingalls (Princeton, N.J.: D. Van Nostrand, 1956), p. 48.
21. For an especially valuable study of the continued activities of pirates and Chinese government cooperation with the British navy to halt piracy, see John K. Fairbank, *Trade and Diplomacy on the China Coast* (Stanford: Stanford University Press, 1964), chap. 18.
22. Grace Fox, *British Admirals and Chinese Pirates, 1832–69* (London: Kegan Paul, Trench, Trubner and Co., 1940), pp. 110–11. Dr. Fox's chart of British naval successes against pirates also shows the amount of money expended for bounties, a practice then authorized by the British government. The amount awarded during this period totaled 91,725 pounds sterling.
23. Lord Charles Beresford, *The Breakup of China* (New York: Harper and Bros., 1899), p. 251.
24. U.S. Government, *The Present Condition of China*, document A, based on a Japanese White Paper of July, 1932, chap. 13.
25. Alfred Thayer Mahan, *The Influence of Sea Power Upon History, 1660–1783* (Boston: Little, Brown, and Co., 1890), pp. 72–73.

CHAPTER 5. IMPERIAL NAVIES UP TO THE OPIUM WAR

1. John K. Fairbank, "A Preliminary Framework," in *The Chinese World Order*, ed. John K. Fairbank (Cambridge: Harvard University Press, 1968), p. 3.

2. "Han Shu" [Han history], chap. 74, p. 2, quoted by Lien-sheng Yang, "Historical Notes on the Chinese World Order," in Fairbank, ed., *The Chinese World Order*, p. 28.

3. Wei Yuan and Lin Zexu, "Haiguo Tuzhi" [Illustrated record of the maritime nations], 1844, pp. 3b and 13. Cf. Mao Zedong, "On Protracted War," *Selected Military Writings of Mao Tse-Tung* (Peking: Foreign Languages Press, 1968), p. 246.

4. Lawrence D. Kessler, *K'ang-hsi and the Consolidation of Ch'ing Rule, 1661–84* (Chicago and London: University of Chicago Press, 1976), pp. 39–46; Xie Guozhen, "Removal of Coastal Population in Tsing Period," *Chinese Social and Political Science Review*, vol. 15 (January 1932), pp. 578–84.

5. Song Shi [Song history], chaps. 167 and 186, ref. by Jung-pang Lo, "The Emergence of China as a Sea Power During the Late Sung and Early Yuan Periods," *Far Eastern Quarterly*, vol. 14, no. 4 (August 1955), p. 491.

6. T.F. Wade, "The Army of the Chinese Empire: Its Two Great Divisions, the Bannermen or National Guard, and the Green Standard or Provincial Troops," *Chinese Repository*, vol. 20 (July 1851), p. 378 fn.

7. An excellent discussion of this procedure is found in James Ferguson Millinger, *Ch'i Chi-kuang Chinese Military Official: A Study of Civil-Military Roles and Relations in the Career of a Sixteenth-Century Warrior* (Ann Arbor: University Microfilms, 1968), pp. 18–19.

8. Zhu Shijie, "Xiaoliuqiu Manzhi" [Discursive notes on little Liuqiu], ca. 1763, p. 6, trans. Laurence C. Thompson, "The Junk Passage Across the Taiwan Strait: Two Early Chinese Accounts," *Harvard Journal of Asiatic Studies*, vol. 28 (1968), p. 178.

9. For the best example, see the anti-opium activities of Lin Zexu as detailed in Hsin-pao Chang, *Commissioner Lin and the Opium War* (New York: W.W. Norton and Co., 1964), chaps. 5–6.

10. See James Ferguson Millinger, *Ch'i Chi-kuang*, pp. 18–19.

11. Ibid., pp. 27–30.

12. Wade, "The Army of the Chinese Empire," pp. 379–80.

13. Good examples are contained in Gideon Chen, *Lin Tse-Hsu* (New York: Paragon Book Reprint Corporation, 1968), chap. 2.

14. See Gu Jiguang, "Fubing Zhidu Kaoshi" [A study of the Fubing militia], pp. 96–214, ref. in Ch'i-ch'ing Hsiao, *The Military Establishment of the Yuan Dynasty* (Cambridge, Mass.: Council on East Asian Studies, 1978), p. 4.

15. For example see Ch'i-ch'ing Hsiao, *The Military Establishment*, pp. 17, 204 fn, and 364. Also see Ho Ke-En, "The Tanka and Boat People of South China," in *Symposium on Historical Archaeological and Linguistic Studies on Southern China, Southeast Asia and the Hong Kong Region,"* ed. F.S. Drake (Hong Kong: Hong Kong University Press, 1967), p. 123.

16. Jung-pang Lo, "The Emergence of China," pp. 491–2.

17. "Yuan Shih 98" [Yuan history], trans. Ch'i-ch'ing Hsiao, *The Military Establishment*, pp. 22, 72–74.

18. Ch'i-ch'ing Hsiao, *The Military Establishment*, pp. 17, 20.

19. Wade, "The Army of the Chinese Empire" (May, June 1851), pp. 250–300.

20. Ibid. (July 1851), pp. 363–427.

21. Ibid., pp. 318, 325, and 372–80.

22. See Ch'i-ch'ing Hsiao, *The Military Establishment*, p. 175 fn63.

23. A valuable study on Chinese military organization is Richard J. Smith, "Chinese Military Institutions in the Mid-Nineteenth Century, 1850–60," *Journal of Asian History*, vol. 8, no. 2 (1974), pp. 122–61.

24. See Romeyn Taylor, "Yuan Origins of the Wei-so System," in *Chinese Government in Ming Times*, ed. Charles O. Hucker (New York: Columbia University Press, 1969), p. 38.

25. Jung-pang Lo, "The Decline of the Early Ming Navy," *Oriens Extremus*, no. 5, 1958, p. 150 fn2.

26. This figure is arrived at by combining the naval figures of Lo, ibid., and land-based figures contained in Ryusaku Tsunoda and L. Carrington Goodrich, *Japan in the Chinese Dynastic Histories* (South Pasadena, 1951), p. 112.

27. Wade, "The Army of the Chinese Empire" (May, June 1851), pp. 372–80.

28. Jung-pang Lo, "The Early Ming Navy," p. 161.

29. Wade, "The Army of the Chinese Empire," p. 374.

30. Richard J. Smith, "Chinese Military Institutions," p. 150.

31. Cf. ibid., and Millinger, *Ch'i Chi-kuang*, p. 19.

32. A detailed description of Qi's coastal defense system is discussed in Millinger, *Ch'i Chi-kuang*, pp. 68–71.

33. Cf. Tsunoda and Goodrich, *Chinese Dynastic Histories*, p. 129, and Wei Peh T'i, "Internal Security and Coastal Control: Juan Yuan and Pirate Suppression in Chekiang, 1799–1809," *Ch'ing-shih wen-t'i* [Problems in Qing history], vol. 4, no. 2 (December 1979), p. 86.

34. Earl Swisher, "Shih Lang," and Fang Chao-ying, "Shih Shih-lun," in *Eminent Chinese of the Ch'ing Period, 1644–1912*, ed. Arthur W. Hummel, vol. 2, (Washington, D.C.: U.S. Govt. Printing Office, 1944), pp. 653–54.

35. Henry Noel Shore (Baron Teignmouth), *The Flight of the Lapwing* (London: Longmans, Green, and Co., 1881), pp. 234–5.

36. Gideon Chen, *Lin Tse-Hsu*, p. 36.

37. Ibid., pp. 44, 56, 60.

38. Paul Pelliot, "Le Hoja et le Sayyid Husain de l'Histoire des Ming," in *T'oung Pao* [The journal], no. 38 (1948), pp. 107 fn42, 93 fn14.

39. See Albert M. Craig, John K. Fairbank, and Edwin O. Reischauer, *East Asia: Tradition and Transformation* (Boston: Houghton Mifflin Co., 1973), pp. 246–50.

40. Carlo M. Cipolla, *Guns, Sails, and Empires* (New York: Pantheon Books, 1965), pp. 115 fn2, 115–6.

41. Two books on these respective operations are particularly valuable: John E. Wills, Jr., *Pepper, Guns, and Parleys: The Dutch East India Company and China, 1622–81* (Cambridge: Harvard University Press, 1974); Grace Fox, *British Admirals and Chinese Pirates, 1832–69* (1940; reprint ed., Westport, Ct.: Hyperion Press, 1973).

42. Gideon Chen, *Tseng Kuo-Fan* (New York: Paragon Book Reprint Co., 1968), p. 69.

43. Wade, "The Army of the Chinese Empire," pp. 373–4.

44. Ta-tuan Ch'en, "Investiture of Liu-Ch'iu Kings in the Ch'ing Period," in *The Chinese World Order*, p. 140.

45. G.R.G. Worcester, *The Junks and Sampans of the Yangtze* (Annapolis: Naval Institute Press, 1971), pp. 21–22.

46. George Fadlo Hourani, *Arab Seafaring* (Princeton, N.J.: Princeton University Oriental Studies, 1951), pp. 108–9.

47. George Macartney, *An Embassy to China*, ed. J.L. Crammer-Byng (England: Longmans, 1962), p. 275.

48. Shen Gua, "Mengi Bitan" [Dream pool essays], ca. 1089 A.D., chap. 2, par. 19, trans. Joseph Needham, *Science and Civilisation in China*, vol. 4 (Cambridge: At the University Press, 1971), p. 660.

49. "Songhui Yaogao" [Drafts for the history of the administrative statutes of the Song dynasty], collected by Xu Song, ca. 1809, Bing section, chap. 29, p. 316, 32a, trans. by Jung-pang Lo, "The Early Ming Navy," p. 575.

50. Needham, *Science and Civilisation*, vol. 4, p. 576.

51. *Zhongguo Haijun Lishi* [A naval history of China], 2d ed. (Taibei, 1970), chap. 1, pp. 10–11.

52. *Taiping Yulan* [Imperial encyclopedia: Taiping reign], ca. 983 A.D., chap. 315, p. 2a, cited in Needham, *Science and Civilisation*, vol. 4, p. 679.

53. J.C. De Mendoza, *The History of the Great and Mighty Kingdom of China*, ed. G.T. Staunton (London, 1853), introduction.

54. Zheng Ruozeng, "Chouhai Dubian" [Illustrated seaboard strategy], ca. 1562, trans. Carlo M. Cipolla, *Guns, Sails, and Empires*, pp. 125–6.

55. John L. Rawlinson, *China's Struggle for Naval Development, 1839–95* (Cambridge: Harvard University Press, 1967), p. 153.

56. Trans. Gideon Chen, *Lin Tse-hsu*, pp. 3–4.

57. W.H. Hall, Captain, RN, *The Nemesis in China* (London: Henry Calburo, 1846), p. 130.

58. Ibid., p. 91.

59. Details of the treaty and its impact on China are contained in John King Fairbank, *Trade and Diplomacy on the China Coast* (paperback ed., Stanford: Stanford University Press, 1969), chap. 6.

60. Charles Gutzlaff, *China Opened* (Smith Elder, and Co., 1938), p. 455.

CHAPTER 6. THE TOTTERING IMPERIAL FRAMEWORK AND NAVAL SELF-STRENGTHENING

1. "Shichao Shengxun" [Sacred edicts of the ten emperors], chap. 109, quoted in Gideon Chen, *Lin Tse-Hsu* (New York: Paragon Book Reprint Corporation, 1968), p. 54.

2. "Shengwu Ji" [Record of imperial military exploits], chap. 14, quoted in John King Fairbank, *Trade and Diplomacy on the China Coast* (Stanford: Stanford University Press, 1969], p. 29.

3. John L. Rawlinson, *China's Struggle for Naval Development, 1839–95* (Cambridge: Harvard University Press, 1967), pp. 7–11.

4. The careers of the three, Zuo Zongtang, Zeng Guofan, and Li Hongzhang, are documented in *Eminent Chinese of the Ch'ing Period*, ed. Arthur W. Hummel (Washington, D.C.: U.S. Government Printing Office, 1944), pp. 762, 751, and 464.

5. Jack J. Gerson, *Horatio Nelson Lay and Sino-British Relations, 1854–64* (Cambridge: East Asian Research Center, Harvard University, 1972), pp. 50–53.

6. Ibid., pp. 39, 68, 155, 142.

7. *The Times* (London, January 11, 1864).

8. Quoted in Ssu-yu Teng and John K. Fairbank, *China's Response to the West* (New York: Atheneum, 1973), p. 80.

9. Gideon Chen, *Tso Tsung T'ang* (New York: Paragon Book Reprint Corporation, 1968), p. 9.

10. For translations of Zuo's letters and memorials, see ibid., pp. 11–13.

11. The spokesman of the conservative opposition was a Mongol official named Wo-ren, whose life is described in *Eminent Chinese*, pp. 861–3. Excerpts from his 1867 memorial to the emperor objecting to Western learning is translated in Teng and Fairbank, *China's Response*, pp. 76–77.

12. Prosper Giquel, *L'arsenal de Fou-tcheow*, trans. H. Lang (Shanghai, 1874), p. 10.

13. Knight Biggerstaff, *The Earliest Modern Government Schools in China* (Ithaca: Cornell University Press, 1961), pp. 210–11.

14. Ibid., p. 212.

15. *L'arsenal*, p. 10.

16. Biggerstaff, *Modern Government Schools*, p. 213.

17. Rawlinson, *China's Struggle*, p. 48.

18. Ibid.

19. Biggerstaff, *Modern Government Schools*, pp. 214–6.

20. Ibid.

21. Details of this educational mission are contained in Yung Wing, *My Life in China and America* (New York, 1909), chap. 17.

22. A brief but interesting discussion of the mission with photos appears in John K. Fairbank, Edwin O. Reischauer, and Albert M. Craig, *East Asia: Tradition and Transformation* (Boston: Houghton Mifflin Company, 1973), pp. 593–5.

23. Biggerstaff, *Modern Government Schools*, p. 229.

24. Ibid.

25. Yung Wing, *My Life*, p. 207.

26. *Who's Who in China, 1925* (Shanghai, 1925), pp. 728–9.

27. Biggerstaff, *Modern Government Schools*, p. 233.

28. Ibid.

29. Ibid., p. 234.

30. Ibid., p. 236.

31. Li Chien-nung, *The Political History of China, 1840–1928*, trans. by Ssu-yu Teng and Jeremy Ingalls (1956; reprint ed., Stanford: Stanford University Press, 1967), pp. 116–21.

32. Captain Chabaud-Arnault, "Combats in the Min River," trans. by Lt. E.B. Barry, *U.S. Naval Institute Proceedings*, vol. 11, no. 32 (1885), pp. 298–305.

33. Li Chien-nung, *Political History of China*, p. 129.

34. Fairbank, Reischauer, Craig, *East Asia*, p. 600.

35. "Zhouban Yiwu Shimo" [The complete account of the management of barbarian affairs], 1930, trans. in Immanuel C.Y. Hsu, "The Great Policy Debate in China, 1874: Maritime Defense Vs. Frontier Defense," *Harvard Journal of Asiatic Studies*, vol. 25 (1964–65), p. 215.

36. Immanuel C.Y. Hsu, ibid., pp. 218, 220.

37. Ibid., pp. 221–22.

38. Ibid., pp. 222–23.

39. Quoted in ibid., p. 219.

40. Ibid., p. 221.

CHAPTER 7. THE RUSH TO MODERNIZE, 1874–94

1. Quoted in Stanley F. Wright, *Hart and the Chinese Customs* (Belfast: Wm. Mullan and Son, 1950), p. 478.

2. "Zhouban Yiwu Shimo" [The Complete Account of the Management of Barbarian Affairs], Tongshi period, 99:14b–15a, trans. Immanuel C.Y. Hsu, "The Great Policy Debate in China, 1874: Maritime Defense vs. Frontier Defense," *Harvard Journal of Asiatic Studies*, vol. 25 (1964–65), p. 215.
3. A detailed description of these purchases is contained in John L. Rawlinson, *China's Struggle for Naval Development, 1839–95* (Cambridge: Harvard University Press, 1967), pp. 68–71, and Appendix C.
4. J.W. King, *The Warships and Navies of the World* (Boston: A. Williams and Co., 1881), pp. 429–31.
5. An experimental torpedo boat, built in England, arrived in China in August 1879. It was steel, possessed six water-tight compartments, and carried three spar-torpedoes. The craft was 52 feet long, 7 feet at the beam, and had a top speed of 16 knots. (King, *Warships and Navies*, p. 432).
6. Mr. Wright comments that "Bridgeford got into personal touch with Li Hung-chang, to whom the hint was dropped that while he could accept Hart's advice and plans, it was not necessary to leave the execution of any scheme in Hart's hands. By the end of 1881, it was clear that Hart's services as an agent for the purchase of arms and gunboats would no longer be required" (*Chinese Customs*, p. 177).
7. Rawlinson, *China's Struggle*, p. 249. Mr. Rawlinson gives the purchase price as 6.2 million marks.
8. Stephen S. Roberts, "The Imperial Chinese Steam Navy, 1862–95," *Warship International*, no. 1 (1974), pp. 31, 44.
9. Rawlinson, *China's Struggle*, pp. 250–51.
10. Roberts, "Chinese Steam Navy," p. 44.
11. Ibid., p. 26.
12. John K. Fairbank, Edwin O. Reischauer, and Albert M. Craig, *East Asia Tradition and Transformation* (Boston: Houghton Mifflin Company, 1973), pp. 588–9.
13. John K. Fairbank and Ssu-yu Teng, *China's Response to the West: A Documentary Survey, 1839–1923* (New York: Atheneum, 1973), p. 112.
14. Lt. Col. Rheinhold Wagner, "Two Memoranda Regarding the Defenses, Harbours, and Railways Required by China," *Royal United Service Institution Journal*, vol. 42, no. 246 (August 1898), pp. 941–66.
15. Rawlinson, *China's Struggle*, p. 147.
16. Ibid., p. 148.
17. Ibid., p. 157. Also see Bao Zenpeng, *Zhongguo Haijun Lishi* [A naval history of China], (Taibei: Chinese Naval Publication Office, 1951), pp. 231–2.
18. Knight Biggerstaff, *The Earliest Modern Government Schools in China* (Ithaca: Cornell University Press, 1961), p. 238.
19. D. Pratt Mannix to Secretary of the Navy William H. Hunt, in L.R. Marine 1881, Record Group 80, letter dated 15 November 1881.
20. D. Pratt Mannix to U.S. Commandant of the Marine Corps, in L.R. Marine 1882, Box 199, Record Group 127, letter dated 15 November 1882.
21. Quoted in Paul H. Clyde, *United States Policy Toward China* (New York: Russell and Russell, 1964), pp. 159–74.
22. Vice Admiral F.R. Fremantle, "Naval Aspects of the China-Japan War," *Royal United Service Institution Journal*, vol. 40, no. 216 (February 1896), pp. 123–4.
23. Quoted in Wright, *Chinese Customs*, pp. 481–2.
24. The incident is recounted in more detail in Rawlinson, *China's Struggle*, pp. 163–5.
25. Trans. in Li Chien-nung, *The Political History of China, 1840–78*, (1956; reprint ed., Stanford: Stanford University Press, 1967), p. 125.
26. Arthur W. Hummel, *Eminent Chinese of the Ch'ing Period* (Washington, D.C.: U.S. Govt. Printing Office, 1944), pp. 384–6; Rawlinson, *China's Struggle*, p. 133.
27. See Stanley Spector, *Li Hung-chang and the Huai Army* (Seattle: University of Washington Press, 1964), p. 308, table 18.
28. William F. Tyler, *Pulling Strings in China* (London: Constable and Co., 1929), p. 89.
29. Rawlinson, *China's Struggle*, pp. 159–60.
30. Edwin A. Falk, *Togo and the Rise of Japanese Sea Power* (New York: Longmans, Green, and Co., 1936), pp. 131–2.
31. Bao Zenpeng estimates that between 1889 and 1894 the Navy Board contributed about 20,000 taels for the Summer Palace (*Zhongguo Haijun Lishi*, pp. 214–5).
32. Alexander Michie, *The Englishman in China*, 2 vols. (Edinburgh and London, 1900), vol. 2, p. 399.
33. Henry Noel Shore (Baron Teignmouth), *The Flight of the Lapwing* (London: Longmans, Green and Co., 1881), p. 234.
34. *Imperial Chinese Navy List, Peiyang Squadron* (Tientsin, 1888).

35. J.O.P. Bland, *Li Hung-chang* (New York: Henry Holt and Co., 1917), p. 233.
36. Fremantle, "Naval Aspects," p. 123.
37. The translation of Zuo's memorial is contained in Denby to Bayard, *Foreign Relations of the United States* (U.S. State Department, 1885), pp. 178–80.
38. See Ensign Frank Marble, "The Battle of Yalu," *U.S. Naval Institute Proceedings*, vol. 21, no. 3 (1895), p. 494.
39. Ibid.

CHAPTER 8. DISASTER AT YALU:
THE SINO-JAPANESE WAR, 1894–95

1. This phrase was originated by the nineteenth–century scholar, Feng Guifen, and popularized by Zhong Zhitong in the 1890s. See Ssu-yu Teng and John K. Fairbank, *China's Response to the West* (1954; reprint ed., New York: Atheneum, 1973), p. 50.
2. Quoted in Noel F. Busch, *The Emperor's Sword* (New York: Funk and Wagnalls, 1969), p. 34.
3. United States, Department of State, *China Despatches*, Yong to Frelinghuysen, vol. 65, no. 230 (August 8, 1883).
4. Quoted in Zenone Volpicelli, *The China-Japan War* (London: Sampson Low, Marston and Co., 1896), appendix D.
5. Quoted in Ensign Frank Marble, "The Battle of the Yalu," *U.S. Naval Institute Proceedings*, vol. 21, no. 3 (1895), p. 518.
6. Ibid.
7. Ibid., p. 516.
8. Ibid., pp. 480, 486.
9. Ibid., pp. 511, 518.
10. William F. Tyler, *Pulling Strings in China* (London: Constable and Co., 1929), p. 50.
11. Tyler, *Pulling Strings*, p. 52.
12. U.S. Navy Department, Office of Naval Intelligence, Captain Du Boulay, British War Office Intelligence Division, file no. F-6-C, reg. no. 2252 (1896).
13. Quote attributed to Philo Norton McGiffin, in Vice-Admiral the Honourable Sir E.R. Fremantle, "Naval Aspects of the China-Japan War," *Journal of the Royal United Service Institution*, vol. 40 (February 1896), p. 132.
14. J.O.P. Bland, *Li Hung-chang* (New York: Henry Holt and Co., 1917), p. 233.
15. Tyler, *Pulling Strings*, p. 51.
16. Marble, "Battle of Yalu," p. 492.
17. John L. Rawlinson, *China's Struggle for Naval Development, 1839–95* (Cambridge: Harvard University Press, 1967), p. 182.
18. Quoted in Marble, "Battle of Yalu," p. 517.
19. Ibid., pp. 490–3, 503.
20. Ibid., pp. 491–2.
21. Ibid., pp. 497–8.
22. Marble, "Battle of Yalu," pp. 517–8.
23. McGiffin, "Battle of Yalu," p. 602.
24. Vladimir, *The China-Japan War*, pp. 276, 291, 296.
25. See Paul H. Clyde and Burton F. Beers, *The Far East* (Englewood Cliffs, New Jersey: Prentice Hall, 1971), pp. 189–90.
26. Quoted in ibid., p. 193.

CHAPTER 9. REFORM AND REVOLUTION:
CHINA'S NAVY, 1896–1911

1. For a detailed bibliography of Yan Fu, see Howard R. Boorman, ed., *Biographical Dictionary of Republic of China* (New York: Columbia University Press, 1967), pp. 41–47. Also see Ssu-yu Teng and John K. Fairbank, *China's Response to the West* (1954; reprint ed., New York: Atheneum, 1973), pp. 149–50.
2. Quoted in Teng and Fairbank, *China's Response*, p. 150.
3. Quoted in ibid., p. 129.
4. The *Haitian* is described in *The Engineer*, (December 1897), p. 595. It ran aground a few years later off Shanghai and sank (1904). The *Haiji* is discussed in H.T. Montague Bell and

H.G.W. Woodhead, *The China Yearbook, 1912* (Nendeln/Liechtenstein: Kraus Reprint, 1969), pp. 260–1.

5. "New Chinese Warships," *The Engineer* (February 1897), p. 201.
6. Information on these vessels is contained in Paul Siverstone and C. de Saint Hubert, *World Ship Society Warships Supplement*, no. 39 (August 1975), pp. 14–15.
7. Lord Charles Beresford, *The Breakup of China* (New York: Harper and Brothers Pubs., 1899), pp. 284–5.
8. "The Situation of the Chinese Army on the 1st of March, 1910," *Journal of the Royal United Service Institution* (September 1910), p. 1193.
9. In 1910 Sun Yat-sen controlled four modern anti-Manchu army divisions on the Yangzi. See memorandum of conferences between Sun Yat-sen and Homer Lea, quoted in F.L Chapin, "Homer Lea and the Chinese Revolution" (senior thesis, Harvard University, 1950), pp. 118–9. Also see William F. Tyler, *Pulling Strings in China* (London: Constable and Co., 1929), p. 233.
10. Li Zhejin, *Zhongguo Jindai Haijun Shihua* [Contemporary chinese naval history] (Taibei: Xinya Publishing Co., 1967), p. 78.
11. Information on Sa's early career is contained in ibid., pp. 77–79.
12. Radm. Kemp Tolley, *Yangtze Patrol* (Annapolis: Naval Institute Press, 1971), p. 168.
13. U.S. Navy Department, Office of Naval Intelligence, "Reorganization of the Chinese Navy, 1909," U.S. naval attaché in Peking, report no. 136 (November 11, 1909).
14. U.S. Navy Department, Office of Naval Intelligence, "Regulations of the Chinese Navy, 1910–11," U.S. naval attaché in Peking, report no. 105 (December 24, 1910).
15. For example, see list of officers of the imperial Chinese navy in U.S. naval attaché, "Reorganization of the Chinese Navy," report no. 136.
16. Paul H. Clyde and Burton F. Beers, *The Far East* (Englewood Cliffs, N.J.: Prentice Hall, 1971), pp. 215–6.
17. *Japan Mail* (August 16, 1905).
18. U.S. Navy Department, Office of Naval Intelligence, "Chinese Students in Japanese Schools, 1909–18," U.S. naval attaché in Peking, report no. 210 (December 10, 1918).
19. "Disputed Islands in the South China Sea: Part II," *Office of Naval Intelligence Review*, declassified (June 1956), p. 239.
20. See U.S. Navy Department, Office of Naval Intelligence, "Regulations of the Chinese Navy, 1910–11," U.S. naval attaché in Peking, report no. 25 (March 16, 1911).
21. Hugh Trevor-Roper, *The Hermit of Peking* (New York: Alfred A. Knopf, 1977), pp. 172–3.
22. Tyler, *Pulling Strings*, pp. 194–5.
23. Details of the commission are contained in H.S. Brunnert and V.V. Hagelstrom, *Present Day Political Organization of China* (1910; reprint ed., Taipei: Ch'eng wen Publishing Co., 1971), pp. 64–67.
24. For a more detailed description of the U.S. visit, see William Reynolds Braisted, *The United States Navy in the Pacific, 1909–22* (Austin: University of Texas Press, 1971), pp. 82–85.
25. Meribeth E. Cameron, *The Reform Movement in China, 1898–1912* (Stanford: Stanford University Press, 1931), p. 99.
26. A copy of the Bethlehem Steel contract is contained in U.S. Navy Department, Office of Naval Intelligence, "Shipment of Arms and Ammunition to China, 1929–30," U.S. naval attaché in Peking, report no. M-7-215-29 (February 15, 1929).
27. The entire memorial is contained in U.S. Navy Department, Office of Naval Intelligence, "Reorganization of the Chinese Navy, 1910–11," U.S. naval attaché in Peking, classification no. E-9-d, reg. no. 947 (June 12, 1911).
28. U.S. naval attaché, "Reorganization of the Chinese Navy," report no. 136.
29. U.S. naval attaché, "Reorganization of the Chinese Navy," classification no. E-9-d, reg. no. 947.
30. Ibid.
31. T'ang Leang-Li, *The Inner History of the Chinese Revolution* (London, 1930), pp. 77–78.
32. Li Zhejin, *Zhongguo Jindai Haijun Shihua*, p. 78.
33. Ibid., pp. 79–80.
34. Quoted in Edwin J. Dingle, *China's Revolution, 1911–12* (New York, 1912), pp. 100–2.

CHAPTER 10. DISSENSION AND DECAY, 1912–37

1. Andrew J. Nathan, *Peking Politics, 1918–23* (Berkeley: University of California Press, 1976), p. 67.
2. U.S. Navy Department, Office of Naval Intelligence, "Organization Navy Board, China,"

U.S. military attaché in Peking, report no. 955 (December 28, 1912). See also H.T. Montague Bell and H.G.W. Woodhead, *The China Yearbook, 1913* (Nendeln/Liechtenstein: Kraus Reprint, 1969), pp. 294–7.

3. Paul Siverstone and C. de Saint Hubert, "The Chinese Navy, 1870–1937," *World Ship Society Warships Supplement* (August 1975), pp. 13–14.

4. Bao Zenpeng, *Zhongguo Haijun Shi* [A naval history of China], (Taibei: Chinese Naval Publication Office, 1951), pp. 223–6.

5. U.S. Naval Department, Office of Naval Intelligence, "The Chinese Navy: General Data, 1907–37," commanding officer of the USS *Whipple*, file no. E-9-b, reg. no. 11981 (1924).

6. U.S. Navy Department, Office of Naval Intelligence, trans. of *Zhongguo Haijun Sanhao* [Chinese navy no. 3], U.S. naval attaché, report no. 122–47 (August 11, 1947).

7. Bao Zenpeng, *Zongguo Haijun Shi*, p. 240. Also see Li Zhejin, *Zhongguo Jindai Haijun Shihua* [Contemporary chinese naval history] (Taibei: Xinya, 1967), p. 188.

8. U.S. Navy Department, Office of Naval Intelligence, "Characteristics of Chinese Officers, 1921–3," U.S. naval attaché in Peking, report serial 501 (August 26, 1921). Also see William Reynolds Braisted, *The United States Navy in the Pacific, 1909–22* (Austin: University of Texas Press, 1971), p. 657.

9. "A Reflection on the Chinese Navy," *Peking Leader* (supplement for 1919). Forwarded in U.S. Navy Department, Office of Naval Intelligence, U.S. naval attaché in Peking, report no. 232 (April 12, 1920).

10. Chao-ying Shih and Chi-hsien Chang, *The Chinese Yearbook 1936–37* (Nendeln/Liechtenstein: Kraus Reprint, 1968), p. 971.

11. Li Zhejin, *Zhongguo Jindai Haijun Shihua* [Contemporary Chinese naval history], (Taibei: Xinya, 1967), p. 137.

12. Information on the careers of these three admirals can be found in *Who's Who in China, 1925* (Shanghai, 1936), pp. 640–1, 544–5, and 487–8.

13. J.O.P. Bland, *Li Hung-chang* (New York: Henry Holt and Co., 1917), pp. 248–9.

14. U.S. Navy Department, Office of Naval Intelligence, "The Chinese Navy: General Data, 1907–37," U.S. naval attaché in Peking, report serial no. 203 (June 23, 1927).

15. U.S. Navy Department, Office of Naval Intelligence, "The Chinese Navy: General Data, 1907–37," commanding officer of the USS *Whipple*, file no. E-8-d, reg. no. 14993 (June 13, 1924).

16. U.S. Navy Department, Office of Naval Intelligence, "The Chinese Navy: General Data, 1907–37," U.S. naval attaché in Peking, report serial no. 203 (June 23, 1927).

17. Information for this section is based upon U.S. Navy Department, Office of Naval Intelligence, "Political Conditions in China, 1922," file no. C-9-e, reg. no. 15102-B (June to September 1922).

18. Quoted from a letter of June 22, 1922 to the U.S. secretary of state in ibid.

19. Li Zhejin, *Zhongguo Jindai Haijun Shihua*, op. cit., pp. 182–3.

20. An outline of the plan is described in U.S. Navy Department, Office of Naval Intelligence, "Policies of Nationalist [Kuomintang] Government: China, 1928–33," U.S. naval attaché in Peking, report serial 468 (December 14, 1928).

21. U.S. Navy Department, Office of Naval Intelligence, "Political Conditions: China, 1928–29," U.S. naval attaché in Peking, report serial no. 42 (February 2, 1929).

22. U.S. Navy Department, Office of Naval Intelligence, U.S. naval attaché in Peking, report serial no. 455, file no. C-10-g, reg. no. 19502–B (December 6, 1928).

23. U.S. Navy Department, Office of Naval Intelligence, "Shipment of Arms and Ammunition to China, 1929–30," commander of the U.S. Asiatic Fleet, report no. 353–49 (November 8, 1929).

24. U.S. Navy Department, Office of Naval Intelligence, "Political Conditions: China, 1933–4," U.S. naval attaché in Peking, report no. 374 (November 24, 1933).

25. U.S. Department of the Navy, Office of Naval Intelligence, U.S. naval attaché in Peking, report no. 47 (February 1933).

26. U.S. Department of the Navy, Office of Naval Intelligence, "Ships, China: General Information, 1935–37," U.S. naval attaché in Peking, report no. 262 (July 15, 1935).

CHAPTER 11. THE NAVY AND FOREIGN RELATIONS, 1912–37: PART I

1. Hugh Trevor-Roper, *The Hermit of Peking* (New York: Alfred A. Knopf, 1977), p. 174.

2. Printed in "Professional Notes," *U.S. Naval Institute Proceedings*, vol. 40 (July–December 1914), p. 1178.

3. Most of this section is based on William F. Tyler, *Pulling Strings in China* (London: Constable and Co., 1929).

4. Ibid., p. 226.
5. Data on Li Dingxin's background is taken from *Who's Who in China* (Shanghai, 1925), pp. 487–8 and U.S. Navy Department, Office of Naval Intelligence, "Characteristics of Chinese Officers, 1921–23," U.S. naval attaché in Peking, report no. 501, (August 26, 1921).
6. Tyler, *Pulling Strings*, p. 234.
7. Ibid., p. 136.
8. A copy of the Sino-British naval contract is contained in U.S. Navy Department, Office of Naval Intelligence, "British Naval Missions to China, 1929–34," U.S. military attaché in Peking, report no. 7654 (January 23, 1930).
9. An excellent account of Chiang K'ai-shek's employment of German advisors is contained in F.F. Liu, *A Military History of Modern China, 1924–49* (Princeton: Princeton University Press, 1956), chaps. 7 and 10.
10. According to Mr. Liu, the German industrial firm, Hapro, had contracted for twelve submarines to be delivered to China. Moreover, Hapro had also planned to provide the Chinese with cruisers and other small combatants (*Military History*, p. 102).
11. U.S. Navy Department, Office of Naval Intelligence, "China's Foreign Advisors," U.S. naval attaché in Peking, report no. 22 (January 20, 1936).
12. During the course of researching U.S. Navy involvement in China, the author found that Dr. William Braisted had already done the job superbly. Much of this section is based on his *United States Navy in the Pacific, 1909–22* (Austin: University of Texas Press, 1971), 2 vols.
13. William R. Braisted, "China, the United States Navy, and the Bethlehem Steel Company, 1909–29," *Business History Review*, vol. 42, no. 1 (Spring 1968), p. 52 fn11.
14. U.S. Navy Department, Office of Naval Intelligence, "China's Foreign Advisors," U.S. naval attaché in Peking, report no. 46 (February 4, 1936).
15. On 13 October 1913, a British newspaper announced that Rear Admiral Arthur Christian was to be appointed naval advisor to the Chinese government (contained in U.S. naval attaché, "China's Foreign Advisors," report no. 22).
16. The ships were ordered in November 1913. See "Professional Notes," *U.S. Naval Institute Proceedings*, vol. 40 (July–December 1914), p. 1177.
17. Braisted, *United States Navy*, p. 273.
18. Ibid., p. 283.
19. Quoted in Braisted, *United States Navy*, p. 656.
20. Wei Han's early background is described in John R. Rawlinson, *China's Struggle for Naval Development, 1839–95* (Cambridge: Harvard University Press, 1967), p. 286. Also see *Who's Who in China, 1935* (Shanghai), p. 174.
21. U.S. State Department, memorandum by MacMurray (April 12, 1922), Record Group 59, file no. 89334/201.
22. Braisted, *United States Navy*, p. 662.
23. Gillis to Henry R. Carse, quoted in William R. Braisted, "China, the United States Navy, and the Bethlehem Steel Company, 1909–29," *Business History Review*, vol. 42, no. 1 (Spring 1968), p. 64 fn73.

CHAPTER 12. THE NAVY AND FOREIGN RELATIONS, 1912–1937: PART II

1. An important classified Soviet document regarding conditions in the Chinese navy was stolen by Chinese soldiers during a raid upon the Soviet military attaché's office in Beijing on 6 April 1927. The forty-three-page document was translated and forwarded in U.S. Navy Department, Office of Naval Intelligence, "The Chinese Navy, 1928," U.S. naval attaché in Peking, report no. 466 (December 12, 1928).
2. Ibid., p. 39.
3. Ibid., p. 41.
4. A description of foreign Communist involvement at Huangpu is contained in F.F. Liu, *A Military History of Modern China 1924–49* (Princeton: Princeton University Press, 1956), chaps. 1–4.
5. U.S. Navy Department, Office of Naval Intelligence, report no. 466, pp. 20–21.
6. Smirnov may have been known as Jiajie, or Mr. Grey. See U.S. naval attaché, "The Chinese Navy," report no. 466.
7. See the summary in C. Martin Wilbur and Julie Lien-ying How, *Documents on Communism, Nationalism, and Soviet Advisers in China, 1918–27* (New York: Columbia University Press, 1956), pp. 215–16.

8. Li Zhilong's brief stint as head of the navy is described in a handwritten confession extracted by the Kuomintang military following his arrest on 20 March 1926. See *Documents on KMT-CCP Cooperation, Party Purges, and Worker-Peasant Movement* (Hoover Collection, Stanford University), vol. 1, 2980/6482.

9. Wang Mougong was the officer arrested. See the excellent article by Tien-wei Wu, "Chiang Kai-shek's March Twentieth Coup d'Etat of 1926," *Journal of Asian Studies*, vol. 27, no. 3 (May 1968), pp. 585–602.

10. Li Zhilong's confession in *Documents on KMT-CCP Cooperation*.

11. Tien-wei Wu, "March Twentieth Coup," p. 600.

12. Li Zhejin, *Zhongguo Jindai Haijun Shihua* [Contemporary Chinese naval history] (Taibei: Xinya, 1967), pp. 190–6.

13. Recounted in ibid., pp. 154–5.

14. Kato Haku Denki Henson Iinkai, *Kato Takaaki* (Tokyo, 1929), vol. 2, pp. 192–3.

15. U.S. Navy Department, Office of Naval Intelligence, "Chinese Students in Japanese Schools, 1909–18," U.S. naval attaché in Peking, report no. 210 (December 10, 1918).

16. The report also states that "Japanese influences are attempting to control it [the Chinese navy] or put it out of business" (U.S. Navy Department, Office of Naval Intelligence, U.S. Asiatic Fleet intelligence officer, confidential report no. 62, [July 13, 1920]).

17. Bao Zenpeng, *Zhongguo Haijun Shi* [A naval history of China], (Taibei: Zhongguo Congshu, 1970), 2 vols., preface.

18. U.S. Navy Department, Office of Naval Intelligence, "Political Conditions in China, 1927," commanding officer of the USS *Pittsburgh*, intelligence report serial 339–4 (December 28, 1927).

19. Kenneth Scott Latourette, *A Short History of the Far East* (New York: The MacMillan Co., 1946), p. 550.

20. See *The Chinese Economic Bulletin*, vol. 12, no. 10 (March 10, 1928); vol. 12, no. 14 (April 7, 1928); and vol. 12, no. 15 (April 14, 1928).

21. "The Present Condition of China," (Tokyo, 1932; reprinted by the U.S. Government Printing Office, July 1932), part 1, p. 29.

22. U.S. Navy Department, Office of Naval Intelligence, "Political Conditions: China, 1937," U.S. naval attaché, report no. 237 (June 18, 1937).

23. U.S. Navy Department, Office of Naval Intelligence, "Chinese-Japanese Relations, 1932–35," U.S. naval attaché in Tokyo, report no. 60 (March 8, 1935).

24. U.S. Navy Department, Office of Naval Intelligence, "Ships, China: General Information, 1935–37," U.S. naval attaché in Peking, report no. 496 (December 30, 1935).

25. Ibid., report no. 367 (November 3, 1936).

26. Ibid., report no. 223 (June 17, 1935); report no. 262 (July 15, 1935).

27. "Zhongguo Xin Haijun" [China's new navy], September, 1947, trans. and forwarded in U.S. Navy Department, Office of Naval Intelligence, "China: Navy: Historical Information . . .," U.S. naval attaché in Nanking, serial 201–47 (December 29, 1947), p. 9.

CHAPTER 13. TARNISHED TRADITIONS, LEND-LEASE, AND CIVIL WAR, 1944–49

1. "The Chinese Navy, Past and Present," *Office of Naval Intelligence Review*, declassified (January 1947), p. 28.

2. See "A Study on Changes of Naval Officers' Training," *Zhongguo Haijun* [Chinese navy], nos. 4 and 5, trans. and forwarded by the U.S. naval attaché in Nanking, U.S. Navy Department, Office of Naval Intelligence, serial 8–48 (January 27, 1948).

3. Tai Chi-hua, "The Naval Status of the Different Nations in the Pacific," *Zhongguo Haijun*, nos. 4 and 5, trans. and forwarded by the U.S. naval attaché in Nanking, serial 8–48 (January 1948).

4. Tai Chi-hua, "The Naval Status," p. 1.

5. Memorandum for the Joint Chiefs of Staff, December 8, 1943. Quoted in Lee Stretton Houchins, "American National Involvement in the Chinese Civil War, 1945–49," (Ph.D. dissertation, American University, 1971), pp. 211–2.

6. An analysis of the European-versus-Pacific attitude in the U.S. Navy is contained in Vincent Davis, *Postwar Defense Policy and the U.S. Navy, 1943–46* (Chapel Hill: University of North Carolina Press, 1966), pp. 76–80.

7. "News from London," *Zhongguo Haijun*, no. 1, in U.S. Navy Department, Office of Naval Intelligence, U.S. naval attaché in Nanking, declassified report serial 86–47 (May 13, 1947). The original group consisted of 26 officers and 214 enlisted men. However, 35 men failed the physical exam and I.Q. tests.

8. Yien Yu, "News Brevities About the Taking Over of the FU-PO," *Zhongguo Haijun*, no. 2., trans. and forwarded by U.S. naval attaché in Nanking, serial 8–48 (January 27, 1948).

9. By January 1948, the Nationalist government had promulgated a list of the call, kilocycle, and broadcasting times of the three naval meteorological broadcasting stations on Pratas Island (Dongsha), the Paracel Islands (Xisha), and the Spratly Islands (Nansha) (see "News of the Month," *Zhongguo Haijun*, nos. 4 and 5, p. 1).

10. "A Voyage to the South," *Zhongguo Haijun*, no. 3, forwarded by U.S. naval attaché in Nanking, serial 122–47 (August 11, 1947).

11. See *The China White Paper, August 1949* (Stanford: Stanford University Press, 1967), pp. 338–51.

12. "The Chinese Navy," p. 28.

13. "U.S. Department of State Bulletin" (February 10, 1946), p. 205.

14. Lee Houchins, "Admirals, Generals, and Commissars" (Draft paper delivered at the Research Colloquium on Modern China on May 12, 1966), p. 4.

15. "Directive to Commanding General, U.S. Forces China Theatre," commander in chief of the U.S. Pacific Fleet, (August 10, 1945), quoted in ibid., p. 5.

16. U.S. Navy Department, Office of Naval Intelligence, U.S. naval attaché in Nanking, declassified report serial 86–47 (May 6, 1947).

17. U.S. Navy Department, Office of Naval Intelligence, commander of the Western Pacific in Tsingtao, declassified report serial 11–C–48 (October 1, 1948).

18. U.S. Navy Department, Office of Naval Intelligence, U.S. naval attaché in Nanking, declassified report serial 23–S–48 (December 16, 1948).

19. U.S. Navy Department, Office of Naval Intelligence, commander of the Western Pacific in Tsingtao, declassified report serial 13–C–48 (October 1, 1948).

20. U.S. Navy Department, Office of Naval Itelligence, U.S. naval attaché in Nanking, declassified report serial 23–S–48 (December 16, 1948).

21. U.S. Navy Department, Office of Naval Intellience, commander of the Western Pacific in Tsingtao, declassified report serial 10–C–48 (August 18, 1948).

22. U.S. Navy Department, Office of Naval Intelligence, commander of the Western Pacific, declassified report serial 3–S–48 (no date).

23. The latter squadron belonged to the Fourth Naval District and was renamed the Sixth Gunboat Flotilla (see U.S. Navy Department, Office of Naval Intelligence, U.S. naval attaché in Nanking, declassified report serial 43–48 [June 21, 1948]; and U.S. naval attaché in Canton, declassified report serial 1–48 [January 14, 1948]).

24. Li Hai, "Naval Officers' Training," p. 3.

25. "Neimo Xinwen" [Inside news], October 1, 1948, trans. in U.S. Navy Department, Office of Naval Intelligence, U.S. naval attaché in Nanking, declassified report serial 82–48 (October 22, 1948).

26. U.S. Navy Department, Office of Naval Intelligence, declassified report serial 186–47 (December 9, 1947).

27. U.S. Navy Department, Office of Naval Intelligence, U.S. naval attaché in Nanking, declassified report serial 130–46 (July 20, 1946).

28. U.S. Navy Department, Office of Naval Intelligence, U.S. naval attaché in Canton, declassified report serial 20–46 (September 27, 1946).

29. U.S. Navy Department, Office of Naval Intelligence, U.S. naval attaché in Canton, declassified report serial 25–46 (July 14, 1947).

30. Captain Zou was second in command aboard the *Zhongshan* in 1926 when its commanding officer, Li Zhilong, was accused by Chiang K'ai-shek of attempting to kidnap him (see U.S. Navy Department, Office of Naval Intelligence, U.S. naval attaché in Nanking, declassified report serial 25–46 [April 2, 1946]; and U.S. naval attaché assistant in Canton, declassified report serial 1–46 [September 2, 1946]).

31. U.S. Navy Department, Office of Naval Intelligence, U.S. naval attaché in Nanking, declassified report serial 151–46 (August 9, 1946).

32. U.S. Navy Department, Office of Naval Intelligence, assistant U.S. naval attaché in Canton, declassified report serial 17–49 (April 14, 1949).

33. U.S. Navy Department, Office of Naval Intelligence, U.S. naval attaché in Nanking, declassified report serial 170–46 (September 12, 1946).

34. Ibid.

35. U.S. Navy Department, Office of Naval Intelligence, U.S. naval attaché in Nanking, declassified report serial 99–48 (December 9, 1948).

36. U.S. Navy Department, Office of Naval Intelligence, quoted by assistant U.S. naval attaché in Canton, declassified report serial 12–48 (February 25, 1948).

37. U.S. Navy Department, Office of Naval Intelligence, U.S. naval attaché in Canton, declassified report serial 56–48 (November 8, 1948).

38. U.S. Navy Department, Office of Naval Intelligence, U.S. naval attaché in Nanking, declassified report serial 96–48 (December 6, 1948).
39. U.S. Navy Department, Office of Naval Intelligence, U.S. naval attaché in Nanking, declassified report serial 43–48 (June 21, 1948).
40. U.S. Navy Department, Office of Naval Intelligence, U.S. naval attaché in Nanking, declassified report serial 78–48 (October 7, 1948).
41. U.S. Navy Department, Office of Naval Intelligence, assistant U.S. naval attaché in Canton, declassified report serial 17–49 (April 14, 1949).
42. U.S. Navy Department, Office of Naval Intelligence, U.S. naval attaché in Nanking, declassified report serial 64–48 (September 2, 1948).
43. Chung Pan [Zhong Ban], "The Lesson of the Cruiser *Chungking*," *Xinwen Tiandi* [World news], March 10, 1949, contained in U.S. Navy Department, Office of Naval Intelligence, assistant U.S. naval attaché in Shanghai, declassified report serial 9–49 (March 25, 1949).
44. An excellently documented summary of the *Chongqing*'s operations is contained in Lee Stretton Houchins, "American National Involvement in the Chinese Civil War, 1945–49," pp. 219–27.
45. Chung Pan, "The Lesson," p. 2.
46. "The Defection of the *Chungking*," *Shen Bao* [The examiner], March 27, 1949, contained in assistant U.S. Navy Department, Office of Naval Intelligence, assistant U.S. Navy naval attaché in Shanghai, report serial 9–49 M (March 25, 1949).
47. U.S. Navy Department, Office of Naval Intelligence, assistant American legation U.S. naval attaché, Hong Kong BCC, declassified report serial 7–S–50 (September 9, 1950). This report contains a debrief of a *Chongqing* seaman who managed to escape to Hong Kong in early 1950.
48. Chung Pan, "The Lesson," p. 2.
49. Assistant American legation, report serial 7–S–50.
50. Ibid.
51. Ibid.
52. Ibid.
53. "Intelligence Briefs," *Office of Naval Intelligence Review*, declassified (July 1949), pp. 39–40.

CHAPTER 14. IN THE IMAGE OF TRADITION: THE CHINESE NAVY, 1949–55

1. Quoted in *Renmin Ribao* [People's daily] (September 27, 1949).
2. Complete text in *New York Times* (June 28, 1950).
3. Loren Fessler, "The October 1949 Battle of Quemoy," *American Universities Field Staff Series*, vol. 16, no. 17 (December 1969), pp. 231–46.
4. "The Southeast China Coast Today," *Office of Naval Intelligence (ONI) Review*, declassified (February 1953), p. 58.
5. Referenced in ibid., p. 59.
6. This is the beginning of the PRC's issuance of the "serious warnings," which by the early 1970s had reached several hundred in number ("China Coast," p. 52).
7. "The Bright Light Illuminating the Sea: Commanders and Fighters of the PLA Navy cherish the Memory of Chairman Mao," in *Foreign Broadcast Information Service: China* (*FBIS-CHI*), (October 17, 1977), p. 11.
8. Quoted in *Communist China, 1949–59*, vol. 1 (Hong Kong: Union Research Institute, 1959), pp. 229, 234.
9. U.S. Navy Department, Office of Naval Intelligence, U.S. naval attaché in Taibei, declassified report serial 121–52 (July 2, 1952).
10. U.S. Navy Department, Office of Naval Intelligence, assistant U.S. naval attaché in Hong Kong, declassified report serial 9–S–50 (November 30, 1950).
11. "Observation Stations and Radar Station Commended," in *Survey of China Mainland Press* (November 30, 1954).
12. "Guard the Sea Frontier With a Loyal Heart," in *FBIS-CHI* (May 4, 1971), p. c5.
13. "I Defend Hsisha for the Motherland," in *FBIS-CHI* (August 16, 1976), p. h5.
14. "The Struggle for the Coastal Islands of China," *ONI Review*, declassified (December 1953), p. 4.
15. "An Unsuccessful Nationalist Raid," *ONI Review*, declassified (June 1954), p. 253.
16. U.S. Navy Department, Office of Naval Intelligence, U.S. naval attaché in Taibei, declassified report serial 45–S–54 (June 11, 1954).

17. Complete details of the *Taiping* attack are in U.S. Navy Department, Office of Naval Intelligence, U.S. naval attaché in Taibei, declassified report serial 45–S–54 (December 1, 1954).
18. U.S. Navy Department, Office of Naval Intelligence, U.S. naval attaché in Taibei, declassified report serial 14–55 (March 1, 1955).
19. "The Communist Assault on Ichiang," *ONI Review*, declassified (May 1955), pp. 237–41.
20. *The Case of Peng Teh-huai, 1959–68* (Hong Kong: Union Research Institute, 1968), p. 227.

CHAPTER 15. MODERNIZATION: SINO-SOVIET NAVAL COOPERATION, 1950–59

1. John Gittings, *The Role of the Chinese Army* (London: Oxford University Press, 1967), p. 144. "Chinese Communist Naval Training" recorded that "the evidence indicates that Soviet penetration, particularly in the more technical fields, extends down to the lowest levels and smallest units of the Chinese Communist naval training organization" (*Office of Naval Intelligence [ONI] Review*, declassified [September 1951]).
2. Howard L. Boorman, *Moscow-Peking Axis* (New York: Harper, 1957), pp. 7–8.
3. "People's Air Force and Naval Units Collectively Join SSFA," New China News Agency (NCNA), November 8, 1951, in *Survey of China Mainland Press (SCMP)*, p. 212.
4. NCNA correspondents, "The Bright Light Illuminating the Sea: Commanders and Fighters of the PLA Navy Deeply Cherish the Memory of Chairman Mao," in *Foreign Broadcast Information Service: China (FBIS-CHI)*, (October 17, 1977), p. 11.
5. The Sino-Soviet Friendship Association Headquarters in Beijing claimed that during its first ten years it published 46,566,000 copies of 1,829 books and pamphlets, and organized 204,500 lectures attended by 164,890,000 persons. See *Druzhba* [Friendship], no. 41 (1949), p. 21f.
6. See U.S. Navy Department, Office of Naval Intelligence, U.S. naval attaché in Taibei, declassified report serial 87–S–53 (June 12, 1953), and "Chinese Communist Naval Ports and Bases," declassified, *ONI Review* (July 1954).
7. Peter Cheng, *A Chronology of the People's Republic of China* (Totowa, N.J.: Littlefield, Adams and Co., 1972), p. 17. Also see Strobe Talbott, *Khrushchev Remembers: The Last Testament* (Boston: Little, Brown and Co., 1974), p. 246 fn29.
8. U.S. Navy Department, Office of Naval Intelligence, U.S. naval attaché in Taibei, declassified report serial 40–S–58 (September 28, 1948), enclosure 4, p. 14.
9. U.S. Navy Department, Office of Naval Intelligence, U.S. naval attaché in Taibei, declassified report serial 121–52 (July 2, 1952).
10. "The Chinese Communist Navy," *ONI Review*, declassified (Autumn 1954), p. 39.
11. Ibid., p. 42.
12. "Developments in the Chinese Communist Navy During 1956," *ONI Review*, declassified (Summer 1957), pp. 44–46.
13. Chinese News Service Release, March 27, 1954, in *SCMP*, no. 777 (March 30, 1954), p. 6.
14. "Bright Light Illuminating the Sea," in *FBIS-CHI* (October 17, 1977), p. e12.
15. Quoted in John M.H. Lindbeck, "Organization and Development of Science," *Sciences in Communist China*, ed. Sidney H. Gould (Washington, D.C.: Association for the Advancement of Science, 1961), p. 24.
16. "Chinese Academy of Military Sciences Set Up," NCNA, in *SCMP*, no. 1736 (March 16, 1958), p. 2.
17. Ellis Joffe, *Party and Army: Professionalism and Political Control in the Chinese Officer Corps, 1949–64* (Cambridge: East Asian Research Center, Harvard University, 1967), p. 30.
18. "Naval Units Stationed at Tsing Tao Have Become Powerful Modernized Armed Force," *Tsing Tao Jih Pao* [Qingdao Ribao], in *SCMP*, no. 1653 (November 18, 1955), p. 9.
19. NCNA release, May 21, 1955, in *SCMP*, no. 1053 (May 21–23, 1955), p. 37.
20. See the eyewitness report contained in U.S. Navy Department, Office of Naval Intelligence, U.S. naval attaché assistant in Hong Kong, declassified report serial 7–S–50 (September 9, 1950).
21. For biographic information see Cdr. L. Bruce Swanson, Jr., "The Navy of the People's Republic of China," *Guide to Far Eastern Navies*, ed. Barry M. Blechman and Robert P. Berman (Annapolis: Naval Institute Press, 1978), pp. 160–1.

22. Gene Z. Hanrahan, "Report on Red China's New Navy," *U.S. Naval Institute Proceedings*, vol. 79 (August 1953), p. 852.
23. U.S. Navy Department, Office of Naval Intelligence, U.S. naval attaché assistant in Hong Kong, declassified report serial 7–S–50 (September 9, 1950).
24. Lu Tung-yi [Lu Dongyi], "An Examination of Doctrinaire Tendency in Training Work," *Jiefang Junpao* [Liberation army news], in *Union Research Service*, vol. 6 (October 13, 1956), p. 100.
25. A good overview of early PRC naval training is in "Chinese Communist Naval Training," *ONI Review*, declassified (September 1951), pp. 376–7. Also see Cdr. L. Bruce Swanson, Jr., "People's Republic of China," p. 116.
26. "Communist China Digest," no. 8, trans. in *U.S. Joint Publications Research Service (JPRS)*, no. 1106–D FI 0831 (January 15, 1960).
27. "On Coalition Government," April 24, 1945, in *Selected Military Writings of Mao Tse-tung* (Peking: Foreign Languages Press, 1968), p. 303.
28. Zhou Xihan, "Let Us Inherit and Uphold the Glorious Tradition of Our Army and Strengthen the Building of Our Navy," *Renmin Ribao*, in *SCMP*, no. 1596, (July 30, 1957), p. 17.
29. U.S. Navy Department, Office of Naval Intelligence, U.S. naval attaché in Taibei, declassified report serial 10–S–58 (April 15, 1958).
30. For details on the three fleets, see Swanson, "People's Republic of China," pp. 109–10. For years, the South Sea Fleet headquarters was at Canton; however, it was subsequently moved to Zhanjiang. See Harvey W. Nelson, *The Chinese Military System* (Boulder: Westview Press, 1977), p. 171.
31. See "Conscription Law Made Public," *FBIS-CHI* (February 18, 1955), p. aaa21.
32. "PLA Urged to Adhere to CPR Policies," *FBIS-CHI* (November 29, 1956), p. bbb4.
33. U.S. Navy Department, Office of Naval Intelligence, U.S. naval attaché in Taibei, declassified report serial 10–S–58 (April 15, 1968).
34. William W. Whitson, ed., *PLA Unit History* (Washington, D.C.: Office of the Chief of Military History, 1967), appendix 2, p. 120.
35. "The Chinese Communist Air Force," *ONI Review*, declassified, (Autumn 1953), p. 44.
36. Quoted in *Qingdao Ribao*, October 8, 1956, trans. in *JPRS*, no. DC–47 (March 21, 1958).
37. "The Chinese Communist Naval Air Force," *ONI Review*, declassified (Autumn 1953), p. 46.
38. "The Chinese Communist Naval Air Force," *ONI Review*, declassified (July 1958), p. 309.
39. Quoted in Chang Yi-min (Zhang Yimin), "Building the World's Strongest People's Navy," *Peking Review*, no. 1 (January 3, 1968), p. 42.
40. An excellent discussion of the PRC debate over national defense in the late 1950s is contained in Alice Langley Hsieh, *Communist China's Strategy in the Nuclear Era* (Englewood Cliffs, N.J.: Prentice-Hall, The Rand Corporation, 1962), pp. 49–76.
41. Quoted in ibid., p. 53.

CHAPTER 16. IDEOLOGY VERSUS TECHNOLOGY, 1956–59

1. Edward Crankshaw and Strobe Talbott, *Krushchev Remembers* (Boston: Little, Brown and Co., 1974), pp. 258–9.
2. Ibid., p. 247.
3. Chang Yi-min (Zhang Yimin), "Build the Strongest People's Navy in the World Following the Course Charted by Chairman Mao," in *Foreign Broadcast Information Service: China (FBIS-CHI)* (December 14, 1967), p. ccc6.
4. Ibid., p. ccc7.
5. Cf. Ellis Joffe, *Party and Army Professionalism and Political Control in the Chinese Officer Corps, 1949–64* (Cambridge: Harvard University Press, 1967), p. 36, and U.S. Navy Department, Office of Naval Intelligence, U.S. naval attaché in Taibei, declassified report serial 40–S–58 (September 23, 1958), p. 13.
6. *Jeifanjun Bao* [Liberation army news], January 19, 1957, in *Survey of China Mainland Press (SCMP)*, no. 1514 (April 23, 1957), p. 21.
7. Lu Tung-yi (Lu Dongyi), "An Examination of Doctrinaire Tendency in Training Work," *Jiefangjun Bao*, in *Union Research Service*, vol. 6 (October 13, 1956), pp. 100–2.
8. "Naval Units Stationed at Tsingtao Have Become Powerful Modernized Armed Force," *Tsingtao Jihpao [Qingdao Ribao]* in *SCMP*, no. 1653 (November 18, 1957), p. 9.
9. Ibid.

10. "Conference of Navy Activists Concluded," New China News Agency (NCNA), in *SCMP*, no. 1492 (March 19, 1957), p. 9.
11. "Build Up a Powerful Naval Defense Force," *Renmin Ribao* [People's daily], in *SCMP*, no. 1498 (March 27, 1957), p. 5.
12. Chou Hsi-han (Zhou Xihan), "Let Us Inherit and Uphold the Glorious Tradition of Our Army and Strengthen the Building of Our Navy," *Renmin Ribao* (July 30, 1957).
13. "Absolutely Do Not Eat 'Prepared Food'," *Jiefangjun Bao* (September 20, 1958), p. 1.
14. Ibid.
15. Chu Anping in *Renmin Ribao*, trans. in Roderick MacFarquhar, *The Hundred Flowers Campaign and the Chinese Intellectuals* (New York: Octagon, 1973), p. 51–2.
16. Wei Yijing, "The Party Leadership in Science," *Renmin Ribao*, (July 1, 1958), p. 1.
17. "The Chinese Communist Military Threat to the Offshore Islands," *Office of Naval Intelligence (ONI) Review*, declassified (November 1958), p. 467.
18. U.S. Navy Department, Office of Naval Intelligence, U.S. naval attaché in Taibei, declassified report serial 46–5–58 (September 29, 1958).
19. "Military Threat," *ONI Review*, p. 470–1.
20. Strobe Talbott, trans. and ed., *Khrushchev: The Last Testament* (Boston: Little, Brown and Co., 1974), pp. 261–2.
21. Ibid., p. 262; Peter Cheng, *A Chronology of the People's Republic of China* (Totowa, N.J.: Littlefield, Adams and Co., 1972), p. 91.
22. Edward Crankshaw and Strobe Talbott, *Khrushchev Remembers* (Boston: Little, Brown and Co., 1970), p. 472.
23. Ibid., p. 473.
24. See Cdr. Bruce Swanson, "The PRC Navy: Coastal Defense or Blue Water," *U.S. Naval Institute Proceedings*, vol. 102, no. 879 (May 1976), p. 91.
25. Quoted in Cheng, *A Chronology*, p. 172.
26. J.C. Cheng, ed., *The Politics of the Chinese Red Army: A Translation of the Bulletin of Activities* (Stanford: Hoover Institution, 1966), p. 671.
27. "Intelligence Briefs," *ONI Review*, declassified (November 1961), p. 485.

CHAPTER 17. OLD TRADITIONS, MODERN PRACTITIONERS: COASTAL CONTROL AND THE MARITIME MILITIA

1. Liu Yunzheng, "The Militia in Chinese People's Revolutionary Wars," *Peking Review* (August 21, 1964).
2. New China News Agency (NCNA), Canton release, July 23, 1951.
3. "China's Coastal Fisheries," *Office of Naval Intelligence (ONI) Review*, declassified (December 1955), p. 651.
4. "Red China's Coastal Fleet," *ONI Review*, declassified (June 1954), pp. 228–9.
5. A. Doak Barnett, *Cadres, Bureaucracy, and Political Power in Communist China* (New York: Columbia University Press, 1967), pp. 197–8.
6. "Coastal Fleet," *ONI Review*, pp. 228–30.
7. Ibid.
8. "Fishermen's Cooperation," *China Reconstructs*, vol. 5, no. 9 (September 1956), p. 6.
9. "600 Well-equipped Fishing Boats Leave North Kiangsu for Spring Fishing Season," *Survey of China Mainland Press (SCMP)*, no. 97 (April 21, 1951), p. 32.
10. "PLA Vigilantly Guarding Coast Protect and Help Fishermen to Carry Out Production," *SCMP*, no. 761 (March 4, 1954), pp. 35–36.
11. Jaydee R. Hanson, "China's Fisheries: Scaling Up Production," *The China Business Review* (May–June 1980), p. 26. The best detailed study on China's fishery operations is Jan J. Solecki, *Eonomic Aspects of the Fishing Industry in Mainland China* (Vancouver, Canada: Institute of Animal Resource Ecology Library, The University of British Columbia, 1966).
12. See Luke T. Lee, *China and International Agreements* (Durham, N.C.: Rule of Law Press, 1969), pp. 59–67, 204–8.
13. Hanson, "China's Fisheries," p. 27.
14. Ibid., p. 25. See also Jan J. Solecki, *Economic Aspects*, p. 140.
15. "Protection Call for Resources," *China Trade Report*, vol. 19 (February 1981), p. 3.
16. "Expansion of China's Fishing Industry Illustrated at Exhibition," *SCMP*, no. 3695, pp. 16–17.
17. "China's Naval Units Help Fishery," *SCMP*, no. 1687 (January 3, 1958), p. 9.
18. Quoted in J.C. Cheng, ed., *The Politics of the Chinese Red Army: A Translation of the Bulletin of Activities* (Stanford: Hoover Institution, 1966), p. 537.

19. Chang Yi-min, "Building the World's Strongest People's Navy," *Peking Review* (January 3, 1968), p. 42.
20. Quoted in Cheng, *The Politics of the Chinese Red Army*, pp. 668–70.
21. For example, see the editorial "Implausible Chinese Explanation," in *Japan Times* (April 22, 1978), p. 12. The Japanese also confirmed that the PRC navy was in radio contact with the fishermen. See *Yomiuri Shimbun* (April 20, 1978), p. 2.

CHAPTER 18. SELF-STRENGTHENING AND THE STRATEGY DEBATE, 1960–65

1. The best record of this association is contained in William W. Whitson, *The Chinese High Command* (New York: Praeger Publishers, 1973).
2. *Who's Who in Communist China* (Hong Kong: Union Research Institute, 1969), pp. 205, 304. Information on the origins of the Sixth Ministry of Machine Building is in Chu-yuang Chen, *The Machine-Building Industry in Communist China* (Chicago: Aldine, Atherton, 1971), p. 13.
3. Chao Kuo-hua (Zhao Guohua) and Chiang Yun (Jiang Yun), "Experimental Determination of Inertia Parameters of Moving Body Under Water," *Zhongguo Zaochuan* [Chinese journal of shipbuilding], no. 2 (58), April, 1965, pp. 1–26, trans. in Joint Publication Research Service (JPRS), no. 33,046 (November 26, 1965).
4. Trans. from *Zhongguo Zaochuan*, article nos. 1, 3, and 4, 1963, in *JPRS*, no. 24, 144 (April 9, 1964).
5. See *Zhongguo Zaochaun*, no. 1 (January 20, 1963), pp. 44–59; no. 4 (October 20, 1963), pp. 48–58; and no. 3 (October 20, 1964), pp. 31–51. Also refer to *Zhongxing Jixie* [Heavy machinery], no. 4 (April 9, 1958), pp. 17–27.
6. Ho Yu-sheng (He Yusheng), "Static Characteristics of Hydrofoil Craft," *Zhongguo Zaochuan*, no. 1, pp. 30–35.
7. *Guide to Far Eastern Navies*, ed. Barry M. Blechman and Robert P. Berman (Annapolis: Naval Institute Press, 1978), pp. 386–7.
8. Ibid., pp. 96, 386.
9. Ibid., pp. 103, 384.
10. Ibid., pp. 98, 106, 372, 378.
11. J.C. Cheng, ed., *The Politics of the Chinese Red Army: A Translation of the Bulletin of Activities* (Stanford: Hoover Institution, 1966), pp. 639–40.
12. Ibid.
13. "Submarines in the Adriatic with Chinese Crews," *Messaggero* (May 25, 1965). Also see "Alarming Information: Submarines in Albania Run by Chinese," *Il Tempo* (May 25, 1965); and "Albania Seen Getting China Sub Base Aid," *Washington Post* (January 6, 1964), p. A12.
14. "Alarming Information," *Il Tempo*.
15. *The Politics of the Chinese Red Army*, pp. 26, 331–4.
16. Ibid.
17. Ibid., pp. 333–4.
18. Ibid., p. 334.
19. *Nanfang Ribao*, [Southern daily], March 3, 1964, in Survey of China Mainland Press (SCMP), no. 3179, ref. in David G. Muller, Jr., "The Politics of the Chinese People's Navy" (Masters essay, Center for Chinese Studies, University of Michigan, December, 1974), p. 43.
20. "Submarine Crew Develop Glorious Tradition of PLA by Firmly Upholding Three Major Democratic Practices," *Renmin Ribao*, June 8, 1965, in *SCMP*, no. 3482 (June 22, 1965), pp. 7, 8.
21. "A New Type of Military School," *Peking Review* (January 10, 1969), pp. 17–20.
22. "Naval Committee Defeats Lo Ruiqing's Line," New China News Agency (NCNA) news release (December 5, 1967).
23. For example, see "South Sea Fleet Promotes Educated Cadres to Higher Positions," Canton Provincial Service, October 2, 1980, trans. in *Foreign Broadcast Information Service: China (FBIS-CHI)* (October 3, 1980), pp. P3–P4.
24. "A Certain Naval Unit in Ch'ung-ming Island Reclaim Over 6,000 Mou of Land on Barren Beach," *Dagong Bao*, Peking, in *SCMP*, no. 2749 (May 8, 1962), pp. 13–14.
25. Ibid.,
26. "Shorter Training Period for Submarine Specialists," NCNA (July 28, 1968).

27. Ref. in Peter Cheng, *A Chronology of the People's Republic of China* (Totowa, N.J.: Littlefield, Adams and Co., 1972), p. 146.
28. Ibid., p. 152.
29. Harvey W. Nelsen, *The Chinese Military System* (Boulder: Westview Press and London: Thorton Cox, 1977), p. 64.
30. Lo Jui-ching (Lo Ruiqing), "Commemorate the Victory over German Fascism! Carry the Struggle Against U.S. Imperialism Through to the End," *Peking Review* (May 14, 1965), pp. 14–15.
31. A well detailed discussion of the debate is contained in Uri Ra'anan, "Peking's Foreign Policy Debate, 1965–66," *China in Crisis*, ed. Tang Tsou, vol. 2 (Chicago: University of Chicago Press, 1968), pp. 23–71.
32. "Report on the Problem of Lo Jui-ch'ing's Mistakes," by the Work Group of the CCP Central Committee, trans. Ying-mao Kau, *The Peoples Liberation Army and China's Nation Building* (White Plains, N.Y.: International Arts and Sciences Press, Inc., 1973), p. 298.
33. "Chinese Navy Sinks Chiang Warship," *Peking Review* (November 19, 1965), p. 3.
34. "The Problem of Lo Jui-Ch'ing's Mistakes," p. 298.
35. Ibid., pp. 290–1.
36. Li Tso-p'eng (Li Zuopeng), *Strategy: One Against Ten Tactics: Ten Against One* (Peking: Foreign Languages Press, 1966), pp. 4, 6, 40.
37. Quoted in Ra'anam, "Peking's Foreign Policy Debate," p. 55.
38. Ibid., pp. 57–58.

CHAPTER 19. THE NAVY AND THE GREAT PROLETARIAN CULTURAL REVOLUTION, 1966–68

1. Quoted in Peter Cheng, *A Chronology of the People's Republic of China* (Totowa, N.J.: Littlefield, Adams and Co., 1972), p. 224.
2. A detailed description of Su Zhenhua's career is contained in *Guide to Far Eastern Navies*, eds. Barry M. Blechman and Robert P. Berman (Annapolis: Naval Institute Press, 1978), pp. 155–6. Also see *Xinhua* news release, February 15, 1979, in *Foreign Broadcast Information Service: China (FBIS-CHI)* (February 16, 1979), pp. e1–e5.
3. Peter Cheng, *A Chronology*, p. 214.
4. Contained in *Survey of China Mainland Press (SCMP)*, no. 3625 (January 27, 1966), p. 23. The best source on Mai Xiande is found in *Battle Hero Mai Hsien-teh* (Peking: Foreign Languages Press, 1967).
5. New China News Agency (NCNA), Peking, June 24, 1966, in *SCMP*, no. 3736 (July 12, 1966), p. 3.
6. For example, see Junichi Konno, "The Past Year in Peking," *Akahata*, November 23, 1967, trans. in *FBIS-CHI* (December 8, 1967), p. ccc10.
7. NCNA release, November 13, 1966, in *SCMP*, no. 3823 (November 18, 1966), p. 6.
8. Ibid.
9. From a Shanghai radio broadcast, contained in *FBIS-CHI* supplement (May 24, 1967), p. 32.
10. From a Qingdao Domestic News Service release, in *FBIS-CHI* (April 5, 1967), p. ddd6–7.
11. "May Seventh Directive Bears Fruit: New Men—Sailors as Well as Workers—Are Brought Up," in *Renmin Ribao*, May 7, 1969, trans. in *SCMP*, no. 4421 (May 22, 1969). Also see "Storm in the Port of Shanghai," *China Reconstructs*, vol. 16, no. 4 (April 1967), p. 31.
12. *Yomiuri Shimbun* (February 21, 1967, morning edition).
13. NCNA release, July 28, 1968, trans. in *Summary of World Broadcasts: The Far East* (BBC Monitoring Service, August 3, 1968), p. B116.
14. See "Radio Talk Describes Conscription System in China," in *FBIS-CHI* (April 17, 1974), p. e9.
15. Minoru Shibata, "I Was Deported," *Sankei* (Tokyo), September 29, 1967, trans. in *FBIS-CHI* (October 4, 1967), pp. ccc13–16.
16. Hangzhou Provincial Service, November 9, 1967, trans. in *FBIS-CHI* (November 14, 1967), p. ddd1.
17. See Wuhan Provincial Service, October 22, 1967, in *FBIS-CHI* (October 24, 1967), pp. ddd10–11; and Shanghai City Service, October 13, 1967, in *FBIS-CHI* (October 16, 1967), p. ddd1.

18. William W. Whitson, *The Chinese High Command* (New York: Praeger Publishers, 1973), p. 257.
19. NCNA Domestic Service, December 9, 1978, in *FBIS-CHI* (December 11, 1978), p. e14.
20. Beijing news release, July 24, 1967, trans. and summarized in *FBIS-CHI* (July 27, 1967), p. ccc4.
21. See biographical data on Admiral Fang in *Guide to Far Eastern Navies*, p. 159. Also see NCNA news release, October 26, 1967, in *SCMP*, no. 4050, October 30, 1967.
22. NCNA International Service, August 22, 1967, in *FBIS-CHI* (August 24, 1967), pp. ccc1–2.
23. "Eradicate Slavish Comprador Philosophy, Develop Large-Scale Shipbuilding," *Hsinhua News Agency*, Hong Kong, vol. 26 (June 29, 1970), p. 35.
24. *Renmin Ribao*, December 18, 1967.
25. *VWD Montan* (West Germany), November 16, 1970, quoted in *Kikai Kogyo Kaigai Joho* [Foreign information of Machine Industry] (Tokyo, February 1, 1971), p. 107.
26. *Wenwei Bao* (Hong Kong, August 20, 1968), p. 1.
27. *Aomen Ribao* (Macao, November 11, 1971), p. 4.
28. NCNA International Service, December 2, 1967, quoted in *FBIS-CHI* (December 4, 1967), p. ccc5.
29. NCNA Domestic Service, December 2, 1967, in *FBIS-CHI* (December 6, 1967), p. ccc6.
30. Ibid.
31. NCNA International Service, December 2, 1967, in *FBIS-CHI* (December 4, 1967), p. ccc2.
32. Peking Domestic Service, December 6, 1967, in *FBIS-CHI* (December 8, 1967), p. ccc9.
33. Chang Yi-min (Zhang Yimin), NCNA International Service, December 24, 1967, in *FBIS-CHI* (December 27, 1967), pp. ccc6–11.
34. Ibid., pp. ccc6, ccc11.
35. Ibid., pp. ccc8, ccc10.
36. "Commemorating the Fifteenth Anniversary of the Great Supreme Commander Chairman Mao's First Inspection of the Fleet," *Peking Review* (March 8, 1968), pp. 5–6.
37. NCNA International Service, April 25, 1968, in *FBIS-CHI* (April 26, 1968), pp. b1–2.
38. NCNA, Peking, June 30, 1968, in *SCMP*, no. 4212 (July 8, 1968), pp. 29–30.
39. NCNA, Peking, July 20, 1968, in *SCMP*, no. 4225 (July 25, 1968), p. 19.
40. NCNA Domestic Service, Peking, August 14, 1968, trans. in *FBIS-CHI* (August 29, 1968), p. b3.
41. NCNA International Service, Peking, September 4, 1968, in *FBIS-CHI* (September 5, 1968), p. b1.
42. "May Seventh Directive Bears Fruit," *SCMP*, no. 4421, p. 7.
43. Chu-yuan Cheng, "The Effects of the Cultural Revolution on China's Machine-Building Industry," *Current Scene*, vol. 8, no. 1 (January 1, 1970).
44. Data on these vessels can be found in *Guide to Far Eastern Navies*, pp. 367, 370–1, 377–8, 386.
45. Observations of the R-class submarine are reported in Desmond Wettern, "PRC Navy Close-up," *U.S. Naval Institute Proceedings* (March 1981), p. 126.
46. NCNA International Service, November 15, 1967, in *FBIS-CHI* (November 16, 1967), p. ccc1.
47. *Record of Proceedings of a Court of Inquiry . . . Relating to the Seizure of USS Pueblo. . .*, vol. 1 (U.S. Navy Judge Advocate General Office), p. 243.

CHAPTER 20. THE EMERGENCE OF NEW STRATEGIC RELATIONSHIPS, 1969–72

1. All of the information on Chinese naval construction in this paragraph is taken from *Guide to Far Eastern Navies*, eds. Barry M. Blechman and Robert P. Berman (Annapolis: Naval Institute Press, 1978), pp. 362–97.
2. Commander Bruce Swanson, "The PRC Navy: Coastal Defense or Blue Water?" *U.S. Naval Institute Proceedings* (May 1976), p. 95.
3. New China News Agency (NCNA) news release, September 18, 1968, quoted in Hemen Ray, "China's Initiatives in Eastern Europe," *Current Scene*, vol. 7, no. 23 (December 1, 1969), p. 10.
4. The Sino-Tanzanian connection is described in George T. Yu, *China and Tanzania: A Study in Cooperation Interaction*, China Research Monographs no. 5 (University of California, Berkeley: Center for Chinese Studies, 1970). Also see William Beecher, "Improved Missile in China Reported," *New York Times* (February 1, 1972), p. 6.

5. Fred S. Hoffman, "Chinese Trying to Get Ceylon Port Facilities," *Washington Star* (March 20, 1971).
6. "A Criticism of the Theory of Making the Electronics Industry the Center," August 12, 1971, trans. in *Foreign Broadcast Information Service: China (FBIS-CHI)* (August 18, 1971), pp. b8–13.
7. NCNA news release, December 25, 1976, in *FBIS-CHI* (December 27, 1976), pp. e6–9.
8. Peking Domestic Service, April 19, 1971, trans. in *FBIS-CHI* (April 20, 1971), p. a1.
9. NCNA International Service, September 20, 1971, in *FBIS-CHI* (September 21, 1971), p. a2.
10. NCNA International Service, May 31, 1971, in *FBIS-CHI* (June 1, 1971), pp. a16–17.

CHAPTER 21. POLITICAL OPPOSITION AND THE ASCENDENCY OF THE MARITIME SPIRIT, 1973–77

1. Roger Glenn Brown, "Chinese Politics and American Policy: A New Look at the Triangle," *Foreign Policy*, no. 23 (Summer 1976), p. 13.
2. New China News Agency (NCNA) International Service, December 29, 1971, in *Foreign Broadcast Information Service: China (FBIS-CHI)* (December 29, 1971).
3. For example, see "U.S.-Soviet Scramble for Hegemony in South Asian Subcontinent and Indian Ocean," *Peking Review* (January 14, 1972).
4. News release, August 29, 1973, in *FBIS-CHI* (August 30, 1973), pp. a8–9.
5. See UN General Assembly Resolution 2832 (December 16, 1971); 2992 (December 15, 1972); and 3080 (December 19, 1973).
6. NCNA news release, December 4, 1973, in *FBIS-CHI* (December 7, 1973), p. a9.
7. *Guide to Far Eastern Navies*, ed. Barry M. Blechman and Robert P. Berman (Annapolis: Naval Institute Press, 1978), p. 364.
8. "PRC Navy Close-up," *U.S. Naval Institute Proceedings* (March 1981), p. 125.
9. "FCAFE Group Reports on RP Oil Deposits," *Manila Times* (July 16, 1971), p. 19.
10. Data on PRC merchant-shipping purchases are taken from various daily issues of *Lloyd's Registry of Shipping*, London. Also see *Guide to Far Eastern Navies*, pp. 145–7.
11. *China Trade Report* (Hong Kong: Far Eastern Economic Review), vol. 19 (January 1981), p. 8.
12. NCNA Domestic Service, July 21, 1978, trans. in *FBIS-CHI* (July 25, 1978), pp. e19–20.
13. "Statement by the Spokesman of the Ministry of Foreign Affairs of the People's Republic of China," January 11, 1974, in *FBIS-CHI* (January 14, 1974), p. a1.
14. *New York Times* (January 21, 1974).
15. Beijing Domestic Service, March 16, 1974, trans. in *FBIS-CHI* (March 22, 1974), p. b1.
16. An excellent summary of the Chinese political situation in this period is contained in *Asia Yearbook, 1976* (Hong Kong: Far Eastern Economic Review), pp. 138–42.
17. NCNA Domestic Service, March 14, 1977, trans. in *FBIS-CHI* (March 16, 1977), pp. e1–3.
18. Ibid., p. e3.
19. NCNA Domestic Service, March 14, 1977, p. e3.
20. NCNA, September 15, 1977, in *FBIS-CHI* (September 16, 1977), p. e18.
21. Ibid.
22. *China News Summary*, no. 634 (October 6, 1976), p. 4.
23. Victor Zorza, "The Peking Struggle Over the Military," *Washington Post* (May 21, 1976).
24. Beijing Domestic Service, February 5, 1977, trans. in *FBIS-CHI* (February 7, 1977), pp. e5–9.
25. *Renmin Ribao*, June 25, 1978, trans. in *FBIS-CHI* (July 7, 1978), pp. e8–10. Also see Su Zhenhua's speech on Yaowenyan's activities in *FBIS-CHI* (August 30, 1978), p. e24.
26. Beijing Domestic Service, May 19, 1976, in *FBIS-CHI* (May 21, 1976), p. l7.
27. *Guangming Ribao*, June 17, 1976, trans. in *FBIS-CHI* (July 2, 1976), pp. a18–19.
28. Dr. James Schlesinger, "Inside China Now," *U.S. News and World Report* (October 18, 1976), pp. 40–42.
29. Beijing Domestic Service, May 25, 1977, trans. in *FBIS-CHI* (May 27, 1977), p. e5.

CHAPTER 22. THE NEO-MARITIME SPIRIT: DIRECTIONS AND IMPLICATIONS

1. For example, see V. Shagin, "The Navy in the Expansionist Plans of Peking," *Morskoy Sbornik*, no. 3 (1979), pp. 68–71; and V. Stepanov, "Beijing's Buildup," *Voyennyye*

znaniya, no. 8, pp. 30–31, trans. in *Joint Publication Research Service (JPRS)* 76847 (November 20, 1980).

2. An example of IMF loans is reported in John T. Norman, "China May Get $845 Million Loan from IMF," *Asian Wall Street Journal Weekly* (March 2, 1981).
3. Charles N. Dragonette, "The Dragon At Sea: China's Maritime Enterprise," *U.S. Naval Institute Proceedings,* Naval Review Issue (May 1981), page 80.
4. *China Trade Report* (Hong Kong: Far Eastern Economic Review, January 1981), p. 8.
5. "An International Force in the Making: Soviet Style?" *Far Eastern Economic Review* (February 6, 1981), p. 46.
6. Phijit Chong, "Quickening Oil Search," *China Trade Report* (January 1980), p. 2.
7. *Xinhua* news release, September 29, 1979, in *Foreign Broadcast Information Service: China (FBIS-CHI)* (September 20, 1979), pp. 12–4.
8. *Guide to Far Eastern Navies,* ed. Barry M. Blechman and Robert P. Berman (Annapolis: Naval Institute Press, 1978), p. 102.
9. Ibid., pp. 103–4. The figure is based upon projected building rates since 1978.
10. Ibid., p. 96.
11. *Xinhua,* May 9, 1980, in *FBIS-CHI* (May 9, 1980), p. e1.
12. Ti Tsung-heng (Di Zongheng); "Communist, Nationalist Naval Strength Assessed," *Ming Bao,* February, March, April 1977, trans. in *JPRS* 71527 (July 1978), pp. 37–38.
13. Chang Yi-min (Zhang Yimin), "Building the World's Strongest People's Navy," *Peking Review* (January 3, 1968).
14. "The Undersea Dragon," *Peking Newsletter,* trans. in *FBIS-CHI* (April 18, 1977), pp. e5–6.
15. Liu Derong, Xu Nengrong, and Xu Yinglin, "Shanghai Naval Unit Scores New Achievements in Combat Training and Coastal Defense Construction," trans. in *FBIS-CHI* (February 11, 1980), p. o3.
16. Quoted in *China Trade Report* (January 1981), p. 9.
17. George Lauriat, "China: Shipping Survey," *China Trade Report* (February 1980), p. 12.
18. Wolfgang Bartke, *Who's Who in the People's Republic of China* (Armonk, N.Y.: M.E. Sharpe, 1981), p. 473.
19. *China Trade Report* (October 1980), p. 7.
20. See Deng's interview in *Forbes* (June 9, 1980). One of the best Chinese assessments of the Soviet military strategy appeared in *Renmin Ribao,* January 11, 1980, trans. in *FBIS-CHI* (January 15, 1980), pp. c1–6.
21. For examples of Chinese views, see "What Does Soviet Invasion of Afghanistan Tell Us?" January 18, 1980, trans. in *FBIS-CHI* (January 21, 1980), p. c1; Yu Pang, "What's Moscow After?" *Beijing Review,* no. 4 (January 28, 1980), pp. 9–10; Tan Wenrui, interview with *Der Spiegel,* trans. in *FBIS-CHI* (February 22, 1980), pp. a1–9; and Guo Ping, "A Hundred Days after the Afghan Incident," *Xinhua,* April 5, 1980, trans. in *FBIS-CHI* (April 7, 1980), pp. c1–2.
22. George Lauriat, "Another Coming Conflict of Comrades Ahead," *Far Eastern Economic Review,* October 5, 1979, p. 58.
23. "Moscow Peace and Progress in Mandarin to Southeast Asia," February 24, 1979, trans. in *FBIS-Soviet* (February 27, 1979), p. c7.
24. Contained in *Xinhua* release, January 30, 1980, in *FBIS-CHI* (January 31, 1980), pp. e1–13.
25. Jiang Yuanchun, "Soviet Strategy for East Asia," *Beijing Review* (March 23, 1981), p. 20.
26. For example, see Deng Xiaoping's interview in *Yomiuri Shimbun* (March 30, 1980), p. 3.
27. "Lessons to be Drawn from Afghanistan," *Beijing Review* (February 4, 1980), p. 10.
28. Tan Wenrui, *FBIS-CHI* (February 22, 1980), p. a9.
29. For a discussion of the article, see Cheah Cheng Hye, "Bridging the Strategic Gap," *Far Eastern Economic Review* (April 25, 1980), pp. 30, 32.
30. Yang Dongliang, "A Tentative Analysis of the 'Debate on Coastal Defense Versus Land Border Defense'," *Guangming Ribao,* February 10, 1981, trans. in *FBIS-CHI* (March 5, 1981), p. 17.
31. For an example of the uncertainty, see Xu Xiangqian, "Strive to Achieve Modernization in National Defense. . . ," *Hongqi,* no. 10 (October 2, 1979), pp. 28–33.

PRINCIPAL WORKS CITED

CHINESE SOURCES (authors and titles in Pinyin)

BOOKS

Bao Zenpeng. *Zheng He Xiaxi Yangzhi Baochuan Kao* [A study of the treasure ships used by Zheng He on the western sea voyages]. Taibei: Zhonghua Congshu, 1961.
————. *Zhongguo Haijun Shi* [A naval history of China]. 1st ed. Taibei: Chinese Naval Publications Office, 1951. 2d ed. Taibei: Zhongguo Congshu, 1970.
Li Zhejin. *Zhongguo Jindai Haijun Shihua* [Contemporary Chinese naval history]. Taibei: Xinya, 1967.
Shen Shixing, ed. *Da Ming Huidian* [History of the Ming administrative statutes]. 5 vols. Taibei, 1964.
Xie Jinluan, ed. *Taiwan Wenxian Congkan* [Taiwan literature collection]. Taibei, 1962.

PERIODICALS

Guangming Ribao. Beijing.
Honggi [Red flag]. Beijing.
Ho Ke-en. "The Tanka or Boat People of South China." *Journal of Oriental Studies* 5 (1965): 1–39.
Remin Ribao [People's daily]. Beijing.
Zhongguo Haijun [China's navy]. 1947–49.

MANUSCRIPTS

Cao Yubian. "Haifang Tuyi" [Proposals for coastal defense with maps]. Washington, D.C.: Library of Congress, Orientalia Manuscript Division.
Dong Tiangong. "Taihai Jianwen Lu" [Record of things seen and heard in the Taiwan Sea]. Tabei: Taiwan Wenxian Congkan [Taiwan literature collection], vol. 129, 1961.
"Ming Shi Lu" [Veritable records of the Ming dynasty]. Mimeograph of the original manuscript. Taibei.
Wei Yuan, and Lin Zexu. "Haiguo Tuzhi" [Illustrated record of the maritime nations]. Washington, D.C.: Library of Congress, Orientalia Manuscript Division.
Zheng Ruozeng. "Chouhai Tubian" [Illustrated seaboard strategy]. Washington, D.C.: Library of Congress, Orientalia Manuscript Division.

Zhong Tingyu. "Ming Shi" [Ming dynasty history]. Mimeograph of the original manuscript. Taibei.

SOURCES IN TRANSLATION (authors and titles in Wade-Giles)

BOOKS

Brunnert, H.S., and Hagelstrom, V.V. *Present Day Political Organization of China, 1912.* Translated by A. Beltchenko and E.E. Moran. 1912. Reprint. Taibei: Ch'eng Wen, 1971.

Cheng, J.C., ed. *The Politics of the Chinese Red Army: A Translation of the Bulletin of Activities.* Stanford: Hoover Institution, 1966.

Kau Ying-mao, et al. *The Political Work System of the Chinese Communist Military: Analysis and Documents.* Brown University, 1971.

———. *The People's Liberation Army and China's Nation Building.* White Plains: International Arts and Sciences Press, 1973.

Li Chien-nung. *The Political History of China, 1840–1928.* Translated by Ssu-yu Teng and Jeremy Ingalls. 1956. Reprint. Stanford: Stanford University Press, 1967.

Li Tso-peng. *Strategy: One Against Ten Tactics: Ten Against One.* Peking: Foreign Languages Press, 1966.

Mao Tse-tung. *Selected Military Writings.* Peking: Foreign Languages Press, 1968.

Mills, J.V.G., ed. and trans. *Ying-Yai Sheng-Lan: The Overall Survey of the Ocean's Shores.* Cambridge, England, 1970.

Teng, S.Y., and Fairbank, J.K. *China's Response to the West.* 1954. Reprint. New York: Atheneum, 1973.

Tsunoda, R., and Goodrich, L.C. *Japan in the Chinese Dynastic Histories.* South Pasadena, 1951.

Wilbur, C.M., and How, J.L. *Documents on Communism, Nationalism, and Soviet Advisors in China, 1918–27.* Translated from the Russian. New York: Columbia University Press, 1956.

PERIODICALS

Beijing Review. Beijing.

Foreign Broadcast Information Service Daily Report and Supplement (China). Washington, D.C.

Joint Publications Research Service Reports. Washington, D.C.

Survey of China Mainland Magazines. Hong Kong.

Survey of China Mainland Press. Hong Kong.

Xie Guozhen. "Removal of Coastal Population in Early Tsing [Qing] Period." Translated by Ch'en T'ung-hsieh. *The Chinese Social and Political Science Review* 15 (January 1932).

SOURCES IN ENGLISH

BOOKS

Barnett, A.D. *Cadres, Bureaucracy, and Political Power in Communist China.* New York: Columbia University Press, 1967.

Bartke, W. *Who's Who in the People's Republic of China.* Armonk, N.Y.: M.E. Sharpe, 1981.

Beresford, Lord Charles. *The Breakup of China.* New York: Harper, 1899.

Biggerstaff, K. *The Earliest Modern Government Schools in China*. Ithaca: Cornell University Press, 1961.

Blechman, B.M., and Berman, R.P., eds. *Guide to Far Eastern Navies*. Annapolis: Naval Institute Press, 1978.

Boorman, H.L., ed. *Biographical Dictionary of Republican China*. New York: Columbia University Press, 1967.

Braisted, W.R. *The United States Navy in the Pacific, 1909–22*. Austin: University of Texas Press, 1971.

Cameron, M.E. *The Reform Movement in China, 1898–1912*. Stanford: Stanford University Press, 1931.

Chang Hsin-pao. *Commissioner Lin and the Opium War*. New York: W.W. Norton, 1964.

Chen, G. *Lin Tse-Hsu*. New York: Paragon Book Reprint Corporation, 1968.

———. *Tseng Kuo-Fan*. New York: Paragon Book Reprint Corporation, 1968.

Cheng, P. *A Chronology of the People's Republic of China*. Totowa, N.J.: Littlefield, Adams, 1972.

Crankshaw, E., and Talbott, S. *Krushchev Remembers*. Boston: Little, Brown, 1970.

Dolan, R.E. *A Comparative English-Chinese Dictionary of Military Terms*. Washington, D.C.: Defense Intelligence Agency, 1981.

Drake, F.S., ed. *Symposium on Historical Archaeological and Linguistic Studies on Southern China, Southeast Asia, and the Hong Kong Region*. Hong Kong: Hong Kong University Press, 1967.

Fairbank, J.K. *Trade and Diplomacy on the China Coast*. 1953. Reprint. Stanford: Stanford University Press, 1964.

———. *The United States and China*. New York: Viking Press, 1970.

Fairbank, J.K., ed. *The Chinese World Order*. Cambridge: Harvard University Press, 1968.

Fairbank, J.K., Reischauer, E.O., and Craig, A.M. *East Asia Tradition and Transformation*. Boston: Houghton Mifflin, 1973.

Fox, G. *British Admirals and Chinese Pirates, 1832–69*. 1940. Reprint. Westport, Ct.: Hyperion Press, 1973.

Gittings, J. *The Role of the Chinese Army*. London: Oxford University Press, 1967.

Hall, W.H. *The Nemesis in China*. London: Henry Calburo, 1846.

Herrick, R.W. *Soviet Naval Strategy*. Annapolis: United States Naval Institute, 1968.

Hsiao Ch'i-ch'ing. *The Military Establishment of the Yuan Dynasty*. Cambridge: Council on East Asian Studies, Harvard, 1978.

Hsieh, A.L. *Communist China's Strategy in the Nuclear Era*. Englewood Cliffs, N.J.: Prentice Hall, 1962.

Hummel, A.W., ed. *Eminent Chinese of the Ch'ing Period, 1644–1912*. Washington, D.C.: U.S. Government Printing Office, 1944.

Jane's Fighting Ships. Annual edition.

Joffe, E. *Party and Army: Professionalism and Political Control in the Chinese Officer Corps, 1949–64*. Cambridge: East Asian Research Center, Harvard, 1967.

Kessler, L.D. *K'ang-Hsi and the Consolidation of Ch'ing Rule, 1661–84*. Chicago: The University of Chicago Press, 1976.

Klein, D.W., and Clark, A.B. *Biographic Dictionary of Chinese Communism, 1921–65*. Cambridge: Harvard University Press, 1971.

Liu, F.F. *A Military History of Modern China, 1924–49*. Princeton: Princeton University Press, 1956.

Manchuria Year Book. Tokyo, 1931.

Mote, F.W. *Intellectual Foundations of China*. New York: Alfred A. Knopf, 1971.

Nathan, A.J. *Peking Politics, 1918–23*. Berkeley: University of California Press, 1976.

Needham, J. *Science and Civilisation in China*. Vol. 4. Cambridge: At the University Press, 1971.

Nelsen, H.W. *The Chinese Military System*. Boulder: Westview Press, 1977.

Neumann, C.Q. *History of the Pirates Who Infested the China Sea From 1807 to 1810*. London, 1831.

Nicholas, C.W., and Paranavitana, S. *A Concise History of Ceylon*. Colombo: Ceylon University Press, 1961.

Powell, R.L. *The Rise of Chinese Military Power, 1895–1912*. Princeton: Princeton University Press, 1955.

Purcell, V. *The Chinese in Southeast Asia*. London: Oxford University Press, 1951.

Rawlinson, J.L. *China's Struggle for Naval Development, 1839–95*. Cambridge: Harvard University Press, 1967.

Shore, H.N. *The Flight of the Lapwing*. London: Longmans, Green, 1881.

So Kwan-wai. *Japanese Piracy in Ming China During the Sixteenth Century*. Michigan State University Press, 1975.

Solecki, J.J. *Economic Aspects of the Fishing Industry in Mainland China*. Vancouver: The University of British Columbia, 1966.

Spector, S. *Li Hung-chang and the Huai Army*. Seattle: University of Washington Press, 1964.

Talbott, S. *Khrushchev Remembers: The Last Testament*. Boston: Little, Brown, 1974.

Trevor-Roper, H. *The Hermit of Peking*. New York: Alfred A. Knopf, 1977.

Tyler, W.F. *Pulling Strings in China*. London: Constable, 1929.

Volpicelli, Zenone [Vladimir]. *The China-Japan War*. London: William Clowes, 1896.

Waley, A. *Three Ways of Thought in Ancient China*. 1939. Reprint. New York: Doubleday, n.d.

Whitson, W.W. *The Chinese High Command*. New York: Praeger, 1973.

Who's Who in China. 1925 and 1936 editions. Shanghai.

Who's Who in Communist China. Hong Kong: Union Research Institute, 1969.

Wills, J.E. *Pepper, Guns, and Parleys: The Dutch East India Company and China, 1622–81*. Cambridge: Harvard University Press, 1974.

Woodhead, H.G.W., ed. *The China Yearbook*. 1912–39 editions. Kraus Reprint. Nendeln/Liechtenstein: A Division of Kraus-Thomson Organization, 1969.

Worcester, G.R.G. *The Junks and Sampans of the Yangtze*. Annapolis: Naval Institute Press, 1971.

Wright, M.C. *The Last Stand of Chinese Conservatism: The T'ung-Chih Restoration, 1862–74*. Stanford: Stanford University Press, 1957.

Wright, S.W. *Hart and the Chinese Customs*. Belfast: William Mullan, 1950.

PERIODICALS

Braisted, W.R. "China, the United States Navy, and the Bethlehem Steel Company, 1909–29." *Business History Review* 42 (Spring 1968): 50–56.

The China Business Review. Washington, D.C., 1977–81.

China Trade Report. Hong Kong, 1979–81.

Chinese Economic Bulletin. Peking and Shanghai, 1927–29.

Chinese Economic Journal. Peking and Shanghai, 1927–28.

Chinese Economic Monthly. Peking and Shanghai, 1925–26.

Far Eastern Economic Review. Peking and Shanghai, 1925–26.

Fei Hsiao-tung. "Peasantry and Gentry: An Interpretation of Chinese Social Structure and Its Changes." *American Journal of Sociology* 52, no. 1 (July 1946): 1–17.

Fessler, L. "The October 1949 Battle of Quemoy." *American University Field Staff Series* 16, no. 17 (December 1969).

Hanson, J.R. "China's Fisheries: Scaling Up Production." *The China Business Review* 7, no. 3 (May–June 1980): 25–30.

Hsu, I.C.Y. "The Great Policy Debate in China, 1874: Maritime Defense Versus Frontier Defense." *Harvard Journal of Asiatic Studies* 25 (1964–65): 212–28.

Hsu Yun-ts'iao. "The Revamping of Oceangoing Sea Routes Made in the Yuan and Ming Dynasties and Repercussions in Southeast Asian History." *Chinese Culture* 19, no. 3 (September 1968): 49–55.

Lo Jung-pang. "The Controversy Over Grain Conveyance During the Reign of Qubilai Qagan, 1260–94." *The Far Eastern Quarterly* 13 (1953): 263–85.

———. "The Decline of the Early Ming Navy." *Oriens Extremis*, no. 5 (1958): 149–68.

———. "The Emergence of China as a Seapower During the Late Sung and Early Yuan Periods." *The Far Eastern Quarterly* 14, no. 4 (August 1955): 489–503.

Marble, F. "The Battle of the Yalu." *United States Naval Institute Proceedings* 21, no. 3 (1895): 479–521.

McGiffin, P.N. "The Battle of the Yalu." *Century Magazine* (August 1895): 585–604.

Roberts, S.S. "The Imperial Chinese Steam Navy, 1862–95." *Warship International*, no. 1 (1974): 19–55.

Silverstone, P., and deSaint Hubert, C. "The Chinese Navy, 1870–1937." *World Ship Society Warships Supplement*, no. 39 (August 1975): 11–16, and no. 40 (November 1975): 29–32.

Skinner, G.W. "Marketing and Social Structure in Rural China: Part I." *The Journal of Asian Studies* (November 1964).

Smith, R.J. "Chinese Military Institutions in the Mid-Nineteenth Century, 1850–60." *Journal of Asian History* 8 (1974).

Swanson, B. "An Introduction to Chinese Command, Control, and Communications." *Signal* 32, no. 8 (May–June 1978): 46–108.

———. "The PRC Navy: Blue Water or Coastal Defense?" *United States Naval Institute Proceedings* 102, no. 879 (May 1976): 82–107.

———. "The PRC Navy and Chinese Foreign Policy." *Survival* 21, no. 4 (August–September 1978): 146–55.

Thompson, L.C. "The Junk Passage Across the Taiwan Strait: Two Early Chinese Accounts." *Harvard Journal of Asiatic Studies* 28 (1968).

Wade, T.F. "The Army of the Chinese Empire: Its Two Great Divisions, the Bannerman or National Guard, and the Green Standard or Provincial Troops." *Chinese Repository* 20 (1851): 25–422.

Wagner, R. "Two Memoranda Regarding the Defenses, Harbors, and Railways Required by China." *Royal United Service Institution Journal* 42, no. 246 (August 1898): 941–66.

Wang Yi-t'ung. "Official Relations Between China and Japan, 1368–1549." *Harvard-Yenching Institute Studies* 9 (1955): 1–19.

Ward, B.E. "A Hong Kong Fishing Village." *Journal of Oriental Studies* 1 (1955): 196–214.

Wei Peh T'i. "Internal Security and Coastal Control: Juan Yuan and Pirate Suppression in Chekiang, 1799–1809." *Ch'ing-shih wen-ti* [Problems in Qing history] 4, no. 2 (December 1979): 83–112.

Wettern, D. "PRC Navy Close-up." *United States Naval Institute Proceedings* 107, no. 3 (March 1981): 122–27.

Wu Tien-wei. "Chiang K'ai-shek's March Twentieth Coup d'Etat of 1926." *Journal of Asian Studies* 27 (May 1968): 585–602.

UNPUBLISHED

Millinger, J.F. "Ch'i Chi-kuang Chinese Military Official: A Study of Civil-Military Roles and Relations in the Career of a Sixteenth-Century Warrior." Ph.D. dissertation, Yale University, 1968.

Muller, D.G. "The Politics of the Chinese People's Navy." Masters essay, University of Michigan, 1974.

Navy Department, Office of Naval Intelligence (declassified)
China Reports Series, 1894–1937
U.S. Naval Attaché Reports, 1909–63
"Naval Review," 1946–63

(NOTE: All U.S. Navy Department reports referenced in this work as well as others related to Chinese maritime matters have been reproduced and are available in Special Collections, Nimitz Library, U.S. Naval Academy, Annapolis, Maryland. The original documents are at the U.S. Navy Archives, Navy Yard, Washington, D.C.)

INDEX

monarchy, 133; background, 145; involvement with William Tyler, 145–47; and U.S. commitment to build ships and train Chinese sailors, 151
Lifanyuan, 14
Li Hongzhang: and the Chinese education mission, 78; and the strategy debate of 1874–75, 83–84; and naval modernization, 85–102; and Korea, 104–5; and the Battle of Yalu, 105; and the Treaty of Shimonoseki, 111–12; attempts to revive the navy, 115; Japanese tribute to, 119; honored by Fujian naval clique, 134; attacked by radicals in 1976, 272; and PRC assessment of, 285
Liji, 157–59
Lijin, 130
Li Lisan, 173
Lin Baoyi: "honors" incident with Japanese navy, 159–60
Lin Biao: and the PRC Navy red and expert policy, 224–25; and research on engines, 226; and the "red" phase, 230–31; and the 1964–65 strategy debate, 234–36; and 1967 naval congress, 246–47; and defense spending, 255; and the Ninth Party Congress, 257–58; and dispute over PRC foreign policy, 258–61; death of, 261
Ling fu, 178–79
Linqing, 3
Lin Taizeng, 96
Lin Xiangguang, 177
Lin Zexu, 70
Lin Zhiping, 68
Lin Zun: relieved for smuggling, 176; defects, 182; made deputy director of Nanjing naval school, 199
Lisui, 157–59
Liu Buchan, 96, 107
Liu Guanxiong: background and support for constitutional monarchy, 133; and the Bethlehem Steel contract, 148
Liu Haotian, 258
Liu Kunyi, 102, 114
Liuqiu Islands (Okinawa), 14, 47; shipwrecked sailors and Japanese suzerainty, 81–82
Liu Shaoqi: loses influence, 238; opposes large-scale shipbuilding, 244–45
Liu Yongkou: arrested, 176
Li Yuanhong: student at Tianjin naval academy, 92; attempts to enlist Sa Zhenping's aid, 124–25
Li Zhilong, 156–57
Li Zongxi, 87–88
Li Zuopeng: as a Lin Biao protégè, 225; and the 1964–65 strategy debate, 235–36; replaces Su Zhenhua, 241; and 1967 naval congress, 246; named navy first political commissar and member of politburo, 258; purged, 261
Localism: described, 65–66

Lo Fenglu, 113
Longqi, 50
Lo Ruiqing: criticizes Mao's protracted-warfare strategy, 191; on Public Security Force coastal-defense responsibilities, 204; and navy fishermen, 221; and the 1964–65 strategy debate, 233–36; criticized during cultural revolution, 246; rehabilitated, 271
Los Angeles, USS, 213
Louchuan, 67
Luda-class destroyer: built in China, 255
Lu Dongge, 180
Lu Renlin: purged, 243
Luzhou, 45

Macartney, Halliday, 89
McGiffin, Philo Norton, 105–10
MacMurray, John V.A., 150
Madame Mao: and radicals, 238; joins with PLA, 243; attends 1967 naval congress, 246; member of politburo, 258; member anti–Lin Biao coalition, 261; attacks new naval policies, 270–72
Ma Dejian, 129
Mahan, Alfred T., 53
Ma Huan, 36–40
Mai Xiande, 240
Major port: defined, 21–22
Malaysia, 45–46
Maldive Islands, 40
Manchuria: annexation of Chinese, 153–54
Mannix, Captain D. Pratt: U.S. marine advisor to Chinese navy, 93
Mao Zedong: discourse on pirates, 49; early naval goals of, 183; defines PRC Navy responsibilities, 187; seeks naval aid from the Soviet Union, 193; visits navy headquarters, 193; visits Jiangnan Shipyard and various warships, 196–97; impact on PRC naval organization, 201; army building defended as goal for navy, 211; and Great Leap Forward, 212; orders attack on Matsu and Quemoy, 212–13; opposes joint Sino-Soviet naval command, 214; shortens military education, 242; and 1967 naval congress, 246–47; orders army to restore order, 248; inspects the fleet, 249; and PRC foreign policy, 259–61
Marble Boat: empress dowager's construction of, 99
Maritime China: early influence of, 17–27, 33, 58–59; Ming decline of, 40–43; influence on PRC, 191–92, 206, 215, 270, 284–85
Maritime Customs. *See* Chinese Maritime Customs
Maritime militia: origins of, 61–62; role and activities of, 216–23
Marketing: in ancient China, 2
Matang, 166

Qing Empire

- - - - - Provincial Boundaries
∿∿∿∿∿ Great Wall
· · · · · Canals
―――― Rivers

Frontier 1689–1859
Settled by Treaty of Nerchinsk

HEILONGJIANG

JILIN

SHENGJING

Albajin

Dongjiang

Haishengwei
(Vladivostok)

OUTER MONGOLIA

INNER MONGOLIA

ZHILI

Beijing

Port Arthur
(Lushun)
Dalian

Yantai
Weihai

Qingdao

SHANDONG

JIANGSU

Shanghai

Nanjing

Hangzhou

Ningbo

Wenzhou

ZHEJIANG

Tanzhou

Funing

GANSU

SHANXI

SHAANXI

HENAN

ANHUI

HUBEI

Wuhan

JIANGXI

FUJIAN

Fuzhou

Xinghua
Quanzhou
Xiamen (Amoy)
Shantou

Duanshui
Qiong
TAIWAN
Taiwanfu
Penghudao

XINJIANG

XIZANG

SICHUAN

GUIZHOU

HUNAN

GUANGDONG

Canton
Guangzhou Wan

YUNNAN

GUANGXI

Leizhou
Qiongzhou

Haikou

Frontier 17th–18 Ct.

Yellow River

Red River

Yangzi River

Xi River